Palgrave Studies in Prisons and Penology

This is a unique and innovative series, the first of its kind dedicated entirely to prison scholarship. At a historical point in which the prison population has reached an all-time high, the series seeks to analyse the form, nature and consequences of incarceration and related forms of punishment. Palgrave Studies in Prisons and Penology provides an important forum for burgeoning prison research across the world.



More information about this series at
http://www.palgrave.com/gp/series/14596

Jennifer Turner • Victoria Knight
Editors

# The Prison Cell

## Embodied and Everyday Spaces of Incarceration

palgrave
macmillan

*Editors*
Jennifer Turner
Department of Geography and Planning
University of Liverpool
Liverpool, UK

Victoria Knight
School of Applied Social Sciences
De Montfort University
Leicester, UK

Palgrave Studies in Prisons and Penology
ISBN 978-3-030-39913-9 ISBN 978-3-030-39911-5 (eBook)
https://doi.org/10.1007/978-3-030-39911-5



This Palgrave Macmillan imprint is published by the registered company Springer Nature Switzerland AG.
The registered company address is: Gewerbestrasse 11, 6330 Cham, Switzerland

*This book is dedicated to Willow Jane Easton-Wooff*

# Acknowledgements

The origins of this book hark back to 2016 in Odense, Denmark. I am grateful to Jennifer for entertaining the idea that resulted in this very book. We both agreed that the prison cell demanded scrutiny. At the end of our conversation at the drafty Danish bus station, we agreed to pursue this work. I'd like to thank Jennifer for her determination, patience and professionalism in creating this work. I'd also like to thank the contributors for their insights, our publisher Palgrave Macmillan and series editors. I am personally grateful to Professor Rob Canton and Professor Dave Ward for their scholarly advice and patient reviewing when needed. Lastly my lovely daughters, Olive and Lois.

Victoria Knight (Leicester, November 2019)

I would like to echo Victoria's thanks to all of our contributors—many of whom have been negotiating tricky logistics around access to prison spaces and complex collaborations to deliver their chapters. These, of course, are in addition to the many challenges presented by balancing academic and personal lives. We are grateful to everyone for working so hard towards and being so understanding of our rigid timetable and for your positive responses to our most pedantic editorial instructions! We very much appreciate the support of Palgrave Macmillan, including that from Josie Taylor and the series editors in the development of the book proposal and from Liam Inscoe-Jones to facilitate delivering it on time.

Thanks also to Professor Ben Crewe for your warm encouragement via the Afterword. It is also important to thank the other scholars who submitted abstracts, who we were unable to include in this volume. These suggested chapters also offered rich, diverse and important contributions but were simply too numerous for the book. We apologise to those colleagues for not being able to showcase their work on this occasion but thank them for the support and interest in the volume, which served to reinforce our confidence in the need for this collection specifically dedicated to the prison cell. We hope that this book will provide a platform for the development of associated work in this important area and look forward to seeing it in print elsewhere. I would personally like to thank Professor Kimberley Peters for her support in offering her expertise for additional reviewing. Finally, I would like to thank Victoria for her willingness to open up her own initial ideas to develop this collaboration and for making the whole process both intellectually stimulating and a genuine pleasure to be part of. Oh, and for digging out her A Level Biology notes to entertain my most abstract ideas...

Jennifer Turner (Liverpool, November 2019)

## Praise for *The Prison Cell*

"Just as cells are the building blocks of all organisms so too are they the foundation of carceral life. They are places of pain, dislocation and resistance but also of sanctuary, play and domesticity. In this innovative, informative and intriguing book the cell is placed under the penal microscope to reveal connections and layers of meaning that would otherwise remain hidden."

—Professor Ian O'Donnell, *University College Dublin, author of* Prisoners, Solitude, and Time

"Anyone thrown into a prison cell begins to live in the shadow of madness, according to the writer and imprisoned revolutionary, Victor Serge. This vivid collection of essays challenges the reader to think into these shadows and search for new meanings and fresh understanding of incarceration. The editors introduce a fascinating analogy and disturbing sense of scale by likening the prison cell to the microscopic biological cell. Just as prison cells "symbolically represent the monolithic values of the prison", so are they the living tissue of carceral space, literally "the containers of prison life". International in scope and enlivened by a diversity of voices, including those of prisoners, this impressively edited collection is a major and innovative contribution to studies of incarceration. Read it, borrow it, share it. Bring light to the shadow."

—Dr Rod Earle, *School of Health, Wellbeing and Social Care, The Open University*

## Contents


1 **Dissecting the Cell: Embodied and Everyday Spaces of Incarceration** 1
*Jennifer Turner and Victoria Knight*

**Part I The Nucleus** 21

2 **'The Solitude of the Cell': Cellular Confinement in the Emergence of the Modern Prison, 1850–1930** 23
*Helen Johnston*

3 **Prison Cells as a Grounded Embodiment of Penal Ideologies: A Norwegian-American Comparison** 45
*Jordan M. Hyatt, Synøve N. Andersen, and Steven L. Chanenson*

4 **The *Kubol* Effect: Shared Governance and Cell Dynamics in an Overcrowded Prison System in the Philippines** 71
*Raymund E. Narag and Clarke Jones*

5 'I Feel Trapped': The Role of the Cell in the Embodied and Everyday Practices of Police Custody 95
*Andrew Wooff*

Part II Cytoplasm 119

6 A 'Home' or 'a Place to Be, But Not to Live': Arranging the Prison Cell 121
*Irene Marti*

7 Prison as Palimpsest: The Dialectics of the Cell and Everyday Life 143
*The ACE Steering Committee*

8 Power in 'No-Cell' Detention: Spatial Restriction and Domestication of Space for Foreign Detainees in Romania 165
*Bénédicte Michalon*

9 A Family Cell: Visual Ethnography in a Prison 'Mothers' Section' 187
*Rossella Schillaci*

Part III The Cell Membrane 213

10 Serving Time with a Sea View: The Prison Cell and Healthy Blue Space 215
*Jennifer Turner, Dominique Moran, and Yvonne Jewkes*

11 Hearing Behind the Door: The Cell as a Portal to Prison Life 239
*Kate Herrity*

12 Prison Cell Spaces, Bodies and Touch 261
*Elisabeth Fransson and Francesca Giofrè*

13 **PrisonCloud: The Beating Heart of the Digital Prison Cell** 283
*Jana Robberechts and Kristel Beyens*

14 **Carceral Projections: The Lure of the Cell and the Heterotopia of Play in *Prison Escape*** 305
*Hanneke Stuit*

**Correction to: Prison Cell Spaces, Bodies and Touch** C1

**The Cell: Afterword** 327

**Index** 333

# Notes on Contributors

**Synøve N. Andersen** works as a researcher at the Unit for Social and Demographic Research at Statistics Norway and is an Associate Professor in the Department of Criminology and Sociology of Law at the University of Oslo. Her work focuses on quasi-experimental analyses of Norwegian correctional and family policies, comparative criminal justice and the dynamics of co-offending networks and criminal careers.

**Another Chance at Education** is a group of authors that includes twelve men imprisoned in a maximum security facility and nine individuals—five of them undergraduate students—involved in higher education at the University of Oregon who work with them. ACE serves as a steering committee for the University of Oregon Prison Education Program's efforts within the prison, and its participation in the national Inside-Out Prison Education Exchange Program, which brings together incarcerated and campus-based students for college classes within penal settings.

**Kristel Beyens** is Full Professor of Criminology and Penology and director of the Research Group Crime & Society (CRiS) at the Criminology Department of the Vrije Universiteit Brussel (Belgium). Her research focuses on contemporary evolutions in punishment, with special attention for penal decision-making and the implementation of prison sentences and community sanctions.

**Steven L. Chanenson** is Professor of Law at Villanova University Charles Widger School of Law. During AY 2019–2020, he was the Crane Fellow at the Program in Law and Public Affairs of Princeton University. Previously, he was the chair of the Pennsylvania Commission on Sentencing. He is also a managing editor of the *Federal Sentencing Reporter*, the leading professional journal of brief commentary on sentencing law, theory and reform.

**Elisabeth Fransson** is a sociologist and an Associate Professor at the University College of Norwegian Correctional Service, Norway. Her research includes prison architecture and philosophies of correctional care, transitions into and out of prison and studies of children and youths in prison. Her current publications include articles about the Norwegian Youth Units, internet rape and court cultures. She is co-editor of *Prison, Architecture and Humans* (2018).

**Francesca Giofrè** holds a PhD and is an architect and associate professor in the Faculty of Architecture, Sapienza University of Rome, Italy. Her research focuses on innovation in the design and building process, design for all and healthy cities. In particular, research within this framework attends to health and social architecture. In 2019 she worked on the renovation of a section of Rebibbia Prison, Rome. Her publications include *Prison, Architecture and Humans* (2018) co-edited with E. Fransson and B. Johnsen.

**Kate Herrity** obtained her PhD in 2019 for her thesis "Rhythms and routines: Sounding order and survival in a local men's prison using aural ethnography". Particular interests include sound and music in prisons, sensory criminology and research methods. Awarded the *Prison Service Journal* annual prize for outstanding article for "Music and identity in Prison: music as a technology of the self", Kate is turning her PhD thesis into a monograph alongside a number of other publications.

**Jordan M. Hyatt** is an Assistant Professor in the Department of Criminology and Justice Studies, Drexel University. His work focuses on randomised and quasi-experimental evaluation of correctional programming, comparative penology and the development of evidence-based criminal justice policies.

**Yvonne Jewkes** is Professor of Criminology at the University of Bath and Visiting Professor of Criminology at the University of Melbourne. She has been carrying out prison research for over 20 years and has spent the last decade researching and writing about prison architecture and design and their potential to rehabilitate. She has recently held two Economic and Social Research Council grants to study these topics and has worked as a consultant to prison architects and senior prison service personnel around the world. Her work on various aspects of imprisonment has appeared in many publications, including *Prisons and Punishment* 3 volumes (2008) and (with Ben Crewe and Jamie Bennett) *The Handbook on Prisons* 2e (2016). With Ben Crewe and Thomas Ugelvik, she is founding editor of the journal *Incarceration* and a series editor of *Palgrave Studies in Prisons and Penology*. She is also the author of the bestselling *Media and Crime* 3e (2015) and *Media and Crime* in the USA (with Travis Linnemann, 2017).

**Helen Johnston** is Professor of Criminology at the University of Hull. Her work particularly focuses upon the history of imprisonment, both local prisons and convict prisons, licensing and early release mechanisms and prison architecture. She has led and collaborated on funded projects supported by the ESRC, AHRC, British Academy and the Leverhulme Trust. Her work on these areas has appeared in many publications, including *Crime in England 1815–1880* (2015) and *Victorian Convicts* (with Godfrey and Cox, 2016).

**Clarke Jones** is a criminologist and senior research fellow based at the Research School of Psychology at the Australian National University. Over the past 14 years, he has conducted ethnographic prison/jail studies in the Philippines on high-risk offenders and applied this research to train staff from the Bureau of Corrections and the Bureau of Jail Management and Penology in correctional reform. Together with Raymund Narag, much of this research has culminated in *Inmate Radicalisation and Recruitment in Prisons* (2018).

**Victoria Knight** is a Senior Research Fellow at De Montfort University. She is a prison sociologist interested in media and digital use in prison settings. Her work has appeared in various journals and books, and she has authored *Remote Control: Television in Prison* (Palgrave Macmillan, 2016).

**Irene Marti** studied social anthropology and sociology at the Universities of Basel and Neuchâtel in Switzerland. Since 2013 she is a member of the Prison Research Group (PRG) at the University of Bern, Switzerland (http://prisonresearch.ch/). She is a PhD candidate at the University of Neuchâtel and is working as a research assistant at the Institute of Penal Law and Criminology at the University of Bern.

**Bénédicte Michalon** is a Senior Research Fellow at the French National Centre for Scientific Research (CNRS), Bordeaux. She works on detention and house arrest for foreigners, and asylum seekers housing in rural areas, with main fieldwork in Romania and France. She coordinated the interdisciplinary team TerrFerme into spatial readings of confinement (http://terrferme.hypotheses.org/). She is a member of the Institut Convergences Migrations (http://icmigrations.fr/) as well as of the Migreurop network (http://www.migreurop.org).

**Dominique Moran** is Professor in Carceral Geography at the University of Birmingham, UK, and a co-director of the University's Centre for Crime, Justice and Policing. She is interested in theorisations of the 'carceral', and her research focuses on lived experiences of carceral spaces. Founder of the Carceral Geography Lab, she is the author of *Carceral Geography: Spaces and Practices of Incarceration* (2015) and an editor of *Carceral Spaces* (2013), *Historical Geographies of Prisons* (2015), *Carceral Spatiality* (Palgrave, 2017) and *The Palgrave Handbook of Prison and the Family* (Palgrave, 2019).

**Raymund E. Narag, PhD** , is Assistant Professor of Criminology and Criminal Justice in Southern Illinois University. He has conducted numerous culturally sensitive trainings for the Bureau of Corrections (BuCor) and the Bureau of Jail Management and Penology (BJMP) to popularise best practices attuned to the Philippine penal and criminal justice conditions.

**Jana Robberechts** is a PhD researcher at the Research Group Crime & Society, Department of Criminology, Vrije Universiteit Brussel (Belgium), where her focus is on digitalisation in prisons.

**Rossella Schillaci** is a PhD student in Digital Media at NOVA University of Lisbon, within the international program in collaboration with the University of Texas in Austin and integrated at iNOVA Media Lab, with a scholarship from the Fundação para a Ciência e a Tecnologia (FCT). She teaches visual anthropology in University workshops and has co-founded the independent production company Azul (www.azulfilm.com) where she has made several prize-winning documentary films, working on the themes of cultural traditions, migrations, identities and imprisonment.

**Hanneke Stuit** is Assistant Professor in Literary and Cultural Analysis at the University of Amsterdam and a Researcher at the Amsterdam School of Cultural Analysis (ASCA). She is interested in spaces deemed peripheral in the globalised present, specifically prison spaces and the narratives and metaphors generated in, about and around those spaces. Focusing on contemporary South Africa (*Ubuntu Strategies: Constructing Spaces of Belonging in Contemporary South African Culture* (Palgrave, 2016)), she also researches the affective and political effects of renditions of the rural in the cultural imagination.

**Jennifer Turner** is a Senior Lecturer in Human Geography at the University of Liverpool. Her research is concerned with spaces, practices and representations of incarceration, past and present. She is the author of *The Prison Boundary: Between Society and Carceral Space* (Palgrave Macmillan, 2016) and co-editor of *Carceral Mobilities: Interrogating Movement in Incarceration* (2017).

**Andrew Wooff** is Lecturer in Criminology at Edinburgh Napier University. His articles on police custody, rural policing, police education and the special constabulary have appeared in many journals and books. He is a member of the Scottish Institute for Policing Research and the Police Custody Standards Board.

# List of Figures


| | | |
|---|---|---|
| Fig. 1.1 | A simple animal cell. (Source: Produced by author) | 3 |
| Fig. 3.1 | A typical cell at SCI Phoenix. (Source: Authors' collection) | 53 |
| Fig. 3.2 | A typical cell at Halden Prison. (Source: Authors' collection) | 56 |
| Fig. 3.3 | The bathroom and personal storage area in a typical cell at Halden Prison. (Source: Authors' collection) | 57 |
| Fig. 5.1 | A photograph of Bishop Auckland police station in Durham (not the case study location), which illustrates the stark nature of a police custody cell. (Source: Hill 2017) | 112 |
| Fig. 6.1 | An empty prison cell. (Source: Andreas Moser, JVA Lenzburg) | 124 |
| Fig. 6.2 | A homely furnished prison cell. (Source: Andreas Moser, JVA Lenzburg) | 128 |
| Fig. 6.3 | Personalisation of the cell through decoration. (Source: A prisoner, JVA Lenzburg). (Note: The pictures were taken by prisoners during walking interviews whereby I asked them to show me 'their' prison and taking pictures of places and objects that are of any relevance for them) | 130 |
| Fig. 6.4 | A prisoner's 'kitchen'. (Source: A prisoner, JVA Lenzburg) | 132 |
| Fig. 6.5 | 'To have it as nice as possible'. (Source: A prisoner, JVA Lenzburg) | 134 |
| Fig. 9.1 | A 2-year-old child inside the prison 'nursery'. (Source: Schillaci (2016)) | 187 |
| Fig. 9.2 | Children with their educators going back into Turin prison from the 'outside' nursery. (Source: Schillaci (2016)) | 190 |

Fig. 9.3 Children saying hello through bars at 8:00 pm when they got locked. (Source: Schillaci (2016)) 192
Fig. 9.4 The corridor of the nursery section with the gate at the end. (Source: Schillaci (2016)) 194
Fig. 9.5 The interior of a family cell. (Source: Schillaci (2016)) 195
Fig. 9.6 Child eating standing on the chair as she cannot reach the table. (Source: Schillaci (2016)) 198
Fig. 9.7 The table with the camping stove. (Source: Schillaci (2016)) 199
Fig. 9.8 One of the tricycles used by children in the prison. (Source: Schillaci (2016)) 202
Fig. 9.9 A child in the corridor near all the iron windows open. (Source: Schillaci (2016)) 203
Fig. 9.10 Children playing at the window. (Source: Schillaci (2016)) 204
Fig. 9.11 A mother speaking with a prisoner officer through the gate that closes her section. (Source: Schillaci (2016)) 205
Fig. 12.1 Cell and corridor: the distribution (Source: F Giofrè) 268
Fig. 12.2 Sketch of the cell by Fabiana, prisoner in Rebibbia, Italy 270
Fig. 14.1 Image of a prisoner escaping from their cell used on *Prison Escape*'s home page (Source: Sander Erdmann/Prison Escape) 310

# List of Tables


| | | |
|---|---|---|
| Table 4.1 | Inmate leadership titles and roles in the Philippines | 78 |
| Table 14.1 | Overview of game stages in ***Prison Escape*** | 308 |

# 1

# Dissecting the Cell: Embodied and Everyday Spaces of Incarceration

Jennifer Turner and Victoria Knight

> It is all too easy now to underestimate cells. We have known about them for such large fractions of our lives that, for the most part, we cease being aware of how remarkable they really are. (Alberts et al. 1994: xxxiii)

The remarkable cells that Bruce Alberts and his colleagues were considering as 'underestimated' were biological cells: the critical components, building blocks and hinge-points around which life itself is determined. As Alberts et al. (1994) explain, cells are the basis of all living things. These are 'small membrane-bound compartments filled with a concentrated aqueous solution of chemicals' that we must study 'to learn … how they are made from molecules and … how they cooperate to make an organism as complex as a human being' (Alberts et al. 1994: 3). By

J. Turner (✉)
Department of Geography and Planning, University of Liverpool, Liverpool, UK
e-mail: jennifer.turner@liverpool.ac.uk

V. Knight
School of Applied Social Sciences, De Montfort University, Leicester, UK
e-mail: vknight@dmu.ac.uk



J. Turner, V. Knight (eds.), *The Prison Cell*, Palgrave Studies in Prisons and Penology,
https://doi.org/10.1007/978-3-030-39911-5_1

examining any plant or animal structure microscopically, we will see that it consists 'of more or less distinct units—cells—which … in large numbers make up the structure or organ' (Mackean and Jones 1975: 6). Already, we can begin to see conceptual similarities to a prison—an 'organism' comprised of multiple rooms that are, largely, the same in each given prison establishment. These rooms, which are most commonly known as prison 'cells' typically represent the space around which life in prison is located, arranged and orchestrated both in terms of physical logistics and punitive philosophy. It is important that the prison cell is not considered as directly comparable—intellectually or actually—to the biological cell. Unlike its biological counterpart, the prison cell is not a natural occurrence. The use of cellular confinement is a *socio-political and economic construction* that, throughout the history of imprisonment, has been instrumental in shaping the organisation of carceral space as one of reform, separation, deterrence and isolation from the world outside of prison.

The very naming of the prison 'cell' is taken-for-granted in most literature that focuses upon this particular carceral space. Although practitioners and scholars researching and working in some contemporary prison spaces—particularly those in the more-exceptional penal landscape of Nordic countries or establishments that incarcerate children—revere the term 'room' as a way to demonstrate progressive action in certain institutions, 'cell' is the most commonplace of terminologies. Yet, unlike the notion of the 'carceral', which finds its Latin roots linked directly to incarceration, the etymology of cell does not find such a history secured in punitive philosophy. Drawing from its French roots, a cell is described as a chamber or storeroom. One the one hand, given such a definition, it is possible to see how the word 'cell' has come to be used for the naming of the room in which prisoners are detained. On the other hand, the biological cell, discovered by Robert Hooke in 1665, also found suitable this term, deriving from the Latin word for 'small room'. In adopting the word 'cell', the biological cell, then, became known as the container for human life.

Typically, as the cells of any biological organ 'are usually specially developed in their size, shape and chemistry to carry out one particular function there is, strictly speaking, no such thing as a typical cell'

(Mackean and Jones 1975: 7). Yet, all animal cells have three certain features in common: each consisting of 'an outer *membrane* enclosing a mass of *cytoplasm* in which is contained a *nucleus*' (ibid.: 7, emphasis added) (see Fig. 1.1). If we extend the analogy to carceral space, we might consider the cell membrane to represent the walls of the individual cell; the nucleus is the individual prisoner housed within it; and the mass of cytoplasm is all the other matter that is contained within the walls of the cell. The nucleus determines the form and function of a cell; the cytoplasm facilitates cell reactions; and the membrane prevents the cell contents—the prisoner—from mixing with the outside medium. All of these components are critical to the successful functioning of the overall structure—in this case, the working of the prison itself. In this respect, we may draw parallels between biological and carceral space. Whilst overarching penal rhetoric may vary country-by-country, the walls of a prison cell serve the purpose of the prison; that is to hold individuals securely and largely prevent contact with the outside world. Neither should the contents of a cell come into contact with those of neighbouring cells. Whilst it is necessary to acknowledge that the two hold fundamental differences, the biological cell provides a conceptual apparatus for interrogating and making sense of the prison cell.

Moreover, and continuing the analogy, a biological cell membrane is permeable; it permits but more so relies on transfers (Wood 1974: 39). As Mackean and Jones outline,

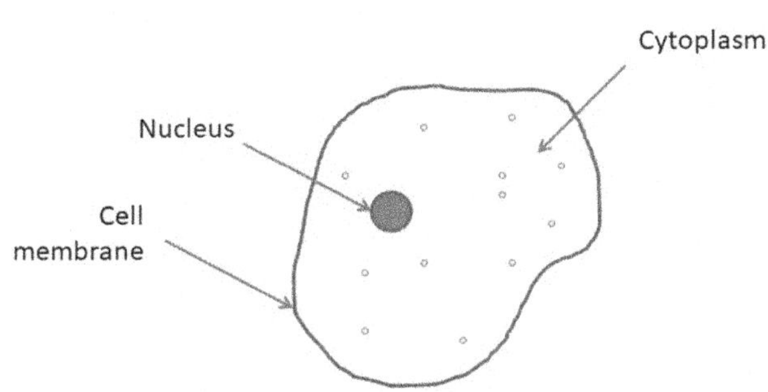


**Fig. 1.1** A simple animal cell. (Source: Produced by author)

> Although each cell can carry on the vital chemistry of living, it is not capable of existence on its own. A muscle cell cannot obtain its own food or oxygen. These materials are supplied by the blood and transported or made available by the activities of other specialized cells. Unless individual cells are grouped together in large numbers and made to work together by the co-ordinating mechanisms of the body, they cannot exist for long. (Mackean and Jones 1975: 11)

For the most part, transfers in the case of biological cells take place in a controlled manner (usually from an area of high concentration to an area of low concentration). However, there are also processes that take place, which go against the gradient. This is known as active transport, where particles are said to 'interfere' with the conventional workings of the cell (Wood 1974: 41). This process allows us to reflect on the workings of the prison cell whereby acceptable transfers may enter and leave the cell: food, letters, library books; and others may cross the cell membrane in a manner that goes against the grain: contraband such as drugs, alcohol or mobile telephones. Accordingly, although there are other spaces of significance in and around the prison establishment, the 'life' work of prison—eating, sleeping, washing, ageing, socialising, working, learning, entertaining, 'rehabilitating'—is predominantly carried out in the space of the cell: the 'container' of much prison life.

In short, the prison cell and the tripartite system of a biological cell arguably demonstrate similarly functioning components. The biological cell as analogy allows us to interrogate the nature and systems of carceral space—two of the foci noted as central concerns of carceral geographies (Moran 2016). It also provides an opportunity to (re)consider complex biological theorisations of spatial relationships (such as biological systematics) that explain relationships between organisms, which may have fallen out of favour since the poststructuralist turn, that challenge grand structures and essence in favour of a world shaped by emergence that is ever becoming (Cosgrove 1989). This work does not argue for a return to biological analysis, to be clear, but it does contend that we might interrogate space differently through drawing such analogies, with the recognition that such spaces are not collapsible or intrinsically comparable. Subsequently, thinking of the cell and unpacking the term through its biological 'traits' provides much purchase for interrogating the processes of emergence, development and experience of carceral spaces.

This is necessary, for although the prison cell has become one of the central components of incarceration, it has received surprisingly sparse treatment from academics. Much work from a variety of disciplines—such as criminology, carceral geography, sociology, penology, psychology, and architecture—has, of course, explored cell spaces as part of their empirical and conceptual appraisals of carceral space more generally. Such work is wide-ranging and it is almost impossible to highlight all examples here. However, it is important to note that studies of cells in the context of incarceration cover a variety of empirical settings, which range from prison and police cells (Baksheev et al. 2010) to holding cells in extradition camps (Schneider 2004). The academic focus on cells has also come from a variety of different foci: security and safety (Cox and Skegg 1993; Reid et al. 2012), architecture (Fairweather and McConville 2013), technology (Knight 2017), time and space (Leal and Mond 2001), racial tensions (Trulson and Marquart 2010), the neoliberal economy (Mitchelson 2014), and the media presentation of carceral space (Fiddler 2007). There is also a wealth of work on former carceral spaces, such as sites of penal tourism where cells are often the stage on which 'edutainment' narratives play out (Wilson et al. 2017). However, although the cell is a focus, its definition and significance as a central component for and through which carceral life is manifest is largely ignored. Important work that attempts to theorise carcerality (Moran et al. 2018) or the prison boundary (Turner 2016), tackles issues related to the cell, but such work has not directed particular attention to the scale of the cell or on what an interrogation of that particular space/spatiality reveals for our wider understandings of prisons and other carceral spaces.

It is well documented in several key texts focussing on prisons (whether academic, policy-directed or practitioner-led) that the cell is ordinarily the primary space in which prisoners spend most of their day and will fulfil this function for a number of months, years and decades. For example, research often reveals significant time spent 'behind the door' in a cell space, which can often extend to 23 hours a day for prisoners in maximum security facilities (see Sykes 2007 among many examples). Of course, being a space in which most time is spent does not automatically make it worthy of discussion. The cell warrants further attention because it is the space at the centre of prison experience. Beyond the practical aspects of everyday life noted above, research that explores the wider lived experience of carceral spaces indicates that the cell is also a space for individual resistances, personalities to be enacted, post-release plans to be concocted, and dreams and aspirations to be explored and manifested (see, for example, Crewe 2012; Ugelvik 2014). In the current climate of contemplating rehabilitative strategies and fostering societal understanding of prison and reform, it is pertinent to interrogate the everyday and embodied experiences of incarceration and, of course, the spaces/spatialities in which they take place. Thinking through the balance of rehabilitative strategy and wider management of the prison estate leads to other considerations of the cell as intrinsic to and bound within decision-making processes about the wider prison system. In the UK, architects and planners of new-build prisons have come to replicate a standard model for the prison cell across the estate (Moran et al. 2016) in an attempt to regulate and make cost-effective the custodial environment. Now, a generic cell design—often constructed through Building Information Modelling software—is part of a governmental strategy to regulate the estate to ensure safety and security for both staff and prisoners. More than this, using standardised designs, manufacturing processes and regular suppliers for the physical components of the cell space nationwide ensures that the Ministry of Justice in the UK, for example, can benefit from economies of scale, policies and procedures can be replicated across the estate, and the experience of the prison cell can be regulated through its standardisation. Cells have become the most easily replicable part of the prison estate. They are firmly embedded into the library of prison 'parts', so much so that some architects have admitted that they no longer spend time focussing on these areas of the prison—instead hoping to win bids with unique configurations of houseblocks or innovative technological advances to reduce staffing or heating costs, for example (Moran et al. 2016). However, in doing so, policy-makers often diminish the significance and individuality of the embodied and everyday practices that are critical to the lived experience of carceral space.

Accordingly, in seeking to highlight the 'remarkable' nature of cell space, *The Prison Cell* focuses upon this central institution of carcerality.

Building upon recent work on carceral atmospheres (Turner and Peters 2015), cell capacities (Peters and Turner 2018) and extending work, for example, that considers the importance of objects in carceral lives/cell spaces (Baer 2005; Schliehe 2017) this volume explores the intricate material, human and more-than-human connections that make cell space function. To this end, the cell analogy, and thinking of the nucleus, cytoplasm and cell membrane of the *prison* cell permits a deep interrogation of this central, but oddly overlooked, space. The book brings together a series of chapters that negotiate the complexities of this type of carceral space and address the significance of the cell in relation to the embodied and everyday experiences of incarceration. Furthermore, the work in this volume highlights the importance of the prison cell as a space that is crucially connected to wider carceral space, recognising cells as more than simply static entities and instead imbued with and embroiled within practices and processes of carceral movement and mobilities (Turner and Peters 2017). We highlight the array of processes and practices that shape carceral life from this perspective to provide a unique volume that advances our understandings, conceptualisations and experiences of the space of the cell. As we have considered, the cell is an intriguing space—a space many researchers find difficult to access practically, safely, decently, morally and ethically. And, yet, the cell symbolically represents the monolithic values of the prison where it largely remains uncontested, often free from scrutiny and direct observation by staff, other prisoners and prison visitors like researchers. As a response to this, this collection extends discourses about the cell and offers novel accounts of the cell in its various forms and in varying contexts. Together this book offers readers a captivating journey deep inside the cell to characterise it as a distinctive, complex and powerful space that has, above all, become positioned as central to incarceration as a process and tool for penal power.

## The Chapters

This body of work offers new insights for scholars, researchers and practitioners. All of the contributions are theoretically informed and draw from extensive and rich data. Our collection offers readers a potential framework, as a metaphor, for understanding the centrality of the cell's role in the system of containment and punishment, as well as wider imaginations of the penal system. Imaginations of the cell are steadfast, often rooted in cultural expectations—as cultural artefacts that are communicated through television, literature and film—of how punishment and incarceration is administered and experienced. Moreover academic studies, particularly in criminology, are grounded in Western ideologies and too often our view of the prison and the cell are aligned to cultural contexts. These imaginations are, in many ways, challenged by the intensive scrutiny contributors have offered. This volume draws upon a multitude of international case studies from a global collective of authors across a range of disciplines (including criminology, penology, anthropology, sociology, geography, literary and cultural studies, media studies, architecture and law) to critique these persistent ontologies by provoking renewed and extended understandings of the prison cell as an everyday and embodied experience of imprisonment.[1] Here these insights offer rich discussions about the ways in which humans respond to the prison at large; through sensory engagements with the physical environment and the people around them in experiences that often include both adaption and resistance to surroundings.

## Part I: The Nucleus

In this section we introduce chapters that speak to the underpinning mechanisms and aims of imprisonment such as forms of power and philosophical interpretations. Here the chapters interrogate the role of the cell as a conduit of power—where the cell is inherently interlinked with the overarching ideology or management principles of the wider penal system.

In Chap. 2, Helen Johnston takes the reader on a historical journey highlighting how English penal philosophies of the early nineteenth century focused upon the prison cell. Johnston outlines how the cell was constructed as a space of transformation, isolation, conflict and punishment; a site in which the individual offender would, in theory, reflect upon and repent their sins and alter their future behaviour. In revealing the relationship between this particular space and the wider institutional agenda, this chapter explains how the use of the cell as a pivotal part of the disciplinary regime has persisted in the modern prison.

Leading on from this, in Chap. 3, Jordan Hyatt, Synøve Andersen and Steven Chanenson further demonstrate how attending to contemporary carceral design provides a perspective on the prevailing ideological and pragmatic goals within penal systems. Hyatt et al. compare the distinct penal ideologies of Norway and the United States through in-depth focus on cells in a newly-constructed prison in each country. Here, they identify a contrast between utilitarian punishment goals like reintegration and 'normality' through environmental-based rehabilitation and the primacy of efficiency and other non-utilitarian correctional goals across both contexts. In highlighting the myriad nuances of the Norwegian and United States' approach to cell design in their new-build prisons, this chapter reveals the prison cell as a space that clearly communicates the contemporary priorities of the prison system.

In Chap. 4, we turn to the prison cell in the context of The Philippines where Raymund Narag and Clarke Jones attend to multiple occupancy cells where prisoners are themselves deputised as part of a leadership structure called the *mayores* system to help with custodial, rehabilitative and administrative tasks. This chapter draws upon qualitative data gathered over 20 years to demonstrate how traditional Filipino culture imported into prison reinforces a shared governance model that impacts how prisoners experience cell life and constructs the cell as a disciplinary tool (Foucault 1977), which, although somewhat contra to Western versions of inadequacy in terms of its infrastructural resources and levels of overcrowding, results in positive outcomes for the prison system in this particular context.

The focus then shifts to the police cell—which exists as both a detainee's first encounter with carceral cell space and as a liminal space 'betwixt and between' life within and outside of the criminal justice system—where, in Chap. 5, Andrew Wooff reveals how cells in police custody suites in the UK play a central role in police practice. Wooff argues that police custody has, until recently, been treated in a fairly monolithic way and is, instead, a complex and multi-faceted environment. In this chapter, Wooff draws on observations and interviews with police officers and custody staff to reveal the police custody cell as a space of monitoring risk and managing emotional turmoil.

## Part II: Cytoplasm

The next section of our book interrogates how prisoners and detainees respond to their confinement within the boundaried parameters of the cell space itself. The contributors' insights provide novel readings of the performative concept of being a prisoner through focus on the embodied and everyday experiences of life in imprisonment in the cell.

In Chap. 6, Irene Marti's ethnographically-informed study explores the experience of long-term prisoners in Switzerland who have been given indeterminate sentences and offers insights into the prisoners' ways of inhabiting a cell. Despite furnishing and maintenance being highly constrained by the prison's regime, this chapter explores the prisoners' individual ways of (re)arranging their prison cell. Here, Marti reveals how prisoners ascribe new meanings and values to the prison cell and create personal and intimate space as a way of inhabiting a cell in a life situation that is characterised by a high degree of uncertainty.

Following this, another interpretation of the prison cell is offered in Chap. 7 by the Another Chance at Education (ACE) Steering Committee. Here, this collaborative team of writers (including university undergraduates, academic faculty members and serving prisoners) co-produced their examination of dimensions of the cell as experienced by men in a maximum-security penitentiary in the United States. In particular, ACE opens up the cell as an emotional landscape, which posits them as mutable spaces, often exhibiting many things simultaneously that are particular to their occupant(s). In exemplifying the complexity of prison cells as a dynamic and significant space within the prison, this chapter reveals them as not only constraining spaces, but also sites and sources of ingenuity and agency.

Bénédicte Michalon also interrogates power relationships through her examination of cells in immigration detention centres in Romania in Chap. 8. She examines the cell as a source of tension between spatial restriction and domestication of space in a situation where cells are typically multi-occupancy. Cells in this context are also used for disguising power relationships; under the pretext of respect for their privacy, the detainees are driven to treat the cell as a domestic space. Their relations to this imposed spatial unit are characterised by their heterogeneity. Domestication of the cell therefore does not appear to be a process of emancipation, but rather a subtle but efficient way of maintaining order within the cell's walls.

In Chap. 9, Rossella Schillaci extends our enquiry into the prison cell as a space for everyday interaction by drawing upon research produced as part of the documentary film *Imprisoned Lullaby* to interrogate the suitability of cell life for children in a prison mothers' unit in Italy. The chapter reveals how mothers must overcome several obstacles in raising their children within the prison environment, particularly in relation to the physical landscape of the prison cell and the daily routine of mother- and childhood that must be contained within it, such as washing, eating and sleeping. Schillaci explores how both mothers and children adopt several strategies to use the cell as a space to build intimate relationships. However, despite these deliberate goals of transforming prison life, such intentions rarely attempt to construct the prison cell as a 'home'. Instead, all long-term emotional and material connections to this 'cursed' space are deliberately avoided.

## Part III: The Cell Membrane

In the final section of the book we present a series of chapters that illuminate what we might term the prison cell boundary. The chapters in this section focus on cell experiences that are tied to spaces outside of it—other cells; connecting corridors; and spaces outwith the prison, among others—to explore how inside of the cell and the outside of the cell symbiotically dis/connect. In particular, these chapters address how experiences of the prison cell are developed through sensations and human connections.

Jennifer Turner, Dominique Moran and Yvonne Jewkes explore the significance of sensory interactions with blue space through the bars of a prison cell window in Chap. 10. Much previous literature has explored how the architecture of incarceration impinges on the lives of those residing in carceral space and rarely considers the prison environment as a therapeutic space. Drawing on notions of therapeutic landscapes and data collected from a UK prison in a coastal town where many cells have a view of the sea, Turner et al. theorise the prison as a nurturing rather than punitive environment by examining the relationship between the prison cell and the lived experience of blue space. In doing so, this chapter reveals the possibilities for both the disciplinary theorisation of therapeutic blue space and the micro-scale health benefits that may be generated by a reconsideration of prison siting and environmental outlook, particularly from the prison cell.

In contrast, moving away from previous studies that have employed a primarily visual approach to prison research, in Chap. 11, Kate Herrity draws on a research project on the significance of sound in prison using aural ethnography in a local men's prison in the UK. Herrity highlights how sounds such as cell door banging and music permeate life in the prison. In particular, these auditory experiences foreground cell life and, for some, offer a source of sanctuary and/or enforce practices of 'sousveillance' within the cell. In registering the sensory experiences that take place 'beyond our line of sight' this chapter adds texture and depth to our understanding of life in prison.

Extending focus to another of the senses, Elisabeth Fransson and Francesca Giofrè explore the significance of touch in Chap. 12. The chapter draws upon material generated as part of a comparative study in two female prisons in Italy and Norway and disrupts traditional understandings of the prison cell as an isolated unit within the prison by exploring various prison cells, their boundaries and extensions. Here, Fransson and Giofrè take inspiration from considerations of sensuous architecture and the philosophy of touch to explore the intersection of spaces inside cells and those outside of them such as corridors and thresholds. In doing so, this chapter not only reveals the value of taking an embodied approach to prison studies but moves beyond an often limited and singular understanding of what a prison cell is and can be.

The prison cell is not simply linked to spaces within the prison but also inherently connected to spaces outside of the institution too. In Chap. 13, Jana Robberechts and Kristel Beyens discuss their research into the digitalisation of the prison cell through the introduction of information and communication technologies, which offer a variety of methods for prisoners to communicate within and beyond the walls of the prison.

This ethnographic study of a Belgian prison equipped with the digital platform *PrisonCloud* interrogates the impacts of this increasingly multi-functional digital cell upon physical and social interactions. Drawing upon observations and interviews with prisoners, prison officers and administrative staff, this chapter interrogates the impact of the relocation of activities within the everyday regime, such as telephone calling and booking medical appointments, inside of the cell. Accordingly, Robberechts and Beyens reveal how the use of in-cell digital technology has the potential to alter prisoner-staff interactions in addition to reinforcing the prisoner's position of dependency, as well as generating new forms of isolation.

Also recognising the relationships between prison cells and the spaces beyond them, Hanneke Stuit takes us, in Chap. 14, into the world of real-life games to explore one example of how the prison cell enters into our cultural imaginations. In this final empirical chapter, Stuit's close reading of the *Prison Escape* game, in the former prison in Breda, the Netherlands highlights how the space of the cell is deployed as an entry point into understanding the prison. The game, where as many as 200 players are locked inside the former prison and tasked with escaping from it, evokes popular imaginations of the prison and panoptic architecture. Here, principles of play rely on a metaphorically constructed, fantastical lure of the prison cell, which engineers resistance to the landscape of surveillance. Stuit posits the prison cell as a heterotopic, liminal space of play offering an embodied, if limited, experience of incarceration which foregrounds reflection on the mechanics of intensified surveillance.

## Moving Forwards

Returning at the end of this chapter to Alberts et al.,

> Cells are small and complex: it is hard to see their structure, hard to discover their molecular composition, and harder still to find out how their various components function. An enormous variety of experimental techniques have been developed to study cells, and the strength and limitations of these techniques have largely determined our present conception of the

> cell. Most of the advances in cell biology—including the most exciting ones of recent years—have sprung from the introduction of new methods. (Alberts et al. 1994: 143)

Just like the biological cell described here, the prison cell is often regarded simply as 'the cell'—yet without careful attention it is hard to understand its structure, composition and how it may function in relation to the larger 'whole' of the prison and to penal philosophy. More so, although there have been attempts to research or 'study' the prison cell, these shape our present understandings and there remains a need to introduce new methods to help us grapple with, make sense of, and understand the cell for academic and policy purposes. As with cell biology, without continued development of, and adaption to, our approach to the study of prison cells, our very conception and understanding of them is limited. Through this collection we have offered some consolidation of what the cell is, what it does and how it is experienced in a variety of different empirical and theoretical perspectives in different contexts. The prison cell is revealed as a crucial yet complex component in regimes of incarceration. It is a paradoxical space where power and resistance converge, which is both anaesthetising and overwhelming in terms of sensory experiences and simultaneously removed from and interlinked with, spaces surrounding it in and beyond prison. The body of work presented in this volume is wide-ranging and strong in its contribution to this field of interest. However, it is, unsurprisingly, incomplete and we hope that new knowledge and modes of inquiry continue to develop to interrogate this critical space. In particular, this contribution draws from an array of disciplines and the eclectic lenses applied in this book highlight the need to open new ontological pathways to enhance our understanding of the cell, perhaps most importantly in multi-disciplinary ways. By way of conclusion to this introductory chapter, we offer four trajectories for development in this area.

Our first consideration builds upon the very metaphor of the biological cell that is set out in this introduction. Considering the prison cell as a set of components akin to nuclei, cytoplasm and cell membranes offers a new conceptual tool to unpack and underpin the complex actions, reactions and interactions of the space of the cell. Much like recent work that has driven the interrogation of the specificity of the 'carceral' itself (see Moran et al. 2018), forward-going analysis of the prison cell may be enhanced further through a (re)consideration of the theoretical and conceptual foundations of the 'prison cell' as a tool for deployment both within an academic and a policy-orientated scope. What does the prison cell consist of? What does this definition include and/or exclude and does this change the scope of research attention to it? In this volume, although we include the likes of cells in immigration detention (which are the focus of Michalon's study in Chap. 8) collectively here under the previously-mentioned renewed scope of the carceral (Moran et al. 2018), in doing so there are key distinctions between these and traditional spaces of the prison that could still be unpacked further from a conceptual point of view. The biological prison cell, so to speak, reminds us to look more closely at minute, forgotten details, and calls our attention to embodied and everyday experience of carceral life. There may be other conceptualisations beyond the biological cell analogy that offer similar, and/or varied, considerations of this complex landscape.

Secondly, and likely in conjunction with any progression of our conceptual toolbox, we offer a plea to extend the empirical range and scope of research associated with prison cells. If our understandings of what exactly the prison cell is and where it can be found are augmented, the potential range of the field of study also increases. We now have the capacity to study a range of different aspects of the prison cell from its sonic properties (as in Herrity's work in Chap. 11) to its architectural design (explored in relation to the view from prison cell windows by Turner et al. in Chap. 10) and its percolation into other cultural artefacts related to the prison (such as in the escape game noted by Stuit in Chap. 14). As will be highlighted in this volume, there is a range of context-specific manifestations of the prison cell but only some of which have we been able to exemplify within this collection. In particular, difficulties of access to not only prison spaces but, also, restrictions on academic scholarship in some countries may have a bearing upon the geographical range of such studies. Particular types of cells are far more closed than others. We could, for example, extend our enquiries to spaces such as detention camps and military prisons but these spaces are often even more 'closed' than traditional prisons as research sites. Recent work, such as Moran et al.'s (2012) work on prisoner transportation also reveals significant difficulties in appraising carceral space in contexts—here Russia—where the specificities of the geographical landscape and infrastructure present quite significant challenges. Whilst there may be immovable obstacles surrounding some of the practical issues associated with access, there are, perhaps, some considerations to offer in relation to how our work may evolve methodologically to respond to these challenges.

In addition, although this volume has illuminated the prison cell as vitally connected to other areas of the prison, much of this connection is revealed by the recognition that, methodologically, most discussion of the prison cell takes place outside of the cell itself. Although some authors have been given favourable access to these spaces (such as that which facilitated the documentary film that became the basis for Schillaci's work in Chap. 9), for reasons of security, prisoner management and researcher safety, interviews with prisoners often take place outside of the cell. In a similar vein, it is also very difficult to capture experiences of cells at certain time periods within the cycle of incarceration. For example, as Wooff (Chap. 5) highlights, the transient and often unpredictable nature of police cells presents clear challenges to accessing participants who may only spend hours in that particular carceral space. Indeed, the in-depth analysis of work such as that offered here by Narag and Jones (Chap. 4) is predicated on a number of years of ethnographically-informed research. These challenges may also apply to researchers interested in other transitory cell spaces such as prison reception areas, first-night centres and, at the other end of the journey, rooms in half-way houses and temporary accommodation offered around the time of release. Here, the practicalities of research converge with ethical considerations surrounding informed consent and the tensions of conducting research with individuals who may be experiencing acute distress in that particular location at that particular time. In the first instance, we may consider the value of historical accounts (such as Johnston's in Chap. 2) and existing data sets—which are often available as data sets acquired through public funding are usually required to be submitted to an archive for future use—are an invaluable tool for tracing philosophical, political and cultural understandings of incarceration without the invasive nature of the creation of 'new' knowledge. However, where the nature of the research enquiry makes this impractical, we could push further for the inclusion of a much wider range of voices from within carceral space. As the contribution by ACE (Chap. 7) will demonstrate, co-creative techniques that celebrate co-authorship and co-production of knowledge from 'within' the prison cell could be offered as a way to explore these spaces more effectively. Taking lead from Robberechts and Beyens (Chap. 13), modes of digitisation—which enable new interactions from within the prison cell—may present new opportunities and new challenges for researchers reaching participants who dwell inside cell spaces.

Finally, we use this volume to call for an extension of the relationship between our empirical knowledge and the policy developments related to it. As many of our chapters contend—most notably in the chapters offering comparative case studies such as those offered by Hyatt et al. (Chap. 3) and Fransson and Giofrè (Chap. 12)—there is a clear relationship between penal philosophy and the prison cell; in terms of its physical landscape, the regime that it serves and the possibility and capabilities it can achieve. Many of the chapters in this collection reveal not only shortcomings of the prison cell—perhaps in terms of its suitability as a space for dealing with particular groups of residents such as young families or prisoners who are likely to spend extended periods in these kinds of spaces (such as in Marti's interrogation in Chap. 6 of prison cells for prisoners with indeterminate sentence)—but also the positive associations with this space. In a penal environment where loss of liberty is deliberately and acutely felt, further interrogation of the space in which prisoners spend most of their daily lives is likely to illuminate many occasions of poor and good practice that have a wider implication for our understandings of the nature and purpose of carceral spaces more generally.

In sum, the prison cell, whilst a central part of carceral life, has not achieved focused scrutiny because it is so pervasive, so central, so taken-for-granted. It is both commonly accepted, yet critically unacknowledged at the same time. Therefore, serious interrogation of this space is often lacking. It is precisely because the cell is so discernible that we are in danger of missing the everyday, the mundane and the ordinary features of incarceration. It is our intention that this volume provides a foundational point from which to continue and expand our understandings of the space of the prison cell: arguably—whether for good or otherwise—the fundamental building block of life in prison.

## Note

1. The scope and geographical extent of the book has resulted in a variety of different terminology to describe the various spaces of, and individuals involved in, incarceration. We appreciate that these terms can often be interpreted differently depending on the disciplinary and geographical situation in which they are received but have retained the use of language common to the academic and social context from which the research emerges.

## References

Alberts, B., Bray, D., Lewis, J., Raff, M., Roberts, P., & Watson, J. D. (1994). *Molecular Biology of the Cell*. New York, NY: Garland.

Baer, L. D. (2005). Visual Imprints on the Prison Landscape: A Study on the Decorations in Prison Cells. *Tijdschrift voor economische en sociale geografie, 96*(2), 209–217.

Baksheev, G. N., Thomas, S. D., & Ogloff, J. R. (2010). Psychiatric Disorders and Unmet Needs in Australian Police Cells. *Australian & New Zealand Journal of Psychiatry, 44*(11), 1043–1051.

Cosgrove, D. (1989). A Terrain of Metaphor: Cultural Geography 1988–1989. *Progress in Human Geography, 13*(4), 566–575.

Cox, B., & Skegg, K. (1993). Contagious Suicide in Prisons and Police Cells. *Journal of Epidemiology & Community Health, 47*(1), 69–72.

Crewe, B. (2012). *The Prisoner Society: Power, Adaptation and Social Life in an English Prison*. Oxford: Oxford University Press.

Fairweather, L., & McConville, S. (2013). *Prison Architecture*. London: Routledge.

Fiddler, M. (2007). Projecting the Prison: The Depiction of the Uncanny in the Shawshank Redemption. *Crime, Media, Culture, 3*(2), 192–206.

Foucault, M. (1977). *Discipline and Punish: The Birth of the Prison*. London: Vintage.

Knight, V. (2017). *Remote Control: Television in Prison*. London: Palgrave Macmillan.

Leal, W. C., & Mond, D. (2001). From My Prison Cell: Time and Space in Prison in Colombia, an Ethnographic Approach. *Latin American Perspectives, 28*(1), 149–164.

Mackean, D., & Jones, B. (1975). *Introduction to Human and Social Biology*. London: John Murray.

Mitchelson, M. L. (2014). The Production of Bedspace: Prison Privatization and Abstract Space. *Geographica Helvetica, 69*(5), 325–333.

Moran, D. (2016). *Carceral Geography: Spaces and Practices of Incarceration*. London: Routledge.

Moran, D., Piacentini, L., & Pallot, J. (2012). Disciplined Mobility and Carceral Geography: Prisoner Transport in Russia. *Transactions of the Institute of British Geographers, 37*(3), 446–460.

Moran, D., Turner, J., & Jewkes, Y. (2016). Becoming Big Things: Building Events and the Architectural Geographies of Incarceration in England and Wales. *Transactions of the Institute of British Geographers, 41*(4), 416–428.

Moran, D., Turner, J., & Schliehe, A. K. (2018). Conceptualizing the Carceral in Carceral Geography. *Progress in Human Geography, 42*(5), 666–686.

Peters, K., & Turner, J. (2018). Unlock the Volume: Towards a Politics of Capacity. *Antipode, 50*(4), 1037–1056.

Reid, S. E., Topp, S. M., Turnbull, E. R., Hatwiinda, S., Harris, J. B., Maggard, K. R., Roberts, S. T., Krüüner, A., Morse, J. C., Kapata, N., & Chisela, C. (2012). Tuberculosis and HIV Control in Sub-Saharan African Prisons: "Thinking Outside the Prison Cell". *Journal of Infectious Diseases, 205*(Suppl 2), S265–S273.

Schliehe, A. (2017). Constraint Locomotion: Of Complex Micro-scale Mobilities in Carceral Environments. In J. Turner & K. Peters (Eds.), *Carceral Mobilities: Interrogating Movement in Incarceration* (pp. 115–130). London: Routledge.

Schneider, D. (2004). Human Rights Issues in Guantanamo Bay. *The Journal of Criminal Law, 68*(5), 423–439.

Sykes, G. M. (2007). *The Society of Captives: A Study of a Maximum Security Prison*. Princeton, NJ: Princeton University Press.

Trulson, C. R., & Marquart, J. W. (2010). *First Available Cell: Desegregation of the Texas Prison System*. Austin, TX: University of Texas Press.

Turner, J. (2016). *The Prison Boundary: Between Society and Carceral Space*. London: Palgrave Macmillan.

Turner, J., & Peters, K. (2015). Unlocking Carceral Atmospheres: Designing Visual/Material Encounters at the Prison Museum. *Visual Communication, 14*(3), 309–330.

Turner, J., & Peters, K. (Eds.). (2017). *Carceral Mobilities: Interrogating Movement in Incarceration*. London: Routledge.

Ugelvik, T. (2014). *Power and Resistance in Prison: Doing Time, Doing Freedom*. London: Palgrave Macmillan.

Wilson, J. Z., Hodgkinson, S., Piché, J., & Walby, K. (Eds.). (2017). *The Palgrave Handbook of Prison Tourism*. London: Palgrave Macmillan.

Wood, D. W. (1974). *Principles of Animal Physiology*. London: Arnold.

# Part I

## The Nucleus

The nucleus is a large spherical or ovoid body enclosed in the cytoplasm but separated from it by a membrane similar to the cell membrane… It is the nucleus that ultimately determines the shape and function of the cell. (Mackean and Jones 1975: 8)

# 2

# 'The Solitude of the Cell': Cellular Confinement in the Emergence of the Modern Prison, 1850–1930

Helen Johnston

In Western societies, during the nineteenth century, the newly established 'modern' prison used the architecture, physical structure of the prison and, notably, the prison cell to induce conformity and reflection and to punish those confined within. In England, from the 1830s, when the prisons began to routinely use cellular confinement under the separate system of discipline, until the 1920s and 1930s when prison regimes were slowly ameliorating, the cell was established as a pivotal part of the prison and its architecture. Once established, the cell would persist as the conventional and most enduring feature of prison design and organisation as well as the most notable space in the prisoner experience. This chapter will explore the beginnings of the use of cellular confinement in late-eighteenth and early-nineteenth-century England. It will then examine the changing philosophies and practices that embedded 'the cell' in the prison architecture and routine of the nineteenth century and early

H. Johnston (✉)
Department of Criminology and Sociology, University of Hull, Hull, UK
e-mail: H.Johnston@hull.ac.uk



J. Turner, V. Knight (eds.), *The Prison Cell*, Palgrave Studies in Prisons and Penology,
https://doi.org/10.1007/978-3-030-39911-5_2

twentieth-century prison as well as considering the experience that cellular confinement engendered.

In order to uncover these experiences, this chapter draws on a range of historical evidence from archival research that documents the English prisoner experience. Primarily, it draws upon prison administrative records for local and convict prisons (governor journals, internal prison records, for example) and government documentation in the form of official investigations and annual reports through the Parliamentary Papers. It also explores a range of published material from the period including autobiographical accounts of prisoners (and social commentators) and newspaper reports. Overall, this rich range of archival material will provide the basis for demonstrating how the cell was established as a pivotal part of the prison experience and indeed how it was able to endure the various changes in dominance of different justifications for punishment over time. In addition, it will argue that the use of isolation and solitude remained a central feature of the cell experience for prisoners well into the twentieth century, a feature often overlooked in historical research on prison in this period.

## Prison 'Reform' in the Late Eighteenth Century

The 'birth' of the prison at the end of the eighteenth and beginning of the nineteenth century saw the transition of prisons from a place of detention to a place where 'transformation' or 'change' could occur within the minds of those confined (Foucault [1975] 1991; McConville 1998a; McGowen 1998). The regimes, routines and practices within prison, as well as the architecture and design of prisons would become central to this (Jewkes and Johnston 2007). In the early phase of prison reform, the architectural development and design of prisons was heavily influenced by ideas about the physical health of prisoners as well as the moral environment that the prison was seeking to create (Evans 1982). In England, key reformers such as John Howard and Elizabeth Fry had pointed to the poor conditions and physical health of inmates; the spread of diseases like gaol fever in the pre-reform gaols and houses of correction; and to the debauched and corrupting moral environment (Howard [1777] 1929;

Fry 1827; McConville 1981, 1998a; McGowen 1998). Both physical and moral health would influence the changes in prison design that would ultimately inform the idea that the 'cell' or cellular confinement offered the potential to address both of these concerning elements.

There was widespread prison building in late-eighteenth-century England, as at least 45 new gaols or bridewells were newly constructed (Evans 1982). However, this activity happened at the local level; there was no government involvement in prison at this time as most of the more serious offenders were either executed or sentenced to transportation overseas. In local prisons, prison architecture and design focused on the prevention of the spread of physical disease. Prisons were often constructed using arcades with sleeping cells or rooms above, with the idea of circulating air and providing ventilation or expelling 'putrid' air, which was then believed to be the source of disease (Evans 1982; Jewkes and Johnston 2007).

The proposals for the first government penitentiary were contained within the 1779 Penitentiary Act, which occurred in the aftermath of the American War of Independence as the American colonies could no longer take convicts previously transported there. The 'Panopticon' prison design, as proposed by Jeremy Bentham, appeared in response to this government call for a new penitentiary (under a tender within the 1779 Act). Bentham's Panopticon design was based on ideas of surveillance, inspection and observation. The proposed six-storey circular structure building where prisoners, in cells facing a central observation tower, would be in view of the guards at all times. The Panopticon was never built despite Bentham's continued efforts (Semple 1993; McConville 1981) and neither were the proposed government penitentiaries, instead, the discovery of Australia had led to the establishment of a new penal colony where over 160,000 convicts would be sent before its cessation in 1867 (Godfrey and Cox 2008; Johnston 2015). Yet the ideas about cellular confinement and a space or place for penance remained and were to reignite as a central part of discussion in the early decades of the nineteenth century.

The use of the prison cell would become a focal point of philosophical discussions and architectural concerns in the early nineteenth century. This discussion and the subsequent practice would have a profound and enduring effect on the ways which determined how prisoners would be confined. In 1811, the Holford Committee again proposed a government penitentiary. The penitentiary would hold prisoners before they were transported overseas. Central to the proposed regime was solitary confinement or seclusion in cells. The Committee reviewed existing arrangements of this nature at local prisons across the country, notably focusing on systems used at Gloucester Penitentiary and at Southwell House of Correction in Nottingham. Indeed, the Committee concluded that 'many offenders may be reclaimed by a system of Penitentiary imprisonment; by which Your Committee mean a system of imprisonment, not confined to the safe custody of the person, but extending to the reformation and improvement of the mind, and operating by seclusion, employment and religious instruction' (Holford Committee 1810–1811: 6). Millbank Penitentiary opened on the banks of the River Thames in 1816 and its regime centred on cellular seclusion and isolation. Those held at Millbank were subject to this system of isolation before being transported to Australia. However, it was blighted by problems of staffing and outbreaks of disease, as well as debates about the use of solitary confinement and its effects on those subject to it (McConville 1981; Wilson 2002, 2014). Millbank's demise was relatively swift as the attention of commentators had already begun to shift and was increasingly influenced by experiments into such practices used in prisons in the United States that, as will be demonstrated, placed the 'cell' at the centre of debates about how prisoners' behaviour might be changed.

## Separation and Silence: Isolation and Contamination

By the 1820s and 1830s, cellular confinement was a major source of discussion in England informed also by practice from across the Atlantic. In America, at Walnut Street prison and then Cherry Hill penitentiary, in Philadelphia, Pennsylvania and at Auburn prison in the State of New York, two contrasting systems of discipline were in operation. At these two locations experiments in the methods of the separate system in

Pennsylvania and the silent system in New York were being undertaken. Both systems aimed to change offenders by limiting the contact that they had with other prisoners and, therefore, the potential for further 'moral contamination' but each relied on different practices to do so. The separate system advocated the use of isolation in cells where prisoners were confined alone to work, eat and sleep. The architecture of cellular confinement was therefore central to this approach. Prisoners were only able to leave the cell for exercise or to attend services in the chapel. Outside of the cell, they were instructed to wear masks or caps with low peaks to obstruct recognition by other inmates (Ignatieff 1978; Forsythe 1987). The competing silent system relied on silence at all times, so, whilst prisoners might sleep in cells alone at night, during the day they worked in silent association with others. Thus under the silent system cellular isolation was only used at night. It was thought that these systems would induce prisoners to reflect upon their previous behaviour to reduce the morally-corrupting influence of the prison environment and encourage them to repent their sins and turn away from life of crime. As is implied, religion was also a significant feature of the approaches, though noticeably more so in the separate system where the prison chaplain had a key role. Isolation and silence would allow for reflection, repentance: within the separate cell they would be solitary, reminiscent of monastic existence. Visits by the chaplain would break the silent monotony. It was within the space of the cell that this religious transformation would take place, as the chaplain of Parkhurst recounted:

> It is [in their cells] that I get into their spirit and worm out their individual traits and temptations, then that I can apply the Gospel remedy to each lad, that I can listen to their regrets on account of past conduct, and to their little tales of home scenes and recollections. It is there that I can calm the troubled mind and cool the fiery temper roused by an imagined injustice. (Cited in Forsythe 1987: 47)

In 1835, the government appointed inspectors of prisons, one of whom, William Crawford, had visited the penitentiaries in the US operating both these systems of imprisonment. He presented a detailed report demonstrating his support for the separate system.

Subsequently, Crawford and another inspector, Reverend Whitworth Russell, both advanced the benefits of the separate system and perhaps inevitably due to their influence, 'separation … was thought to be the panacea for increasing crime' (Tomlinson 1978: 62). Reporting on the Eastern Penitentiary in Pennsylvania, Crawford wrote:

> the cells are ranged on each side of the corridors in the wall of which is a small aperture and iron door to each cell: through this aperture the meals of the prisoner are handed to him without his seeing the officer, and he may at all times be thus inspected without his knowledge. … A privy is constructed in each cell in such a way as to preserve the purity of the atmosphere, and prevent the possibility of communication from cell to cell. … In the arched ceiling of each cell is a window for the admission of light. The cells are eleven feet nine inches long, seven feet six inches wide, and sixteen feet high to the top of the arched ceiling. … On arriving in his cell the hood is removed, and he is left alone. There he may remain for years, perhaps for life, without seeing any human being but the inspectors, the warden and his officers … For the first day or two the convict is not allowed to have even a Bible … It is not, however, until solitude appears to have effectually subdued him that employment of any kind is introduced into his cell. (Crawford 1834: 10)

It was during this period that the cell was embedded within both the philosophies of punishment and the architecture of the prison. The organisation of prison and the idea of holding prisoners in cellular confinement was fixed and has largely remained in Western societies ever since. In England, the overwhelming majority of prisons were under the control of local authorities and not the government. The degree to which they were interested in these new philosophies of punishment and prison 'reform' varied considerably. Though, as Tomlinson has observed, the use of classified association from 1823 ensured greater focus on the individual prisoner and 'the ultimate in classification was to keep every single prisoner in his own separate cell' (1978: 62).

Under the Prison Act 1839, the separate system was regularised for use in all local prisons. Despite this, variation was still evident in practice: the separate system was quickly implemented in some local areas, but other regions held strong to the silent system or lacked any real system at all beyond classifying prisoners according to their gender and crime (DeLacy 1986; Forsythe 1983; Johnston 2015; Saunders 1986). To encourage conformity and uniformity in practice, the legislation also required all new separate cells to be inspected and approved for use by a government prison inspector. The Act stated that the cells must be of a sufficient size, as well as lighted, warmed and ventilated and fitted with means by which the prisoner could communicate with staff. By the 1860s, the use of cellular confinement became the norm for most prisons as the government pressed for more uniform practice across the country.

The second government penitentiary, Pentonville, had the separate system built into its very architecture and fabric—opening in 1842—and was to be a 'model' for the system. As Ferguson observed:

> What a contrast to the pandemonium of associated criminals does the visitor perceive who enters for the first time the walls of the Model Prison at Pentonville! Instead of the noise and bustle of the old Newgates—absolute stillness; a few silent warders only scattered here and there in the large and lofty corridors containing a triple tier of cells, which range the whole length of these galleries! … contrived to secure the complete isolation of 500 individuals from each other. They are fed at the same moment, rest at the same hour, are out in masses in the open air. They are catechized in the school, and respond in the chapel—yet man knows not man. There is continuity, but no neighbourhood; and the very names of the prisoners are lost in the mechanism which assigns numbers in their stead. (1847: 183)

As the above quote emphasises, the unregulated and noisy associating rooms of the past (represented by Newgate) were to be replaced by the regulated corridors of cells, cell upon cell, all identical and all silent. The architecture of the prison and the cell construction ensured that prisoners were 'prevented from ever seeing each other; and, as silence will be in all cases maintained, they will be separated as though they are miles apart' (*Illustrated London News* 1843, cited in Davie 2016: 456).

Yet criticism quickly appeared in the press about both Pentonville and the separate system more generally. Notably, the new regime was seen as a potential source of mental illness in prisoners as well as being unnecessarily severe (Ignatieff 1978; Johnston 2006). As the Pentonville experiment progressed, periods of separation were reduced from an initial 18 months down to 12, and then eventually to 9 months, as evidence emerged of the temporary and permanent effects of cellular isolation. Although there was diverse practice in the many local prisons across the country in terms of their adoption of the separate system, it remains the case that by the early nineteenth century, the prison cell had become the central focus of penal philosophy and practice. The cell was established as a space of potential transformation in which, under the correct conditions, prisoners could reflect on their own behaviour and past criminal life, repent for their crimes and look at God for salvation and a new law-abiding future. In 'the solitude of the cell … alone with God and a wounded conscience, the unhappy man is forced to exercise his powers of reflection, and thus acquires a command over his sensual impulses which will probably exert a permanent influence' (Ritchie 1854, cited in Priestley 1999: 37).

The separate system had been criticised even before Pentonville had opened, but criticism of it was widespread by the 1850s (Henriques 1972; Johnston 2006). Yet, such criticism was contradictory. On the one hand, commentators argued that the long periods of isolation in cells were detrimental to the mental health of prisoners and too severe for them to endure. On the other, it was argued that the regime was too soft; that prisoners duped or manipulated prison chaplains into believing their religious conversion and that isolation was not complete. Some commentators maintained that other aspects of the regime such as the diet or material conditions were too generous in comparison to that of the workhouse or those of the honest poor labourer outside prison. As one such critic observed, 'They provide for Bill Sykes[1] and his friends … well aired and ventilated, clean, tidy, winter-warmed, snug and cheerfully lighted places of abode' (cited in Tomlinson 1978: 65). Indeed, the construction of or adapting a prison to the separate system was very expensive; each cell had to be sufficiently well ventilated, heated, preventing sound, contain a wash basin and water closet/toilet as well as being large enough for labour as well as eating and sleeping.

By this time though, the prison cell was confirmed as the central space in which prisoners would experience their incarceration and around which all other aspects of the internal prison architecture should be organised. As will be explored, although the separate system and its reformatory aims were lost in the subsequent years, the cell was permanently established as fundamental to the organisation and architecture of the prison and central to the daily regime. In the following decades, the call for increasingly severe prison regimes to quell public anxieties about crime and criminality saw the cell refashioned as a space of isolation. Instead of a place of potential transformation through solitude and religion, it became central to a regime based on silence, labour and sparse diet designed to deter both new and persistent offenders.

## Deterrence and Isolation

By the mid-century, there were growing concerns about crime and recidivism as well as the decline in the use of transportation to Australia (Bartrip 1981; Davis 1980; Sindall 1990). In combination with the growing criticism of the separate system outlined above, penal regimes and prison practices became increasingly dominated by a more deterrent philosophy of punishment. This emphasis on deterrence would prevail at least until the end of the nineteenth century and a major investigation into prisons, provided by the Gladstone Committee in 1895.

The decline of the transportation of convicts to Australia from the 1850s had also ensured that new measures to house convicted criminals were needed in England. To this end, the convict prison system was established where prisoners who would previously have been transported would instead serve long prison sentences known as penal servitude. Therefore, from this period until the mid-twentieth century, there existed two systems of imprisonment; short sentences (less than two years, but overwhelmingly offenders served sentences of less than one month) were served in local prisons administered by local authorities, and long sentences termed 'penal servitude' which were served in government-run convict prisons.

By the 1860s, concerns about increasing crime, recidivism and the effectiveness of imprisonment in reforming offenders had influenced the idea that prison conditions need to be more severe (Johnston 2015; McConville 1995, 1998b). Both the Penal Servitude Act 1864 and the

Prison Act 1865 led to increasingly harsher or more severe sentencing and prison policies undermined by a view that a more deterrent system was required. This translated into longer minimum sentences for new and repeat offenders and severe living conditions based on the notion of 'hard labour, hard board, hard fare' aiming to achieve maximum deterrence in prison regimes. For those in local prisons, this entailed long hours of hard labour (at the crank or treadwheel, for example, both pointless repetitive activities), minimal diets and sparse living conditions. The separate cells still existed in prisons but they were re-fashioned into this new regime—the cell became a focal part of the deterrent regime—becoming sites of isolation for deterrent rather than reformatory purposes.

Auto/biographical accounts from prisoners appeared more widely in the latter decades of the nineteenth century and they demonstrate how the dull, poorly-lit, sparse environment was experienced. Mrs Maybrick wrote:

> I stepped forward, but started back in horror. Through the open door I saw, by the dim light of a small window that was never cleaned, a cell seven feet by four. "Oh, don't put me in there!" I cried. "I cannot bear it." For answer the warder took me roughly by the shoulder, gave me a push and shut the door. (1905: 67)

Similarly, Frank Henderson—also a first time entrant to the prison system—described the prison's 'silent and grim gates, [where] the cell door was closed behind me, the lock was turned, and I and the reality were left alone. About that dark cheerless cell, its cold bare walls, its grated windows, its massive door, there was to me an awful certainty' ([1869] 2007: 18).

By this time, discussions about the isolation of prisoners had come to the conclusion that nine months' isolation was the most that prisoners could or should endure. However, for most prisoners, this policy was largely irrelevant. The majority of the prison population were short term prisoners serving less than 28 days. Sentences of this length would be served in separation, with labour (such as oakum picking or turning the crank or making sacks or rope) carried out in the cell. Sentences were short but served in harsh, sparse conditions and, for a significant proportion of these prisoners, these conditions would be endured repeatedly as they experienced the revolving door of imprisonment. Recidivism was of considerable concern in the latter decades of the nineteenth century and the motivation for such harsh prison conditions. But, as McConville (1995) has observed, these regimes were unremittingly severe in character.

Therefore, local prisons, as today, turned over the largest numbers of prisoners, either on remand or serving short sentences or indeed holding those to be moved on to the long-term convict system. Administrative records for prisons in the nineteenth century are peppered with the interactions and conflicts between prisoners and the rules in these prisons. Given the central part the cell played in the regime, it was often the case that prisoners' infractions of the rules would take place in the cell space. Common disciplinary offences occurred in cells; smashing windows panes, breaking prison property and shouting and singing from the cell were regular offences against the prison rules. Prisoners sometimes smashed or broke the meagre institutional items that they were provided with. In local prisons, where the turnover of the prison population was high, records are often patchy and do not necessarily survive but do offer us a glimpse into prisoners' experiences.

Visiting magistrates' (monthly visitors to the prison who acted as external inspectors or overseers) records, for HMP Liverpool for example, cite numerous evidence of ill-discipline within the prison but also reveal the frustrations of those confined within. The experience of Elizabeth Hughes perhaps epitomises the emotions of offenders who experienced the revolving door of imprisonment. Elizabeth had been committed to prison for one month for offences relating to prostitution. Warder Bell reported that the prisoner had been received the previous night at about 7 o'clock. She continued,

> I heard the breaking of glass. I went to the prisoner's cell and saw her jumped off the table—some of the cotton she was working at and some of her clothing was on fire. I opened the door and ordered her out, she refused. She took up the blanket and threw it on the fire—I brought her out by force—14 panes of glass in her cell were broken. (Extract from 347/

MAG/1/3/3, Visiting Committee Reports (VCR), HMP Liverpool, 8 October 1889)

Hughes interrupted the officer's report of the incident when she remarked, 'Is that all you have to say? I'll do it again'. The officer continued 'When I went in there was no one but myself—others afterwards came in—I did not strike you in the face. You were taken out by force, it was necessary'. Hughes stated, 'I did it because I'm tired of coming to prison. I was only out five hours. I'm tired of my life' (Extracts as above). Hughes was placed in a punishment cell for seven days and on 'punishment diet no 1' (bread and water) for this offence.

In the latter decades of the century, committals for drunkenness were at a high and this began a national debate on what to do about inebriacy and those who were repeatedly confined for drunken behaviour. Then, as in previous decades, those committed for such offences often spent their lives between the prison, the street and the public house and the after effects of drinking followed them into the prison cell. Records of local prisons testify to the frustrations of those detained and the initial experiences of detention in the cell. Many reported for disciplinary offences often expressed that the 'drink was not out of them' or that they were suffering what we would now call withdrawal symptoms. In July 1898, Winifred McCormack was charged with breaking 12 panes of glass in her cell window. She admitted the damage stating that she was 'in the horrors of drink at the time', that it was night and she could not get medicine (Extract from 347/MAG/1/3/3, VCR, HMP Liverpool, 29 July 1898). Similarly, Ann Ward was charged with breaking 14 panes of glass in her cell window in December 1898. She told the Committee, 'I am very sorry I had been drinking "very heavy"' (Extract from 347/MAG/1/3/3, VCR, HMP Liverpool, 21 December 1898). Whilst the frustrations of these experiences were experienced in the local prison cell as distress or resistance, they were at least short term. But for those serving long prison sentences, the seclusion and isolation and lack of family contact were much more enduring.

## The Cell: Isolation and Loneliness in Long-Term Imprisonment

Prisoners' experiences in the long-term estate were slightly different from those of the local prison inmates discussed above. Those confined in the long-term system were not committed directly to these prisons and therefore were not going into cells directly from the courts. They were not therefore suffering from immediate entry shock to the prison or suffering the instant effects of confinement. Those confined in the convict prison system would first be committed to a local prison and then would be removed to the convict prison estate, as all the convict prisons were in London and the South of England. Under a sentence of penal servitude, separation had evolved into the first stage of the sentence as separate confinement for up to nine months, usually served in Millbank and Pentonville convict prisons.

Records of prisoners in the convict system of course present similar evidence to the frustrations of short-term prisoners, but this was also compounded by the geographical and physical isolation of being placed in the long term system. For prisoners from the North of England and the Midlands, the likelihood of visits from family or friends was limited by the long geographical distance and by expense. Only 12.4 per cent of all convicts ever received a visit and, for those with multiple sentences, this significantly declined as relationships with those outside fractured (Johnston and Godfrey 2013; Johnston 2019). In the local system, even by the 1920s, no visits were permitted until eight weeks into the sentence (B.2.15 1924).

Detailed analysis of their whole prison record as well as reconstructing their lives also allows us to see other evidence about their lives and the pressures they were facing. For example, although in the initial years of the convict system there had been short-lived prison nurseries, women confined in the convict prisons after the mid-1860s were unable to have children with them inside prison. Depending on the age of the child, those women without partners or people to care for them would find their children sent to workhouses or confined to terms in industrial schools under the Industrial Schools Act 1866 due to their mother's offending (Johnston 2019). Evidence from these records demonstrates the frustration and anxiety that lack of family contact or 'bad' news (deaths in the family or loss of employment) from home could have on those in prison. Families and loved ones on the outside were often living in precarious situations, renting rooms or lodging, perhaps moving around seeking employment, and therefore many letters were returned as 'not found at that address' or 'addressee unknown'. Perhaps unsurprisingly, for those in the convict system who had served multiple sentences their connections to those on the outside diminished with each sentence. The frustration, upset and sometimes distress of bad news were experienced by the prisoner within the isolation of the cell (Johnston 2019).

The second stage of penal servitude was served on the public works, during the mid to late nineteenth century, at a range of prisons built or adapted for this purpose: Brixton, Chatham, Chattenden, Dartmoor, Fulham, Parkhurst, Portland, Portsmouth and Woking. Cells in these establishments varied enormously but all of this development was overseen or directed by Joshua Jebb, initially the Surveyor-General from 1844 then the first Director of the Convict Prisons from 1850. Jebb firmly believed that 'separation is the only basis on which the discipline of a prison can exist' (cited in Forsythe 1987: 45). Some of these prisons were adapted but those entirely constructed also incorporated different types of cells. For example, at Chatham, Portland and Dartmoor, temporary cells made from corrugated iron sheets were used. Whilst prisoners spent the day working at the quarries or on naval dockyards, their night-time accommodation were cells separated by corrugated iron. From the Directorate's point of view, this offered a portable construction and was cheaper financially. Thus, cell construction was not as fixed as might be expected. These cells remained in use until the mid-1890s when they were replaced; whilst they had offered an immediate solution for Jebb in constructing the long-term prison system in the 1850s and 1860s, they were small. They were only 206 cubic feet in size, which was about a quarter of the size of the 819 cubic feet dimensions of a standard night and day cell. This was justified since convicts occupied these cells from 5 p.m. to 7 a.m. and during days when the weather was too bad to work (PCOM 7/3). Yet, the construction must have also allowed prisoners the possibility of communicating through the partition walls as well as exposing them to the cold and the heat during the more extreme weather periods of the year.

By the early 1890s there was increasing criticism of the prison system. Du Cane's tight hold over the system (as both Director of the Convict Prisons and the local prisons after they were centralised in 1877) was a major source of criticism due to his autocratic and militaristic approach to leadership (Forsythe 1990; Harding 1988; McConville 1995). There was also concern that the deterrent approach had gone too far. As an anonymous writer of a series of articles that appeared in the *Daily Chronicle* in 1894 summarised, the system was devoid of hope and reform, characterised by an endless monotonous regime. He observed; 'our local prison system … enhances the faults of solitary confinement, and is marked more conspicuously than it by many terrible evils, cannot be maintained on its present military and purely centralised basis' (29 January 1894: 5). In calling for a Royal Commission to inquire into the prison system, the 'Special Correspondent' (thought to be Reverend W. D. Morrison, chaplain of Wandsworth Prison) argued that:

> The ponderous iron gates, that hide more human misery than any other corner the civilised world contains, rarely open to receive a critical visitor. More perhaps might go if more knew or cared. But few know or care. The great machine rolls obscurely on, cumbrous, pitiless, obsolete, unchanged. The silent world—silent save when on some Sunday morning hundreds of voices may be heard in melancholy chorus of prayer or song—goes on receiving new citizens and discharging old ones, like the greater world around it. (*Daily Chronicle*, 23 January 1894: 5)

By June 1894, the Home Secretary had appointed a Departmental Committee on Prison chaired by Herbert Gladstone. The committee collected a vast amount of information and evidence from those who worked in prisons as well as ex-prisoners. In 1894, the imprisonment of Oscar Wilde for offences under the Criminal Law Amendment Act also drew public attention to the prison system; during the years of his incarceration, he also published ferocious criticism of the brutality of the prison system (Wilde [1898] 2002).

The landmark Gladstone Committee report in 1895 did ameliorate some aspects of the severity of the prison system and advocated a combination of deterrence and rehabilitation in penal policy. Regarding separate confinement, Du Cane continued to urge the view that 'cellular isolation was essential to the prevention of contamination and "that a great number of prisoners … are below par mentally … the thing to do with them … is to put them under control permanently"' (cited in Forsythe 1990: 26). The Committee did not agree that separate confinement induced reflection in prisoners, but they largely supported Du Cane's position that it was a 'deterrent; and a necessary safeguard against contamination' (1895: 20). Therefore, in the first few decades of the twentieth century, prison regimes were marked by continuity rather than any significant change and cellular isolation remained the dominant feature of the prisoner experience (Bailey 1997; Brown 2013; Forsythe 1990). Most of the Gladstone Committee's recommendations applied to the long-term prisoners and thus, the majority of the daily prison population housed in local prisons were still subject to cellular isolation or separation and silence in daily regimes. Thus, despite Gladstone's discussions, the common prisoner experience was one of cellular seclusion. Brocklehurst wrote, in 1898, of his 28-day sentence of solitary confinement:

> Imagine a blind man denied human intercourse, with power of motion only in a space 14 feet by 7, whose only contact with a limited outside world comes through the ceiling, walls and iron door, and you can form a faint idea of what life in prison must be. A prisoner sees nothing beyond the limits of his cell; feels only its discomforts; tastes the prescribed prison fare; hears limited sounds of his strange environment; and smells little beyond the scent of creosote as it exhales from the oakum. (Cited in Anderson and Pratt 2008: 181–182)

In 1910, the Chairman of the Prison Commission, Evelyn Ruggles-Brise, and the Home Secretary, Winston Churchill, attended the opening night of a controversial play by John Galsworthy called *Justice*, which criticised the prison system but notably focused upon the effects of separate confinement, continuing a recurrent debate that had persisted for the last seven decades (Nellis 1996). These events demonstrated the contested and often contradictory ways in which policies were implemented even in periods which are often regarded as more enlightened or progressive such as Churchill's tenure (Bennett 2008).

Thus debate about separate confinement and its effects continued in the 1920s and 1930s. The unofficial inquiry into the prison system, *English Prisons To-day* was published in 1922. It was compiled by two ex-prisoners Stephen Hobhouse and A. Fenner Brockway—who were conscientious objectors to the First World War—and drew together a large amount of evidence on separation as well as prison conditions more broadly. By the 1920s the cell was still pretty sparse. Hobhouse and Brockway's report on the prison system in 1922 explains that:

> The warder unlocks the door leading into the great hall of the prison, and, with his bunch of jangling keys at hand, he accompanies the new inmate to the cell destined for his home. Here his name becomes lost, and he assimilates himself to the cell by buttoning on to his coat the unsightly yellow badge, inscribed with some such device as "A.3.21" or "C.2.8", which had been hanging over the door of the empty cell. The warder sees that the cell water-can has been replenished and that the cleaning materials are not exhausted. The door is banged and double locked, and the prisoner is left alone with his thoughts.
>
> The cage in which he now finds himself is a stern and bare little room, of which the measurement are as a rule seven feet by thirteen and nine feet high. Its furniture consists of a wooden table (either movable or fixed), a small stool without a back, and a bed-board. The window is so high up that it is necessary to stand on the stool to look out of it, and this, to make matters worse, may be regarded as a punishable offence. (Hobhouse and Brockway 1922: 96)

Similarly, Florence Maybrick, imprisoned for the murder of her husband in 1889, found separate confinement 'by far the most cruel feature ... it inflicts upon the prisoner at the commencement of her sentence, when most sensitive to the horrors which prison punishment entails, the voiceless solitude, the hopeless monotony, the long vista of to-morrow, to-morrow, to-morrow stretching before her, all filled with desolation and despair' (1905: 75).

The debate about the use and the extent of separate confinement continued into the early decades of the twentieth century, although some aspects of this were curtailed by the recommendations of the Gladstone Committee since most of their recommendations applied to long term prisoners. Despite some amelioration for long term prisoners, separate confinement was not abolished for all prisoners until 1931. The bulk of the prison population, located within the local prison system, therefore continued to spend the majority of their incarceration isolated in their cells. Whilst sentences were short, due to the progressive stage system (prisoners moving through 28-day stages based on time and behaviour) this meant that most of their prison experience was confinement with in their cell at the first stage.

## Conclusion

During the nineteenth century, the emergence of the modern prison placed the cell at the centre of the new penal philosophies and practices. Since that time, it has remained pivotal in the organisation of prisons and 'the physical hub of the new prisoner's unfamiliar future' (Priestley 1999: 27). In the early years, the cell had been a space for moral reflection and religious enlightenment but, as Forsythe observes, the 'remarkable feature of the history of cellular isolation was its persistence as an article of faith amongst prison disciplinarians in England long after the fundamentalist and extreme faith in its powers of moral regeneration had evaporated' (2004: 768). The persistence of the cell was secured by its capacity to accommodate the changing or dominant disciplinary regimes over time; more reformative in the 1820s and 1830s as shown, but also at the centre of more severely deterrent prison regime dominated by isolation, silence and exacting suffering on the prisoner in the latter decades of the century.

The dominance of practices of separation across decades of the modern prison experiment also challenges the widely-held views of the 1920s and 1930s as a 'golden age of penal reform'. Under the direction of Alexander Paterson, one of the Prison Commissioners, this period is held to epitomise liberal views on imprisonment; namely that people should be sent to prison '*as* punishment rather than *for* punishment' (Ruck 1951: 23).

But the use of separation or separate confinement and its persistence in prison regimes demonstrates the deeply rooted ways in which the cellular confinement was central to the regime and how regimes were very slow to adapt and often considerably contested (Brown 2013; Forsythe 1990). Indeed, even after the initial period of separation, those in local prisons and those in convict prisons would still spend, routinely, between 16 and 17 and a half hours per day in a cell (Hobhouse and Brockway 1922).

Separation through cellular isolation continued as penal administrators clung to the use of cellular confinement as a mechanism of discipline and control and in the belief that it offered both the prevention of moral contamination and the opportunity for reflection. The Victorian prison architecture remained and, as one chairman of the Prison Commission observed, 'nothing less than dynamite could rid us of these grimy and forbidding fortresses' (Scott 1959: 85, cited in Forsythe 2004: 768).

## Note

1. Bill Sykes was a notorious habitual criminal in the popular novel *Oliver Twist* by Charles Dickens serialised in 1837–1839.

## References

Anderson, S., & Pratt, J. (2008). Prisoner Memoirs and Their Role in Prison History. In H. Johnston (Ed.), *Punishment and Control in Historical Perspective* (pp. 179–198). London: Palgrave Macmillan.

Anon. (1894). Our Dark Places. *The Daily Chronicle*, January 23 and 29.

B. 2.15. (1924). *Among the Broad-Arrow Men: A Plain Account of English Prison Life*. London: A & C Black, Ltd.

Bailey, V. (1997). English Prisons, Penal Culture, and the Abatement of Imprisonment, 1895–1922. *Journal of British Studies, 36*(3), 285–324.

Bartrip, P. (1981). Public Opinion and Law Enforcement: The Ticket of Leave Scares in Mid-Victorian Britain. In V. Bailey (Ed.), *Policing and Punishment in Nineteenth Century Britain* (pp. 150–181). London: Croom Helm.

Bennett, J. (2008). The Man, the Machine and the Myths: Reconsidering Winston Churchill's Prison Reforms. In H. Johnston (Ed.), *Punishment and Control in Historical Perspective* (pp. 95–114). London: Palgrave Macmillan.

Brown, A. (2013). *Inter-war Penal Policy and Crime in England: The Dartmoor Convict Prison Riot, 1932*. London: Palgrave Macmillan.

Crawford, W. (1834). *Report of William Crawford Esq., on the Penitentiaries of the United States* (593). Vol. XLVI.349. Parliamentary Papers. London: Home Office.

Davie, N. (2016). *The Penitentiary Ten: The Transformation of the English Prison, 1770–1850*. Oxford: Bardwell.

Davis, J. (1980). The London Garotting Panic of 1862: A Moral Panic and the Creation of a Criminal Class in Mid-Victorian England. In V. A. C. Gatrell, B. Lenman, & G. Parker (Eds.), *Crime and the Law: A Social History of Crime in Western Europe since 1500* (pp. 190–213). London: Europa.

DeLacy, M. (1986). *Prison Reform in Lancashire 1700–1850*. Stanford, CA: Stanford University Press.

Evans, R. (1982). *The Fabrication of Virtue: English Prison Architecture, 1750–1840*. Cambridge: Cambridge University Press.

Ferguson, R. (1847). Pentonville Prisoners. *Quarterly Review, 82*, 175–206.

Forsythe, B. (2004). Loneliness and Cellular Confinement in English Prisons, 1878–1921. *British Journal of Criminology, 44*(5), 759–770.

Forsythe, W. J. (1983). *A System of Discipline: Exeter Borough Prison, 1819–1863*. Exeter: Exeter University Press.

Forsythe, W. J. (1987). *The Reform of Prisoners, 1830–1900*. London: Croom Helm.

Forsythe, W. J. (1990). *Penal Discipline, Reformatory Projects and the English Prison Commission 1895–1939*. Exeter: Exeter University Press.

Foucault, M. ([1975] 1991). *Discipline and Punish: The Birth of the Prison*. London: Penguin.

Fry, E. (1827). *Observations on the Visiting, Superintending, and Government of Female Prisoners*. London: John & Arthur Arch.

Gladstone Committee. (1895). *Report from the Departmental Committee on Prisons* (C.7702) (Vol. LVI). London: Home Office.

Godfrey, B., & Cox, D. (2008). The "Last Fleet": Crime, Reformation and Punishment in Western Australia, Australian and New Zealand. *Journal of Criminology, 41*(2), 236–258.

Harding, C. (1988). 'The Inevitable End of a Discredited System?' The Origins of the Gladstone Committee Report on Prisons, 1895. *The Historical Journal, 31*(3), 591–608.

Henderson, F. ([1869] 2007). *Six Years in the Prisons of England.* Charleston, SC: BiblioBazaar.

Henriques, U. R. Q. (1972). The Rise and Decline of the Separate System of Prison Discipline. *Past and Present, 54*, 61–93.

Hobhouse, S., & Brockway, A. F. (1922). *English Prisons To-day.* London: Longmans, Green & Co.

Holford Committee. (1810–1811). *Report from the Committee on the Laws Relating to Penitentiary Houses* (199: Reports of Committees). London: Home Office.

Howard, J. ([1777] 1929). *The State of the Prisons.* London: Dent.

Ignatieff, M. (1978). *A Just Measure of Pain.* London: Macmillan.

Jewkes, Y., & Johnston, H. (2007). The Evolution of Prison Architecture. In Y. Jewkes (Ed.), *Handbook on Prisons* (pp. 174–196). Cullompton: Willan.

Johnston, H. (2006). "Buried Alive": Representations of the Separate System in Victorian England. In P. Mason (Ed.), *Captured by the Media: Prison Discourse in Popular Culture* (pp. 103–121). Cullompton: Willan.

Johnston, H. (2015). *Crime in England, 1815–1880: Experiencing the Criminal Justice System.* Abingdon: Routledge.

Johnston, H. (2019). Imprisoned Mothers in Victorian England, 1853–1900: Motherhood, Identity and the Convict Prison. *Criminology & Criminal Justice: An International Journal, 19*(2), 215–231.

Johnston, H., & Godfrey, B. (2013). The Costs of Imprisonment: A Longitudinal Study. *ESRC End of Award Report, RES-062-23-3102.* Swindon: ESRC.

Maybrick, F. (1905). *Mrs Maybrick's Own Story: My Fifteen Years Lost.* London: Funk & Wagnalls.

McConville, S. (1981). *A History of Prison Administration, 1750–1877.* London: Routledge & Kegan Paul.

McConville, S. (1995). *English Local Prisons: Next Only to Death, 1860–1900.* London: Routledge.

McConville, S. (1998a). Local Justice: The Jail. In N. Morris & D. J. Rothman (Eds.), *The Oxford History of the Prison: The Practice of Punishment in Western Society* (pp. 266–294). Oxford: Oxford University Press.

McConville, S. (1998b). The Victorian Prison: England, 1865–1965. In N. Morris & D. J. Rothman (Eds.), *The Oxford History of the Prison: The Practice of Punishment in Western Society* (pp. 117–150). Oxford: Oxford University Press.

McGowen, R. (1998). The Well-Ordered Prison: England, 1780–1865. In N. Morris & D. J. Rothman (Eds.), *The Oxford History of the Prison: The*

*Practice of Punishment in Western Society* (pp. 71–99). Oxford: Oxford University Press.
Nellis, M. (1996). John Galsworthy's *Justice*. *British Journal of Criminology, 36*(1), 61–84.
Priestley, P. (1999). *Victorian Prison Lives: English Prison Biography 1830–1914*. London: Pimlico.
Ruck, S. K. (1951). *Paterson on Prisons*. London: Frederick Muller.
Saunders, J. (1986). Warwickshire Magistrates and Prison Reform, 1840–1875. *Midland History, XI*, 79–99.
Semple, J. (1993). *Bentham's Prison: A Study of the Panopticon Penitentiary*. Oxford: Clarendon.
Sindall, R. S. (1990). *Street Violence in the Nineteenth Century: Media Panic or Real Danger?* Leicester: Leicester University Press.
Tomlinson, M. H. (1978). 'Prison Palaces': A Re-appraisal of Early Victorian Prisons, 1835–1877. *Historical Research, 50*(123), 60–71.
Wilde, O. ([1898] 2002). *De Profundis: The Ballad of Reading Gaol and Other Writings*. London: Wordsworth.
Wilson, D. (2002). Millbank, the Panopticon and Their Victorian Audiences. *The Howard Journal, 41*(4), 364–381.
Wilson, D. (2014). *Pain and Retribution*. London: Reaktion Books.

# 3

# Prison Cells as a Grounded Embodiment of Penal Ideologies: A Norwegian-American Comparison

Jordan M. Hyatt, Synøve N. Andersen, and Steven L. Chanenson

## Introduction

The design and furnishing of prison cells can have a profound effect on how incarceration is experienced. This is not accidental, as myriad decisions are made during the construction process for new prisons specifically to shape the usage and meaning of these spaces. While many such decisions are pragmatic, others are ideological, reflecting the goals and

J. M. Hyatt (✉)
Department of Criminology and Justice Studies, Drexel University, Philadelphia, PA, USA
e-mail: jhyatt@drexel.edu

S. N. Andersen
University of Oslo, Oslo, Norway

S. L. Chanenson
Villanova University, Villanova, PA, USA



J. Turner, V. Knight (eds.), *The Prison Cell*, Palgrave Studies in Prisons and Penology,
https://doi.org/10.1007/978-3-030-39911-5_3

priorities of the correctional and social systems in which the prison is situated (c.f. Johnston 2000; Jewkes and Johnston 2007). Carceral spaces, including cells, can be considered an explicit and static manifestation of the correctional goals prevalent at the time of its design, including those that pertain to the balance between punishment and rehabilitation.

Prison architecture evolves over time (Johnston 2004; this volume), though often slower than the ideals and pragmatic reforms that both shape the day-to-day functioning of correctional systems and which may diverge from the official, stated goals of imprisonment. Examining the architectural features of a prison space can thus provide insight into the intended character of a penal institution at the time it was built. This approach also provides an opportunity to compare similar spaces across jurisdictions and over time. Differences in the social, political, and economic structures that support penal systems often make comparative penological analyses challenging (Tonry 2015) and, by examining the built environment of prisons in general and of the cell in particular, a common language for such comparisons can emerge.

This chapter focuses on the physical design and use of the cells in two diverse systems: the United States, as represented by Pennsylvania, and Norway. In Pennsylvania, we focus on SCI Phoenix, the newest correctional institution in the Pennsylvania system. In Norway, we examine Halden Prison, which was designed explicitly to reflect the modern ideals of the Norwegian Correctional Service (NCS). We examine the context of incarceration, the stated goals of the respective prison agencies, and the physical living environment of those incarcerated. Thus, the cell becomes a lens through which prevailing correctional goals and philosophies can be examined and compared.

The foundations for this comparative analysis are based upon data derived from four main sources: (1) official documents from correctional agencies; (2) media articles; (3) a series of interviews conducted with prison leaders at both institutions, and; (4) field notes taken during several visits to both facilities. Interviews were conducted in a semi-structured format with the governor (Norway) and superintendent (Pennsylvania), parallel leadership positions, at the two facilities during 2018–2019. Site visits were conducted on multiple occasions between 2015 and 2019 at both facilities.

## Cell Architecture and Penal Ideology

The design of a correctional environment can strongly influence the subjective impressions of the carceral spaces, as well as the ways those spaces are used and the complex interactions between the incarcerated persons and the authority of the state unfold (Moran and Jewkes 2011). The physical environment can encourage hope, facilitate rehabilitation, or reinforce a sense of justified retribution, institutionalisation, and deprivation (Hancock and Jewkes 2011). In short, the architecture of a prison space embodies the complex, intangible forces—sociological, political, and philosophical—that shape the punishment process.

In one taxonomy, there are two broad categorical classifications for the philosophical purposes of punishment: utilitarian (e.g. rehabilitation, deterrence) and non-utilitarian (e.g. retribution, just desert) (see e.g. Frase 2005).[1] For present purposes, the word utilitarian indicates that particular elements of the experience of incarceration are explicitly intended to facilitate desistance from crime, increase community reintegration, and/or encourage other positive outcomes. These approaches are often lauded as "humane" and are reflected in cell-based experiences that further the incarcerated person's rehabilitation. For present purposes, non-utilitarian elements of punishment are those that are not designed to change future behaviours but are, instead, tied in a retributive way to the past actions of the offender (e.g. the severity of the offence). Within the penal environment, this philosophical emphasis can produce cell-based experiences that reflect practical requirements of the penal system (e.g. cost, security)—potentially at the expense of the incarcerated person's rehabilitative experience. Though not necessarily the stated intent in this context, an emphasis on practical aspects of non-utilitarianism (e.g. efficient population management) can create a living environment that has the potential to functionally and subjectively take on retributive characteristics.

Many correctional systems announce that they pursue seemingly incompatible philosophies in the design of their cells and the facilities in which they are located. Attempting to classify any cell or correctional system as purely or, even predominantly, rehabilitative or retributive, glosses over the complexities of the modern correctional experiences and contemporary hybrid theory (Morris 1974). For example, in describing Halden Prison, Governor Høidal notes that even a facility recognised as humane must balance these goals:

> Rehabilitation is important. We punish but … we will use the time in our prison to help [prisoners] to be better persons and to help them to be motivated to be rehabilitated… In Norway, we also focus on security…what [we] call the static security, that's the walls, the bars, the cameras… And we have what we call organisational [security], and that's how we organise the prison and the environment. (A. Høidal, interview, 2018)

By recognising this complexity while examining the nature of a prison cell—an environment informed by many of these same complexities—it is possible to explore how societies were balancing these incarcerative goals with regard to the design of the environment in which carceral time was to be experienced. Examining the cell can thus illustrate the extent to which incarceration is designed to advance one philosophical approach over another: to rehabilitate and to help (utilitarian) or to manage and to punish (non-utilitarian).

## Jurisdictional Backgrounds and Context

Pennsylvania is one of 50 American states, each enjoying a high degree of independence in setting penal policy. It is located in the Northeastern part of the United States and is the fifth largest state by population with more than 12.8 million people. At 725 per 100,000 people, the incarceration rate is higher than the United States' average (Prison Policy Initiative n.d.). For those individuals sentenced to state prison in 2017, the average minimum sentence was 2.8 years and the average maximum term was 6.5 years (Pennsylvania Commission on Sentencing 2018).[2]

Among other options, Pennsylvania law allows offenders to be sentenced to a fixed term of incarceration, incarceration for the balance of the offender's natural life, and to execution, although a *de facto* moratorium on capital punishment is in place.

The Pennsylvania Department of Corrections (DOC) is a state-level agency with an annual budget of more than $2.2 billion and which currently incarcerates approximately 46,000 individuals in 24 prisons called State Correctional Institutions (SCIs) and one boot camp. The DOC, as expressed in its mission statement,

> ...operates as one team, embraces diversity, and commits to enhancing public safety... Our mission is to reduce criminal behavior by providing individualized treatment and education to inmates, resulting in successful community reintegration through accountability and positive change. (Pennsylvania Department of Corrections 2019a: n.p.)

This core mission is integrated into the operation of SCI Phoenix; the Superintendent of the facility describes how local efforts to implement rehabilitative, utilitarian goals are ongoing throughout the incarceration process: '[R]e-entry begins on the day of reception... [a]nd that's a fairly new philosophy for us' (T. Ferguson, interview, 2019).

Located more than 3700 miles (6000 km) from Pennsylvania, in the Northern part of Europe, Norway currently has a population of just over 5.3 million people. It is a social democracy with a universal welfare system; unemployment is relatively low and trust in governmental institutions is high (Esping-Andersen 1990). The egalitarian history and security provided by the welfare states in Norway were pivotal in shaping the current prison system (Pratt and Eriksson 2011). This justification can be extended to include the design and contents of penal living areas.

The NCS is responsible for carrying out all penal sanctions in Norway. NCS is a nationwide governmental agency, housed under the Ministry of Justice and Public Security, with an annual budget of approximately USD 570 million (5 billion NOK). As of December 2017, the total prison capacity was 4127 individuals. The Norwegian incarceration rate is approximately 44 per 100,000 adults. Norwegian prison sentences are relatively short; in 2017, 56 per cent of incarcerated people were released after 90 days of incarceration, and 86 per cent returned home within one year. The maximum sentence length is 21 years for almost any offence[3] (Norwegian Correctional Service n.d.-a).

The explicit goal of the NCS is to 'is to ensure a proper execution of remand and prison sentences, with due regard to the security of all citizens, and attempts to prevent recidivism by enabling the offenders, through their own initiatives, to change their criminal behaviour' (Norwegian Correctional Service n.d.-a: n.p.). Moreover, the 'principle of normality' lies at the very core of the NCS (Høidal 2018; Vollan 2016). The normality principle means that an incarcerated person's existence in prison should mirror, as much as is possible, the existence of a citizen elsewhere in society (Norwegian Correctional Service n.d.-a). According to NCS leadership,

> The principle of normality is valid per se because it supports a humane approach in the execution of sentences. The penalty shall be felt as a penalty, but still be executed in a way that reduces the negative impact of being incarcerated … [T]he normality concept is closely linked to the principle that deprivation of liberty is the actual penalty, and that other rights are to be observed as much as possible… Supporting the principle of normality means organizing a daily routine in prison that, as far as possible, reflects daily activity in society outside the walls. (Vollan 2016: 91)

## Framing the Facilities

Pennsylvania's SCI Phoenix, located 35 miles (56 km) outside of Philadelphia, opened in July 2018. Designed to confine 3830 people in the general population (Pennsylvania Department of Corrections 2019b), Phoenix took more than a decade and a reported USD 400 million to build (DiStefano 2018). Phoenix was constructed to meet several goals, primarily couched as practical. In preparation for its opening, the Secretary of Corrections noted, '[Phoenix is] energy efficient, it accommodates individuals with disabilities, but beyond that it has great sight. If you're a corrections officer, it's really important that you can see everything' (Dennis 2018). The primacy of functionality was intentional; the facility was explicitly designed to 'suppor[t] the DOC in housing more inmates to better fit the Department of Corrections' population needs while reducing operational costs' (Heery n.d.: n.p.).

As a newly constructed prison, the DOC had an opportunity to build a facility in line with their overt correctional needs and philosophies, which, as noted by Superintendent Ferguson (interview, 2019), emphasises the functionality of the prison: 'I don't want to say [Phoenix is] punitive because I don't ever think that we've been punitive, but I think that we have become more aware in what [it] needs to look like [to operate]'. She also notes that, in constructing Phoenix, the emphasis was on designing a facility that could manage the large population by using 'the appropriations provided to put us in the best technology, [give] us the best technology[,] short lines of sight, the ability to segregate the population in the event of an emergency, [and] control access points'.

SCI Phoenix is a campus comprising 20 individual buildings spread out over 2.5 square miles (647.5 hectares), including 15 nearly identical housing units. The facility is surrounded by multiple levels of fencing topped with razor wire; the perimeter border is about 1.5 miles (2.4 km) long. The fields around the facility are occasionally visible through the barriers. This reflects a change from its predecessor facility, SCI Graterford. 'The only time [a prisoner] had to go outside at SCI Graterford [was] if you chose to go outside for recreation. Here, you have to go outside for everything' (T. Ferguson, interview, 2019). For example, in this facility, residential and common spaces are designed in a way that 'make it easier, and ultimately less expensive, to transport inmates to and from court' (Heery n.d.: n.p.). Phoenix contains an extensive network of video cameras in public spaces. The scope of the surveillance network underscores a pervasive emphasis on formal measures of control.

Halden Prison is located near Halden, a small city in the Southeast of Norway. It opened in 2010 and is currently Norway's second-largest facility with 252 prison cells. Halden cost approximately 2.2 billion NOK (USD 250 million) to build. As a newly designed and constructed prison, Halden is an explicit attempt to embody what the principle of normality could look like in practice (Kriminalomsorgen 2019: 20). Governor Høidal notes the centrality of this mission:

> We punish, but when a person is in prison we will use the time in our prison to help them to be better persons and to help them to be motivated to be rehabilitated. [Therfore,] they wanted to try to make the prison system more like society on the outside…. [so] when they designed Halden prison they wanted to make a prison that did not necessarily look like a prison; it can be a campus, could be a hospital, it can be a school, or another [kind of] institution… The Minister of Justice told the architects…that it should be a high-security prison. So, the main thing for the architects was that it should be "hard" with security, but it should also be "soft" to take care of [the prisoners]. (A. Høidal, interview, 2018)

In this instance, ideology trumped some pragmatic limitations, including the fiscal concerns that have influenced subsequent construction projects. Halden was the first Norwegian prison to use an interior designer (Norwegian Correctional Service n.d.-b), with many architectural and aesthetic choices reflecting this influence. Located in a dense forest, Halden Prison is surrounded by a circular, 0.87 mile (1.4 km) long and 19.6 ft (5.17 m) high perimeter wall made of solid concrete. The wall is topped with a rounded bolster to prevent anyone from scaling it, and there are security cameras and other sensors placed at regular intervals along its length. The wall is omnipresent, blocking all views of the surroundings, and, as 't]he prison's defining feature… [it] is visible everywhere the [prisoners] go, functioning as an inescapable reminder of their imprisonment' (Benko 2015: n.p.).

Like Phoenix, Halden is a multi-structure prison. There are a total of seven buildings within the walls, including two multi-level housing units (Høidal 2018). These buildings are arranged in a semi-circular design and surround a large copse of trees (Statsbygg 2010). There is heavy usage of earthy tones and natural or unprocessed materials, including wood and unpainted metal, in both the construction of the buildings themselves and for interior furnishing. Such materials can, in contrast with the concrete and stainless steel found in many other prisons throughout the world, create an uncommon sense of lightness, space, and openness (Hancock and Jewkes 2011; Moran et al. 2016). This was an intentional aesthetic choice made by both the designers and correctional leaders involved in the creation process (Erik Arkitekter n.d.; Statsbygg 2010). A concentric arrangement of secure perimeters is also evident at Halden.

## A Comparative Examination of Prison Cells

At SCI Phoenix, a typical cell is 81 $ft^2$ (7.53 $m^2$) and is designed to house two individuals[4] (see Fig. 3.1). At its longest, the cell is 12 ft 8 inches (3.86 m) from front-to-back and 7 ft (2.13 m) across at its widest. The door to the cell is made of thick metal and contains a window to the living unit that must remain clear at all times. Ferguson notes that '[t]hey

**Fig. 3.1** A typical cell at SCI Phoenix. (Source: Authors' collection)

have to have windows for security reasons in case there are some issues related to things for tactical purposes… You have to have the ability to see in there' (T. Ferguson, interview, 2019). The colour palette is neutral and in keeping with the design and aesthetics of the rest of the facility. The walls are a uniform, institutional yellow colour, the same as the majority of the other spaces occupied by incarcerated persons. All of the furniture within the cell is constructed of seamless, welded, and unpainted stainless metal. The construction of the space, with high ceilings and bright lights, challenges stereotypes of prisons as dark spaces, though this illumination and openness feel sterile and functional, rather than appealing, as it leaves no corner unexposed or obscured.

Each cell contains the same basic fixtures. All furniture in the unit can neither be moved nor adjusted. A bunk bed is secured in place at the corner formed by the side wall and the back of the room. Each of the identical bed spaces has a slight recess where the incarcerated person's mattress fits neatly. The other pieces of furniture in the cells include a small desk with two round, backless stools secured to the wall opposite the bed. Next to the desk is a cabinet and a small shelf is bolted to the wall in the vicinity of the sink/toilet combination, as is a small electronic intercom through which staff can be contacted if needed. There is little confusion with regard to the function of the cell's layout; the necessities for basic living are present, though they are structured to facilitate control, security, and observation. One cannot mistake a cabinet bolted to the floor and made of robust metal to be anything other than a traditional American carceral fixture.

Phoenix was designed to facilitate "lines of sight" for correctional staff and the cell's environment reflects this prioritisation. Accordingly, only limited personalisation of the space is permitted. With the exception of photographs and letters, most personal property in the cells must be purchased from the DOC, supplementing the sense of uniformity in light of prevailing security concerns.

Most of the light in the cells at Phoenix comes from the overhead fluorescent illumination, which is controlled by staff at the central command desk and operated on a set schedule. Each cell has a single window, located on the back wall and roughly opposite from the entry door. The window is tall and narrow with dimensions of approximately seven inches

(0.17 m) wide by 53 inches (1.34 m) high. These windows have no bars, are made of thick, unbreakable glass and cannot be opened. Accordingly, the windows give off an indirect light for most of the day. These windows do, therefore, not appear to be designed to provide a view or a sense of space; rather they reinforce a sense of just how close—but completely unreachable—the outside truly is.

The bathroom facilities reflect a similar calculation, prioritising near-constant monitoring over individual needs and, perhaps, dignity. Within Phoenix's cells, there is a metal combination toilet and sink, with the bowl of the sink resting at the top of what would be the water reservoir on a standard toilet. There are no knobs on the sink or the toilet; the toilet flushes and water is dispensed when buttons are pressed. The construction of the entire unit is therefore seamless, preventing access to the plumbing where contraband could be hidden. Located near the entrance to the cell, the toilet is in full view of the occupants of the cell, as well as any staff or individuals who may be looking in through the window in the door. The showers are located in the common areas, most often in a set of stalls located at the end of each tier of cells.

At Halden Prison, each cell is designed to house one person and is roughly 86 ft$^2$ (8 m$^2$), with an additional 21 ft$^2$ (2 m$^2$) dedicated to an adjoining bathroom (see Fig. 3.2). This layout was intentional and seen as meaningful, as the governor observes:

> It's also very important for the design of the prison cell that it should look like, well, a small, hotel room. [M]any of the visitors who can come here and look at the prison say [this]. So I think it was important that the room should [not feel like a prison]. [I]t's very important, especially [that] toilets [are] placed outside the room. Other prisons [built] in the 70's [in Norway], they didn't have toilets in the rooms, but that part of the normality principle now; you have [a] private [bathroom]. (A. Høidal, interview, 2018)

The bathroom has a wooden door with no observation window and is adjacent to the cell's entrance. Immediately after the bathroom, there is a wooden closet with space for both personal items and a small refrigerator. Beyond that is a low, wooden bed frame that is secured to the wall and custom-designed to eliminate any small spaces where items could be

**Fig. 3.2** A typical cell at Halden Prison. (Source: Authors' collection)

hidden (A. Høidal, interview, 2018) (see Fig. 3.3). A small light is located on the wall, controlled by the incarcerated person, often above the bed. A rectangular desk, lacking drawers, sits in front of the window. The accompanying chair is free-standing and upholstered. A low bookcase is affixed to the wall across from the bed. All furnishings in the cell are made of the same blonde-coloured beech wood. The walls are painted in a soft palette of green, blue and grey colours intended to have a calming and stress-reducing effect (Statsbygg 2010: 16).

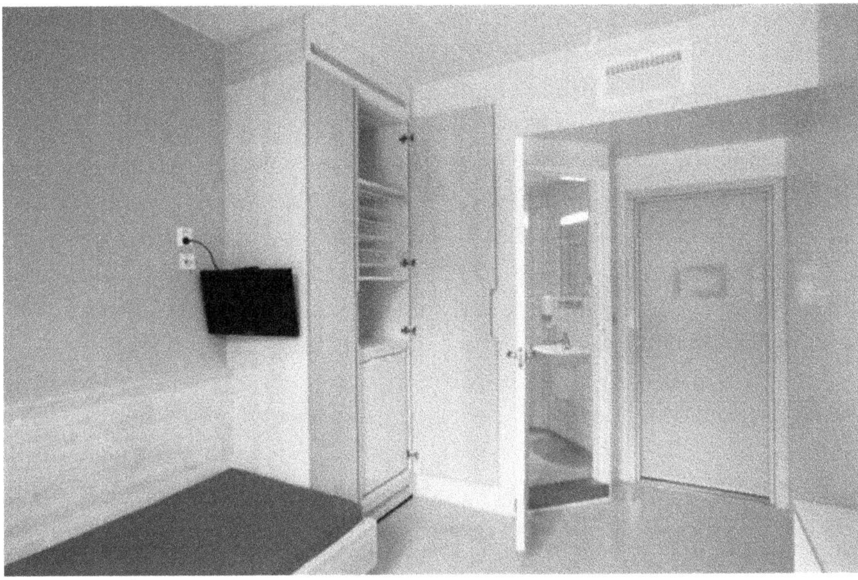

**Fig. 3.3** The bathroom and personal storage area in a typical cell at Halden Prison. (Source: Authors' collection)

At Halden, each cell features a large rectangular window that is 2.55 ft by 5.64 ft (0.78 m by 1.72 m) and located behind the desk and in line with the entry door. There are no bars on this window, though it is comprised of thick, unbreakable glass. Most cells, by design, offer a view of the woods at the centre or the trees at the periphery of the prison campus. Thick fabric curtains, accessible from within the cell, are affixed to the window. Governor Høidal notes that:

> [The cells] have a big window and they look out into the forest. So, it's a nice view from the window of Halden Prison; it's very green. [However] many inmates cover the windows with curtains because they don't want to look out because...: It's too nice I think, they want to be out. (A. Høidal, interview, 2018)

A small grate, running the length of the vertical side of the window, can be opened to allow for fresh air and a slight breeze to enter the cell; the grate is controlled at the resident's discretion. These choices are intentional; architects designed Halden in a way that would expose both staff and incarcerated people to natural light (Erik Arkitekter n.d.; Statsbygg 2010). The private bathrooms in each Halden cell contain a porcelain toilet and sink that is mounted to the wall, as is common in most homes. The shower stall has hardware that parallels what is available in the community (Norwegian Correctional Service n.d.-b). The bathroom space is fully tiled and has a standard glass mirror. Policies relevant to privacy are similarly intended to embody the normality principle. In this case, and as noted above, this means that the bathroom has a full, opaque door that can be shut at the incarcerated person's discretion.

At Phoenix, security and control are paramount concerns, including at the level of the cell. Superintendent Ferguson notes that 'the housing unit design at SCI Phoenix [was] very deliberate.... Phoenix got it right'. She added that 'from a correctional mindset when you walk into Phoenix, if you [are] from a correctional profession, you can't help but love the place. It'll leave you in awe' (T. Ferguson, interview, 2019). The cell doors in Phoenix are constructed of thick, grey, painted metal with a small, vertical window located in the upper portion. This window is unobstructed at all times. A small hatch located in the middle of the door, operated only from the outside of the cell, allows food and other items to be passed into the cell. A similar hatch, located at floor level, allows for the cell to be drained, in case of flooding. The cell door is controlled by correctional officers at all times and opens by sliding along tracks embedded within the walls. Cell residents cannot control their doors.

Halden, despite efforts to encourage reintegration through normality, is a correctional facility. Safety is addressed through both "static" (e.g. locks, cameras) and "dynamic" (e.g. incarcerated person-officer relationships) measures, where the latter remains a top priority (Høidal 2018). Incarcerated people remain under near-constant surveillance and security procedures except when they are actually in their cells. The cell doors at Halden are made of thick metal painted in a light grey colour. In their construction, they are similar to the doors at SCI Phoenix, though the observation window is, by default, covered with a metal hatch. Governor Høidal (interview, 2018) notes that they intend that prisoners have 'total privacy... we don't [usually] check the prisoners [when in their cells] or in the night'. Officers can open all doors, though they are trained to knock before opening doors and rarely watch cell occupants surreptitiously. The doors can also be closed (and locked from the outside) by the incarcerated persons and, after the workday is over, they are permitted to return to their cells where they may close the door to obtain a measured amount of privacy.

Interestingly, and despite manifest differences in the layout and fixtures, leaders in both Pennsylvania and Norway hold that the individuals that live in these spaces accept the cell environment as usual and acceptable, given the context and alternatives. At Halden, Høidal argues that the efforts to build a cell that aids in rehabilitative efforts have been successful (but, see e.g. Brottveit (2018) and K. (2018) for more critical accounts):

> [Prisoners] think they have what they need in the cells, they think they have privacy, they can go in and lock the door... in the daytime from the outside. ... But they can go into the cell and be private, and I think the other inmates respect that if you want to be alone you can be alone and read or look at football on the tv or whatever. I think the [prisoners] are quite satisfied with the standard of the room; they have what they need. (A. Høidal, interview, 2018)

Ferguson reflects on a more tacit acceptance of the living environment at Phoenix, as well as the different populations housed within:

> [F]or the inmates... the physical design is more tolerated by long-term offenders than short-term offenders. I think that those in long-term sentencing seem to adapt better to the actual physical plant, meaning 'this is what you've got, these are the neighborhoods and the house, I'm gonna make the best of what I got. (T. Ferguson, interview, 2019)

These perceptions underscore the gulf between the implementation of cell design, as well as the implications for the foundational goals behind the broader system, in these two correctional contexts.

## Understanding Commonalities and Differences in Function and Design

Despite their differences, corrections in Pennsylvania and Norway share a common historical foundation in the Pennsylvania Model of prison design (Johnston 2000). This model was adopted worldwide, including in Philadelphia's Eastern State Penitentiary (Johnston 2004) and Oslo Prison in Norway (Langelid and Fridhovd 2019). Philosophical shifts in Norway (Pratt and Eriksson 2011), as well as logistical hurdles and ideological challenges in Pennsylvania (Rubin 2015), forced both systems to repudiate their shared approach to prison construction and embark upon divergent paths.

Interestingly, Phoenix and Halden enjoyed contemporaneous design and planned construction trajectories, although Phoenix opened almost eight years after Halden because of myriad administrative and construction challenges (DiStefano 2018). Given that the design process took place at approximately the same time, the developers and leaders in both nations had access to the same research on rehabilitation and correctional efficacy as well as the same building techniques, and were furthermore subject to contemporaneous macro-level fiscal pressures. Halden cost approximately USD 250 million to build and Phoenix was constructed with a budget of approximately USD 400 million. At Phoenix, with at least 3830 standard cells, this translates to approximately USD 103,000 per cell (or USD 51,500 per bed); at Halden, on the other hand, USD 992,000 was apportioned per single-occupant cell. Though a useful, if roughly-estimated[5] metric, the differences within the resultant prison cells cannot be predominantly attributed to fiscal factors; differences in cells were also driven by ideology and the resulting allocation of resources.

As in every high-security prison, safety—manifested as a high degree of control over all aspects of incarcerated people's lives—is paramount in both facilities. Both Phoenix and Halden exist, at their core, to manage people. Both boast an extensive web of cameras and officers keeping a watchful eye on the perimeter and the incarcerated persons, highlighting the clear differentials in power and agency between those imprisoned and staff. As Foucault noted, the goal is to create a state of constant visibility and scrutiny to allow for the free exercise of the penal authority (Foucault 1977: 201). For example, consider the similarities in the architecturally designed ability to monitor people in their cells and the differences in the functional use of that power. In both facilities, staff have the physical ability to look in the cells whenever they want; a power reflected in the layout of the cell, the doors with hatches and the electronic surveillance systems. It has been argued, after all, that the source of power derived from the gaze of the other comes from the subjective knowledge that one is being watched (Crossley 1993). Clearly, Phoenix staff can see more because the toilet is on display within the cell while the bathroom at Halden lies behind an opaque door that can be shut. Yet, the basic point—that people incarcerated in both Norway and America may be observed in the closest thing they have to a private refuge—remains.

The physical differences presage the policy distinctions. At Phoenix, closing the cell door only does so much for the resident; the window on the cell door is always available to the staff as well as others passing by. At Halden, closing the cell door is very much like closing the door to an apartment in society; the observation window is shut by default. The staff must take an affirmative step to see inside the cell. This is where Halden's security needs may, under appropriate circumstances, trump its rehabilitative goal of normality. Staff at Halden report that they rarely open the hatch (A. Høidal, interview, 2018).

Within the cells, the overnight experience in the two institutions presents a revealing contrast, highlighting the interaction between cell design, correctional needs, and the experience of living in these spaces. At Phoenix, staff are required to engage in a counting process several times while the incarcerated people are attempting to sleep. The staff are instructed to look in the cell and visually verify both "flesh and movement" for everyone. If they cannot do so by extending their gaze into the cell with the light from the pod, they will shine a flashlight into the cell and bang on the cell door until they have seen all that they must. At Halden, staff leave the housing unit once the incarcerated persons are locked in their cells for the night; a small number of officers operate a central security centre from a different building overnight. Just as no one normally checks on most adults during the night outside of the prison environment, Norwegian officers generally do not peer into the cell again until they unlock it in the morning. In short, there is an interaction between the physical structure of the cells and the ways in which the cells are managed by the prison authorities.

The architectural differences between the two facilities can be stark. At Phoenix, the totality of structures and supervision seems to suggest that while the design of the cells is not supposed to be part of the retributive punishment overtly, it is also not taking on much of a direct, functional role in the rehabilitative process. These are cells for the storage of human beings during their incarceration. For example, the choice to design cells with exposed toilets values efficiency and safety through near-constant monitoring over competing—and potentially incompatible—notions of privacy and dignity. The cells and physical environment at Halden, in contrast, give primacy to the normality principle and reflect more of a rehabilitative purpose of punishment. For example, the choice to design cells with obscured toilets values notions of privacy and dignity over competing—and potentially incompatible—interests in security.

Even areas of philosophical agreement can produce different results. For example, at Halden, "static security" measures are similar to those at Phoenix: locks, metal detectors, cameras, and walls form a perimeter around cells. These restrictions are perceived as necessary for both security purposes and to create a foundation for a living environment onto which the normality principle can be mapped; they are both functional and means to an end. In Pennsylvania, many of these same ideological decisions are similarly purposeful. They, however, reflect the needs of a drastically different system that must house, feed and monitor correctional populations that are many times larger, and where safety for incarcerated persons and staff remains of paramount concern.

At the same time, the construction of the cells and housings units reflect a design choice with clear implications for how incarcerated persons experience incarceration. In Pennsylvania, the focus on the cell has revolved around the short term (the functioning of the prison) and the facility level, not on the long-term (rehabilitation of the individual) and the societal level (rates of recidivism). American penal institutions have largely focused on incapacitation, that is, removing offenders from the community for the duration of their sentence, as a significant correctional objective. Alternatively, an overt and expressed focus on rehabilitation has been the hallmark of Norwegian corrections since the 1980s (Pratt and Eriksson 2011; Høidal 2018). The principle of normality has become essential because, according to NCS leadership, 'it reflects [societal] values' (Vollan 2016: 93). However, although the Norwegian context has been constructed with an eye towards the normality principle, Halden is still a prison. At Phoenix, where control and observation are more overt and the lack of privacy apparent, there is a degree of transparency that may be obfuscated when an austere metal chair is replaced by a cushioned couch.

Normality in Norwegian corrections, as Engbo (2017: 332) notes, carries a meaning most often related to 'words like social reintegration and rehabilitation'. Taking the replication of a community-like environment as a core tenet, the cells at Halden appear to strive towards that goal, providing many obvious examples. These spaces are permitted, within the rules of the facility, to provide a form of customisation, comfort, and autonomy paralleling that of an apartment in the community. The furniture and toilets in the cells are almost identical to those found in many Norwegian homes. The goal, according to Norwegian prison officials, is to create an experience in the cell that adheres to the principle of normality as much as is possible, suggesting once again the primacy of a rehabilitative purpose of punishment. While aspects of control and the subsequent deprivation of some liberties, are unavoidable, the construction of the cell in light of normality is seen as an effective way to blunt this impact and preserve the rehabilitative nature of the experience at Halden. Normality may, intended or otherwise, become a veneer over the realities of a high-security prison environment. For many who are imprisoned, the most damaging 'pains of incarceration' are a consequence of the basic nature (and goals) of confinement inherent in all prisons (Hancock and Jewkes 2011). While providing a modicum of fresh air and a bathroom may, on the surface, appear well-positioned to ameliorate these harms, this is not universally accepted. Even a liberal conceptualisation of a custodial environment can be perceived as unfair and overly burdensome (Shammas 2014), and being locked into a cell, even one that looks like a hotel room, can be seen as restrictive and, at times, torturous.

Phoenix provides a counterfactual that is much more common in correctional spaces worldwide. Nothing in the cells is intended to be "normal", nor to reflect a sense of community-based living; the systematic preference for an environment that was designed to facilitate the non-utilitarian, retributive processes of incarceration over humanity is apparent. These tensions are reflected in the design of the bathrooms. For instance, the externally visible location of the toilets in the two-person cells is accepted by DOC as a security and control matter, especially in the context of efforts to reduce drug smuggling and violence. Privacy is sacrificed to preserve safety. Phoenix, moreover, views the improved safety of using a metal—as opposed to ceramic (which can be broken into sharp pieces)—toilet or sink as more important than whatever negative effects may be associated with its institutional message. Halden was designed to weigh these factors differently (A. Høidal, interview, 2018). For instance, at Halden staff are implicitly willing to take what some might view as security risks for the sake of the normality principle and an opportunity to foster rehabilitation by providing those individuals with the level of privacy most non-incarcerated people have in the bathroom (A. Høidal, interview, 2018).

Another area where experiences within the cell environments differ is with regard to the ability of an incarcerated person to interact with nature. This can have a profound effect on the quality of life and health (Moran and Turner 2018). At Halden, ensuring this level of engagement was a key goal for the architect, as they clearly state that, '[n]ature is actively involved as a social rehabilitative factor in the architecture' (Erik Arkitekter n.d.: n.p.). Within the cells, this is apparent in the ability to access fresh air through a secure grate and through the placement of large, clear windows facing a copse of trees in almost every cell within the facility. Phoenix, though providing more natural light than older American prisons, offers only a narrow, slit window in its cells. Like Halden, Phoenix was constructed in a manner that was intended to be "green", employing many cutting-edge, environmental friendly measures. The focus has been on energy efficiency, recycling policy and on the reduction of costs associated with older methods of heating, cooling and operating a correctional facility. This reflects an approach that prioritises the reduction of resource consumption—and the sustainability of the correctional system—over the size of the facility or substantive nature of the prison experience (Moran and Jewkes 2014). Little of the natural world is visible from Phoenix's cell; Pennsylvania prioritises the functioning of the system over and above any utilitarian aspects of incarceration, while their Norwegian counterparts consider access to nature to be potentially rehabilitative (cf. Moran and Turner 2018) and, therefore, a meaningful element of incarceration. As a result, incarcerated person in the two facilities are likely to experience this interaction with nature quite differently.

Finally, it is worth restating the perspectives on which these descriptions and observations are based. In both cases, prisons and correctional systems are described with the language from those that control the system and describe an environment as it was intended to be perceived. In many cases, especially with regard to Halden, these conclusions are echoed in media around the globe. While these descriptions provide insight—and an opportunity for comparison—key voices are missing. For instance, one individual formerly imprisoned at Halden found the colours, intended to be soothing (see Statsbygg 2010), to be unimportant; the beechwood furniture offensive in its blandness; and the bathroom minimally tolerable (K. 2018). Others have described many of the features of the cells at Halden, discussed here as humane and normal, as ineffective and oppressive, especially during long periods of confinement in the cell itself (Brottveit 2018: 209). While similar subjective descriptions of the experience of residing in the cells at Phoenix are not yet available, it is reasonable to assume that the level of relative deprivation, abundance of visual scrutiny and profuse formal control are unlikely to foster more positive perceptions of those cells. What is clear is that the ways the cell is experienced and how it is intended to be perceived, can drastically diverge; these perspectives should therefore be heard and considered.

## Conclusion

Both Pennsylvania's SCI Phoenix and Norway's Halden prison were built with an expressed intent of simultaneously confining and improving the lives of those who are imprisoned; this is reflected in their nearly parallel mission statements. These goals are mediated or encouraged by the environments in which the incarcerated persons reside. For example, Pennsylvania's more control-oriented approach to the carceral environment is dictated by a more retributive legal structure and society. Non-utilitarian goals of efficiency and security are paramount inside those prisons. Norway's rehabilitative emphasis is facilitated by a social welfare system and levels of public trust that are largely unparalleled. These priorities are reflected in the design of prison cells and, in turn, communicated to those who must reside within. This does not mean that rehabilitation is unimportant to Pennsylvania correctional officials, nor that the Norwegians are unconcerned with security. Tellingly, the DOC leadership has made it clear that as the Department of Corrections, it must strive to correct the behaviour of incarcerated people (T. Ferguson, interview, 2019), while their peers in Norway stress the need to provide security for the communities within and outside of the prison walls (A. Høidal, interview, 2018). Indeed, the leaders of both Phoenix and Halden independently described their overall goals in similar terms—to improve public safety by improving the behaviour of the people in their charge. The layout and furnishing of the cells in each facility mirror the very different approaches taken to achieve this goal, the balance each society strikes between these at-times competing interests, and the perceived role of the cell in promoting desistance from crime.

While no one aspect of life in custody—physical or programmatic—can define the experience of incarceration, prison cells provide an important piece of the puzzle. Carceral design choices—made with increasing intentionality by correctional officials, policy-makers, and architects—reflect the ideologies that are prevalent at the time the plans are drafted. As 'the design of the prison environment is crucial to its operation and to the impact it has on the achievement of correctional goals for incarcerated people, staff and public users' (Fairweather 2000: 47), the manner in which these spaces reflect an overarching penal ideology should also be considered. The messages communicated by the cells in both Pennsylvania and Norway speak volumes about the goals and means within each system and reverberate far beyond the prison walls.

## Notes

1. We focus our discussion here on the rehabilitative aspects of utilitarianism. A smaller literature exists that discusses the prison environs as deterrent in itself (e.g. Nagin 2013). This aspect of utilitarian punishment did not arise in this examination of these two prisons and their design processes.
2. Sentences are a range, with defendants spending at least the minimum—and no more than the maximum—in prison.
3. A 30-year sentence is possible for war crimes. One other exception is so-called preventive detention, which is a functionally indefinite sentence used only for the most dangerous and high-risk offenders (see e.g., Norwegian Correctional Service n.d.-a).
4. Consistent with legal and operational requirements, including the Americans with Disabilities Act, a small number of cells are designed for one occupant. Single-celling is also used to prevent physical assaults and other victimisation (T. Ferguson, interview, 2019).
5. These rough calculations simply divide the estimated budget by the total number of general cells. This is a very rough proxy for the allocation of resources per cell, as it fails to take into account construction of additional, non-standard cells, the size and nature of the remainder of the facility, material and labour costs, as well as myriad of other factors appropriately employed in a cost-benefit analysis.

## References

Benko, J. (2015). The Radical Humaneness of Norway's Halden Prison. *New York Times*. Retrieved September 11, 2019, from https://www.nytimes.com/2015/03/29/magazine/the-radical-humaneness-of-norways-halden-prison.html.

Brottveit, G. (2018). The Becoming of Punishment as an Unpredictable and Moveable Torment. In E. Fransson, F. Giofrè, & B. Johnsen (Eds.), *Prison, Architecture and Humans* (pp. 29–35). Oslo: Cappelen Damm Akademisk.

Crossley, N. (1993). The Politics of the Gaze: Between Foucault and Merleau-Ponty. *Human Studies, 16*(4), 399–419.

Dennis, M. (2018). Officials Cut Ribbon to Graterford Prison Replacement—SCI Phoenix. *The Mercury*. Retrieved October 2, 2019, from https://www.

pottsmerc.com/news/officials-cut-ribbon-to-graterford-prison-replacement-sci-phoenix/article_7b0f4744-0360-57bf-8403-9b76aa4f9dc7.html.

DiStefano, J. (2018). Pa.'s $400 million Prison Opening Delayed. *The Philadelphia Inquirer*. Retrieved September 11, 2019, from https://www.philly.com/philly/blogs/inq-phillydeals/sci-phoenix-graterford-state-prison-delay-not-june-30-20180629.html.

Engbo, H. J. (2017). Normalisation in Nordic Prisons—From a Prison Governor's Perspective. In P. Smith & T. Ugelvik (Eds.), *Scandinavian Penal History, Culture and Prison Practice* (pp. 327–352). London: Palgrave Macmillan.

Erik Arkitekter. (n.d.). *Halden Fængsel*. Retrieved September 14, 2019, from http://erik.dk/projekter/halden-faengsel/.

Esping-Andersen, G. (1990). The Three Political Economies of the Welfare State. *International Journal of Sociology, 20*(3), 92–123.

Fairweather, L. (2000). Psychological Effects of the Prison Environment. In L. Fairweather & S. McConville (Eds.), *Prison Architecture: Policy, Design and Experience* (pp. 31–48). Oxford: Architectural Press.

Foucault, M. (1977). *Discipline and Punish: The Birth of the Prison*. New York, NY: Vintage.

Frase, R. (2005). Punishment Purposes. *Stanford Law Review, 58*, 67–83.

Hancock, P., & Jewkes, Y. (2011). Architectures of Incarceration: The Spatial Pains of Imprisonment. *Punishment & Society, 13*(5), 611–629.

Heery International, Inc. (n.d.). *SCI Phoenix New Correctional Facility*. Retrieved May 22, 2020, from https://www.heery.com/projects/sci-phoenix-new-correctional-facility/.

Høidal, A. (2018). Normality behind the Walls: Examples from Halden Prison. *Federal Sentencing Reporter, 31*(1), 58–66.

Jewkes, Y., & Johnston, H. (2007). The Evolution of Prison Architecture. In Y. Jewkes (Ed.), *Handbook on Prisons* (pp. 174–196). Portland, OR: Willan Publishing.

Johnston, N. (2000). *Forms of Constraint: A History of Prison Architecture*. Chicago, IL: University of Illinois Press.

Johnston, N. (2004). The World's Most Influential Prison: Success or Failure. *The Prison Journal, 84*(4 Suppl), 20S–40S.

K., J. (2018). Humanity Rather than Materialism: A Short Essay About the Prison Environment. In E. Fransson, F. Giofrè, & B. Johnsen (Eds.), *Prison, Architecture and Humans* (pp. 29–35). Oslo: Cappelen Damm Akademisk.

Kriminalomsorgen. (2019). *Halden Prison: Punishment That Works - Change That Lasts!*. Retrieved March 26, 2020, from https://issuu.com/omdocs/docs/magasin_halden_prison_issu.

Langelid, T., & Fridhovd, I. M. (2019). Straffegjennomføring i Noreg: eit kort historisk oversyn. In K. G. Westreim & H. M. K. Eide (Eds.), *Kunnskapsbasert Straffegjennomføring i Kriminalomsorgen i Norge* (pp. 29–52). Oslo: Fagbokforlaget.

Moran, D., & Jewkes, Y. (2011). Linking the Carceral and the Punitive State: A Review of Research on Prison Architecture, Design, Technology and the Lived Experience of Carceral Space. *Annales de Géographie, 2*, 702–703.

Moran, D., & Jewkes, Y. (2014). "Green" Prisons: Rethinking the "Sustainability" of the Carceral Estate. *Geographica Helvetica, 69*(5), 345–353.

Moran, D., Jewkes, Y., & Turner, J. (2016). Prison Design and Carceral Space. In Y. Jewkes, B. Crew, & J. Bennett (Eds.), *Handbook on Prisons* (pp. 114–130). New York, NY: Routledge.

Moran, D., & Turner, J. (2018). Turning over a New Leaf: The Health-Enabling Capacities of Nature Contact in Prison. *Social Science & Medicine, 231*, 62–69.

Morris, N. (1974). *The Future of Imprisonment.* Chicago, IL: The University of Chicago Press.

Nagin, D. (2013). Deterrence in the Twenty-First Century. *Crime and Justice, 42*(1), 199–263.

Norwegian Correctional Service. (n.d.-a). *About the Norwegian Correctional Service.* Retrieved September 11, 2019, from https://www.kriminalomsorgen.no/information-in-english.265199.no.html.

Norwegian Correctional Service. (n.d.-b). *Halden Prison: Punishment that Works—Change that Lasts!* Retrieved September 14, 2019, from https://haldenfengsel.no/wp-content/uploads/2019/04/Magazine_Halden_Prison_prew6-Engelsk-versjon-2018-pages-3-4.pdf.

Pennsylvania Commission on Sentencing. (2018). *2017 Annual Report.* Retrieved September 11, 2019, from http://pcs.la.psu.edu/publications-and-research/annual-reports/2017/view.

Pennsylvania Department of Corrections. (2019a). *Mission Statement.* Retrieved September 11, 2019, from https://www.cor.pa.gov/About%20Us/Pages/CONTACT%20US%20-%20About%20Us.aspx.

Pennsylvania Department of Corrections. (2019b). *SCI Phoenix.* Retrieved September 11, 2019, from https://www.cor.pa.gov/Facilities/StatePrisons/Pages/Phoenix.aspx.

Pratt, J., & Eriksson, A. (2011). Mr. Larsson is Walking Out Again. The Origins and Development of Scandinavian Prison Systems. *Australian & New Zealand Journal of Criminology, 44*(1), 7–23.

Prison Policy Initiative. (n.d.). *Pennsylvania Profile.* Retrieved September 11, 2019, from https://www.prisonpolicy.org/profiles/PA.html.

Rubin, A. T. (2015). A Neo-Institutional Account of Prison Diffusion. *Law & Society Review, 49*(2), 365–400.

Shammas, V. L. (2014). The Pains of Freedom: Assessing the Ambiguity of Scandinavian Penal Exceptionalism on Norway's Prison Island. *Punishment & Society, 16*(1), 104–123.

Statsbygg. (2010). *Halden Fengsel.* Ferdigmelding 686/2010. Retrieved September 14, 2019, from https://www.statsbygg.no/files/publikasjoner/ferdigmeldinger/686_HaldenFengsel.pdf.

Tonry, M. (2015). Is Cross-national and Comparative Research on the Criminal Justice System Useful? *European Journal of Criminology, 12*(4), 505–516.

Vollan, M. (2016). «Mot normalt»? Normalitetsprinsippet i norsk straffegjennomføring. *Tidsskrift for Strafferett, 16*(4), 447–461.

# 4

# The *Kubol* Effect: Shared Governance and Cell Dynamics in an Overcrowded Prison System in the Philippines

Raymund E. Narag and Clarke Jones

## Introduction

The Philippine correctional system is now the most over-crowded system in the world (IPCR 2018) with its prisons[1] registering an average over-crowding rate of 582 per cent. Though already overcrowded prior to President Rodrigo Duterte's 'war on drugs', the inmate population has increased by more than 67 per cent (from 120,000 to 200,000) in just two years (2016–2018). A bottleneck in the criminal justice system has also now formed for offenders in pre-trial detention, where they spend an average period of 512 days before cases are decided by the courts. Consequently, some facilities now register overcrowding rates of more than 2000 per cent. This means that cells that could comfortably house up to 10 inmates, now accommodate as many as 200 (BJMP 2018).

R. E. Narag (✉)
Southern Illinois University, Carbondale, IL, USA
e-mail: rnarag@siu.edu

C. Jones
Australian National University, Canberra, ACT, Australia





J. Turner, V. Knight (eds.), *The Prison Cell*, Palgrave Studies in Prisons and Penology,
https://doi.org/10.1007/978-3-030-39911-5_4

Making matters worse, the rapid growth in the inmate population has not been matched with corresponding increases in cell space, personnel, and resources to safely and securely house inmates (Narag 2018).

The rapid growth in the inmate population combined within limited personnel and resources negatively affects the living conditions of inmates, the working conditions for staff, and the health and well-being of both guards and inmates alike. A custodial personnel to inmate ratio of 1:7 is prescribed in the BuCor Modernization Law of 2013. Yet, the actual ratio currently stands at 1:80 and is further stretched to 1500 if shift patterns and leave of absences are included. The Manila City Jail Male Dormitory, for example, which was designed for 1200 inmates has more than 6000 inmates and is ordinarily guarded by only 12 custodial officers on a regular shift. Operational resources are also lacking. Prisons have limited budget for facility maintenance and operational activities. The food budget for each inmate is set at PhP 60 (USD 1.10) per day which, by most accounts, is insufficient to buy food for all the inmates in the heavily overcrowded multi-occupancy cells. Therefore, inmates are forced to rely on families to bring in food during visitations and, in some prisons, inmates grow their own produce for sale and distribution. On entry into a prison, inmates are provided with a yellow t-shirt and toiletries (soap and toothpaste), after which they are expected to provide for themselves. The budget for medicine and medical services are also severely limited to PhP 5 (USD 0.10) per person per day, making sick inmates dependent on visitors and volunteer groups for medical assistance. In many cases, personnel utilise their own money to transport sick inmates to the hospital. Only around 5 per cent of inmates are provided with beds in the cells, with the majority sleeping on floors, in stairwells, or on makeshift hammocks. Coupled with a lack of ventilation, and in some cases running water, several inmates die due to skin rashes, heart attack, tuberculosis, and other communicable diseases (Chavez 2018). In Metro Manila's 43 jails alone, around 40 inmates die each month due to disease. While there are variations in cell conditions—on account of the legal status of the inmates (remand versus convicted); facility population size (ranging from less than 100 inmates to 26,000 inmates); location (accessible urban areas versus remote rural communities) and other important variables—the overall description is the same: correctional facilities in the

Philippines are extremely overcrowded, under-staffed, and under-resourced resulting in both inmates and correctional officers suffering from material and resource deprivations.

Using western standards, it would be easy to conclude that the Philippine correctional system is failing or has failed. With the high levels of congestion in the cells, one would expect to see frequent rioting, escapes, and serious assaults (Franklin et al. 2006; Gaes and McGuire 1985). Indeed, extant western prison literature suggests that prisons facing extreme material deprivations are difficult to govern (DiIulio 1987). Additionally, by western correctional standards, the determination of a successful prison or jail facility includes 'the provision of a safe and secure environment' where an offender's quality of life meets basic welfare needs (Management and Training Corporation Institute 2006: 1). Furthermore, a successful prison 'must have programs that prepare the offenders for re-entry into society, thus protecting the public from further effects of crime upon the release of the offenders from custody' (Management and Training Corporation Institute 2006: 1). Criminologists have also produced a range of performance measures for evaluating prisons, using variables like rates of prison violence, the quality of prison health care, the degree of overcrowding, and rates of recidivism (Volokh 2013).

The western literature also suggests that the inadequacy of goods and services induce the formation of illegitimate inmate coping mechanisms that undermine the capacity of prison administrators to manage the cellblocks (Sykes 1958). For example, due to lack of goods and services, an underground prison economy develops that facilitates the entry of contraband and compromises prison security (Kalinich and Stojkovic 1985). The lack of personnel and resources also lead to a vacuum of governance (Darke 2014; Skarbek 2010, 2016) where powerful inmate gangs take control of the day-to-day cell administration (Butler et al. 2018; Dias and Darke 2016). These gangs may take over the entire prison system, capturing the loyalty of the inmates and undermining the legitimacy of prison staff. In Sao Paolo, Brazil, for example, due to overcrowding, insufficiency of personnel, and state repression, a powerful prison gang emerged in 80 per cent of the prison system and has taken over its management (Darke 2018; Dias and Darke 2016). This penological knowledge induces the articulation of policies that advocate for the removal of inmates' role in governance, the suppression of gangs and other inmate groups, and the non-utilisation of inmates' pre-prison skills and resources.

As will be later explained, these scenarios have not been realised due to a range of inmate coping mechanisms, some of which are tied to the importance of Filipino cultural norms, such as communal living, family and friendship support networks, and sharing of food. The Philippine correctional system has also not manifested into a system where the presence of overbearing prison gangs (called *pangkats*) run the facilities. In all cases, correctional officers still have some operational control (Jones et al. 2015). Even though inmates in prisons are usually members of prison *pangkats*, the facilities continue to function relatively free from major disturbances, and recidivism is low despite the multiplicity of deficits (Narag and Jones 2017). Additionally, despite these deficits, inmates have developed unique coping mechanisms to improve their quality of cell life, improve safety, and provide opportunities for rehabilitation. These coping mechanisms have largely formed from the importation of outside Filipino cultural values and traditions into the cells, which have come to form a unique microcosm of Filipino life commonly found outside of prisons.

Through longitudinal, participant observation studies and interviews, this chapter provides a unique understanding of how prison personnel and inmates deal with these harsh realities of cell life in the Philippine correctional system. We explore how Filipino inmates define what is meant by living in a cell. At the outset, it must be mentioned that cells in the Philippines are multi-occupancy cells by design, which ideally could accommodate between 4 and 10 inmates. However, in reality, the cells accommodate as many as 200 inmates, which is a stark contrast to the single occupancy (or two inmate) cells in western developed countries. This multi-occupancy nature of the cells, where inmates live communally, has a direct bearing on how cells are managed and operated and affects how Filipino inmates experience cell life.

Similar to the 'mutations' (Martin et al. 2014: 9) exhibited by some prison systems in contexts of resource deficits (Garces et al. 2013), we describe how Filipino correctional officers and inmates alike develop necessary and mutually acceptable mechanisms to cope with the hardships of prison cell life. Specifically, we document the 'give and take' relationships that develop to overcome the 'pains of imprisonment' (Sykes 1958); the organisational structures and informal processes that sustain coping mechanisms; and the cultural narratives employed by both inmates and staff that are commonly drawn upon to justify specific courses of action. We then describe the evolution of a staff-inmate shared governance system where specific inmates take on active roles managing fellow inmates in the multi-occupancy cells, which includes providing safety and security, opportunities for rehabilitation, and administrative and supportive functions to aid their fellow prisoners. These informal coping mechanisms all take place with the guidance and direction of correctional officers.

We argue that these unique cell dynamics and coping mechanisms contribute to the development of a liveable space despite the harsh material conditions. We further argue that the Filipino cultural values of *damayan* (helping one another), *bayanihan* (community spirit), and *padrino* (patron-client relationship) are imported (Irwin and Cressey 1962) into the prisons. These values help to mediate the nature of staff-inmate relations and differentiate it from other types of prison governance that developed in other parts of the world. Specifically, we differentiate the developmental nature of Philippine 'shared governance' model from the predatory Latin American 'self-governance' model where inmates had developed strong oppositional values against the custodial guards (Darke 2014). As will be explained in the conclusion of this chapter, these dynamics characterise how Filipino inmates experience life in the multi-occupancy cells, which is quite different from how inmates in other countries experience cell life. Highlighting the positive ramifications of this emergent 'customary order' (Aguirre 2005), this chapter concludes with a discussion of the limitations and sometimes futility of introducing western-based correctional management models (Garces et al. 2013) that are not attuned to the Philippine cell realities and are therefore rejected by the guards and inmates alike. In most cases, these western models of correctional management try to take all leadership responsibilities away from the inmates, strip prisoners of identity, limit guard-inmate interactions, and reduce opportunities for family visitations.

## A Note on Data Collection

The authors of this chapter have extensive engagement with the Philippine correctional system. The first author was himself once a detainee for almost seven years while undergoing trial for a crime he did not commit in one of the most crowded jails in Metro Manila. He had a first-hand experience of the intricacies and dynamics of the cell life in a male-only adult jail. After eventually being declared not guilty by the trial court, he took interest in prison reform and has since been an advocate for the past 20 years, documenting and writing extensively about his experiences both behind bars and now outside as an active correctional reformist. The second author has conducted ethnographic research in Philippine correctional facilities over the past 10 years and has been a regular visitor involved in training and advising correctional officers working in the adult male prisons and jails. Both researchers have conducted ethnographic research in over 50 correctional facilities (including remand jails and prisons for convicted felons) and, combined, have conducted over 85 semi-structured and unstructured interviews with male inmates and over 120 semi-structured interviews with correctional officers over a ten-year period (2007–2017). While there are significant variations on how inmates and correctional officers live their lives in the Filipino prison facilities, in this chapter, the authors provide a silhouette of the common life behind bars.

## Vibrancy Amidst Scarcity

Instead of failing, due to the material resource scarcities we described previously, cells in the Philippine demonstrate vibrancy amidst scarcity. Most cells we visited were clean and tidy, and some cells were colourfully painted and decorated. Inmates are usually respectful—they address visitors with 'sir' and 'ma'am', they answer questions deferentially, and they are compliant with the directions of the correctional staff. Despite overcrowding, inmates make way for visitors to pass, making sure that visitors will not feel harassed.[2] Despite physical difficulties, inmates' faces are generally upbeat, and many inmates are eager to share experiences and exchange pleasantries with other inmates or visitors. During weekends, cells are usually festive, with visitors bringing food, children running around the corridors, and inmates from other cells or cell blocks called *brigades* trying to sell clothes, equipment, and other personal belongings. We commonly hear from first-time visitors and volunteers that 'they feel safer in the prisons than in the streets'. Upon entering the prison for the first time, a prison volunteer recounted:

> At first, I was shocked. I never thought inmates would be out of their cells moving around freely. My image of a prison is that inmates are in their cages. But I saw inmates crisscrossing the yard, selling different products and handicrafts. There is a bakery managed by inmates [...] I see placards greeting the *bosyo* of a brigade on his birthday and a *pangkat* (gang) celebrating its anniversary like a fiesta. And there was a basketball tournament and an inmate *mayores* speaking to the participants urging them to be sportsmen [...] like a true politician [...] it is surreal, I thought I was just entering another *barangay* (village). (Prison volunteer, Female 1)

Overall, there is a sense of tranquillity in the cells, as most inmates seem to just get along with each other. While this may vary between facilities, our observations and interviews with inmates and correctional staff in different facilities suggest that the description pictured above represents the normal situation of the cells. This lead us to the question: what explains this resiliency in the face of resource scarcity? What are the coping mechanisms utilised by inmates and prison staff to overcome the scarcities of the cell? What makes the coping mechanisms in the Philippine cells different from the coping mechanisms developed in other countries with similar levels of resource deprivations? Below, we describe the dynamics of these coping mechanisms and the rationale utilised by correctional officers and inmates to justify their existence.

## Dynamics and Rationale of the *mayores* System

One of the most ubiquitous characteristics of Filipino cells is the *mayores* system. Although the exact titles vary, this is an intricate inmate leadership structure (see Table 4.1).

**Table 4.1 Inmate leadership titles and roles in the Philippines**

| Cell leadership title | Responsibility |
|---|---|
| *Mayor de mayores* | Head of the *Mayors (brigada or cell block)* |
| *Mayor* | Head of the cell |
| Vice *Mayor* | Deputy head of cell |
| Chief *Bastonero* | In-charge of discipline |
| *Kulturero* | In-charge of head-counting |
| Chief *Buyonero* | In-charge of cleanliness |
| Chief Jury | In-charge of conflict mediation |
| Chief *Mahinariya* | In-charge of night security |

The names of inmate leaders and their positions are prominently displayed on the cell walls and these leadership roles impact significantly on cell life. In bigger facilities, a brigade structure also develops where a *mayor de mayores* (leader of the *mayors*) is created. Supported by a cadre of leaders, the *mayor de mayores* is in-charge of a group of five to six cells in the brigade. Our interviews reveal that, to be an inmate leader, one must have a good standing among the correctional officers and inmates. An inmate leader in a BuCor prison mentioned:

> It is not the BuCor who created the system of *nanunungkulan* (inmate leaders). It is the inmates themselves. We chose to govern ourselves. Because it is overcrowded, inmates get bored and fights can easily break out. Everybody suffers. So we took upon ourselves to create rules. We have rules inmates need to follow… However, to be effective, you need to have the endorsement of the staff. And be respected by your fellow inmates. (Inmate leader, Male 1)

In most facilities, leaders are elected by their fellow inmates but their positions need to be endorsed by the correctional staff. The inmate leaders (also called *nanunungkulan*) are informally deputised by the correctional officers to perform custodial functions, such as implementing cells rules and regulations, mediating conflicts among the inmates, enforcing disciplinary infractions, and maintaining the upkeep of the cells and brigades. They also informally perform rehabilitation functions, such as making sure inmates participate in educational and spiritual programmes and generating resources for sports, educational and cultural activities.

Correctional officers also utilise inmate *trusties*[3] to supplement these programmes. *Trusties* are selected by the cell leaders and are assigned to work for personnel to augment the correctional officers in clerical and administrative work. In bigger facilities, *trusties* also supplement rehabilitation activities by serving as teachers in the Alternative Learning Systems (ALS), medical assistants for health services, and paralegal aides that assist inmates in their criminal cases. Thus, inmates who are teachers, nurses, lawyers, engineers, and other professions from the outside are highly sought after by the inmate leaders and correctional officers for their expected professional contribution to the facilities and to the daily operations of the cells.

Based on our interviews with *mayors* and senior correctional officers, the *mayores* system is purportedly designed by both the correctional officers and inmates to cope with the lack of personnel. Correctional officers admit that they utilise the inmate leaders as 'force multipliers' (BuCor custodial officer, male 2). Accordingly, it is easier for them to call the inmate leaders and task them to disseminate information, instead of calling inmates individually. This way, they are 'unburdened of their tasks'. Additionally, most correctional officers frame the use of inmate leadership 'as a form of rehabilitation for the inmates', which, by their accounts, gives inmates roles in governing the cells where inmates can 'develop leadership skills that they can utilise in the outside world'. Accordingly, it keeps them busy and pre-occupied, thus reducing boredom and conflict (Conley 1980). A prison rehabilitation officer surmised:

> Some inmates are college-educated. We have one inmate who taught computer studies in a University. He has helped us design software that tracks the participation of inmates in our activities. His software can also monitor inmates who have visitors […] Just imagine if he stays in his cell doing nothing. His talents will be wasted. (Prison Rehabilitation Officer, Female 1)

When asked why inmates are utilised as classification officers, a prison rehabilitation officer answered:

> Why not? They are college graduates. They have relevant education. They have writing skills. We utilise them so that they can be busy while they are

> here. […] So, we use them to help supplement our workforce. (Prison Rehabilitation officer, Male 3)

By giving inmates roles, they also surmise that inmates are 'trusted', which is an important mechanism for inmates to keep a positive self-identity (Goffman 1961). Thus, a unique characteristic of the correctional management in the Philippines is the evolution of the *makatao* (humanistic) approach: correctional officers compensate the material deprivations by developing personalised and intimate relationships with inmates. In the BuCor, for example, the official organisational slogan is: 'we are your family, friends and sanctuary' (Narag and Jones 2017).

Thus, in our multiple visits to prisons, it is common to observe inmate leaders spending time in wardens' offices casually discussing 'problems of the community' over a cup of coffee. In the Philippines, the warden is usually the head of the prison, so their direct contact with inmate leaders provides him or her with valuable information about cell dynamics, how their inmates are coping, and whether there are any potential issues arising in the cells. It is also not unusual to see inmates doing administration work, such as typing up inmate records in the document offices. These types of administrative positions are usually prestigious and usually sought after as they can provide advantages and power over other inmates. For example, one inmate with accounting qualifications in New Bilibid Prison rose to gang leadership status after he was given the role of helping look after the prison's financial records. We also regularly observed former inmates being employed by wardens as drivers, cooks, and utility workers in the same facilities upon release. A custodial officer confessed:

> Let us be honest, without the inmate leaders and trusties, this Bureau will breakdown. That is why, the moment they arrive, we always ask "who among these inmates can be utilised?" In this Bureau, we don't have enough lawyers, whereas, among the inmates, how many of those are lawyers. They can help our paralegal offices. (Custodial officer, Male 8)

As a result, we observed that inmate leaders take their positions seriously. Our interviews suggest that inmates take pride in being inmate leaders and they are conscious of their roles in correctional management. An inmate leader commented,

> The reason why I want to be a *nanunungkulan* (leader) is because I get the chance to speak to important people. I had never talked to a congressman and senator before, but in the prison, I talked to them and I represent my fellow inmates. (Inmate leader, Male 4)

Our interviews further suggest that inmates try not to engage in activities that destroy the trust accorded to them by the wardens and subordinate correctional officers. The majority of the inmate leaders see themselves as *katuwang* (appendages) of the correctional management. Inmate leaders actively participate in solving problems, such as, overflowing septic tanks, malfunctioning water and electrical systems, and other maintenance needs. In some facilities, inmate leaders contribute to the payment of electrical, water, and cable expenses. Thus, a defining characteristic of the inmate leadership structure in the Philippines is its developmental or rehabilitative nature, where inmate leaders take pride in their position of responsibility and even learn leadership skills that can help them upon release. Therefore, inmates tend to strive to take on leadership roles in their cells, which not only provides them with benefits but also helps with keeping individual prison violations to a minimum. The oppositional culture (Jacobs 1977), which is commonly noted in other prison systems, is notably absent. Though this setup is susceptible to abuse by individual corrupt guards and inmate leaders, as will be described later, there are systematic efforts to overcome these abuses in most cells and cell blocks. As will be expounded below, the *mayores* system reflects the Filipino culture of *bayanihan* (heroism) where individuals with talents and skills are expected to lead community members for mutual benefits.

## Dynamics and Rationale of the *kubol* System

Another pervasive trait of Filipino cells is the presence of *kubols*, *tarima* (makeshift beds), and other improvised housing arrangements. Correctional officers tacitly allow inmates to construct *kubols* within the facilities. Inmates petition officers for building materials to be brought into the facilities, where they can either add on new space to existing facilities or construct layers of beds to maximise space within a single cell. The *kubols* provide a sense of privacy for the inmates, particularly during visitation hours when visitors are permitted inside the cells or stay overnight for conjugal visits. In the process, inmates claim ownership of their *kubols* and personalise them: decorate them like their own house, display family pictures, and regain their personal space. Though not all inmates can have instant access to *kubols* and *tarimas* due to the lack of space, owning one is within the reach of everyone: inmates who have stayed the longest (and if they display good behaviour) are prioritised when previous owners are released or transferred to other facilities. With informal supervision from staff, cell space becomes privatised and sold on to other fortunate inmates as a form of *kubol* real estate.

Interviews with correctional officers suggest that they allow inmates to construct *kubols* for 'humanitarian considerations'. Correctional officers are sympathetic to the conditions of the inmates and they are cognisant of the congestion levels that have reached subhuman conditions. A prison custodial officer opined:

> Look, government does not have money. We have been requesting for money to have a building refurbished or a facility constructed. But the request does not get approved in Congress or if approved, it is not released by DBM (Department of Budget and Management) on time. So we just allow inmates to construct facilities. Anyway, when they get released, that property belongs to the BuCor. Should we not allow that? […] if we don't allow, where will the inmates sleep? […] These inmates are people too! (Prison Custodial Officer, Male 1)

Thus, for the correctional officers, allowing inmates to construct *kubols* addresses the inadequacy and failure of the government to provide more accommodation. Correctional officers argue that since it is the inmates themselves who paid money for the *kubols*, then it is not an additional cost to the government. They consider it as a form of Build Operate and Transfer (BOT) scheme, where inmates build the facility, operate it while they are still in prisons, and transfer ownership to the authorities upon release. In the process, inmates are invested in keeping their *kubols*. They have a stake in cell conformity—a disorderly cell may invite the attention of the warden, which can lead to the destruction of the *kubols*. Additionally, if found worthy of having a *kubol*, correctional officers may also allow inmates to construct other facilities, such as prayer rooms, schools, basketball courts, and other amenities. Based on an informal, unstated agreement, correctional officers allow the use of these inmate-made facilities if 'it does not compromise the safety and security of the jail or prison' (Jail warden, Male 3). Thus, the defining trait of the *kubol* scheme is its role to create more accommodation space, relieve congestions, and extend government resources. Unlike in other prison systems where privatisation and commercialisation of housing structures arise (Darke 2014; Skarbek 2010), *kubols* in the Philippines are still state regulated. While abuses do occur, such as the constructions of very elaborate *kubols* (sometimes with flat-screen televisions, air-conditioning, private bathrooms, and queen-sized beds), correctional officers consciously regulate the construction, sale and use of the *kubols* and other inmate-constructed structures. As will be explained in more detail, the *kubol* dynamics capture the social ordering of the inmates: those with bigger and more elaborate *kubol* spaces enjoy considerable esteem but they have higher expectations to become model cell citizens.

## Dynamics and Rationale of the *rancho* System

A third common trait among Filipino cells is the *rancho* system. *Rancho* (also called *kasalo*) is a mechanism where inmates with resources are paired with inmates without resources. Inmates with regular visitors and those who can access money from the outside are considered *very important preso* (VIPs [4]). Inmates without visitors and without access to resources are called *buyoneros*. A *rancho* usually consists of two to three VIPs and four to six *buyoneros*. The *rancho* serves as the basic family unit in the cells. In a cell of 100 inmates originally designed to house just four, there could be as many 10–15 *ranchos*. VIPs in the *rancho* provide for the food, clothing, medicine, toiletries, and other needs of *buyoneros* in the rancho. In return, the *buyoneros* cook food (which is usually provided raw by the staff), wash clothes, and run errands for the VIP inmates. When a *rancho* member gets sick, other members have the responsibility to take care of their sick member. VIP inmates may bring cash (as much as PhP

2000 [USD 40] per week of visit) and may initiate a business inside the facility (selling snacks to inmates and visitors, engaging in livelihood activities, etc.) and utilise the *buyoneros* as business employees. VIP inmates with *kubols* may also share them with their *buyonero* members when the *buyoneros* receive visitors. Aside from economic and material support, the *rancho* also provides social and emotional support to cell members. *Rancho* members also prepare inmates for court trials by conducting mock hearings, provide transportation money to released *ranchomates*, and comfort members undergoing personal problems. Older members of the *rancho* are called *Tatay* (father) or *Kuya* (older brother) and are given higher esteem compared to the younger members. The most senior inmates (usually 60 years and above) and those who are infirm are exempted from cell duties. The pseudo-family structure of the *rancho* ensures that the inmates toe the line: if the family members are difficult to get along with or they are not good *rancho* or cell citizens, they can be expelled from the *rancho* or the cell. An inmate in a Metro Manila Jail confided:

> No one will help an inmate except a fellow inmate. You are with them day in and day out. Your *ranchomates* are your family because they are there all the time. Sometimes, you disagree but that is natural. You must contribute and sacrifice for the family so everyone gets better. If you don't, then like a family, they will gossip about you. (Inmate leader, Male 15)

Correctional officers encourage the formation of the *rancho* system. Our interviews suggest that correctional officers facilitate the use of inmate *rancheros* (food distributors) so they can equitably distribute food. They justify the role of the VIPs in terms of food and resource augmentation. From the 120 correctional officers we interviewed, there was unanimous agreement that without inmate resources, the majority of the inmates would be physically emaciated. A jail gate officer intimated:

> It is important to allow inmates bring food inside. I know it is a lot of work searching food for contrabands but it is part of Filipino culture to share food. It is their happiness [...] If you eat home-made foods, it reminds you of home, your mother or wife. (Jail Chief Gater[5], Male 2)

In the process, inmates have access to outside food and lessen their deprivation of goods and services. Thus, in almost all correctional facilities, a *talipapa* (cell store) emerges where canned goods, condiments, fresh meat, vegetables, medicine, soap, kitchen wares, and other necessities are sold. Correctional officers may also allow VIP inmates to bring in appliances, such as electric fans, cooking utensils, television sets, and other appliances, if these are 'communally used by their *ranchomates*' (BJMP regional director, Male 5). The entry of these materials provides an opportunity for inmates and staff to collectively overcome the substandard conditions. Correctional officers draw resources from the VIP inmates to bring sick inmates to hospitals, administer rehabilitation programmes, to paint the cells, and so on. Thus, the defining trait of the *rancho* system is its role as a 'communal resource'. While the *rancho* scheme is also susceptible to abuse by corrupt correctional staff and inmates for their personal gain, there are built-in mechanisms to overcome abuses. As will be elaborated upon later, the *rancho* system embodies the Filipino cultural values of *damayan* where inmates are expected to contribute to the wellbeing of every member of the cell community.

## Tying the Coping Mechanisms Together: Staff-Inmate Shared Governance

The formation of the inmate leaders, the constructions of the *kubols*, and the dependence on the *rancho* resources are indeed ubiquitous characteristics of the multi-occupancy cells in the Philippines. Their pervasive presence suggests that correctional officers have fully incorporated these informal practices in their management regimes. These coping mechanisms are simultaneously designed and negotiated by the correctional officers and inmates as a response to the shared experience of material deprivations. The developmental nature of this 'give and take' relationship translates to a collaborative form of *staff-inmate shared governance*, where correctional officers take command of the facilities but with maximum participation accorded to the inmates. Inmates are given a leeway on how to manage the cells if they support and conform to the direction and authority of the correctional officers.

However, the emergence of inmate coping mechanisms is not unique to the Philippines. Contemporary and historical studies document the prevalence of the roles of inmate elites in prison governance (Aguirre 2005; Darke 2013; King and Valensia 2014; Marquart and Crouch, 1984; Oleinik 2006; Skarbek 2010). However, what differentiates the Philippine model is that these other types of governance structures are more likely to result in violent tensions within a facility, which affects the overall quality of life inside the cells and the overall security of a facility itself. For example, contemporary studies in some Latin American prisons describe the formation of predatory model of *inmate self-governance*, which arose due to the abandonment by the correctional staff of their roles in managing the cells (Biondi 2017; Darke 2013, 2014, 2018; Dias and Darke 2016; King and Valensia 2014). Prison officers have confined themselves to just guarding outside perimeters, with the primary role of making sure that inmates did not escape (Darke 2014). In inmate self-governance, inmate leaders have developed a very strong pro-inmate ideology that has taken root inside the prison cells, which challenges the ideological basis of prison authority. An oppositional culture (Jacobs 1975) creates a divide between inmates and staff. Coupled with the emergence of violent gangs, which have co-opted the inmate leadership structure, inmates often engage in brutal displays of power (Biondi 2017). This display of power symbolically undermines the prison authority's claim as the sole wielder of the use of force. Such extremes have not developed in the Philippines, which is evident by the low number of inmate infractions in the cells. In contrast to prisons in countries in Latin American where inmate self-governance is prevalent, prison authorities in the Philippines are actively engaged in the management of the cells, despite the low ratio of guards to inmates, and the lack of space and resource. They still have the ultimate control of the use of force. A prison custodial officer declared:

> Inmates are on a long leash. We allow them to feel as if they are free, but, if we have to, we can shorten the leash to restrict their freedom. Ultimately, we are in control but play their game. (Prison custodial officer, Male 5)

Additionally, the formation of *pangkats* is developmental in nature in that they can provide leadership role models for other inmates. The *pangkats'* main mantra, as stated in the *Pangat Magna Carta*, is to respect the authorities and to keep the peace in the cells (*igalang ang mga empleyado*). These observations led us to the following questions: what led to the formation of shared, instead of self-governance, in the Philippines? Are cultural values imported from the outside responsible in determining the type of inmate governance in countries with similar levels of resource deprivations?

## Emergent Findings: The Impact of Outside Cultural Values On Staff-Inmate Shared Governance in the Philippines

Our analysis of observational and narrative data suggests that the developmental and collaborative nature of the staff-inmate shared governance scheme is made possible by the Filipino values and norms that are imported inside the prison cells. The cultural values imported inside mediate the impact of the coping mechanisms. This differentiates the developmental nature of Philippine staff-inmate shared governance model with other forms of governance described previously.

Scholars suggest that inmates bring with them their pre-prison characteristics and outside indigenous cultural values inside the cells (Irwin and Cressey 1962; King and Maguire 1994). Scholars on Filipino culture suggest that the Philippines can be characterised by horizontal and vertical social relations. Horizontal relations pertain to the collectivist nature of Filipino society. In this type of relationships, Filipinos give premium to *damayan* (helping one another) and *bayanihan* (community spirit) (Enriquez 1993). Group needs are given primacy over individual needs. This is best captured by the Filipino saying, *ang sakit ng kalingkingan ay sakit ng buong katawan* (the pain of the pinky finger is a pain of the whole body). It is also manifested by the traditional respect given to authorities and older people by virtue of seniority. Vertical relations, on the other hand, pertain to the enduring effects of colonial mentality. Accordingly, the various colonial governments utilised the Filipino elites in the subjugation of the Filipino masses, creating a cultural divide between socioeconomic classes that endured up to the present day (Hutchcroft 1998; Ileto 1979; McCoy 2009). In these types of relationships, Filipinos give premium to patron-client associations, where individuals at the lower status give deference to individuals in the higher socioeconomic status.

These outside cultural values are manifested in the *mayores*, *kubol*, and *rancho* systems. The collectivist culture dictates that the *mayor* is considered the 'father of the cell' and he is culturally expected to provide for the needs of the children (cell members). Thus, cultural tenets, like *tayo ay pamilya* (we are family) are regularly invoked by the cell leaders to mobilise support from cell members. Inmates are expected to offer their talents and resources for the upkeep of the cells. On the other hand, inmates naturally submit to the authority of the inmate leaders. Undermining the authority of duly elective representatives and creating group discord (*baryo-baryo*) are considered violations of this cultural mandate. This cultural imperative thus pre-empts animosity between inmates and inmate elites. In the same vein, the jail warden is considered the 'father of the whole facility'. Using this Filipino cultural tenet, the warden can also invoke compliance among inmates as 'members of the jail family'. The warden can thus call upon inmates to volunteer their services to augment prison operations. This cultural bind prevents the formation of an oppositional culture (Jacobs 1975) between inmates and staff. Instead, a personalistic patron-client relationship develops between inmates and staff. In this setup, staff extend privileges to subservient and loyal inmates in exchange of their continuing compliance to prison rules and regulations.

The construction and use of the *kubol* and the formation of the *rancho* system are also consistent with Filipino cultural values. Though the *kubol* is assigned to a particular inmate, other inmates can regularly use the *kubols* by invoking the ethic of *damayan*. It is similar to the practice of a host sharing the best rooms in their house when a visitor stays overnight. This limits the privatisation and commercialisation of the *kubols*. The *ranchomates* are also expected to behave in a particular decorum. Members of the *rancho* are expected to protect the good image of the *rancho* as wayward activities of one member may put the entire *rancho* in a bad light. For example, a *ranchomate* who perennially misses a headcount due to oversleeping will reflect poorly on the leadership and unity of the *rancho*. A VIP inmate who exploits the labor of a *buyonero* will be frowned upon by other *ranchos*. These cultural mandates serve as built-in mechanisms that curb the potential abuses in the *rancho* system.

## Conclusion: The Cell as Experienced by the Filipino Inmates

Filipino inmates thus experience cell incarceration in a contextually-determined setting. The cell becomes a microcosm of life outside the facilities. The porousness of the facilities suggests that they can re-create their pre-prison lives inside the cells. Inmates' pre-prison characteristics are fully recognised and valued, and serve as their initial card in negotiating their life within the community. Lawyers will be addressed as 'attorneys,' teachers will be called 'sirs' by inmates and correctional staff alike. Inmates can engage in self-help mechanisms that nurture their 'agentic' (Aguirre 2005) engagement in cell and prison life. They are not mere recipients of the actions of the prison authorities, rather, they co-articulate and co-implement the visions and policies of the facility. This setup provides mechanisms for inmates to preserve their self-identity (Goffman 1961), which is usually corroded in institutional security-laden settings. Furthermore, inmates who abide by the rules of the customary order can rise to the ranks of inmate leadership, acquire bigger spaces, and enjoy prestige in the cell and prison community. This provides an opportunity for inmates to normalise their conditions (Gutierrez 2012), where good work is recognised and rewarded and bad actions are frowned upon and penalised. Thus, the cell becomes a disciplinary tool (Foucault 1977) to inculcate the importance of following the rules, respecting authority, understanding other peoples' concerns before making imprudent actions, and navigating through tense and depriving conditions. Inmates who do not or cannot follow the informal rules will remain on the lower rung of the social hierarchy. This daily grind, experienced in very compact settings, eventually impacts the behaviour of the inmates inside the cells and long after they are released. Indeed, inmates who had stayed in prisons for a couple of years speak of the leadership and survival skills called *diskarte*, which they 'learned inside the prison' and are useful in free-world living. Even among inmates who stayed in detention centres and jails for only a few days and weeks speak highly of the importance of following the rigid rules. They surmise, ironically, that if Philippine laws are respected and followed with the same passion and regularity as cell rules and regulations, Philippine society will be peaceful and progressive. Though by default, and not by design, the emergent prison practices rehabilitate individuals into valuable members of the society because they inscribe upon them cultural values that give premium to such notions as community, hard work, and respect for others. However, we are not attempting to downplay the problems that occur from time to time in the Philippine cells. As previously noted, the material deprivations take a toll on the physical and mental health of inmates and correctional officers. Though generally subservient, prison disturbances do occur, especially when crowding levels hit critical points.

Additionally, when left unchecked, unscrupulous correctional officers and inmate leaders can work in tandem to abuse the VIP system, engage in the drug trade, and foment violence. Power struggles between and among inmate leaders and correctional officers may also accrue when newly-arrived wardens do not conform to the shared governance scheme. In some facilities where prison *pangkats* are present, the family culture can sometimes mutate to a tribal culture with its attendant rivalry and quest for territory. Indeed, these events happen, which tends to disrupt the equilibrium (Sykes 1958) of the prison climate. However, when such disturbances occur, correctional officers and inmates re-invoke the customary order to establish peace (Jones et al. 2015).

The staff-inmate shared governance model described in this chapter helps with the day-to-day management of correctional facilities in the Philippines. However, reliance on inmate leadership structures and resources is usually considered anathema to principles of modern correctional management. Correctional officers in the Philippines are regularly advised by western experts to abolish the *mayores*, *kubol*, and *rancho* systems. Thus, the operation manuals of the correctional agencies explicitly prohibit the use of the shared governance scheme. This creates ambivalence and confusion among the lower-level officials who recognise and depend on the customary order. Additionally, removing these coping mechanisms without addressing overcrowding, and the lack of personnel and resources, may push the mutation from shared governance to self-governance. As explained at the outset, two years of implementation of the drug war has made the prisons extremely overcrowded. Restrictions on the entry of resources and destruction of *kubols* had been earnestly implemented. While resilient and subservient, our interviews suggest that some inmates may eventually articulate an oppositional ideology that could radically mutate the prison climate in the direction of the Latin American prison experience. As one inmate from a highly restrictive maximum-security facility recently mentioned:

> They have taken away our *kubols*, they reassigned us to different cells, they disallowed our *pangkats* to function, now it is free for all. There are no more rules, *matira matibay* (survival of the fittest). Inmates are patient and they can take the blows. But if there are inmates articulate enough to mobilise us to action, violence will erupt. (Inmate leader, Male 10)

Finally, the staff-inmate shared governance scheme is rooted to the Filipino culture that is imported inside the facility. It is developmental and collaborative in nature. It transforms the cell experience from one of spaces of deprivation and misery into that of a dynamic, supportive community. It promotes self-help and protects the self-identity of the inmates, translating to lower levels of recidivism. Removing these coping mechanisms will further expose inmates to depriving conditions. Thus, instead of doing away with these indigenous structures, we argue that the shared governance scheme must be formalised and fully incorporated into the correctional manuals. By formalising these structures, excesses and abuses can be regulated or curbed.

## Notes

1. In the Philippines, the correctional system is three-tiered. The detention centers are managed by the Philippine National Police (PNP); the jails are managed by the Bureau of Jail Management and Penology (BJMP) and

the Provincial governments; and the prisons and penal farms are managed by the Bureau of Corrections (BuCor). Detention centers and jails officially house inmates undergoing trial, however, due to prolonged pretrial proceedings, majority of inmates end up serving their sentences in these facilities. Thus in the Philippines, detention centers, jails and prisons are interchangeable and are collectively called "*kulungan*". In this chapter, we use the term 'prison' to also mean jails and detention centers.

2. In the Philippines, due to lack of visitation areas, most prisons allow visitors to enter the cells.
3. Inmate leaders (nanunungkulan) and trusties are two different classes of inmates who participate in shared governance. Inmate leaders have political roles; trusties have administrative/clerical roles. They also differ in level of prestige in the inmate community. However, trusties can become inmate leaders if they gain the trust of the inmates in the cells.
4. Preso is Spanish for prisoner.
5. An officer in charge of gate security and of frisking visitors upon entry.

## References


Aguirre, C. (2005). *The Criminals of Lima and Their Worlds: The Prison Experience, 1850–1935*. Durham, NC: Duke University Press.

Biondi, K. (2017). Prison Violence, Prison Justice: The Rise of Brazil's PCC: Could the Origins and Code of Ethics of São Paulo's Largest Prison Gang Offer a New Way to Think About Prison Security Policy in Brazil? *NACLA Report on the Americas, 49*(3), 341–346.

Bureau of Jail Management and Penology (BJMP). (2018). *Data and Statistics*. Retrieved October 13, 2018, from https://www.bjmp.gov.ph/datstat.html.

Butler, M., Slade, G., & Dias, C. N. (2018). Self-Governing Prisons: Prison Gangs in an International Perspective. *Trends Organized Crime*. https://doi.org/10.1007/s12117-018-9338-7.

Chavez, C. (2018). *BJMP Pushing Measures to Address Jail Health Woes*. Retrieved October 13, 2018, from https://news.mb.com.ph/2018/04/22/bjmp-pushing-measures-to-address-jail-health-woes/.

Conley, J. (1980). Prisons, Production, and Profit: Reconsidering the Importance of Prison Industries. *Journal of Social History, 14*(2), 257–275.

Darke, S. (2013). Entangled Staff-Inmate Relations. *Prison Service Journal, 207*, 16–22.

Darke, S. (2014). Managing without Guards in a Brazilian Police Lockup. *Focaal, 2014*(68), 55–67.
Darke, S. (2018). *Conviviality and Survival: Co-Producing Brazilian Prison Order*. London: Palgrave Macmillan.
Dias, C. N., & Darke, S. (2016). From Dispersed to Monopolized Violence: Expansion and Consolidation of the Primeiro Comando da Capital's Hegemony in São Paulo's Prisons. *Crime, Law and Social Change, 65*(3), 213–225.
DiIulio, J. J. (1987). *Governing Prisons: A Comparative Study of Correctional Management*. New York, NY: Free Press.
Enriquez, V. G. (1993). Developing a Filipino Psychology. In U. Kim & J. W. Berry (Eds.), *Indigenous Psychologies: Research and Experience in Cultural Context* (pp. 152–169). Thousand Oaks, CA: Sage.
Foucault, M. (1977). *Discipline and Punish: The Birth of the Prison*. New York, NY: Vintage.
Franklin, T. W., Franklin, C. A., & Pratt, T. C. (2006). Examining the Empirical Relationship between Prison Crowding and Inmate Misconduct: A Meta-Analysis of Conflicting Research Results. *Journal of Criminal Justice, 34*(4), 401–412.
Gaes, G. G., & McGuire, W. J. (1985). Prison Violence: The Contribution of Crowding Versus Other Determinants of Prison Assault Rates. *Journal of Research in Crime and Delinquency, 22*(1), 41–65.
Garces, C., Martin, T., & Darke, S. (2013). Informal Prison Dynamics in Africa and Latin America. *Criminal Justice Matters, 91*, 26–27.
Goffman, E. (1961). *Asylums: Essays on the Social Situation of Mental Patients and Other Inmates*. Garden City, NY: Anchor.
Gutierrez, F. C. (2012). Pangkat: Inmate Gangs at the New Bilibid Prison Maximum Security Compound. *Philippine Sociological Review, 60*, 193–237.
Hutchcroft, P. D. (1998). *Booty Capitalism: The Politics of Banking in the Philippines*. New York, NY: Cornell University Press.
Ileto, R. C. (1979). *Pasyon and Revolution: Popular movements in the Philippines, 1840–1910*. Quezon City, Metro Manila: Ateneo de Manila University Press.
IPCR. (2018). *Highest to Lowest - Occupancy Level (Based on Official Capacity)*. Retrieved October 13, 2018, from http://www.prisonstudies.org/highest-to-lowest/occupancy-level?field_region_taxonomy_tid=All.
Irwin, J., & Cressey, D. R. (1962). Thieves, Convicts and the Inmate Culture. *Social Problems, 10*, 142–155.

Jacobs, J. B. (1975). Stratification and Conflict Among Prison Inmates. *Journal of Criminal Law & Criminology, 66*, 476.

Jacobs, J. B. (1977). *Stateville: The Penitentiary in Mass Society*. Chicago, IL: University of Chicago Press.

Jones, C., Narag, R., & Morales, R. (2015). Philippine Prison Gangs: Control or Chaos? *RegNet Research Paper No. 2015/71*. Retrieved May 29, 2019, from https://ssrn.com/abstract=2586912 or https://doi.org/10.2139/ssrn.2586912.

Kalinich, D. B., & Stojkovic, S. (1985). Contraband: The Basis for Legitimate Power in a Prison Social System. *Criminal Justice and Behavior, 12*(4), 435–451.

King, R. D., & Maguire, M. (1994). Contexts of Imprisonment: An International Perspective: Introduction. *British Journal of Criminology, 34*, 1–13.

King, R. D., & Valensia, B. (2014). Power, Control, and Symbiosis in Brazilian Prisons. *South Atlantic Quarterly, 113*(3), 503–528.

Management & Training Corporation Institute. (2006). *Measuring Success: Improving the Effectiveness of Correctional Facilities*. Retrieved December 14, 2018, from https://www.mtctrains.com/wp-content/uploads/2017/06/Measuring-Success-Improving-the-Effectiveness-of-Correctional-Facilities.pdf.

Marquart, J. W., & Crouch, B. M. (1984). Coopting the Kept: Using Inmates for Social Control in a Southern Prison. *Justice Quarterly, 1*(4), 491–509.

Martin, T. M., Jefferson, A. M., & Bandyopadhyay, M. (2014). Sensing Prison Climates: Governance, Survival, and Transition. *Focaal, 2014*(68), 3–17.

McCoy, A. W. (Ed.). (2009). *An Anarchy of Families: State and Family in the Philippines*. Madison, WI: University of Wisconsin Press.

Narag, R. E. (2018). Understanding Factors Related to Prolonged Trial of Detained Defendants in the Philippines. *International Journal of Offender Therapy and Comparative Criminology, 62*(8), 2461–2487.

Narag, R. E., & Jones, C. R. (2017). Understanding Prison Management in the Philippines: A Case for Shared Governance. *The Prison Journal, 97*(1), 3–26.

Oleinik, A. (2006). A Plurality of Total Institutions: Towards a Comparative Penology. *Crime, Law and Social Change, 46*(3), 161–180.

Skarbek, D. B. (2010). Self-Governance in San Pedro Prison. *The Independent Review, 14*(4), 569–585.

Skarbek, D. B. (2016). Covenants without the Sword? Comparing Prison Self-Governance Globally. *American Political Science Review, 110*(4), 845–862.

Sykes, G. M. (1958). *The Society of Captives: A Study of a Maximum Security Prison*. Princeton, NJ: Princeton University Press.

Volokh, A. (2013). Prison Accountability and Performance Measures. *Emory Law Journal, 63*(2), 339–416.

# 5

# 'I Feel Trapped': The Role of the Cell in the Embodied and Everyday Practices of Police Custody

Andrew Wooff

## Introduction

Once someone has been arrested, they are taken to police custody in order for investigations into the allegations made against them to be examined. Legally, therefore, police custody is the cornerstone of the British criminal investigations process, facilitating decisions taken about whether to charge or release detainees (Skinns et al. 2017b). Until recently, police custody was interpreted as a fairly benign space where detainees were held before decisions were taken. Recent work, however, has argued that far from being a passive experience, the cell becomes a place of emotion where detainees contemplate and consider the impact of detention on their future lives (Wooff and Skinns 2018). Liminality is a useful concept for exploring this emotional uncertainty of being in a cell. More commonly applied in health and education settings (Atkinson and Robson 2012), it refers to the 'interstructural state' in which the

A. Wooff (✉)
School of Applied Sciences, Edinburgh Napier University, Edinburgh, UK
e-mail: A.Wooff@napier.ac.uk



J. Turner, V. Knight (eds.), *The Prison Cell*, Palgrave Studies in Prisons and Penology,
https://doi.org/10.1007/978-3-030-39911-5_5

person is 'betwixt or between' socially constructed identities (Turner 1967). Although I have argued elsewhere that police custody in general can be considered a liminal experience for many detainees (Wooff and Skinns 2018), time in the cell in particular is frequently the period where, emotionally, detainees experience the liminality of custody. Not only are they cut off from the outside physically and metaphorically, but when detainees are in their cell they are acutely aware that the decisions being taken about them will potentially impact on their future life. Jewkes (2011: 278) argues that, in the context of those who are on indeterminate sentences, liminality is frequently experienced when we go from a period of stability to 'one of ambiguity'. The cell in police custody is the space where detainees experience those feelings.

Indeed, environmental psychology can provide theoretical understandings of the impact of the building design on the social interaction among users, with a growing body of scholarship linking prison architecture to the way that prisoners and staff interact (Beijersbergen et al. 2016; Jewkes 2013; Laws and Crewe 2016; Crewe et al. 2014; Liebling 2004; Moran 2013; Moran et al. 2018). Understanding the role of the police custody cell in the way(s) that relationships between risk, emotion and resistance can be managed by staff at the scale of the cell can elucidate understandings of this carceral space. In particular, emotions in police custody tend to be intensified (Wooff and Skinns 2018). These emotions can be heightened by the physical environment of the cell, where the detainee is kept in a highly controlled, windowless and stark space, often uncertain of the outcome of their case. It is also a space where staff exert control over detainees by monitoring, regulating and managing emotions through their (in)actions in a bid to minimise risk to detainees and staff. Frequently the cell is used to de-escalate situations, where detainees who are arrested and are too violent, un-cooperative or incoherent through drink or drugs to be dealt with immediately, are taken straight to the cell. This makes the time a detainee is in a police cell an inherently risky period, where risk of suicide and self-harm is heightened (Williams et al. 2017). As a result, the cell can be a place where the detainee exercises their power in the context of custody, resisting, being violent and, importantly, a place where emotions are actively managed by staff.

As in prison settings there is a complex interaction between risk and emotion, with resistance commonly being the culmination of the emotional turmoil experienced by a detainee in a police custody cell. Following Laws and Crewe's (2016) work on emotion management in prisons, the police custody environment can impact emotionally on the detainee in a number of ways. This includes the cognitive change, which refers to how we 'reappraise or transform' and 'how we think of situations' (Laws and Crewe 2016: 538), but can also refer to the emotional realisation that often occurs when someone is brought in to custody that their life may alter significantly once a decision has been taken about whether to charge or release them. In other words, although the average time someone tends to be held in police is 9–10 hours (Skinns 2011), the particular spaces in a custody suite elicit different emotions and these can cause 'emotional aftershocks' in the life of an individual once they have been released (Wooff and Skinns 2018). The role police staff have in managing these emotional transactions is also significant and it is the police cell that is a site for this.

Although the charge bar[1] and the broader custody environment is important (see Roach Anleu et al. (2015) for a discussion of emotions in courtrooms), particularly in considering 'emotion zones', this chapter focuses specifically on the cell within the custody suite. The cell is where the detainee tends to spend most of their time when they are in police custody: it is where, aside from being interviewed or getting fingerprints and DNA taken (which tends to be brief), the detainee will be held. It is also the site where rights and entitlements can be given or denied, underscoring the lack of control the detainee has in the situation and the power differential between the staff and suspects. Uniquely in the criminal justice estate, police custody cells increasingly have closed-circuit television (CCTV). CCTV is one way that officers manage the risk of detainees self-harming, putting those deemed as a high-risk in cells (where available) with CCTV. However this also raises complex questions about privacy versus risk and the extent to which officers can monitor and intervene to support and manage the emotional turmoil of detainees. The chapter will draw on data gathered as part of a research project examining risk and efficiency in police custody in Scotland and will use the lens of the police custody cell to consider how the emotions of the detainee can be managed by considering the risk posed by the person and inter-relatedly, their emotion as often expressed through forms of resistance. This chapter will argue that understanding the cell as a site of risk, emotion and resistance in a dynamic way allows interrogation of the way(s) that the cell can be used to manage emotion.

## Methodology

The chapter draws on data from a study funded by the Scottish Institute of Policing Research, entitled 'Measuring Risk and Efficiency in Police Custody in Scotland' (2015–2017). In order to develop an understanding of the varying nature of police custody across Scotland, two contrasting case study locations were selected. The urban case study was a large, inner-city custody suite operating a fairly typical management structure with 52 cells. The rural case study operated a dispersed custody model, where the remote rural custody estate was managed by a central urban-based custody Sergeant and team. These contrasting locations offered varying opportunities and challenges and offered insights in to how the cell was a site of risk, emotion and resistance.

This chapter focuses exclusively on how staff manage risk, emotion and resistance in the police cell and draws upon 12 semi-structured interviews with staff and 15 hours of observation across the two custody sites. Participants included Custody Sergeants, Custody Inspectors, Police Constables (PCs) in custody and Police Custody Support Officers (PCSOs). Strategic interviews were also conducted with senior custody managers, at the rank of Superintendent. Non-participant observation was conducted by observing different shifts working in a custody suite on different days and times, including Friday and Saturday nights and recording 'systematic description of events and behaviours' (Marshall and Rossman 2011: 79). Data were transcribed, coded and analysed and thematic analysis allowed themes to be developed such as the ways that risk, emotion and resistance were managed by custody staff via the space of the prison cell.

## The Cell as a Site of Physical and Emotional Risk

Managing risk and 'risky' populations is a core part of the role of working in custody. As Williams et al. (2017) note, a lack of bespoke training on mental health and a 'one-size fits all' approach to risk assessment leads to custody staff feeling under pressure and ill-equipped to deal with the multitude of risks related to health. Those detainees coming into custody frequently have complex healthcare needs that pose a risk to the detainee and also to the staff managing them. As Rekrut-Lapa and Lapa (2014) note, those coming into police custody with mental health issues are over represented compared to the general populations. Hence it is likely that staff are required to manage complex healthcare risks of detainees (see Rekrut-Lapa and Lapa 2014; Skinns 2011; Williams et al. 2017). As this chapter will demonstrate, the custody cell is a site where many of these risks, such as those of self-harm and violence, can be amplified. The cell, then, is a site of increased risk of harm where the 'corrosive effects of the custody environment' (Cummins 2008: 41) can be observable. Staff are therefore tasked with managing and monitoring these acts of harm and the space of the cell is central to this interaction.

Some forms of self-harm in custody can be understood as a form of resistance that allows the detainee to exert some control over the situation (Cummins 2008). Staff practices are significant in order to mitigate further risk of harm and the process of monitoring is central to their work around containment within the cell. In Cummins' (2008: 44) study, he notes that in the cell, the 'most common methods of self-harm used in these incidents were ligatures and head butting/punching the cell walls'. Preventative methods are often deployed such as putting detainees in a rip-proof blue suit. However, interestingly, Cummins (2008) notes that the blue paper suits, in themselves, do not prevent incidents of self-harm taking place. Conversely they discovered that due to the indignity detainees felt while in these suits, being placed in them might actually be a contributory factor towards self-harm (Cummins 2008). Dignity and the conditions of the custody cell, therefore, appear to be important in helping to reduce self-harm in the cell. That is, the cell itself can impact on the emotions of the detainee. As a result, staff have to navigate and respond to these situations.

As this chapter highlights, the cell environment often makes it challenging to effectively manage risk due to the custody estate dating back many years (Skinns et al. 2017b). This impacts directly on the conditions of the cell and type of environment, with older buildings described as 'subterreanean' with a lack of light and ventilation problematic in custody suites across the Police Scotland custody estate (Skinns 2011). The impact of the environment of police custody on staff and detainees is beginning to be examined, with Skinns and Wooff (2020) noting that detainees felt they were treated with more dignity in custody suites in which detainees perceived as having better conditions. As one sergeant explains the cell remains the key space of risk within the custody suite:

> Yes, when a detainee is put in the cell that can be risky. We obviously do risk assessments [these are a set of standard questions asked to all detainees] when we are booking people in and anyone I am worried about I tend to put in the observation cells, and make sure they are being monitored. But sometimes it isn't possible to do a risk assessment straight away or people deteriorate ... you need to constantly be thinking 'what if?' (Sergeant, urban suite)

This quote highlights that risk is the lens through which staff in custody most often view detainees, particularly inside the cells. It shows the importance of considering risk in a dynamic way,[2] but also highlights the cell as a key site of risk within the custody suite. This is particularly the case when detainees are sent 'straight to the cell' (Williams et al. 2017). This tends to happen to detainees who are particularly drunk, heavily under the influence of drugs or are being violent:

> When people are first brought in and they are a potential threat, the cops will have done their part, i.e. they will be maybe handcuffed to the rear, fast strapped on the legs around the knees and the ankles, and if they're going to spit, they'll have a spit hood on the prisoner as well. Generally someone like that isn't going to stand here and give their name, date of birth, whatever, so they are then taken up to a cell with no risk assessment. (PCSO, urban suite)

When a detainee is taken straight to cell, the 'risks are amplified' (Williams et al. 2017). That is, the risk to both the detainee and staff is increased if the detainee is taken to the cell without going through the normal 'booking in' processes. Yet, in these instances, the cell is deployed as a safe space for the detainee to calm down and be closely monitored. Safety of the detainees is compounded by the safety of staff. The risk to staff emerges as both the physical risk that a detainee may harm them because they are being violent and from the wider threat to their livelihoods if someone dies in police custody:

> We're trained, there's officer safety training that we do once a year, and it's about a two man teaming or three man teaming someone into a cell, to get them safely into the cell and unwrapped from handcuffs and restraints and such in a safe way for the prisoner and the staff ... it's about everybody getting out of that cell safe and the prisoner being safe as well. Risk wise, when someone is in a cell and we know they are a spitter or whatever. (PCSO, urban suite)

In this example the cell is an area of risk for the officer especially when a detainee is being violent. This is particularly true in the older custody estate, where cells tend to be enclosed and cramped and it can be hard to carry out approved cell-exit tactics.[3] The cell in these circumstances becomes a key point where the physical (and emotional) risk of harm is heightened to both staff and detainees and the cell becomes a containing space for the staff to manage the emotional outpourings of detainees. Furthermore in older custody facilities, the cell space can be an extra burden for the staff to manage, where the physical design can hinder the approved cell exit tactics by having narrow doorways which reduces the number of staff able to carry out the procedure. In this sense, the police custody cell has the potential to become a physical site of danger for the staff and resistance for the detainee (see later sections). When detainees are put in their cell, they can be placed there for a number of hours before being processed, receiving their rights and accessing an appropriate adult or lawyer as required. Minimising risk in the police custody cell therefore requires careful consideration of the health of detainees, both physically and mentally. As one Sergeant notes, '[managing] that risk is about making the right decision, particularly when they are in cells to avoid the worst scenario of death in custody'.

The risk of harm to a police officer is only one dimension of the cell as a site of risk. As Skinns et al. (2017a) highlight, risk in police custody appears to be more about the risk posed to detainees, usually as a result of a complex set of vulnerabilities. As McKinnon and Grubin (2010) note, mental health issues feature frequently among people coming in to custody, with the police cell being identified as a time of particular risk. One of the best ways to minimise the risks to inmates is through the use of CCTV (Williams et al. 2017). The Royal Commission on Criminal Justice (Doxford 1993) recommended the use of CCTV in custody, while as Newburn and Hayman (2002) note, the Police Complaints Authority recommended CCTV was expanded beyond police custody areas and into individual cells. In Scotland, most custody centres have at least one cell with CCTV, most have two or three cells with CCTV and newer suites are being designed with CCTV in every cell. Naturally, risk assessments and decisions have to be taken about which detainees to put in the cells with CCTV—normally those designated as most vulnerable. All respondents to Williams et al.'s (2017) study suggested that CCTV in cells was invaluable in helping minimise risk in these spaces. In my study, respondents also highlighted the importance of CCTV in helping minimise risk in custody cells, drawing a clear link between the built custody environment, risk in cells and CCTV:

> CCTV is invaluable, but you'll have seen, some of our estate is pretty old … not very modern and lacking in technology. It's not very modern and the cells, well without CCTV you feel a bit blind. As a custody sergeant I'm wary when people are in cells without CCTV, yes PCSOs [police custody support officers] are doing checks, but you never know. CCTV adds a safety net. (Custody Sergeant, urban suite)

CCTV in these circumstances is there to help staff monitor detainees, but it also underlines the social control that it enables. At the scale of the cell, CCTV symbolises the exertion of control by the officers in a space which, albeit temporarily, is someone's private space where they use the toilet, sleep and eat. Although in cases where there are specific worries about a detainee they may be put under 'constant observation' (monitored by a police officer or PCSO at all times), there is a larger group of detainees who may not need immediate healthcare input, but who nevertheless pose a risk of self-harm or alcohol withdrawal (Skinns 2011). The case study locations had limited CCTV provision and, as Skinns (2011: 83) notes, 'CCTV is only as good as the people monitoring them'. In one of our case study locations, police officers were expected to sit in a room and monitor four small TV screen CCTV cameras for up to two hours at a time:

> As the Custody Inspector shows us round what feels like a rabbit warren of corridors and cells, we reach what looks like a cubby hole. In there are four TV screens, not the modern flatscreen type, but old square thick monitors about 14 inches across, two flickering. It is possible to make out the blurry outlines of two detainees. There is a PC in there staring at the four screens with his phone out. Walking in behind, the Inspector snidely remarks that he shouldn't have a phone out whilst on constant observation duty. He says he has been there for two hours, his radio battery has died and he needs relieved by the next shift. He hasn't been able to call the booking in desks because they are too far away and he hasn't been able to leave his constant observation. (Observation notes, urban suite)

The College of Policing (2018) has guidelines on the monitoring of CCTV, with clear evidence that someone should not monitor more than four CCTV monitors at a time and that the monitors should have a clear picture. Additionally, a recent inspection by Her Majesty's Inspectorate of Constabulary in Scotland (2018) noted a number of deficiencies in the monitoring of CCTV in the custody estate in Scotland:

> For example, at one centre we visited, no one was monitoring the CCTV screen on which a detainee should have been constantly observed and, at another centre, we found magazines in an area only used for constant observations, suggesting staff may not be sufficiently focused on their task. Custody staff also told us about officers engaged in constant observations using their mobile phones. (Her Majesty's Inspectorate of Constabulary in Scotland 2018: 15)

These accounts highlight the limitation of CCTV and the challenges of monitoring someone constantly on a small CCTV screen whilst they are located in their cells. Aside from the physical limitations of monitoring CCTV, questions also remain about whether the proliferation of CCTV is entirely beneficial to the detainee or whether it is a mechanism through which the police can be more readily held to account. It enables the cell to be a site of constant observation, where although risk can be minimized by its use, the notion of constantly being observed in a private space could be problematic for some detainees. Such is the routinisation of CCTV being deployed in custody cells, this nuance is rarely considered. Officers routinely talked about CCTV helping reduce the risks to them in relation to CCTV in cells, enhancing their own feelings of safety:

> The cameras are there; I see them as my protection. I know that it protects me. Some of the prisoners know it's there, so they play up to it. But ultimately I'm more concerned for what it would mean for me. So it is my protection. (PC, urban suite)

For this PC the CCTV helps to mitigate against physical risks. Interestingly, whilst CCTV is encouraged in police custody cells, it is not commonplace in prison cells (Allard et al. 2008), perhaps underlining the different purposes of the cell. In custody, advocating the widespread use of CCTV in cells suggests that the right to monitor and surveil a detainee is more important than a right to privacy in the cell. In prisons, the cell represents a (more) private space, with Laws and Crewe (2016: 535) arguing that 'personal cells were used as spaces where more challenging emotions could be processed and ventilated'. However, despite what the application of widespread in-cell CCTV might say about the ways that staff view the custody suite cell, this study identifies the cell as a site of pain—where boredom, anger, fear, shame, guilt and worry coalesce as detainees are forced to spend a lot of time reflecting on what has happened.

## Managing Emotional Turmoil

Because of the nature of police custody, painful emotions are undoubtedly a feature of the detainee journey. Emotions have been considered as 'deviations from rationality' (Mercer 2005: 98) but, as Hughes (2009: 199) argues, emotions are at the heart of human existence and 'take on even greater importance during times of conflict', stress and pressure. Indeed the cell is a space of emotional pain, where detainees regularly vent their frustration and anger; focusing on the way that the cell is a site for this emotional turmoil is important for understanding how emotion management in a custody suite operates.

The cell is a particular spatial context, where connections are imbued with power, a lack of explicit choice and a space where the detainees' bodies and environment are impermanent, but are affected by interactions between and with others in generating new forms of embodied materiality. The design of a police custody cell, for example, is stark, without any form of stimulation. There are no televisions, the cells are painted in beige monotone, books are rarely offered or available, and there is no way of telling the time (see Wooff and Skinns (2018) for further discussion). A mattress is available in most cells, while pillows and blankets are offered to detainees considered not at risk of self-harm.

In contrast to the stark visible nature of the cell, it is often the site of the most colourful emotional outpourings in custody. In part this is because, when in the cell, the detainee is 'behind closed doors' and in the most private sphere in custody, notwithstanding the impact of CCTV discussed above. As Skinns and Wooff (2018) have argued, it is the space in custody where the physical space impacts on the body and the reality of the situation hits home. Indeed, the transition to the cell from other spaces in the custody suite is significant, with different areas of custody eliciting different emotions. Previous work argues that 'emotional realisation tends to happen at the charge desk, whilst cognitive change and a more contemplative mood tends to happen in the cell' (Wooff and Skinns 2018: 11), highlighting the importance of understanding the cell as a space within a custody suite.

This is particularly clear with detainees who experience 'a cognitive change', described by Laws and Crewe (2016) as the ways that we reappraise or transform how we think of specific situations. Police custody cells are the site where this often happens in a police station, because it is the site where people are sent to calm down when they are brought in and are acting violently. As one police officer noted:

> We send them straight to cell if they are being argumentative or violent. It's not worth the hassle. (Custody Sergeant, urban suite)

Not only is this disorientating for the individual—particularly if they wake up from alcohol or drug-related sleep—but the cell becomes a site that is used to try and encourage an emotional change in detainees. Here they are actively encouraged by staff to calm down and manage their emotional outbursts. As one PCSO notes:

> You do see a lot of detainees change when they go to the cell. Sometimes they come in kicking and screaming and within a few minutes are really upset. (PCSO, rural suite)

The cell in this context can be a site of distress, pain and panic. This is something which reinforces the findings of other studies, underlining the importance of understanding painful emotions in this context (Williams et al. 2017; Skinns et al. 2017a). In the study by Skinns and colleagues, a detainee talks of being 'devastated … the fact that I was sitting in that cell, the room just felt like it was closing in on us' (Skinns et al. 2017a: 11), highlighting the link between the physical environment of the cell and the sense of reflection and despair.

These emotions were heightened through the deprivation of particular liberties and staff are thus significant in regulating entitlements. At the time of the observations, the cell represented a place where additional punishment could be metered out by depriving detainees of particular entitlements. This was particularly the case for detainees who were assessed as high risk by staff, with reading material being an example which was given to detainees in an ad-hoc way and used as a way of getting detainees to behave. When asked about reading material in cells, a Sergeant explained:

> We don't routinely give reading material, but if someone is in here for the weekend or has been behaving we'll usually give them something … depends [on behaviour] really. (Sergeant, urban suite)

HMICS (2018) also noted that the provision of books and magazines was dependent on local custody staff. While giving detainees something to read may seem like a small point, the deprivation of small humanising elements of the cell can have a broader implication for understanding power within the custody setting. Beyond this, without the distraction of something to read or do, boredom, claustrophobia and deep self-reflection are more likely (Wooff and Skinns 2018). This is even more apparent with entitlements such as sanitary products and toilet roll:

> When I ask about the toilet roll when we are walking round, a PCSO remarks that 'we don't give it out routinely because of risk of harm', when I ask what sort of harm, he states that 'we had a swallower once.' (Observation notes, urban suite)

Her Majesty's Inspectorate of Constabulary in Scotland (2018) also highlight the importance of maintaining the dignity of menstruating women in custody, highlighting the need for 'providing a varied and adequate supply of sanitary protection, changes of underwear, access to handwashing facilities and more frequent showers' (2018: 19). The inspection highlights a number of deficiencies across the custody estate relating to access to handwashing in cells and a lack of female custody staff at many of the smaller facilities. When in the cell, this means female detainees are often required to ask male staff for assistance. Not only is this lack of provision degrading to the detainee, but serves to underline the way that the physical custody cell can negatively impact on both the body (with a lack of physical sanitary ware) and the mind. Beyond the emotional turmoil caused by being arrested and held in a cell, the deprivation of these particular entitlements also symbolise a broader power being applied by Sergeants in police custody (Wooff and Skinns 2018).

Additionally, the loss of dignity through deprivation of particular entitlements within the cell reinforces the emotional burden that being locked in a cell can impact on the detainee.

Beyond the loss of dignity experienced by some detainees, the deprivation of everyday items can also enhance the emotional isolation felt within a custody cell. For example, the deprivation of a phone, a clock or music can make the detainee feel particularly isolated, reflective and 'in limbo' (Skinns and Wooff 2020; Wooff and Skinns 2018). Time is intimately linked to experiencing liminality, with our sense of time being linked to the organised daily rhythms (Hale et al. 2010). The 'temporal disruptions' through, for example, waking up in a police custody cell disorientated and confused after being arrested, is heightened by a lack of sense of time in the cell. None of the Police Scotland custody cells have a clock, which, alongside the lack of natural light in custody suites, means that detainees (and staff) are often unaware and disorientated when it comes to the time:

> The detainees forever buzz us [from the cell], constantly some of them. Often it is to ask for the time, when they are getting out … but you can't ignore it. (PC, urban suite)

Detainees can press a buzzer to either summon staff or speak via an intercom to staff, on top of being checked at a minimum of hourly. Staff often take a long time to respond to buzzers, especially when it is busy, underlining the isolation of being held in a cell with little mental stimulation, where time tends to pass slowly particularly when reflecting on what life may be like once released from the cell and the 'emotional aftershocks' which may ensue (Wooff and Skinns 2018). The cell here becomes a closed, locked and isolated box. Rather than minimising the emotional turmoil, through the simple action of not responding to buzzers in a timely fashion, staff can heighten the distress among detainees. At least in other spaces in the custody suite outwith the cell, the detainee is accompanied at all times and therefore has the opportunity to communicate with staff.

Time and the liminal nature of being in the police cell, therefore, play an important role in understanding the way(s) that the negative emotions associated with being in custody can be minimised. Not only are detainees deprived of everyday interaction by 'being cut off', but also experience a loss of control over the processes, both metaphorically (they do not know the outcome of the case and the implications of this on their life) and, sometimes, physically (the police using coercive control to force the detainee into complying with processes) (Skinns and Wooff 2020). The way the cell is designed physically and used to exert control by staff leads to it being the site of much emotional uncertainty and anxiety, which both makes it a particularly risky place, but can also lead detainees to resist in different ways.

## The Cell as a Site of Resistance

The custody cell not only provides a space of risk and a space of intensified emotion, but frequently is also a site of resistance. Resistance is a concept which has been discussed at length in both the prisons and carceral geographies literature. As Moran and Jewkes (2015) note, the carceral geographies literature has focused on, among other things, the role of the incarcerated body in creating spaces; and draws on Sibley and Van Hoven's (2009: 1016) call to understand space as 'produced and re-produced on a daily basis'. In particular, Jewkes (2013: 128) notes that 'the powerful construct and exercise their power, but the weak tactically create their own spaces within those places; making them temporarily their own as they occupy and move through them'. The relatively short temporal nature of the police custody environment means that cells are only occupied for, on average, 9 or 10 hours (Skinns 2011). This means that there are limited opportunities (and materials) available for detainees to exercise their power in creating the custody cell as their own.

Thus, resistance in police custody tends to be relatively short lived, most clearly being articulated as physical violence (either to the self or others), banging, shouting and swearing and some more passive forms of resistance in the cell (such as continually pushing the cell buzzer, refusing to leave the cell or damaging the cell). A lack of material goods (pens, pencils, paper) means that bodily fluids can be a form of resistance in custody. Much of the literature on 'dirty protests[4]' focuses on prisons, with, for example, the dirty protests of the troubles in Northern Ireland being highlighted (Aretxaga 1995; Conlon 2016). While dirty protests do occur in police custody—I have seen this situation twice when undertaking fieldwork—they tend to link to the anger and frustration at being deprived certain rights and entitlements (e.g. toilet roll) rather than as part of a wider, more coordinated political statement. It is therefore an overt protest to their containment.

As Skinns (2011) explores, being locked in a police cell is the epitome of a loss of control, highlighted by the imbalance of power relations and the reliance of staff to respond to their requests, particularly personal hygiene items. In Skinns' (2011) study, detainees discussed the impact of being locked up without a rhythm and without any control over any part of the process or the custody cell. Resistance to the processes of police custody, however minor, can reinsert a degree of power over containment, for example, forcing staff to attend the cell frequently or not complying with requests for information. The staff's experiences of dealing with resistance are observable through emotional outburst as described in the previous section. At one point during my observation:

> A young guy, 20 or so, is brought in kicking off and being aggressive. The sergeant at the charge bar asks his name at which point he hurls some abuse and continues to fight and shout. Sergeant instructs him to be taken 'straight to cell' where he is lifted unceremoniously and taken to the first available cell. Two PCSOs follow them down and he splays his arms and legs, refusing to go in to the cell […] The officers perform a 'cell exit' and leave him shouting 'I f**kin hate this, I feel trapped', to which the six staff say 'well you are' with a chuckle… (Observation notes, urban suite)

This is one example of a situation which is repeated across the custody estate on a daily basis. The detainee in this example spent the next five hours banging the cell door, shouting loudly. The lack of empathy shown by staff heightened his agitation. He was monitored on CCTV, but his aggressive nature meant that the risk assessment, fingerprinting and photographing could not be carried out. Over time the staff do their best to negotiate with him:

> Once the detainee has had time to 'calm down', I witness the staff repeatedly make attempts to reason with the young guy, go to the cell and tell him if he calms down he will get out quicker, he'll be able to get a cup of tea and be processed. His anger still apparent through the banging and shouting. (Observation notes, urban suite)

By constantly banging and shouting, detainees highlight their frustration by being in a cell, but also resist the suggested behaviour norm of 'getting your head down' to help the time pass more quickly (see Wooff and Skinns 2018; see also Herrity (2018; this edition) for discussion on the impact of noise in prisons). The noise associated with a detainee banging on the police custody cell door or wall is not always seen as a negative by staff. While the staff acknowledge that detainees who resist by creating a loud noise whilst inside the cell maybe annoying and present a physical risk to staff, the staff recognise that the noise at least symbolises that they are alive:

> It's the silent ones you need to worry about. Or say they've been banging their hand in the cell, I might get the doctor to come and look. More likely than not, I have to say it would be for more psychological stuff. The injuries are easy, because injuries come in, you get them to the hospital, the likes of heart pain, get an ambulance and get them to the hospital. It's more like psychological stuff, people come in and you're a bit concerned have they got psychiatric issues. (Sergeant, rural suite)

This Sergeant recognises that physical harm is observable and treatable, however, the invisible harms present challenging and complex work for staff. As has been explored earlier, the risk of the detainee injuring themselves in the cell is one of the key concerns of custody staff (Williams et al. 2017). Yet this is perceived much easier to manage than those that present with mental health problems.

The cell is also often used as a physical space for passive resistance. Shouting and banging tend to be the most obvious forms of resistance in a police cell, however, more passive forms of resistance were also apparent in the fieldwork. For example, acts of graffiti were apparent in some of the cells that were observed. Graffiti has long been associated with resistance (e.g. Ferrell 1995) since it is a physical marker of an unwillingness to comply with the rules. Police services anticipate such acts of resistance and rules and the repercussions are clearly outlined in cell signage (similar to that in the cell depicted in Figure 5.1), which indicate that if occupants' commit criminal damage they will be charged.

Interestingly, Fig. 5.1 also evokes the idea that the custody cell is a 'home' ('Would you damage your own home?'), a slightly ironic and cruel statement given how desperate many detainees are to be at home (or how many may actually be homeless) and how stark and dehumanising a custody cell environment is. Nevertheless, despite the warnings, graffiti is a fairly regular occurrence in police custody. A lack of writing materials tend to mean that graffiti is scratched in to the paint and on one occasion I witnessed this being picked up on (the limited) CCTV:

**Fig. 5.1** A photograph of Bishop Auckland police station in Durham (not the case study location), which illustrates the stark nature of a police custody cell. (Source: Hill 2017)

> I am sitting with a PCSO who is monitoring a camera, a detainee with his back to the door and blanket round. After a few mins the PCSO says 'I think him in cell 2 is writing on the wall' ... the PCSO rushes down the corridor and I see him going into the cell on the camera. When he comes back he explains the detainee was just scratching at the wall, but 'luckily no damage was done or that would be another charge'. (Observation notes, urban suite)

Similarly cell buzzers tended to create friction between staff and detainees. As Skinns (2011) highlights, this may be about the practicalities of continually having to respond to a persistent detainee buzzer call (or carrying the associated risks of switching it off completely), but control and power were also apparent features of the interactions:

> As a detainee is taken to his cell he becomes more agitated and presses his cell buzzer lots of times. I see a PCSO reasoning with the detainee ... I presume he's asking him to stop ... At first the staff respond fairly quickly, but after repeated buzzing over a period of 45 minutes, staff are less responsive to it. There is a brief discussion about turning it off, but the detainee's cell isn't covered by CCTV so they decide not do this. Instead they stop responding [except to normal checks] and hope the detainee will get bored and stop buzzing which he does. (Observation notes, urban suite)

This interaction shows that the buzzer is a symbol of the way that the physical attributes of the cell can be used as a passive form of resistance, while also underlining the subtle power (beyond the obvious legal power) that the staff have over detainees in this environment. Indeed, as Skinns (2011) notes, being held in a cell is a terrifying prospect for some, something magnified when staff do not respond to buzzer calls. However, for others, annoying the staff by repeatedly ringing the buzzer represents a small opportunity for them to exert some form of power over the staff in the suite. Yet, in the context of the police cell, staff often perceive that such acts, like the graffiti or the repeated buzzing, occur because the detainee is simply bored. Acute boredom is a commonplace experience during cell containment where overcoming this sensation can be a challenge (Armstrong 2018; Knight 2017). However, in this respect, the activities apparently stimulated by boredom are managed by the very recognition and reliance of that particular emotion. Here, staff express their hope that cell occupants will simply 'get bored' of their own acts of resistance.

## Conclusion

Despite the small geographic space occupied by a police custody cell, it is arguably the most important part of a custody suite for understanding the relationship between risk, emotion and resistance in the police custody environment. This chapter has argued that far from being a passive space, the cell is a space through the emotions of the detainee can be managed by considering the risk posed by the person and inter-relatedly, their emotion as often expressed through forms of resistance. The cell is a site of risk for staff, where uncertainty pervades about on-going drug and alcohol withdrawal; the implications of the emotional turmoil that being locked in a cell might have on a detainees; and the impact of forms of resistance, including self-harm, might have on a detainee's well-being.

It is important to consider the agency of the detainee in the custody setting, understanding that space and place determine personal experience and social practice (Sibley and Van Hoven 2009). Moreover, the design of the cell plays an active role in the emotional and embodied experience of the detainee, with the bare walls, lack of basic goods and lack of a sense of time impacting on those in the space. As Wooff and Skinns (2018) note, the physical space of custody at the micro-scale therefore explicitly and implicitly interacts with those that are contained within it, deprived of their liberty. More than this, staff harness police cell space as a tool through which to comprehend (and often alter) the detainees' experiences of emotion, risk and resistance. Understanding the way(s) that power and control are used at the scale of the cell goes some way to supporting and developing a more dignified experience for the detainee, while also acknowledging the importance of mitigating risks within the cell environment. Indeed, beginning to understand the complex links between the painful emotions of detainees, the resistance that they may exhibit and the risk that they present in the police custody cell is an important practical step for improving the police custody cell environment.

## Notes

1. The charge bar is the desk where the Sergeant and booking in officers are located. It is where a detainee is booked in to custody; where details of the arrest are relayed; where a risk assessment is normally carried out; where the rights and entitlements of the detainee are explained; and where a search is carried out. It is also the place where a charging decision is relayed to the detainee. Most of these are raised platforms, which practically allows a better view and therefore control of detainees, but arguably also symbolises the power of the police over suspects (Skinns 2011).
2. Dynamic risk assessment is the process of continually identifying potential issues, assessing risk, taking action to reduce risk, monitoring and reviewing those decisions and accounting for the actions taken.
3. These are the authorised professional practice from the College of Policing which describe how staff remove restraints from detainees within the cell and then exit the cell safely, with minimum risk to staff and detainee.
4. 'Dirty protests' is the vernacular for smearing excrement on the walls of the cell. This rose to particular prominence during The Troubles in Northern Ireland in the late 1970s.

## References

Allard, T. J., Wortley, R. K., & Stewart, A. L. (2008). The Effect of CCTV on Prisoner Misbehavior. *The Prison Journal, 88*(3), 404–422.

Aretxaga, B. (1995). Dirty Protest: Symbolic Overdetermination and Gender in Northern Ireland Ethnic Violence. *Ethos, 23*(2), 123–148.

Armstrong, S. (2018). The Cell and the Corridor: Imprisonment as Waiting, and Waiting as Mobile. *Time & Society, 27*(2), 133–154.

Atkinson, S., & Robson, M. (2012). Arts and Health as a Practice of Liminality: Managing the Spaces of Transformation for Social and Emotional Wellbeing with Primary School Children. *Health & Place, 18*(6), 1348–1355.

Beijersbergen, K. A., Dirkzwager, A. J., van der Laan, P. H., & Nieuwbeerta, P. (2016). A Social Building? Prison Architecture and Staff–Prisoner Relationships. *Crime & Delinquency, 62*(7), 843–874.

College of Policing. (2018). *Detention and Custody: CCTV*. Retrieved July 22, 2019, from https://www.app.college.police.uk/app-content/detention-and-custody-2/buildings-and-facilities/cctv/#continual-cctv-cell-monitoring.

Conlon, K. L. (2016). *"Neither Men nor Completely Women": The 1980 Armagh Dirty Protest and Republican Resistance in Northern Irish Prisons*. PhD thesis, Ohio University.

Crewe, B., Warr, J., Bennett, P., & Smith, A. (2014). The Emotional Geography of Prison Life. *Theoretical Criminology, 18*(1), 56–74.

Cummins, I. (2008). A Place of Safety? Self-harming Behaviour in Police Custody. *The Journal of Adult Protection, 10*(1), 36–47.

Ferrell, J. (1995). Urban Graffiti: Crime, Control, and Resistance. *Youth & Society, 27*(1), 73–92.

Hale, B., Barrett, P., & Gauld, R. (2010). Temporality and Liminality. In B. Hale, P. Barrett, & R. Gauld (Eds.), *The Age of Supported Independence: Voices of In-Home Care* (pp. 45–59). London: Springer.

Her Majesty's Inspectorate of Constabulary in Scotland. (2018). *Inspection of Custody Centres Across Scotland*. Retrieved April 18, 2019, from https://www.hmics.scot/sites/default/files/publications/HMICS20181019PUB.pdf.

Herrity, K. (2018). Music and Identity in Prison: Music as a Technology of the Self. *Prison Service Journal, 239*, 40–47.

Hill, L. (2017). Ever Wondered What Happens If You Get Arrested? Take a Look behind the Bars at the Police Station. *Chronicle Live*. Retrieved April 18, 2019, from https://www.chroniclelive.co.uk/news/north-east-news/what-happens-arrested-jail-police-13333656.

Hughes, B. (2009). Becoming Emotional About International Policing: Exploring the Relationship between Emotions and Policing. *International Peacekeeping, 16*(2), 199–214.

Jewkes, Y. (2011). Loss, Liminality and the Life Course Sentence: Managing Identity through a Disrupted Lifecourse. In A. Liebling & S. Maruna (Eds.), *The Effects of Imprisonment* (pp. 366–390). London: Routledge.

Jewkes, Y. (2013). On Carceral Space and Agency. In D. Moran, N. Gill, & D. Conlon (Eds.), *Carceral Spaces: Mobility and Agency in Imprisonment and Migrant Detention* (pp. 127–132). London: Ashgate.

Knight, V. (2017). *Remote Control: Television in Prison*. London: Palgrave Macmillan.

Laws, B., & Crewe, B. (2016). Emotion Regulation among Male Prisoners. *Theoretical Criminology, 20*(4), 529–547.

Liebling, A. (2004). *Prisons and Their Moral Performance: A Study of Values, Quality and Prison Life*. Oxford: Oxford University Press.

Marshall, C., & Rossman, G. (2011). *Designing Qualitative Research*. London: Sage.

McKinnon, I., & Grubin, D. (2010). Health Screening in Police Custody. *Journal of Forensic and Legal Medicine, 17*(4), 209–212.

Mercer, J. (2005). Rationality and Psychology in International Politics. *International Organization, 59*(1), 77–106.

Moran, D. (2013). Between Outside and Inside? Prison Visiting Rooms as Liminal Carceral Spaces. *GeoJournal, 78*(2), 339–351.

Moran, D., & Jewkes, Y. (2015). Linking the Carceral and the Punitive State: A Review of Research on Prison Architecture, Design, Technology and the Lived Experience of Carceral Space. *Annales de géographie, 2*, 163–184.

Moran, D., Turner, J., & Schliehe, A. K. (2018). Conceptualizing the Carceral in Carceral Geography. *Progress in Human Geography, 42*(5), 666–686.

Newburn, T., & Hayman, S. (2002). *Policing, Surveillance and Social Control: CCTV and Police Monitoring of Suspects*. Cullompton: Willan.

Rekrut-Lapa, T., & Lapa, A. (2014). Health Needs of Detainees in Police Custody in England and Wales: Literature Review. *Journal of Forensic and Legal Medicine, 27*, 69–75.

Roach Anleu, S., Bergman Blix, S., & Mack, K. (2015). Researching Emotion in Courts and the Judiciary: A Tale of Two Projects. *Emotion Review, 7*(2), 145–150.

Royal Commission on Criminal Justice. (1993). *Chairman Viscount Ruciman of Doxford, CMND 2263 Report*. Retrieved August 7, 2019, from https://assets.publishing.service.gov.uk/government/uploads/system/uploads/attachment_data/file/271971/2263.pdf.

Sibley, D., & Van Hoven, B. (2009). The Contamination of Personal Space: Boundary Construction in a Prison Environment. *Area, 41*(2), 198–206.

Skinns, L. (2011). *Police Custody: Governance, Legitimacy and Reform in the Criminal Justice Process*. Oxon: Willan Publishing.

Skinns, L., Rice, L., Sprawson, A., & Wooff, A. (2017a). Police Legitimacy in Context: An Exploration of "Soft" Power in Police Custody in England. *Policing: An International Journal, 40*(3), 601–613.

Skinns, L., Wooff, A., & Sprawson, A. (2017b). Preliminary Findings on Police Custody Delivery in the Twenty-First Century: Is It 'Good' Enough? *Policing and Society, 27*(4), 358–371.

Skinns, L., & Wooff, A. (2020). Pain in Police Detention: A Critical Point in the 'Penal Painscape'? *Policing and Society* [Online First: https://www.tandfonline.com/doi/full/10.1080/10439463.2019.1706506]

Turner, V. (1967). *Betwixt and Between: The Liminal Period in Rites de Passage*. London: Cornell University Press.

Williams, E., Norman, J., & Sondhi, A. (2017). Understanding Risks: Practitioner's Perceptions of the Lottery of Mental Healthcare Available for Detainees in Custody. *Policing: A Journal of Policy and Practice*, *13*(4), 441–454.

Wooff, A., & Skinns, L. (2018). The Role of Emotion, Space and Place in Police Custody in England: Towards a Geography of Police Custody. *Punishment & Society*, *20*(5), 562–579.

# Part II

## Cytoplasm

Under the light microscope, [cytoplasm] appears to be a uniform, semi-fluid, structureless substance containing a variety of particles and occupying most of the space inside the cell. The electron microscope, however, shows that it is by no means a structureless jelly but consists of a variety of folded tubes and passages, called the *endoplasmic reticulum*, which communicate with the external medium and nucleus. (Mackean and Jones 1975: 7)

# 6

# A 'Home' or 'a Place to Be, But Not to Live': Arranging the Prison Cell

Irene Marti

## Introduction

In general, prison scholars describe the prison cell as an ambiguous place. On the one hand, they agree that the cell is probably the only place in prison where prisoners can spend unobserved time and experience privacy and relief from prison pressure (Cohen and Taylor 1972; Toch [1977] 1996; Ugelvik 2014). On the other hand, the cell is seen as not really 'their space' either, because 'nothing is theirs here [in the prison]' (Wacquant 2002: 378). The cell remains a domain that is highly controlled by the prison system. A first look at the inside suggests that the prison cell is a very small and narrow place. In Switzerland, the size of a cell is generally 12 $m^2$; possibilities for movement and activity are therefore very limited. As prisoners are held in single cells, when the doors are locked they have no possibility for (direct) interpersonal communication.

I. Marti (✉)
University of Bern, Bern, Switzerland

University of Neuchâtel, Neuchâtel, Switzerland
e-mail: Irene.Marti@krim.unibe.ch



J. Turner, V. Knight (eds.), *The Prison Cell*, Palgrave Studies in Prisons and Penology,
https://doi.org/10.1007/978-3-030-39911-5_6

Therefore, they are forced to 'do time' alone. Finally, it is the place in prison where individuals have to spend most of their time. From the institutional perspective, the cell is primarily the place where prisoners are supposed to rest.

This chapter 'enters' the prison cell using an ethnographic lens and looks more closely at the individual experience of this particular place by prisoners. In the case study detailed in this research, prisoners are held in indefinite incarceration in Switzerland and therefore do not know if they will ever be released. These offenders committed serious sexual or violent offences and are held, after the duration of their initial sentence, either in prison for security reasons (according to Art. 64 Swiss Criminal Code [SCC]), or in therapy in the case where the offenders are suffering from 'serious mental disorders' (Art. 59 SCC). From a legal point of view, both Art. 64 SCC and Art. 59 SCC are preventive: these are safety 'measures' and not a 'punishment'. However, in contrast to other countries such as Germany, the regime of detention in Switzerland is the same for prisoners held in indefinite incarceration as for those serving finite sentences (Künzli et al. 2016). Due to a more severe practice with respect to the release of high-risk offenders labelled 'dangerous' and categorised as posing an 'undue risk' to society, this prison population has increased since the 1990s (Schneeberger Georgescu 2009). Prison scholars agree that long-term imprisonment has 'profound existential implications' (Crewe et al. 2016: 3). However, prison studies usually focus on prisoners who serve regular sentences and thus will eventually be released, or on those who serve 'real' life sentences where the end date is usually death (Leigey and Ryder 2015).

In an effort to expand the focus of enquiry, this chapter provides insights into how prisoners sentenced to indefinite incarceration in Switzerland *inhabit* the prison cell. While cell furnishing and maintenance is highly constrained by the prison's accommodation regime, it also provides room for manoeuver. Inspired by Michel Lussault and Mathis Stock's (2010) 'pragmatics of space' approach, this chapter explores how prisoners (re)arrange spatial elements and thereby ascribe new meanings and values to the cell and create personal and intimate space. It begins with the presentation of the research context and methodology. Following this is a description of the prison's accommodation regime. The ensuing two sections shed light on two types of arrangements of the prison cell, which reflect the prisoners' different ways of dealing with imprisonment and their uncertain future.

## Research Context and Methodology

The analysis that follows is drawn from ethnographic data (DeWalt and DeWalt 2002) that I generated between 2013 and 2015 using document analysis, participant observation, informal discussions, and in-depth interviews carried out with 22 prisoners (most of them sentenced to indefinite incarceration) in two high-security prisons for male offenders—the *JVA Lenzburg* and the *JVA Pöschwies*—in the context of a study on end-of-life in Swiss prisons.[1] In addition, this chapter draws on further data generated as part of my PhD project on the lived experience of prisoners sentenced to indefinite incarceration. Between 2016 and 2017, I carried out document analysis, participant observation, informal discussions, walking interviews, and in-depth interviews with 19 male prisoners in the same two prisons.[2]

## The Prison's Accommodation Regime

On a national level, no explicit rules exist regarding the material conditions of the prison cell in Switzerland (Baechtold et al. 2016: 159). The standards are mainly defined on the level of each individual institution. However, several cantonal guidelines suggest single-cell occupancy as 'the norm'.[3] Since the revision of the SCC in 2007, the so-called 'principle of normalization' serves as the point of reference for questions concerning the materiality of the cell. Thus, the material conditions of the cell must correspond to 'average living conditions' (Art. 75, para. 2, SCC, my translation). Resulting from this are minimal requirements regarding lighting, ventilation, sanitary facilities, furnishings, and the size of the cell (Baechtold et al. 2016: 159–160). In addition, the Federal Office of Justice has formulated explicit standards that come into force when authorities must decide on subsidies to be allotted to new penal institutions (BJ 2016). For example, 12 $m^2$ has been determined to be the minimum size required for a single cell (Baechtold et al. 2016: 160). In terms of lighting, heating, and sanitary facilities, the norms should correspond to the rules concerning general housing construction in Switzerland. The cells should receive enough daylight, have access to running water, and be equipped with a flushing toilet. They must be furnished with a bed, a chair and a table, and a wardrobe or clothes rack. Finally, the addition of personal objects, namely wall decorations, should be 'generously permitted' (Baechtold et al. 2016: 160, my translation) Fig. 6.1.

**Fig. 6.1** An empty prison cell. (Source: Andreas Moser, JVA Lenzburg)

In the internal rules of the prisons I visited, it is indicated that the prisoners can furnish the cell in a 'homely' manner and have 'personal objects' in their cell (JVA Lenzburg 2011; JVA Pöschwies 2016, my translation). Prisoners are authorised to hang pictures and put up photos on the wall. However, where they can (e.g. on the pin board) and cannot be put (e.g. on the door and the door frame) is clearly defined. It is prohibited to hang pictures that are considered 'shocking', 'defamatory', political, or religious, and to display photos and symbols that have a 'provocative' effect on others. Erotic images are allowed if they do not violate 'the morality of someone with normal sensitivity regarding sexual issues' (JVA Lenzburg 2011, my translation); pornography is prohibited. The prisoners can buy additional furnishings, such as a rug or a reading lamp. However, numbers are limited and they generally must all fulfil specific standards. They can buy plants from the prison garden, but keeping flowers in the cell is forbidden. Stuffed animals are accepted, if they are not bigger than 25 cm. Moreover, it is not permissible to obstruct the view into the cell (e.g. by installing a curtain on the cell door). The use of a towel as a tablecloth is also not allowed. If the prison furniture is not fixed, the prisoners can move it; however, they are not completely free to do so. For instance, furnishings must not be moved to the so-called wet area (where the toilet and the sink are installed), and they must be upright, that is, 'put on their legs' (JVA Pöschwies 2016, my translation). Prison officers regularly have to 'search' the cells for prohibited objects (such as weapons and mobile phones) that prisoners might have illicitly acquired. Finally, prisoners can be transferred anytime and their personal items can be withdrawn—with or without notification.

In addition to the instructions regarding cell furnishing, there are several internal rules regarding the maintenance of the cell: 'The cell and its furnishing must be tidy and clean, and clearly arranged at any time' (JVA Lenzburg 2011, my translation). According to the Oxford English Dictionary, 'tidiness' refers to 'the state or quality of being arranged neatly and in order'. 'Dirt' is defined, according to the same source, as 'a substance, such as mud or dust, that soils someone or something'. However, as emphasised by Douglas (1966: 2), 'there is no such thing as absolute dirt: it exists in the eye of the beholder'. In prison, the order and tidiness of the cell is regularly controlled by prison officers. They are thus the ones who hold the power of definition. Whether a cell is kept 'tidy and clean' is always the result of a subjective assessment, and shaped by the prison officers' individual ways of using authority as well as their impressions and stereotypes regarding certain offenders:

> This morning, I accompanied two prison officers during their assignment to inspect some of the cells while the prisoners were at work. … Whenever a cell was in a perfect order, they named it "military". According to [the first prison officer] this was "especially the case with the Muslim". [The second prison officer] said that "especially the pedophiles" were, in contrast, "extremely grubby". (Fieldnotes 7.4.2016)[4]

These assessments may have powerful consequences. They can lead to remarks in the prisoner's record—for example, 'the cell is overloaded and chaotic' (Fieldnotes 6.4.2016)—and immediate sanctions in case it is decided that the cell order does not correspond to the rules.

All these rules clearly demonstrate that although the cell is considered to be the prisoners' 'personal' space, it remains a domain that is highly regulated by the prison management.

## Prisoners' Ways of Arranging the Cell

Although cell furnishing and maintenance is highly constrained by the prison's accommodation regime, the prisoners' ways of inhabiting the cell are never fully determined by the prison. They use, appropriate and (re) arrange the institutional spatio-temporal order that defines the prison cell through individual practices and thereby create personal and intimate space. Inspired by the geographers Lussault and Stock and their pragmatist approach, inhabiting is here understood both as a way of concretely residing in a cell and more generally as relation to the world. From their perspective, being in the world is not about 'being in space'—in the sense of being on Earth (as in a Heideggerian terminology)—but about 'coping with space' (Lussault and Stock 2010). Yet, the authors prefer the terminology 'doing with' instead of 'coping' as, from their perspective, the expression 'to cope with space' makes sense when space is considered as a problem, which is certainly not always the case. The authors argue that actors may encounter and mobilise space as either a 'problem' or as 'empowerment' (Lussault and Stock 2010: 13). More concretely, by encountering places, actors make use of spatial elements and thereby get 'playfully or in a constrained way … over distances, transgress boundaries and … arrange and … rearrange things, and, through discourses and other kinds of acts shape the quality of places' (Lussault and Stock 2010: 15). Space is therefore both a *condition* and a (material and immaterial) *resource* for practices (Lussault 2007: 215–218). Lussault and Stock further argue that space and action are co-constructed. One the one hand, practices create spatial arrangements and define qualities of places. On the other hand, spatial discourses and imaginaries with spatial content as well as spatial elements (e.g. physical accessibilities and limits) are present in individual practices (Lussault and Stock 2010: 16).

From this analytical perspective, by inhabiting a cell, prisoners automatically (re)arrange it and thus attribute new meanings and values to the cell. The prison cell (and, as I argue, the prison in general) can thus not be reduced to a space in the sense of a (pre-defined) container that contains people, but, as I argue, apprehended as a formally established *set of arrangements of space and (clock) time* that is used and appropriated and constantly (re)arranged by individuals through their everyday practices. Using empirical examples, I illustrate in the following, simply put, two types of arrangements of the prison cell: the cell as 'a home' and the cell as 'a place to be, but not to live'.

## Arranging the Cell Into 'A Home'

During fieldwork, I visited some of the prisoners with whom I established closer connections inside their cells. It began with an invitation from Clément, who was eager to show me his cell:

> Clément welcomed me by saying: "Welcome to my three-room-apartment, reduced to one room". He smiled. His "apartment" indeed looked quite cosy and is well furnished: there are two rugs on the floor, a TV, a stereo system, a computer, a wall clock, pictures on the wall, cooking utensils and a lot of spices. We stepped in and he explained to me how he arranged the three "rooms" or areas (the cooking area, the wash corner, and the living

> area) and talked about his strategies to make the best out of this limited and highly controlled place: "you have to use space to a maximum". (Fieldnotes 8.2.2016)

As this example suggests, the prison's accommodation regime does not prevent prisoners from transforming their cell into something else, for instance, into, as they said, a 'home' (see Fig. 6.2). This arrangement can be carried out through a wide range of techniques: (1) through narratives, (2) through the arrangement and use of objects, (3) through the

**Fig. 6.2** A homely furnished prison cell. (Source: Andreas Moser, JVA Lenzburg)

application of domestic patterns of movement and activities, and (4) by using the senses.

Regarding the prisoners' narratives about the cell, many of them explicitly used to name their cell their 'home', or 'room'. 'I don't say cell, I say: This is my room, my studio (laughs)' (Darko 6.5.2016). Also, they use the expression 'to live' (*leben/wohnen*) regarding their cell, which in German means far more than simply existing. Narratives of the cell as a home might reflect what Tuan ([1977] 2001: 32) considers as a basic human need: the need to 'anchor' one's personality in objects and places. According to the author, '[a]ll human beings appear to have personal belongings and perhaps all have the need of personal place, whether this be a particular chair in a room or a particular corner in a moving carriage' (Tuan [1977] 2001: 32). For Tuan ([1977] 2001: 144), home involves emotions; it is an 'intimate place', a place where people feel safe and cared for and a sense of attachment and rootedness. Home is also related to familiarity. Through 'routine activity' people transform 'unknown space' into 'familiar place' (Tuan [1977] 2001: 73). From this perspective, the transformation of the cell into a home appears as a result of an almost 'natural' process, based on the very basic human need to belong somewhere combined with a process of familiarisation.

These two aspects, the feeling of belonging and familiarity, also came out in the prisoners' narratives. Many prisoners said that the cell became their 'favourite place' in prison because there they could find peace and quiet, away from other prisoners. The expression 'to have got used/accustomed' was also mentioned during the interviews, often followed by the expression that 'this is home now': 'I got used to it, I know everything now [how the prison functions] … I feel myself at home now, so to speak' (Erich 19.10.2017).

Leder (2004) sees a more active intention behind the transformation of the cell into a home. He interprets it as 'reclamation of space' to 'humanize' the prison: 'If spatiality has become constricted, ruptured, disoriented, even reversed, [there are prisoners who] will do what is possible to reverse the reversals. [They] will make of [their] cell a home' (Leder 2004: 58). This takes place not only through narratives, but also through furnishing. Indeed, the prisoners I talked to also made use of the spatial and material elements in the cell to transform it into a home (as illustrated in Fig. 6.2). Even though the possibilities are limited, through the (re)arrangement and usage of particular objects they create what they consider a 'homely ambiance'. They typically put rugs on the floor, buy plants, and put pictures on the wall.

> I want to furnish it so it doesn't look like a cell anymore, but rather a space where one sees that there is someone living in there, there lives a person, a human being, someone who also feels comfortable. So, I want to put a carpet, plants ... things like that. (Leo 23.3.2016)

Leo's statement echoes Ugelvik (2014: 73–75) who defines the transforming of the cell into a home as a 'freedom-creating-action', whereby prisoners challenge their ascribed position as a prisoner and 'making themselves into something other than a prisoner'. The personalisation of the cell, especially through decoration (see Fig. 6.3), is also described as

**Fig. 6.3** Personalisation of the cell through decoration. (Source: A prisoner, JVA Lenzburg). (Note: The pictures were taken by prisoners during walking interviews whereby I asked them to show me 'their' prison and taking pictures of places and objects that are of any relevance for them)

an attempt to express 'personal identity', as a way to 'manoeuvre within the space of the other' (Baer 2005: 215).

I argue that by transforming the cell into a home through narratives, furnishing and decorating, prisoners not only personalise space with the aim to 'humanize' the prison (Leder 2004) and 'to leave their marks on the prison landscape' (Baer 2005: 210), they also manipulate their 'sense of size and spaciousness' (Tuan [1977] 2001: 54). In addition to the acquisition and arrangement of objects, when furniture is not fixed, prisoners usually move it (within the frame of possibilities), such as David, who thereby created 'more space' and a friendlier ambiance:

> I moved the desk a little further down, closer to the window … and the cupboard, I pushed it closer to the bed, so, like this I have more space up there. Because [fellow prisoners], when they come into my cell, they mostly sit on the bed, one on the chair, so if another one wants to join us then he has to bring his own chair or sit on the floor. So, it's practical to have a bit more space up there. (David 2.5.2016)

Through a particular arrangement of furniture and objects, Kurt transformed 'his room' in a way that he sometimes even forgets that he actually is in prison:

> I have birds, which I got from a mate … And I bought plants, and on the floor, I have put a carpet. And on the walls, I hung a few pictures, and my flag, my country flag. Sometimes, when I come into my room, I don't know whether this is my house or prison (laughs). There is no difference at the moment, because I've been here for 10 years, it feels like I was born here (laughs). (Kurt 3.5.2016)

The creation of a 'homely' ambiance can also be something temporary, by 'misusing' prison furniture and objects and transforming them into something else. Very common is the dismounting of the cupboard door to create a table, big enough for four prisoners to enjoy a meal together.

As this last example suggests, the transformation of the cell into a home takes place also through domestic patterns of movement and activities (see also Ugelvik 2014: 118). Prisoners in all the prisons I visited have the possibility to socialise in the evening. During these get-togethers

Fig. 6.4 A prisoner's 'kitchen'. (Source: A prisoner, JVA Lenzburg)

in someone's cell, they mainly engage in cooking (by using 'the kitchen', illustrated in Fig. 6.4) and eating together, watching a movie, or playing games, with the principle aim to create a 'cosy atmosphere' (Hugo 23.3.2016), and to live moments of 'peace' (Clément 24.3.2016) and 'normality' (Louis 22.3.2016). One prisoner told me that he lives 'like a family life' with two younger fellow prisoners, whom he has 'practically adopted' (informal conversation, 8.2.2016). They used to visit him in his cell to eat together, to lie on his bed and relax, to watch a movie, or to listen to music together. Another prisoner told me how he and his 'best friend' in prison celebrated Christmas together by sharing a bottle of wine in his cell that they illicitly bought from a fellow prisoner (Fieldnotes 23.2.2016). Although temporary (at least in prison), according to Tuan ([1977] 2001: 140), human encounters are essential in the experience of home, because, often 'the value of place [is] borrowed from the intimacy of a particular human relationship; place itself offer[s] little outside the human bond'. He argues that although for most people possessions and ideas are important, 'other human beings remain the focus of value and the source of meaning' (Tuan [1977] 2001: 138–139).

Finally, I claim that the transformation of the cell into a home also takes place through a particular use of the senses. There are many prisoners who 'do not see' the bars in front of the window anymore because they do not want to see them. David uses a particular smell to create a homely ambiance—which is also a way to keep memories of his past (and his previous home) alive, invisible for others:

> From time to time I offer myself the luxury of buying a small bottle of eucalyptus oil from the medical service to put a few drops on my pillow. I tell them that this helps me to breathe better, but actually the reason is a sentimental one … My wife used to put eucalyptus leaves in her pillow … It smelled really good. (David 2.5.2016)

Lastly, through music—for instance by playing the guitar or listening to their favourite songs—prisoners transform the cell into a place where they can immerse in their 'own world' (Leo 23.3.2016) and transcend the prison context.[5]

As I have shown in this section, the prisoners' ways of transforming the cell into a home can be regarded as a 'natural' process linked to familiarisation with the environment and getting used to prison. It can also be defined as an attempt to express individuality and to challenge the prisoner status. I argue that to arrange the cell into a home is also rooted in the prisoners' intention to make the best of this situation and not to worry too much about their (uncertain) future. While showing me his cell (illustrated in Fig. 6.5), Erich first pointed to his newly purchased coffee machine, the plants he has, and the pictures he put on the wall, and explained to me: 'This is where I live … and since I have to be in prison, I at least want to have it as nice as possible' (Erich 18.10.2017).

Markus made a similar argument. When I asked him whether the cell is a place he feels comfortable, his response was:

> Well … I feel good in this place, as far as you can say so, because it's *my* place, it's my home. Of course, it's a prison cell, but since I haven't a home outside anymore and will never have one again, I got used to it. It's not a

**Fig. 6.5** 'To have it as nice as possible'. (Source: A prisoner, JVA Lenzburg)

> resignation, it's more … not an adaptation, you come to terms with it somehow, it's somehow a pragmatic decision to take that as your home. And it doesn't bother me. (Markus 28.8.2017)

As Crewe et al. (2016) suggest, this is a typical pattern found by long-term prisoners beyond the early sentence phase. They define it as a way of coping to make the problems of imprisonment more manageable over time: to accept the situation and using it positively. As they argue, long-term prisoners who are further into their sentence experience the present no longer as a form of stasis because life is no longer considered 'on hold' (in the past, or being lived elsewhere) and consider the prison as their 'home' now and 'the only place where life could meaningfully be led' (Crewe et al. 2016: 10). Similar to this, I argue that transforming the cell into a home is also about 'normalising' incarceration and transform it into 'a frame of action' (see Vigh 2008: 11). As Marco told me, to perceive imprisonment as his 'normal life' allows him 'to regain mental free spaces'. It enables him to feel 'safe' and comfortable and to go about his life (Marco 4.5.2016). However, some prisoners mentioned that this requires giving up hope, letting go their pre-prison self, and cutting off their bonds to the outside world as it is too painful to emotionally live in two different worlds. As I illustrate in the following, in contrast to prisoners who transform the cell into a home, I met prisoners who said that they would 'never' want a cell to be their home.

## Arranging the Cell as 'A Place to Be, But Not to Live'

Lars was one of the prisoners with whom I had frequent contact during fieldwork. I spent several days with him, helping him at his work place. At the end of our time together I visited him in his cell:

> In the afternoon, I searched for a prison officer who was willing to escort me to Lars. Once we arrived at his cell, the officer knocked at the door and, after a few seconds, opened it. Lars came to the doorstep and welcomed me … I was surprised: the cell was almost empty! This is not at all what I expected, especially because Lars is one of the prisoners who will probably have to stay in prison for the rest of his life. I noted that he didn't wear shoes and apologised for wearing shoes myself and asked if I should take them off. He declined. I felt a bit lost and uncertain facing this empty cell. No cooking utensils, no pictures, no decoration at all, except the flag of his home canton above his bed, which he mentioned several times during our collaboration. He remained silent, kept looking at me, and I felt the need to start a conversation. I started to comment on what I saw … I then went to the window and asked: "what kind of view do you have?" and he replied: "none, there's just the courtyard". I mentioned that he had hardly any private stuff, like pictures. He then took a photo album out of the cupboard and showed me some pictures of his family. I wanted to know if he had requested a bigger cell [long-term prisoners do have this option] to which he replied "no, I am anyway hardly inside. Just for sleeping. And besides that, with a bigger cell one has much more to do [he refers to the cleaning]". We then had a chat about my project and soon after we said goodbye by shaking hands … Again, at his workplace the following day, Lars explained to me that he doesn't intend to furnish the cell to be "too cosy" … To him, to settle in means "to accept" his situation and this would mean "giving up on himself". (Fieldnotes 17.2.2016)

Lars made clear to me that the cell is a place he does not want to belong to. He did not decorate the cell in a personal way (with exception of the flag), he described it simply as a place he uses for sleeping, a place without any view. At a first glance, he also did not act like a typical 'host' (he did not care whether I took off my shoes or not, did not start a conversation), until he showed me pictures of his family members.

Lars' narrative of the cell as *a place to be, but not to live* is shared by many others. For these prisoners, to transform their cell into a home would basically mean to create a 'cosy' ambiance. For them, to feel comfortable in prison is equivalent to acceptance of incarceration and giving up hope (see also Milhaud 2009: 291). Rolf mentioned in this regard that '[i]t's important for me that I never get used to my cell, and never to incarceration. I don't want that. I must avoid it. Otherwise, I will perish. It would mean abandoning freedom' (Rolf 6.5.2016). Anton told me: 'it makes my hair stand on end when someone starts to talk about his cell by calling it "my room" … for me it's just a cell … It's a place to be, but not to live' (Anton 24.3.2016). In contrast to Leder (2004: 58), who labels such an attitude a 'strategy of escape' by emphasising that prisoners who do not want to feel at home in prison consider their 'true home' to be in the outside world 'albeit one from which they are temporarily exiled', most of the prisoners I met and who share this attitude did not mention their home to be outside. This could be because most of them have lost contact with their families and friends and many of the places they used to know have disappeared. Everything has changed outside over the years. However, some prisoners talked about their dreams of establishing a new life abroad, creating a new home. This is in line with the argument of Cohen and Taylor (1972: 93) who stated that, as for long-term prisoners the future in prison is unthinkable, they rely upon 'ideas about a future life outside to sustain themselves through their temporally undifferentiated days'. But, for the prisoners I talked to, the future is nearly unthinkable in the outside world too. They fear that (in case of release) they will be too old to find a job, and that the pension they would be granted would not be sufficient to live a decent life. Their ideas about a future life consist therefore less of concrete plans and more of dreams and visions:

> A mate of mine whom I have met here and who is now in another prison ... we still stay in touch, we call each other ... when he is on a holiday [temporary release]. And once he is outside, he will go to Brazil, he has a house there. And should I ever get the chance to get out again, I could go to Brazil too, that's already fixed. Here in Switzerland, I will anyway no longer have any chance. (Hugo 25.6.2013)

> Today I had a chat with Marco. [...] He told me about his prospects. He maybe gets Art. 59 or 63, then he would be out even faster. For him, an "intermediate step" would be quite ok. He also told me that he had been doing therapy again for some time now. I asked about his future plans. He wants to work in the IT business, to support customers independently, to repair PCs, of which he understands something. He would like to travel, perhaps emigrate to Belize. He gets a Disability Pension, on which he thinks he could live quite well. He would like to open an Internet cafe that would eventually be operating without him. (Fieldnotes 4.4.2016)

Even though the future is difficult to imagine, most of these prisoners are still 'fighting' against their situation and hoping for their release. They say that fighting is something that keeps them alive; it is a way of resistance. Therefore, they are strongly concentrated on the future and constantly waiting for something that may happen—an appointment at the court, a visit from a lawyer, a transfer to a more open prison and, perhaps, their eventual release. However, because of their strong hope for change and their intense orientation to the (uncertain) future, these prisoners are constantly suffering the 'pains of uncertainty and indeterminacy' (Crewe 2011: 513) and have difficulties giving meaning to their present life in prison. In contrast to prisoners who want their cell not to look like a cell anymore but rather a home, these prisoners do not *call* their cell a home, as they do not want to *feel* at home. In material terms, they also do not want to *arrange* their cells in a homely way; they want the cell to remain a cell.[6] For most of these prisoners' this means to have only few objects and personal items in their cell—sometimes their cells are almost empty (and look similar to a complete empty cell as illustrated in Fig. 6.1). This echoes Leder's (2004: 58) argument that prisoners who do not want to create themselves a home in prison, they want to 'refuse to become complicit with it' and 'orient to the outside world'. As Heinz explains:

> My cell is functionally furnished. I have everything I need … and it's clean. But I didn't put posters on the wall or things like that; I don't want to furnish it like an apartment that suits my personal taste. I keep telling myself: this is not mine. (Heinz 3.5.2016)

Just like Heinz, Anton also emphasised that he arranged his cell in a purely functionally manner: 'It [the cell] is expediently furnished. A computer, a printer, books, envelopes, paper, CDs, a stereo system. But otherwise, nothing else' (Anton 24.3.2016). Not having any (or only a few, but hidden) personal objects can also be understood as a means of protecting one's privacy in the sense of 'reserve' as defined by Cohen and Taylor (1972), which means to not reveal certain personal aspects of oneself. However, there are also prisoners who want to create a home while keeping it 'functionally furnished'. In this case, it is more a matter of personal taste—'I don't have any plants. I'm not that much of a plant person' (Marco 4.5.2016)—or because it is thought to make the room feel smaller when there are too many objects in it.

Nevertheless, the prisoners who disassociate themselves from the prison through their narratives and ways of arranging the cell also expressed feelings of belonging and attachment. This became apparent, for instance, when they were describing to me their feelings after they realised that their cell had just been searched—'like after a burglary' (Anton 24.3.2016). As Jonathan told me:

> I always think: they have been here again. I realise that they have searched the cell and think: they have been here again. Wednesday and Friday I clean the cell, the floor and everything, and then I can see footprints on the floor. That's how I notice that they have been in my cell. (Jonathan 2.5.2016)

Ugelvik (2014), claims that the feeling of 'space belonging to me is [a] practical question […] a room becomes *my* room by me taking residence in it' (Ugelvik 2014: 117). Taking residence in a room or a house is connected to the arrangement of things due to personal needs (and taste). It, therefore, always also 'reflects those who live there, their perceptions, habits and practices' (Ugelvik 2014: 117). Indeed, even though some prisoners may decide not to arrange it in a cosy way and do not want to feel to belong there, they do store and arrange personal objects that they keep in their cell in a way that suits them best. Maybe they have only the very basic items handed out by the prison, such as plates, cutlery and cups, a toothbrush, toothpaste, soap, a towel, clothes, and shoes. But maybe they also have some more 'private' things: a postcard from a friend, photographs of family members (although kept invisible for others), or a note that confirms their next visit.

I argue that the feeling of attachment may also be a result of the fact that the cell is the place where they can be alone and pass unobserved time, where they sleep, have sex (with themselves or fellow prisoners), get dressed, use the toilet (see also Ugelvik 2014: 121)—all activities that are (at least in so-called 'Western' societies) considered as 'intimate' and 'private' and not performed in public (see Hall [1966] 1982). The cell is also the place in prison where they are 'not on show' (Ugelvik 2014: 123); where they can freely express those emotions they usually try to control or hide in front of staff or fellow prisoners. Hence, independently of whether the prisoners intend to transform the cell into a home or not, the cell constitutes (to some degree) a personal and private territory (see also Goffman 1961; Toch [1977] 1996), which, in one way or another, prisoners try to defend by using a wide range of techniques. As I observed, these techniques include trying to influence the frequency and accuracy of cell searches by behaving 'inconspicuously' and thereby strengthening the borders of their personal territory; or getting to know the prison officers' rhythms and routines to be able to catch the right moment to engage in (what they consider as) intimate and private activities.

## Conclusion

As this chapter illustrates, using an ethnographic lens and the concept of *inhabiting* offers the potential to explore the prison cell and, more concretely, the prisoners' ways of residing in it. Here, it is possible to trace the prisoners' subjective experience detached from predefined assumptions and concepts of what the prison cell (as well as the prison as a whole) is and what it does. In the academic literature, the prison is often explored by qualifying it *per se* as a 'bad' or 'dehumanizing' place (O'Donnell

2014: 179) where prisoners face above all a wide range of 'pains' and 'deprivations' (Sykes 1958); and have to find strategies to 'survive' this extraordinary or 'extreme' situation (Cohen and Taylor 1972). Without neglecting these understandings of the prison, using the concept of inhabiting in relation to cell space facilitates an approach to the prison as a place where these people *live* their ordinary everyday lives. It enables the exploration of prisoners' agentic and practical engagement with the cell, and imprisonment in general, without necessarily labelling it 'resistance' or 'adaptation' to the prison environment (as previous research often does). It thus also sheds light on the usually unnoticed, apparently insignificant and banal activities, habits, and routines that prisoners develop and carry out when residing in this place. This particular focus on the prison cell reveals the manifold expressions of the prisoners' ways of dealing with imprisonment, such as focusing on the present, accepting imprisonment and creating a 'home' in prison, or, in contrast, maintaining focus on the future, hope for release and continually expressing distance from the prison and all the spaces that it encompasses.

## Notes

1. The project *End-of-Life in Prison: Legal Context, Institutions and Actors* was funded by the Swiss National Science Foundation (SNSF) (http://www.p3.snf.ch/Project-139296).
2. The PhD project *Living the Prison: An Ethnographic Study of Indefinite Incarceration in Switzerland* was also funded by the SNSF (http://p3.snf.ch/project-159182).
3. In Switzerland's federal political system, legislation in the field of criminal law is a matter for the federal government. The execution of sentences, however, generally falls under the responsibilities of the cantons (FOJ 2010).
4. All fieldnotes and quotations from prisoners have been translated from German by the author. All names have been replaced by pseudonyms.
5. See also Herrity (this volume) for a discussion of the significance of sound in cell space.
6. Here it is important to note that the significance prisoners attribute to the cell can change over time and according to the situation (see also Lussault

and Stock 2010: 17). For instance, during our first meeting within the scope of a formal interview in 2016, Markus vehemently expressed the position that he would never call his cell a home. In 2017, after several more meetings and informal discussions, during the walking interview I conducted with him, he first showed me his cell, which he named 'my home' (Markus 28.8.2017).

## References


Baechtold, A., Weber, J., & Hostettler, U. (2016). *Strafvollzug. Straf- und Massnahmenvollzug an Erwachsenen in der Schweiz* (Dritte, vollständig überarbeitete und erweiterte Auflage. Reihe KJS-CJS, Band 17). Bern: Stämpfli Verlag.

Baer, L. D. (2005). Visual Imprints on the Prison Landscape: A Study on Decorations in Prison Cells. *Tijdschrift voor Economische en Sociale Geografie, 96*(2), 209–217.

Bundesamt für Justiz (BJ). (2016). *Handbuch für Bauten des Straf-und Massnahmenvollzugs*. Retrieved October 31, 2017, from https://www.bj.admin.ch/dam/data/bj/sicherheit/smv/baubeitraege/hb-erwachsene-d.pdf.

Cohen, S., & Taylor, L. (1972). *Psychological Survival: The Experience of Long-Term Imprisonment*. Harmondsworth: Penguin.

Crewe, B. (2011). Depth, Weight, Tightness: Revisiting the Pains of Imprisonment. *Punishment & Society, 13*(5), 509–529.

Crewe, B., Hulley, S., & Wright, S. (2016). Swimming with the Tide: Adapting to Long-Term Imprisonment. *Justice Quarterly, 34*(3), 517–541.

DeWalt, K. M., & DeWalt, B. R. (2002). *Participant Observation: A Guide for Fieldworkers*. Walnut Creek: Altamira Press.

Douglas, M. (1966). *Purity and Danger: An Analysis of the Concepts of Pollution and Taboo*. London: Routledge and Kegan Paul.

Federal Office of Justice (FOJ). (2010). *The Execution of Sentences and Measures in Switzerland*. Retrieved October 31, 2017, from https://www.bj.admin.ch/dam/data/bj/sicherheit/smv/dokumentation/smv-ch-e.pdf.

Goffman, E. (1961). *Asylums: Essays on the Social Situation of Mental Patients and Other Inmates*. Garden City, NY: Anchor Books.

Hall, E. T. ([1966] 1982). *The Hidden Dimension*. Garden City, NY: Anchor Books.

JVA Lenzburg. (2011). *Hausordnung 2011*. Kanton Aargau.

JVA Pöschwies. (2016). *AGE-Info*. Kanton Zürich.

Künzli, J., Eugster, A., & Schultheiss, M. (2016). *Haftbedingungen in der Verwahrung—Menschenrechtliche Standards und die Situation in der Schweiz*. Bern: Schweizerisches Kompetenzzentrum für Menschenrechte (SKMR).

Leder, D. (2004). Imprisoned Bodies: The Life-World of the Incarcerated. *Social Justice, 31*(1/2), 51–66.

Leigey, M. E., & Ryder, M. A. (2015). The Pains of Permanent Imprisonment: Examining Perceptions of Confinement Among Older Life Without Parole Inmates. *International Journal of Offender Therapy and Comparative Criminology, 59*(7), 726–742.

Lussault, M. (2007). *L'homme spatial. La construction sociale de l'espace humain*. Paris: Seuil.

Lussault, M., & Stock, M. (2010). Doing with Space: Towards a Pragmatics of Space. *Social Geography, 5*(1), 1–8.

Milhaud, O. (2009). *Séparer et punir. Les prisons françaises: mise à distance et punition par l'espace*. PhD thesis, Université Michel de Montaigne – Bordeaux III.

O'Donnell, I. (2014). *Prisoners, Solitude, and Time*. Oxford: Oxford University Press.

Schneeberger Georgescu, R. (2009). Im schweizerischen Freiheitsentzug altern: Nicht der Alterskriminelle prägt das Bild des alten Insassen, sondern der langjährige Insasse im Massnahmenvollzug. *Forum Strafvollzug. Zeitschrift für Strafvollzug und Straffälligenhilfe, 58*, 124–127.

Sykes, G. M. (1958). *The Society of Captives: A Study of a Maximum Security Prison*. Princeton, NJ: Princeton University Press.

Toch, H. ([1977] 1996). *Living in Prison: The Ecology of Survival*. Washington, DC: American Psychological Association.

Tuan, Y. ([1977] 2001). *Space and Place: The Perspective of Experience*. Minneapolis, MN: University of Minnesota Press.

Ugelvik, T. (2014). *Power and Resistance in Prison: Doing Time, Doing Freedom*. London: Palgrave Macmillan.

Vigh, H. (2008). Crisis and Chronicity: Anthropological Perspectives on Continuous Conflict and Decline. *Ethnos, 73*(1), 5–24.

Wacquant, L. (2002). The Curious Eclipse of Prison Ethnography in the Age of Mass Incarceration. *Ethnography, 3*(4), 371–397.

# 7

# Prison as Palimpsest: The Dialectics of the Cell and Everyday Life

The ACE Steering Committee

The recent proliferation of work that has introduced and given momentum to research in carceral geography has enriched our understanding of various aspects of incarceration. Scholars in this area have generated insightful engagements with the primary bodies of theory that are often enlisted in the effort to better understand how, why, and where human beings are forcibly enclosed, and some of the ramifications thereof (Moran et al. 2018). In this growing body of literature, there are calls, that are both methodological and ethical, for a fuller representation of the voices and experiences of those who are incarcerated. This chapter is a pioneering effort to respond to that call and to contribute to an examination of various dimensions of carceral realities, as they are

The authors of this chapter are Shaul Cohen (corresponding author), Bianca P., Daniel, Don S., Emily Kalbrosky, Eric, Jaime, Jason Christner, Jimmy, John Knight, Jordan Pickrel, Josh Cain, Julie Williams-Reyes, Kathleen Dwyer, Kehala Hervey, Kosol, Kyle Hedquist, Michael, Phoebe Petersen, Sang Nguyen, and Shannon Fender. Names appear as requested by each participating member of the ACE group. The authors would like to thank Dr. Diane Baxter for her comments on early versions of this chapter.

The ACE Steering Committee (✉)
Department of Geography, University of Oregon, Eugene, OR, USA
e-mail: scohen@uoregon.edu



J. Turner, V. Knight (eds.), *The Prison Cell*, Palgrave Studies in Prisons and Penology,
https://doi.org/10.1007/978-3-030-39911-5_7

understood by a group of men who currently reside in the Oregon State Penitentiary and have collectively served over 250 years of their sentences there and at a number of other prisons in the United States. Our group includes prisoners[1] ranging in age from 27 to 81 years old, who been incarcerated for periods ranging from 8 to 35 years. The sentences of some of the authors have recently been completed; others have a few years to many decades remaining on their time; and some will never be released. These men are joined as authors of the chapter by two faculty members, five students, and two alumni from the University of Oregon who are the 'outside' members of the ACE group (Another Chance for Education) in the Oregon State Penitentiary; together the group has been working for a decade to foster educational opportunities in prisons and juvenile detention facilities in Oregon and elsewhere in the United States.[2]

In this chapter, we focus on the prison cell as we consider the evolving relationship between that construct and its occupants as the years of incarceration accumulate and the prisoners' orientation to their world evolves, drawing attention to the diversity of experiences that occur there. We also address the prisoners' efforts to 'domesticate' the space they inhabit, and ways in which the cell can function as an emblem that supports the emotional needs of the prisoner and serves as a way to project identity in a manner that communicates messages about territory and status to other prisoners and staff (Turner 2016). Our first-hand narrative begins with the cell in the broader construct of prison 'neighbourhoods', and subsequently examines how location and function shape the experience of the cells' occupants and affect those living in close proximity within the institution.

While very appreciative of work in the sub-discipline of carceral geography, from which we have learned much, our reaction to studies to date in this and other disciplines is one of 'yes!, but…'. Theorisation and empirical studies of prisons tend to fall into binaries that don't fully capture the dynamism of the cell in relation to self, power, and place, even when authors are specifically critiquing the simplified descriptions of prison life. Our overarching sense is that the prison environment is frequently so fraught and multifaceted that descriptions in the literature often lose important dimensions of the fluidity, complexity, and simultaneity of opportunities and constraints in which prisoners forge agency, deploy tactics, and nurture and maintain identity. The aspects of the cell we address—prison neighbourhoods, the domestication of the cell, and the evolving nature of the cell for its occupants over time—illustrate our central argument that the space and experiences of this key area of imprisonment are malleable. In this malleability, we find an essential point of contact between the lives of those who are incarcerated and the struggles of less powerful people everywhere; that is, for all that is denied or imposed on the resident of the cell, there is both need and opportunity to shape the place in which we live out our most fundamental existence (Frankl 1959). Whether in a carceral setting or in the 'free world', human adaptability and resourcefulness are powerful forces, despite institutional efforts to limit or eradicate them.

Cells have been discussed as liminal spaces. Authors have rightly pointed to the complicated natures of space and time (Moran 2015), and there is on-going and productive conversation around Foucault's (1977) lack of attention to autonomy (Dirsuweit 1999); Goffman's total institution concept and its scope (1961); and the absolutism of Agamben's bare life (1998). Our hope in this chapter is to avoid the 'reductive binaries' (Earle 2014: 429) that tend to depict prison life as a list of situations and circumstances; instead, we view prison more like a kaleidoscope, with patterns and moments that reflect an on-going process.

Some authors do capture elements of incarceration that are part of the incredible complexity of these worlds. As James notes, the prison cell is 'a space of constant negotiation and uncertainty' (2018: 154) and Moran et al. refer to a 'continuum' of qualities and conditions within the carceral (2018: 677). Both of these observations highlight the 'churn' of the prison experience, something that infuses our understanding of the different functions that cells have because of the agency exercised by their occupants, and the counter current of authority exercised by the state. As Andrew[3] sees it, the cell 'takes on many forms that depend on the needs of the prisoner'. His characterisation shows that, alongside the recognition of the cell as a mechanism of constraint that belongs to the state, it can also be a place of attachment, and these different experiences can reside in a prisoner simultaneously.

Our inside authors have figured out how to 'do time', and thus the personal observations in this chapter should be seen as those of veterans of the system, and we caution against efforts that overly simplify the prison experience, or map too broadly from one situation to another.[4] Foucault's attention to the institutional aspiration to create docile bodies is important (particularly when one considers the level of mental health issues in prisons, and the extremely high rates of medication in use in many of them), but with an eye towards Bourdieu (1990), de Certeau (2011), Jewkes (2013) and Scott (1985), we argue that many incarcerated individuals create their places, their identities, and organise their cells through continual actions of assertion and denial. This may come as a surprise to some, given the extreme conditions of incarceration and the fundamental loss of freedom, but Relph points out that to 'have roots in a place is to have a secure point from which to look out on the world, a firm grasp of one's own position in the order of things' (1976: 38). A person inside a cell is still a person, despite the elements arrayed to deny, diminish or extinguish their selfhood.

As noted by Sibley and Van Hoven 'space within the prison is both transparent and opaque' (2009: 199), and stakeholders act in ways that are visible and invisible. The activity within the cell is an effort to make a place that serves its occupant(s), and which the prisoner endeavours to keep private, at least in part. This happens in dialectic with the continual steps taken by the prison administration—through the process of design, the use of electronic surveillance, and human observation—to make the cell visible, and to maintain a place that is different from that desired by its occupants. At times, this tension feels like a competition, as the residents of the prison—whether individually or collectively—attempt to increase their ability to act and to improve their lot. For its part, the prison administration and the individuals employed by it act to implement their objectives in a fashion that is as safe and effective for them as possible, which is often not in accord with the desires or needs of those in custody. For those in prison, in whatever capacity, there is an unceasing stream of decisions that constitutes a cost-benefit approach to daily activities. While there are some rules that are always enforced (particularly those for more serious violations), it is often uncertain as to which rules will be enforced at a given time, and which rule staff members will apply in some fashion, in some parts of the prison, to some people, for some reason.[5]

To convey the myriad currents that flow through and around this highly complex place, we offer an image that reflects our experiences of cells and their manifold functions: that of the palimpsest—something that is used and reused, inscribed and re-inscribed, in which traces of different layers are evident, though sometimes indistinct or occluded. By this, we mean that the cell is always being written, erased, and overwritten through the intricacies of power, and that the inscription done there by the different stakeholders unfolds sequentially, though much of what transpires does so concurrently. Brian says that for those spending a long period of time in them,

> the cell is predictable in a sense, and we struggle with the sameness and boredom, while at the same time you always feel like you don't know what's going to happen next. I hate the boredom, but sometimes it's better than the alternative. In the end though, it's mostly patterns, ours and theirs [the staff's], blending together.

Chuck adds: 'Some of the time we feel like we control our cells, and sometimes they feel like they control our cells. Really both are true and neither are true a lot of the time'. It is observations such as these that add detail and nuance to earlier studies of this sort, and suggest to us the palimpsest and capture pragmatic elements of the cell in prison life.

In offering commentary on the lives of those who are incarcerated, we add our voices to the analyses of who 'owns' what in the prison; what constitutes agency and autonomy; and what power can mean in these lives (Moran 2015). Without in any way denying or minimising the negative elements of incarceration, we fall within the group that finds at least some 'positives in the carceral experience' (Jewkes 2013: 127), and see the cell as a 'repository of socially and politically relevant traditions and identity which serves to mediate between the everyday lives of individuals and the… institutions which constrain and enable those lives' (Agnew and Duncan 1989: 7). The cell is more, though, than a repository; it is a space in which many of the overarching dimensions of incarceration are enacted, resisted, and contested. Indeed, the cell is an amalgam in which a number of elements combine in ways that yield a variety of individualities amidst the drive for standardisation and anonymity that marks mass incarceration.

This writing draws upon our sustained exploration of the relationship between incarceration, agency, and identity, and our engagement with the literature on prisons and on the policies that shape our work. The chapter is therefore a synthesis of what we learn from the scholarship on incarceration elsewhere, and our individual and shared experiences inside these (and other) prison walls. We include quotations from individual members of the group, but write as a community that has drafted this chapter collectively. Our use of the term 'we' should not be taken to mean that we are unaware of the stark divide that separates the incarcerated members of the group from those living in 'the free world' outside. Rather, it is an affirmation that we form a community of common interest in which we are able to draw upon a range of knowledge that gives us insight, breadth, and strength. It should be noted that our writing process was to break into smaller groups focusing on specific aspects of the cell, and the chapter as a whole represents both consensus and synthesis. While all of those involved in the writing are listed as authors, and the personal quotes included herein come from ACE members, we have created pseudonyms for the attribution of these quotes in order to maintain collective 'ownership' of what is by nature a tapestry of individual experiences.

## The Neighbourhood and the Cell

Where an individual lives within the prison is affected by a number of variables, and, inasmuch as the cell is formally assigned to its occupants by the administration, that determination predominantly resides with the staff. Among the factors that have bearing are the nature of the sentence (length and category of crime), the conduct of the prisoner (though reward and punishment are at times unrelated to or only partially the result of the behaviour of the prisoner), age, physical and mental health, sexual orientation, race, and availability of beds. Neighbourhoods within a prison, like neighbourhoods elsewhere, can provide benefits and contain risks that have little to do with a particular cell and its occupants, but rather reflect patterns or perceptions that adhere to a larger scale than a single dwelling. Though not a prominent aspect of our current circumstances, gang life can be a significant marker of territory and identity, and the dynamics of power related to that form of social organisation can map onto entire prisons, or at the smaller scales of block, tier, or even an individual cell.[6]

One significant aspect of the experience of the cell is encapsulated by our inside authors as 'location, location, location'. A common reference made by both prisoners and staff is that of 'a small town' as a simile for the geography of the prison, where its cell blocks or even individual tiers are compared to neighbourhoods. While the prison has a number of centralised places—the chow hall, the yard, the showers, and the industrial areas—the cell blocks have distinct characters and patterns.[7] Some of the attributes of location are simple, such as desire for proximity to friends and distance from adversaries, for good lighting (more to see by, less to sleep with), comfortable temperatures (like most prisons in the United States, this penitentiary is not air conditioned, and heat—and cold—are distributed unevenly), and regular air flow (which is important since each cell contains a toilet, and access to showers is limited).

In the 'Honours Block' at OSP, there are solid metal doors on the cells (with a window near the top) that can reduce noise and distraction and enhance privacy in comparison with the barred cells on the other block. The Honours Block, which can be earned by serving 5 years without incurring any disciplinary action, is markedly different from the other blocks in that its residents are able to circulate on the open area of their floor during times when prisoners are not restricted to their cells; all of the other blocks lack that configuration, and their inhabitants are locked in their cells when they are not engaged in some activity (work, eating, yard, showers, chapel, visiting, and so on).

Throughout the prison, aspects of location can be specific to the circumstances of the prisoner, an example of which is proximity to the 'box', where the security staff are based on the tier or cellblock. For most prisoners, being close to the box is undesirable in that it reduces privacy, increases risk, and comes with the hustle and bustle of the work of the staff. The only advantage of proximity for the average prisoner is a somewhat diminished risk of theft. However, for the part of the population that is particularly vulnerable to attack—homosexual and transgender prisoners,[8] those convicted of sex crimes, those who collaborate with the administration, and 'snitches', or simply those who are viewed as a target of some sort—being close to the box may provide a measure of security (Copes et al. 2011).

In addition to proximity to the box, the location of the cell on the tier has other important dimensions. Prisoners are prohibited from entering any cell other than their own, and are restricted in their mobility when outside of their cells; thus residing at the far end of a tier can draw even more attention to foot traffic that is outside of the prescribed movement for permitted activity. Non-compliant use of the cell may be less visible in some parts of the prison, but may, at the same time, be all the more suspicious for creating activity where it otherwise would not be concentrated. Foot traffic can also exacerbate the tensions around privacy, and some prisoners prefer a remote location where they will be less frequently observed and disturbed by others. This can mean though that they will pass by more cells on their way to and from other parts of the prison, and in doing so they are 'subject' to seeing what goes on elsewhere. This may be interesting and useful, but it might also be distasteful, and there are things happening that prisoners 'don't want to see, and really shouldn't see' as Charles puts it. And if an individual observes, or is even in a position to observe illicit activity, it creates the possibility of snitching, and of being considered a snitch, thus proximity to other cells can create a variety of hazards for the viewer and the viewed.

## The Cell Diversifies Over Time

While for some the cell remains inherently punitive throughout their incarceration, for many, including the imprisoned authors of this chapter, the experience of the cell evolves as individuals age and mature over the course of their sentence.[9] From the initial experiences of adapting to life in prison to later coping with the losses associated with aging in prison, the cell remains central to the carceral experience and can grow more important over time. It functions as a tool of punishment initially, and this aspect endures in some respects even as the cell can become an office and a home, and has immense power in shaping an individual's experience in prison. As a powerful example of this, DeShaun who is now in his ninth decade of life says that 'The work that I do now is very similar to the work I did on the outside. I have files, paperwork, and preparation notes on my desk in my cell. My cell is the closest thing to the outside I have. I have a radio, TV, and artwork'. For individuals like DeShaun, who is serving a life sentence, reframing the cell to home and office serves a powerful function in claiming control and defining when and how to feel ownership, even in the face of the realities of 'the cell' as the basic unit of confinement.

Eli illustrates some of the mental journey experienced by (some) prisoners, saying, 'I realized that I was only hurting myself by continuing to consider the cell my punishment. Some guys refuse to be comfortable in their cells, but I think I can best improve myself by being as relaxed in my environment as possible, wherever that may be'. Frank captures the shifting geography of the prison for himself as he ages by observing that

> My friends and acquaintances tend to live, work, and socialize in the same small area of confinement that I do now. I used to own this place [i.e., the prison], and knew the goings-on of everything in here as only a prisoner of youth and good health could. The prison yard is for the young and healthy, old men retire to the comforts and security of what the blocks and their cell can give them.

At the beginning of a period of incarceration, the cell can induce feelings of claustrophobia and dread, while at the same time constituting a place outside of the flow of prison traffic: a base of sorts from which a prisoner can have a measure of respite and learn what is necessary to acclimate to prison life, or to the specific ways of a particular prison or place within it. This is necessary in relation to the formal rules of the institution and the unwritten but influential rules of the prisoners themselves that shape the daily geography of the prison and determine what can and cannot be done in different locations (Cresswell 1996). After being sentenced to more than five decades in prison, Gary describes how 'the reality set in that I would never be free again. The cell became a cage, and like any other animal, I knew that I had to adapt to my surroundings if I wanted to live and make the most of my existence'.

One of the elements that is immediately challenging upon incarceration is constant surveillance—both informal and formal—as suggested by Bentham's Panopticon (Foucault 1977). The conceptual 'freedom' that our members discuss in relation to their cells and neighbourhoods also relate powerfully with the mentality required to adapt to shifting priorities and personalities of the prison staff over time. Studies that have begun to outline the 'emotional geography' of carceral spaces comment on the difficulty of maintaining equanimity when faced with the loss of autonomy and aspects of privacy (Crewe 2009; Dirsuweit 1999; Milhaud and Moran 2013; Philo 2001; Sibley and Van Hoven 2009). Though there is a regular turnover in staff, as the period of incarceration grows in length, prisoners become familiar with some of the security officers, and, similarly, officers come to recognise those that they see on a regular basis. The attitudes of staff members, and their overall orientation to their work, have profound implications for those subject to their authority. Thus the 'emotional landscape' of incarceration can include a dialectic between those incarcerated and their captors, and the mood, character, and mental health of the staff have to be recognised as having a significant impact on the experience of those who reside in the facility.

In regard to people passing by a cell or stopping outside of it, three general categories are identified by prisoners: friend, stranger, or enemy. Most of our 'inside' authors classify staff in this fashion and feel more, or less, relaxed during particular shifts depending on who is on duty. With greater experience, prisoners are better able to navigate the differences in approach on the part of the security staff, and thus avoid much of the 'hassle' that can come in response to the actions or attitudes—perceived or real—on the part of the prisoner. This is extremely important in the life of those incarcerated, for while they don't like being observed within their cells, or even having their cells viewed by others, the stakes are much higher when their cells get 'tossed', or searched.

As Hank notes, 'One of the things we have to figure out is how to keep people out of our space'. When the cell is searched, or even simply entered into by staff members, prisoners feel a sense of trespass and violation. They are unable to forbid this practice and know that it can happen at any time, thus their sense of ownership and (relative) emotional safety is compromised by staff entrance to the confines of the cell. Some of the men that have made adjustments to prison life, in general, and to the patterns of specific staff in particular, note the infrequency with which their cells are tossed, and believe that this is because they have accrued social capital with staff and other prisoners. Having social capital, which is an element of the prison 'currency' of respect, helps them maintain territorial boundaries, and this allows a greater sense of ownership of their space (Sibley 1995).

As time passes for the prisoner, so too it passes for those they are connected to on the outside. Among the many pains of incarceration is the particular sense of helplessness and loss that accompanies growing infirmity and the deaths of family members. The grief and rage that can mark the approach and then experience of bereavement is one that our members note as being particularly powerful, and this can accompany the sickness and death of friends behind bars as well. While trauma of this sort is understood and respected by the prison community, Isaac notes the disdain in prison for the showing of emotion 'in public', that is, in the prison's shared spaces like the chow hall, the yard, and the various work and activity areas. The cell thus serves as a sanctuary in which one can mourn in relative privacy. Further, the cells of those who die while incarcerated can remain associated with a former occupant long after their death, and, in that respect, Jose observes that 'the cell can act as a cemetery' as well, even if it's not a burial place.

Kareem points to the importance of possessions for long-term prisoners in maintaining connections with the world outside (Turner 2017), and says that

> as someone who is serving a sentence without the possibility of release, I began to collect a lot of stuff. I had books, cups, lots of photos from home. As the years went by, I would send my family pictures of my "home" [i.e., the prison]: me on the yard, at work, and with my new "family." I want them to see that I have a life, but because of the restrictions on cameras [which aren't allowed on the cell blocks], I can't show them what I've done with my cell.

Kareem's efforts to mark time through the accumulation of possessions, and the communication about that material stake to others, align with

Fiddler's (2010) focus on the importance of memory in the making of space and place. Luke asserts that

> A man's cell is surely part of his identity. It's common knowledge that prisoners don't actually own their own cell in any penitentiary and that they are accustomed to moving quite often, but it is also true that many of the men that become warehoused in this system can spend a couple of decades or more in the same cell. If a man occupies a space for so long does this create a claim of ownership?'

His sentiment highlights the cognitive work of the prisoner, who knows that he is not sovereign, yet feels a right of possession. For those serving long sentences, in particular, this relationship between occupant and cell becomes all the more personal and powerful. As any human being relates to shelter, safety, community, surroundings, neighbours, and so on, the prisoners who face decades of their life confined to one loosely controlled 'home' must map their sense of belonging onto carefully proscribed senses of permanence, ownership, and belonging.

## Domesticating the Cell

The cell can become a locus of agency and an expression of individuality—and of humanity—as the prisoner learns to take advantage of what is allowed, and to extend beyond that in the tension between the possible and the permissible.[10] With time, prisoners learn how to partition the very small area available to them—the cell, part of a cell, or part of a dormitory—and to populate that space in ways that make it personal, and in some respects, to create privacy for some of their most significant possessions (Baer 2005; Moran 2015; Schliehe 2017) and activities. In making such efforts, prisoners must be cognisant of the rules applying to contraband (Gibson-Light 2018; Kalinich and Stojkovic 1985) and prohibited conduct regarding use and modification of prison space. Particularly in shared spaces, infractions make a prisoner vulnerable to official sanction and can constitute a risk for other occupants of the space as well. As noted above, when prison officials enter a cell, the potential harms extend to the entire space, and to all of those living therein. When the administration seizes the property of prisoners, it reduces their cell to the 'standard issue' and strips them, again, of their individuality and accumulated history.

Thus, while privacy and individuality are central desires, steps taken to create them come with a set of practical concerns that generate a cost-benefit dynamic. This is reflected in the dichotomy between wanting to shield some possessions or activities from public view, while using some items or actions to communicate specific messages to those in the proximity of the cell. Matt uses the term 'curb appeal' to suggest the relationship between what is—and what isn't—observed, and the value of the cell for those living within one: if the cell looks good or has desirable items within it, the owner/occupant gets a positive 'bump' in status. For some, this leads to extremely high standards of cleanliness or small modifications such as waxing the floor inside of the cell (Sloan 2012) or arranging artwork for display, like any modifications to a home in order to reflect the personality and status of the resident. Quirks of prison-wide maintenance also come into play, as items such as sinks have been replaced with different models over the years, leading to small elements of difference in some cells, for which the occupants sometimes place great significance in an institution built on sameness.

Within this constrained space, there remain myriad ways of creating self-expression, self-possession, and humanity. While Owen speaks of the importance of photographs—a widely shared sentiment—Pao points out that some images, such as family photos, key moments in life, or personal favourites, are placed or concealed in a manner that reflects a desire to be able to draw upon them while also keeping them private (Milhaud and Moran 2013). In a shared cell, items can 'brand' all of the occupants with whatever associations there may be with the possessions of one individual, such as gang insignia or inflammatory material. Some images, though, afford an opportunity for common ground or mutual appreciation, such as favourite celebrities, military unit insignia, sports triumphs and such, and even with staff members, there are opportunities for human connection in that way. Others note, though, that images can be markers of identity or affiliation with particular communities that may be in conflict or exercise some degree of territoriality within the prison, and thus when such emblems are displayed, they can constitute one of the many fences or borders mentioned above.

Given the tight confines, domesticity touches upon things beyond the visual. The auditory and olfactory have impacts that affect the quality of life and the level of comfort within the cell (see Herrity, this volume, for particular consideration of prison soundscapes). In the Oregon State Penitentiary, headphones are required for watching television or listening to music, but talking, singing, snoring, and other sounds compromise privacy and can be a source of tension and create a feeling of intrusion. Movement within the cell is felt—literally—by those nearby, and is thus subject to negotiation between cellmates. Nate calls this 'the dance', and says that it is an important factor in getting along with neighbours. He points out that if he moves from his (upper) bunk to the ground without care to step lightly, others will complain about the jolts that are transferred from his cell to theirs. And of course, there are issues of hygiene and placement of the body within the cell that are commonly noted, and captured by Kantrowitz (1996: 60) with the phrase 'spatial meticulousness'.

In some places, the cell can serve as a kitchen: some blocks 'cook' with hot tap water, others have access to a microwave oven in a day room available to some of the prisoners. Cell cuisine is an important element of social and economic life (Gibson-Light 2018; Valentine and Longstaff 1998), and is part of what Goffman (1961) terms 'secondary adjustments', ways of coping with and sometimes getting around the restrictions that constrain daily life. As noted by Collins Jr. and Alvarez, with 'a little creativity' with food, prisoners can 'travel to the places of [their] youth by imitating the meals' their families made, and can 'show some appreciation for… friends by hosting a spread that lets [them] all feel like humans rather than numbers for a while' (Collins Jr. and Alvarez 2015: xxi). As with all prison life, these domestic pursuits also hold the risk of conflict—food that is deemed overly 'smelly' or unpleasant can be a source of complaint to neighbours and therefore must be negotiated and renegotiated, and so is again subject to the rules—written and unwritten—that surround each individual in their quasi-private space.

The cell serves other functions of course. Ugelvik (2014: 121) compares the cell to a home and says that 'prisoners must simulate all the rooms... from the most public, such as the hall and dining room, to the most intimate and private, such as the toilet and bedroom', and this is true, though it considerably overstates the material circumstances prior to the incarceration of many prison residents. There is also a divide among prisoners, with some comfortably referring to the cell as their house or home, whereas others vehemently reject that term, insisting that they will never be 'at home' while incarcerated. The cell, though, can be a repository, and Rob says that the things on his shelf, 'four bottles of lotion, deodorant, coffee and creamer offer me a sense of comfort, knowing that I'll be ok for a while, these are assets that I own'. The cell can also be a studio for art or music, and for tattooing, something that is forbidden but offers a way of artistic expression that allows prisoners to make statements of attachment to a place, of longing for family, of protest, of fierceness, and many other things. The cell can also be a place to fight, an 'arena', where violence may escape the attention of the administration, and therefore spare participants (and bystanders) procedural sanction, and possible violent intervention by the staff. In some ways, this reality again both echoes and undermines the analogies to a home in the 'free world' with illicit activities—small and large—taking place in relative privacy.

## Summary

Ugelvik argues that the 'pronoun "my" in "my cell" and "my room" does not reflect any real ownership, that much is clear', and that 'a lot of effort is put into creating the illusion of ownership, the feeling of a private life' (2014: 218). We understand what he is saying, and acknowledge that, in legal terms, his first assertion is correct and that, in some respects, ownership in prison can be illusory. At the same time, this characterisation strips the prison life of authentic meaning and dismisses the agency that prisoners experience as real. This issue is far more than semantic. Sibley notes psychological dimensions in geography and the critical importance of the home as 'a boundary of the self', something that serves a vital function in forming and maintaining the 'sense of individuality' (1995: 94).

Our work emphasises the emotional landscape in a prison, partly in terms of where and how space for feeling and for expressing feelings is created behind bars (Baer 2005; Crewe 2009; Crewe et al. 2014). Sam and Terry share their observation that within the prison there are many unseen borders and fences and that these operate at a range of scales from the institution as a whole to the micro geography of the shared cell, wherein emotion does not have to be suppressed to the same degree. Even there though, emotion is often managed, both because of the pain of incarceration and attendant loss for the individual and for the consequences of being perceived as weak by others as the walls of the cell remain permeable.

The aspects of prison life that we have described in this chapter highlight the complications of living in circumstances that are severely constrained, yet also illustrate the ingenuity—and need—of prisoners in utilising the cell as a source of and location for agency. In shaping the cell in ways that are both permitted and prohibited, prisoners manage to personalise what is intended to be standardised and, in so doing, exercise a measure of power that belies the notion of the docile body. Characterisations that argue that ownership and privacy are either actual—and thus often not part of a prisoners legal status or reliably part of their regular existence—or chimeric, are too reductive and fail to reflect what prisoners do with space and time as they live in particular moments and over the course of lengthy sentences.

In considering the interplay between the letter of the law and the spirit of prisoner life, we find that the concept of attachment helps explain aspects of the carceral experience that we argue constitute agency and give meaning to life and are an area of vital emotional expression and individuality. Antonsich describes the categories of belonging, 'as a personal, intimate feeling of being "at home" in a place' and 'as a discursive resource which constructs, claims, justifies, or resists forms of socio-spatial inclusion/exclusion' (2010: 645). He points to differences between formal characteristics of belonging such as citizenship and the 'personal intimate, private sentiment of place attachment' (2010: 645). As noted above, there are pronounced differences among prisoners in terms of referring to their cell as their home; and feelings about rootedness, possession, and place evolve over time. Yet even for those who reject the nomenclature of home, there are genuine modes of attachment that serve as belonging within the inclusion/exclusion dynamics of incarceration.

In some respects prisons are designed to be placeless, yet in the complicated and overlapping systems of authority—formal and informal—are the mosaics of geography for people without political power (Cohen 2000); the placeless yearn for a place in the worlds they inhabit. For those in prison, this world is the featureless cell, the variegated block and the maze of borders and fences that delineate daily existence but don't completely circumscribe the lives of those living therein. While mechanisms of state power are writing a set of narratives for and about prisoners, many people who are incarcerated, including the inside authors of this chapter, are etching their own versions of self and community as part of the palimpsest that gives character to the cell, the block and the prison.

## Notes

1. Over the years there has been some discussion in our group about what term to use for people who are incarcerated. When we began our prison education work the Department of Corrections used the term 'inmate', which was and continues to be stamped on the clothing of those living here. That term was deemed pejorative by a majority of our group, and we opted to use the term 'prisoner', or one who is held against their will. Recently Oregon has shifted to the term 'Adult in Custody' (though the clothing continues to be marked with 'Inmate' and the Oregon DOC emblem), but that term has not gained much acceptance. Any nomenclature used in this context is political; see for example Hickman (2015) for a review of some of the terms and their implications.
2. Our education work in Oregon's prisons began as part of the national Inside-Out programme, which is based at Temple University. In the spirit of that organisation, our academic courses and other activities in carceral facilities include 'outside' participants who we bring in to participate in shared learning opportunities with people who are incarcerated. The ACE group functions as a steering committee for the University of Oregon's Prison Education Programme, and is composed of individuals who voluntarily take on leadership roles in relation to education specifically and in many other prison programmes as well.

3. All quotes from personal observations have been made anonymous, an aspect of our writing process which we discuss more fully on p.148.
4. It is our sense that the Oregon State Penitentiary is less harsh and has more positive opportunities than many other maximum security prisons that we have been in or read about. It is also important to note that while prisons are highly regimented institutions, they are also in many respects quite arbitrary, thus we represent these experiences as solely our own even within this facility.
5. In Oregon's jails and prisons punishments can be part of the regular judicial system, that is, as a consequence of formal charges and a trial; as part of an internal administrative process; or simply as a decision made by a staff member. At the extreme end of sanctions are the death penalty, additional prison sentences, and the loss of opportunity for earlier release by the parole board. Solitary confinement of varying length is also a very serious threat, as is transfer to another prison, which can be enormously disruptive for a prisoner and for their family. Other consequences can include loss of jobs, fines, suspension of ability to participate in prison club activities or to go outside, and 'celling in', which is a short-term confinement to the cell. In prison physical pain and humiliation can also be administered in different manners and contexts.
6. While gangs are not as influential at OSP as they are in some prisons, they do exist, and their territoriality manifests on the prison yard, in the chow hall, and in some parts of the cell blocks. Beyond specific gang affiliation, race is a significant factor, and African-American and White prisoners do not cell together, which is to say that such a pairing would be unacceptable to some of the population and lead to violence; and the prison administration choses to avoid that dynamic. As in most prisons in the United States, at the Oregon State Penitentiary there is a hierarchy of status that dictates some aspects of social relations, including who can—or cannot—live with whom. The top echelon related to the charges for which an individual was convicted is the taking of another person's life, and the bottom echelon is filled by those convicted of child abuse or rape. Those at the bottom of this pecking order are often targeted, and for that reason and 'guilt by association' they are usually assigned to a cell with others of similar standing. 'Regular' prisoners generally do not want to reside with or even next to those who have this pariah status.
7. At OSP there are the typical jobs preparing food, cleaning, and so forth. There are also jobs for some of the prisoners in the facilities of Oregon

Corrections Enterprises, a quasi-private contractor that operates metal and wood shops, and industrial laundry, and a call centre within the prison. The issue of prison labour is a complex and interesting topic that is beyond the scope of this chapter (see LeBaron 2012). Among our authors are men who work in each of these areas.

8. Discussion of prison culture in relation to LGBTQ individuals is outside the scope of this paper, and the authors recognise the problematic nature of the marginalisation—including 'neighbourhood' marginalisation.
9. See also Marti (this volume) for a discussion of the changing relationship with the prison cell over time and across a prison sentence.
10. See also Michalon (this volume) for a discussion of agency and resistance in cell space.

## References


Agamben, G. (1998). *Homo Sacer: Sovereign Power and Bare Life*. Translated by Daniel Heller-Roazan. Stanford: Stanford University Press.

Agnew, J., & Duncan, J. (1989). *The Power of Place: Bringing Together Geographical and Sociological Imaginations*. Boston, MA: Unwin and Hyman.

Antonsich, M. (2010). Searching for Belonging: An Analytical Framework. *Geography Compass, 4*(6), 644–659.

Baer, L. D. (2005). Visual Imprints on the Prison Landscape: A Study on the Decorations in Prison Cells. *Tijdschrift voor Economische en Sociale Geografie, 96*(2), 209–217.

Bourdieu, P. (1990). *The Logic of Practice*. Stanford, CA: Stanford University Press.

Cohen, S. (2000). An Absence of Place: Expectation and Realization in the West Bank. In A. Murphy & D. Johnson (Eds.), *Cultural Encounters with the Environment: Enduring and Evolving Geographic Themes* (pp. 283–303). Lanham, MD: Rowman & Littlefield.

Collins, C., Jr., & Alvarez, G. (2015). *Prison Ramen: Recipes and Stories from Behind Bars*. New York, NY: Workman Publishing.

Copes, H., Higgens, G., Tewksbury, R., & Dabney, D. (2011). Participation in the Prison Economy and the Likelihood of Victimization. *Victims and Offenders, 6*, 1–18.

Cresswell, T. (1996). *In Place/Out of Place: Geography, Ideology and Transgression*. Minneapolis, MN: University of Minnesota Press.

Crewe, B. (2009). *The Prisoner Society: Power, Adaptation, and Social Life in an English Prison*. Oxford: Oxford University Press.

Crewe, B., Warr, J., Bennett, P., & Smith, A. (2014). The Emotional Geography of Prison Life. *Theoretical Criminology, 18*(1), 56–74.

de Certeau, M. (Ed.). (2011). *The Practice of Everyday Life*. Berkeley, CA: University of California Press.

Dirsuweit, T. (1999). Carceral Spaces in South Africa: A Case Study of Institutional Power, Sexuality and Transgression in a Women's Prison. *Geoforum, 30*(1), 71–83.

Earle, R. (2014). Insider and Out: Making Sense of a Prison Experience and a Research Experience. *Qualitative Inquiry, 20*(4), 429–438.

Fiddler, M. (2010). Four Walls and What Lies Within: The Meaning of Space and Place in Prisons. *Prison Services Journal, 187*, 3–8.

Foucault, M. (1977). *Discipline and Punish: The Birth of the Prison*. New York, NY: Pantheon.

Frankl, V. E. (1959). *Man's Search for Meaning*. Boston, MA: Beacon Press.

Gibson-Light, Michael. (2018). Ramen Politics: Informal Money and Logics of Resistance in the Contemporary American Prison. *Qualitative Sociology, 41*, 199–220.

Goffman, E. (1961). *Asylums: Essays on the Social Situation of Mental Patients and Other Inmates*. New York, NY: Anchor Books.

Hickman, B. (2015). *Inmate. Prisoner. Other. Discussed*. New York, NY: The Marshall Project. Retrieved May 30, 2019, from https://www.themarshallproject.org/2015/04/03/inmate-prisoner-other-discussed.

James, F. (2018). It's Important Not to Lose Myself: Beds, Carceral Design, and Women's Everyday Life within Prison Cells. In E. Fransson, E. Giofre, & B. Johnsen (Eds.), *Prison, Architecture and Humans* (pp. 151–176). Oslo: Cappelen Damm Akademisk.

Jewkes, Y. (2013). On Carceral Space and Agency. In D. Moran, N. Gill, & D. Conlon (Eds.), *Carceral Spaces: Mobility and Agency in Imprisonment and Migrant Detention* (pp. 127–131). Farnham: Ashgate.

Kalinich, D. B., & Stojkovic, S. (1985). Contraband: The Basis for Legitimate Power in a Prison Social System. *Criminal Justice & Behavior, 12*, 345–451.

Kantrowitz, N. (1996). *Close Control: Managing a Maximum Security Prison—The Story of Ragen's Stateville Penitentiary*. Albany, NY: Harrow & Heston.

LeBaron, G. (2012). Rethinking Prison Labor: Social Discipline and the State in Historical Perspective. *Journal of Labor and Society, 15*(3), 327–351.

Milhaud, O., & Moran, D. (2013). Penal Space and Privacy in French and Russian Prisons. In D. Moran, N. Gill, & D. Conlon (Eds.), *Carceral Spaces: Mobility and Agency in Imprisonment and Migrant Detention* (pp. 167–182). Farnham: Ashgate.

Moran, D. (2015). *Carceral Geography: Spaces and Practices of Incarceration.* London: Routledge.

Moran, D., Turner, J., & Schliehe, A. (2018). Conceptualizing the Carceral in Carceral Geography. *Progress in Human Geography, 42*(5), 666–686.

Philo, C. (2001). Accumulating Populations: Bodies, Institutions, and Space. *International Journal of Population Geography, 7*, 473–490.

Relph, E. (1976). *Place and Placelessness.* London: Pion Limited.

Schliehe, A. (2017). Towards a Feminist Carceral Geography? Of Female Offenders and Prison Spaces. In D. Moran & A. Schliehe (Eds.), *Carceral Spatiality: Dialogues Between Geography and Criminology* (pp. 75–112). London: Palgrave Macmillan.

Scott, J. (1985). *Weapons of the Weak: Everyday Forms of Peasant Resistance.* New Haven, CT: Yale University Press.

Sibley, D. (1995). *Geographies of Exclusion: Society and Difference in the West.* London: Routledge.

Sibley, D., & Van Hoven, B. (2009). The Contamination of Personal Space: Boundary Construction in a Prison Environment. *Area, 41*(2), 198–206.

Sloan, J. (2012). 'You can See Your Face in My Floor': Examining the Function of Cleanliness in an Adult Male Prison. *The Howard Journal of Criminal Justice, 51*(4), 400–410.

Turner, J. (2016). *The Prison Boundary: Between Society and Carceral Space.* London: Palgrave Macmillan.

Turner, J. (2017). The Artistic 'Touch': Moving Beyond Carceral Boundaries Through *Art by Offenders*. In D. Moran & A. Schliehe (Eds.), *Carceral Spatiality: Dialogues Between Geography and Criminology* (pp. 135–168). London: Palgrave Macmillan.

Ugelvik, T. (2014). *Power and Resistance in Prison: Doing Time, Doing Freedom.* London: Palgrave Macmillan.

Valentine, G., & Longstaff, B. (1998). Doing Porridge: Food and Social Relations in a Male Prison. *Journal of Material Culture, 3*(2), 131–152.

# 8

# Power in 'No-Cell' Detention: Spatial Restriction and Domestication of Space for Foreign Detainees in Romania

Bénédicte Michalon

## Introduction

Confinement of foreign nationals in detention centres is distinct from imprisonment. It involves, in particular, the use of holding premises that are distinct from prison establishments. Institutionalisation of detention specific to foreign nationals has resulted in the opening of *ad hoc* 'centres' that are not within the remit of prison administrations. The administrations in charge of immigration control have, since the 1970s (in France) and 1980s (in the USA), frequently installed detention centres in existing premises previously devoted to other purposes. Some initially possessed an economic purpose: hangars and warehouses (in Marseille), builders' prefabs (in the Paris region) or shipping containers (e.g. in Italy). Others were of an institutional nature: former prisons (in Berlin), prison wings (in Cyprus) or former accommodation centres for asylum seekers (in the Czech Republic). Finally, detention centres have been installed in civil

B. Michalon (✉)
French National Centre for Scientific Research (CNRS), Bordeaux, France
e-mail: Benedicte.Michalon@cnrs.fr



J. Turner, V. Knight (eds.), *The Prison Cell*, Palgrave Studies in Prisons and Penology,
https://doi.org/10.1007/978-3-030-39911-5_8

buildings, notably in hotels (e.g. in Toronto). The existing architectural aspects therefore guided the material arrangements of such confinement and any interior alterations that may have been made for this purpose. Inside these disparate places, the main living spaces of the detainees (which I shall refer to as 'cells' in this chapter) are most often comprised of communal spaces intended to 'accommodate' several people. The propagation and generalisation of the policy of detaining foreign nationals since the beginning of the 1990s in Europe (MIGREUROP 2017) and even more markedly at the beginning of the twenty-first century throughout the world (Flynn 2014; Nethery and Silverman 2015) have resulted in new dedicated structures being built, for example, in the states that have become members of the European Union since 2004. Collective confinement has continued to be the norm in such detention facilities.

The political will to distinguish places of detention for foreign nationals from prison establishments is also reflected in the use of specific terminology. The official names tend to euphemise their actual purposes and to 'normalise' the conditions that foreign nationals have to endure. Those names highlight supposed purposes of welcome, such as in the case of the 'first aid and reception centre' in Lampedusa (Italy); they also stress accommodation and housing, for instance, in the 'guest houses for foreigners' in Turkey. In the same vein, the cells are also called 'rooms' or 'dormitories'. This language that seeks to dissimulate the constraint is so powerful that it is repeated by the independent agencies that inspect places of deprivation of liberty, as well as by many researchers. Consequently, according to the most broadly used vocabulary, there are no 'cells' in detention centres.

In addition to such spin, there is relative ignorance of the interiors of these premises. Certain works in social sciences have alluded to the role of the material environment in the constraints exerted by the state on confined persons. In particular, they have demonstrated how the spatial layout and the resulting policing practices contribute to the definition, codification and legitimisation of administrative detention (Fischer 2017; Larsen and Piché 2009; Michalon 2015). The works devoted to architectural thinking concerning detention and the space taken up by the cells are nevertheless scarce. They emanate from critical architects who question the role of their discipline in migration policy. Indeed, it occurs that architects are called upon by governments to contribute to better social acceptance of confinement schemes, as was the case for the construction of the detention centre on Christmas Island in Australia (Grinceri 2016). In this case the authorities asked the architects to design a space that was as similar as possible to a domestic space (Anderson and Ferng 2013). While these available publications do not go into the details of the architectural projects and only give limited explanation of what detention cells resemble, they insist on the restricted participation by architects in the debates concerning reinforcement of immigration controls. They also reveal the political desire to 'dematerialise' detention through making it nearly impossible to obtain blueprints, photos or images. These places are just as 'undocumented' as the people within them (Chaks 2016).

This state of knowledge is in stark contrast with the profusion of thinking with regard to cells in prison environments. Indeed, cells have occupied a place of central importance in penitentiary and architectural theories on 'modern' prisons since the start of the nineteenth century. They have progressively been established as the basic spatial unit in western prisons (Besson 2018; Johnston this volume). Other than aiming to standardise detention conditions, cells were intended to make it possible, via isolation and separation, to carry out an initial mission of correction and then dissuasion (Johnston 2010, this volume). They then went on to play a broader security-based role (Cliquennois 2006). Today, this spatial unit is a focus for the discourse of humanising the conditions of imprisonment and the independent agencies that inspect places of detention are calling for the generalisation of individual cells. Social science research has, nonetheless, shown that its architecture is not sufficient in gaining understanding of the place occupied by cells in penitentiary projects. The everyday experiences of prison users show its central role. As such, cells are a common thread in the way that the different players in the prison world experience custody (e.g. see Milhaud and Moran 2013; Narag and Jones, this volume; Scheer 2016). There are a multitude of experiences of cells, influenced by many factors. Consequently, they comprise a social construct (Bony 2015).

Based on these results of research on prisons, it is via analysis of the experience of the two main groups of actors present in detention centres in Romania—namely, confined foreign nationals and police officers of the General Inspectorate for Immigration (*Inspectoratul General pentru Imigrări*, IGI)[1]—that I examine the role of cells in detention schemes. Indeed, they seem to act as a material and symbolic intermediary in the relations of power that characterise the confinement of foreign nationals. More specifically, they contribute to the tension arising from the clash between spatial restriction and domestication of space. This tension is used by the agents of the state to exert their power over the detainees.

The chapter elaborates on the tension between agency and getting detainees to participate to the power dynamics. To begin with, I analyse the manner in which the cell represents a central tool in carrying out their missions for the police officers who are in daily contact with the detainees. I then address the individual relations that the detainees have with this spatial unit in which they spend most of their time. The cell therefore appears as a contradictory space. On the one hand, its maintenance might be considered to give agency to the detainees. But, on the other, it appears as an insidious technique to get detainees to participate in a state-regulated version of what the 'good' behaviour should be. In that respect, the power dynamic is reverted back to the state.

## Researching Detention in Romania

The discussion focuses on Romania as a case study. Two detention centres for foreign nationals were opened in Otopeni and Horia near to Arad in 1999 and 2001, within the scope of negotiations for the country's admission to the European Union. They fall within the remit of the IGI and are intended for the confinement of three categories of foreign nationals: persons who are not or are no longer entitled to residence in Romania, persons who are considered to be a 'threat' to national security and public order, or persons who have received a criminal conviction accompanied by withdrawal of the right of residence and application of an expulsion order.

The two centres are split into several sub-sections. The zone reserved for detainees is made up of actual confinement facilities (cells and immediately adjacent corridors or walkways) and areas occasionally used by the detainees (canteen, courtyard and sports field, infirmary, etc.). Their architecture differs. One is structured around a central corridor that leads into the cells and communal areas; the police control room is located in the middle of this corridor. In the other, of panoptic arrangement, the cells are positioned opposite the control room behind two sets of metal gates and remain visible to the control room. At the time of this research, the first centre had a detention capacity of 160 people, while the other could confine 50 people.[2] Their cells share common features. They are designed for four people. They are sparsely equipped, featuring two bunk beds, a table and a few chairs, a wardrobe and a bathroom. The appearance is uncontestably evocative of a prison: the windows are barred, the doors have an eyehole, and the persons confined must ring a bell to call the police personnel. The first centre also includes cells for 12 people and two solitary confinement cells used to punish.

The empirical data was gathered in Romania over nine months in 2009, 2010 and 2014. I was authorised by the IGI to carry out the survey in the two detention centres, and I conducted interviews with detainees without a police presence or any specific form of surveillance. I was able to hold informal discussions with the personnel during their service and was also authorised to carry out a series of individual interviews with police officers. This data was enhanced by volunteer work performed over six months for a non-governmental organisation (NGO). I was authorised to conduct interviews with people assisted by the NGO on its premises, generally on several occasions and without any presence of NGO employees. I completed this work through interviews with officers of the immigration control schemes. The data analysed herein thus comes from interviews with approximately 30 foreign nationals who were in or had left detention and approximately 20 IGI police officers. At the time of the fieldwork, the detainees' group was largely male; only one woman who had been detained was interviewed. The staff of both centres was also largely male. The analysis developed here therefore concerns a very masculine context; it would probably be different if applied to a more feminised context.

## A Tool for Police Power

In some detention centres, the detainees are, when they leave their cells, in direct contact with the humanitarian workers coming to assist them (Fischer 2017) or the employees of private companies recruited for the maintenance of the premises (Tassin 2016). This is not the case in Romania, where only police officers are permanently present in the detainees' living areas and in physical and/or visual contact with them outside the cells. The cell can be considered a mode of control 'by the walls': the materiality is intended to facilitate the monitoring of prisoners by confining them. The staff are consequently available for other tasks (Demonchy 2004). However, police officers also hold prerogatives which necessarily involve cellular space. Police work appears to be grounded on diverse uses and values of the cell.

### A Space of Categorisation and Assignment

As with any place of deprivation of liberty, arrival at the detention centre is followed by an 'admission ceremony': one of the processes of 'mortification' (Goffman 1961) designed to transform the foreigner into a 'detainee'. This is grounded in a series of physical, administrative and spatial operations: full search, medical examination, then processing of a file by a policeman who allocates the new detainee's cell and bed. Cell assignment strategies differ from one institution to another. In some, detainees can express their preference (Bosworth 2014). In Romania, the police allocate foreign nationals to the cell spaces. In doing so, they impose both a social order (through categorisation) and a spatial order (through distribution) inside. During the fieldwork, the two centres were under-filled. It could allow for individual occupation of the cells. Nevertheless, the managers of the facilities preferred collective occupations. Their choice highlights some concerns of the police and their will to facilitate surveillance by concentrating detainees in space. Indeed, staff were mobilised on tasks outside the detention area as such.

The policy of collective occupation of cells is also a way of materialising the influence of the state on individuals by forcing them to cohabit with strangers. The allocation of detainees to cells—an 'art of distributions' (Foucault [1977] 1995: 141)—appears to be common practice at detention centres for foreign nationals (e.g. see Bosworth 2014; Martin 2012). It is based on different types of categories: official (undocumented foreign nationals, convicted foreign nationals; men, women or families) or unofficial ones. The latter may be due to the staff's cultural or racial stereotypes. For if, in some countries, staff of detention facilities are trained on ethnic and cultural issues and on how to mobilise them in their duties (Khosravi 2009), this is not the case in Romania. A policeman admitted that 'before we didn't know anything about this and it all comes with experience' (Interview, policeman, 2010).[3] Experiences involving grouping together or separating detainees according to categories are part of a learning curve in the day-to-day task of monitoring.

As in other detention centres (Fischer 2017), officers are careful to avoid regrouping in cells that could lead to conflict or protest movements. Conversely, they try to enable relationships that may contribute to calming detainees. As often as possible, people categorised as being from a same cultural or religious group are put together; groups considered by the police officers to have potentially problematic relationships are kept separate:

> Everyone from the ex-Soviet states has problems with coloured people. Therefore, we make sure that they come into contact very infrequently. For example, we don't put them in the same cells. (Interview, policeman, 2009)

When assigning a bed to a new detainee, police officers also take into account the detainee's previous custodial experiences, be they in prisons or detention centres. These past experiences are judged in an ambivalent way. They can be considered to be a stabilising influence:

> Detainees with a previous prison background have a positive effect on the others because they are used to prison, and can explain that a detention centre is not a prison. They help to maintain a balance in the group since they are already acclimatised. (Interview, policewoman, 2010)

However, these prior custodial experiences are also seen as a potential source of tensions. The hypothesis of possible 'cross-contamination' from criminal convicts to other foreign nationals legitimises the police to enforce surveillance: 'They can transfer problematic behaviour to others and teach them things they have learnt in prison that cause problems' (Interview, policeman, 2010). Those detainees are seen as able to introduce 'a kind of dangerous criminal expertise … that can cause friction with police officers, and be at odds with the ideal picture of a placid and accommodating detainee' (Hall 2012: 102). The distribution of detainees in cells is a social and spatial assignment; it is therefore a political choice. It materialises some of the rationales of police work. The cell space participates in an eminently concrete way in relations of power between detainees and staff.

## Cellular Regime and Surveillance

The functions of cellular space in police work go beyond social and spatial distributions and assignments. They determine the monitoring through time management and the imposition of (in)visibility regimes. The experience of the cell is closely intertwined with the schedules of the prisoners (Milhaud 2017) and those of the guards. The detention regime differs significantly between the two facilities in Romania. In one of them, the detainees can only go out three hours a day to eat in the canteen and to move around freely in the common areas. Here the facility's walls are largely entrusted with 'guarding' the detainees; rendering foreign nationals invisible behind the cell walls is the principle that prevails here. Meanwhile, the police officers carry out other tasks. Their day-to-day surveillance activities consist of the opening and closing of the cell doors at the scheduled times, the accompaniment and monitoring of movements in and possibly outside the premises and responding to calls by means of the eyehole fitted to all cell doors. In the morning and evening, they open the cells to count the detainees. In this facility, surveillance mainly involves rendering the detainees invisible during most of the day.

In the other centre, detainees can leave their cell and walk on a corridor closed by railings for most of the day. They can also access a 'leisure' room, located on the lower floor, during the afternoon but have limited time to go out into the courtyard. Here, the surveillance is based on visibility and visual monitoring. This centre is organised on a principle of panoptic architecture, according to which the staff must be able to see what is going on in the cell, which this policeman expresses when he explains that the cell doors remain open during the day because:

> people shouldn't be left alone, and we should always be able to see everything they do … including when it is too quiet. That is when we have to go make sure everything's OK—even if we only go into the corridor. Although they are constantly observed and monitored, people must have their privacy … You need to show you're vigilant, but in as pleasant a way as possible. Detainees must have respect for their privacy, but also know they cannot do whatever they want because they are being watched. (Interview, policewoman, 2010)

However, the doors of the cells are metallic and opaque—unlike the railings in the Benthamian project. Being able to see permanently into the cell means that the door must remain open all day long. The cell here is somehow a space of forced visibility.

The general cell regime may, however, be modified in cases of breaking of rules and regulations, disobeying of policemen's orders and altercations between guards and detainees or amongst detainees. The cell serves to reaffirm police power. In one centre, the person to be punished is transferred to a different floor so that they no longer come into contact with their fellow detainees. In the other centre, the punishment depends on the gravity of the alleged acts: 'The decision to resort to force is only made gradually, and when violence has occurred. Otherwise, we go through a series of stages' (Interview, policeman, 2010). In less serious cases, detainees are kept locked in their cell all day long. For a greater degree of conflict or wrongdoing, policemen can lock the detainees into isolation cells, which are located in the immediate vicinity of 'normal' cells. Solitary confinement cells are commonplace in detention centres. It confirms that foreign nationals' control schemes rely on punitive mechanisms, that the persons under control experience them as punishment and that this alters the notion of justice, as theorised elsewhere (Bosworth, 2012, 2017).

## Imposed Domestication?

The cell can be considered to be of central importance in the work of police officers because it transforms the exercise of power. As emphasised by Milhaud and Moran, the absence of privacy is both a prerequisite and a form of punishment in custodial settings (Milhaud and Moran 2013). Privacy is generally defined by the ability to be alone, at least occasionally (Dirsuweit 1999). An analysis of police work in Romanian detention centres shows that the role of cell space is actually more complex than having or not having the possibility to be alone. The guards describe the cell space as a private space and frequently use the issue of privacy to justify their actions. One could therefore consider, at first sight, that the police grip weakens where the recognition of a private space for the detainees could arise. However, this apparent limitation of surveillance goes with subtle changes of the ways of imposing power over detainees.

First, although police officers are the only ones to be allowed to open and close cell doors, they end up setting limits within areas that come within their remit. The threshold of the cells has a particular symbolic importance. Police officers say that they do not enter cells except when necessary: 'the cells, those are private spaces'. They count detainees from the threshold of the door. The cell door is said to be only crossed for certain reasons (search, conflict between foreign nationals, riot, etc.). However, this practice remains ambiguous: when called by the bell, the guards look inside the cell through the eyehole and talk to detainees through the door. The argument of the private character of this space can be used to keep the cell closed and to make use of the technical objects that incarnate the state's power in the first place.

On a second level, the police discourse about the cell as a private space also expresses what is presented as tolerance vis-à-vis the modifications made to the layout of the cells by the detainees. The director of a centre takes as an example the use of blankets as a prayer rug by the Muslims, a practice which he says he accepts. He explains his tolerance by the issue of privacy: 'It is also a question of privacy. It would be wrong for me to interfere' (Interview, policeman, 2010). Tolerance is, in this case, a relational technique of pacification in detention. As such, it may be considered as a layer of 'soft power', 'made up of both staff-prisoner relationships' and 'that exert influence in relatively light, subtle and disembodied ways' (Crewe 2011: 460).

If these practices are tolerated, it is because they go hand in hand with a third use of the privacy issue by the police. The detainees are responsible for cleaning and tidying their cell and guards check this every morning: 'they are private spaces, I can't ask the cleaning women to take care of them' (Interview, policeman, 2010). The social functions of housework, however, go beyond the issue of privacy. 'It's their place; they have to look after it themselves. It's not a hotel here' (Interview, policeman, 2010): these words show how power is enacted through the obligation to treat the cell space as a domestic space, a private space that is maintained and appropriated. Here the process is similar to that analysed by Pugliese with regard to the detention of foreign nationals in hotel rooms in Australia, which, by making the hotel a place for the power of the state, obliterates the distinction between the custodial and the vernacular (Pugliese 2009). In Romania, the police injunctions to clean the cell space obfuscate voluntarily the line between custodial space and domestic space.

In the detention centres of Romania, the cell is an unavoidable space of police work. The way police officers use it highlights the importance of materiality in the exercise of power, beyond a sole function of holding. The cell is the material support for the social assignment of detainees and for their surveillance. But it is also a way to disguise power relationships. Under the pretext of the respect of their privacy, the detainees are driven to treat the cell like a domestic space. What the police do with the cell partly determines how the detainees live there. What do they do with the injunction to 'domesticate' a space of constraint? Does it hold potential for detainees, or is it just an instrument of domination?

## Domestication of the Cell Space and Upholding of the Institution

Detained foreign nationals spend most of their time in the cell. The personalisation practices in this space are often analysed as means of adaptation or even of resistance, the cell thus being considered as a 'refuge' (Milhaud 2017). However, despite the architectural homogeneity of the cells and even if the guards keep repeating 'They're at home here', the relationships of detainees to this imposed spatial unit prove very heterogeneous. They are situated between low personal investment and a negotiated order. They reflect the discretionary power of institutional actors. The domestication of the cell can only operate within the margins tolerated by the police—and as another layer of 'soft power'.

### A Not-So-Much Appropriated Space

During the fieldwork, the cells observed from the door threshold[4] are hardly modified by their occupants. The guards confirm that few detainees modify their cells. The foreign nationals themselves express only mild criticism of the fitting out of cells, described as 'not so bad as all that'. Space is minimal and detainees are in close proximity, but material conditions are not criticised much because 'we know it's not a hotel here'. Similar to the situation in penitentiaries (Baer 2005; Narag and Jones, this volume), only a minority of detainees has the will, the time and the means for modifying and personalising cell space. In prison, the relationships with the cell vary according to various parameters such as the age of the prisoner, his/her social background, his/her previous experiences and particularly his/her residential and prison experiences (Bony 2015). In detention, three factors seem to explain that few detainees transform the cell space.

First, the sudden nature of the arrest and the lack of explanation about being placed in detention and in a particular cell are felt as particularly violent:

> The policemen didn't ask me any questions or explain anything to me. They just arrested me, brought me some sheets,[5] and said "This is your home" and shut the door. (Interview, former detainee, 2009)

They usually have few personal belongings seeing as arrests are made by surprise: in the street, at their place of work or on the IGI premises, or even during a border crossing. They are largely devoid of personal possessions when they enter the detention centre, and even less so when they enter their cell, where money and other goods are forbidden, according to the technique of 'stripping' (Goffman 1961). However, counterbalancing this way of imposing power depends in part on the possibility of having access to other objects, which few detainees manage to do.

The second reason for the low investment of detainees in the cell is that detention centres are transit places. In 2009 and 2010, foreign nationals remained on average 18 and 20 days in detention,[6] making these places 'inevitable motels', as Michel Foucault said (2001). Moreover, there is a high turnover of detainees which does not occur smoothly and makes the domestication of the cell difficult. The relation to cell space is constantly redefined according to new arrivals and departures. In such a context of short timescales, the detainees most likely to personalise their cells are those who spend several weeks or months there, and this represents a clear minority of the population.

Finally, the cells of the Romanian detention centres are characterised by the very small number of activities that detainees have the right to conduct there. The few daily activities take place outside the cell: meals are taken in a canteen, leisure takes place in collective rooms or outside (e.g. at the time of the fieldwork, cells were not equipped with televisions), the visitors are met in visiting rooms. The cell is the space for its maintenance, phone calls[7] and sometimes cell-to-cell discussions. Detention is also characterised by the low number of activities available to detainees, which limits the interest of leaving the cell. Thus, while in some prison cells there are 'dos and don'ts' organised according to the multitude of activities that are practised in that special space (Bony 2015), cells in detention centres are barely modified and adapted because of the emptiness of time spent there. The cell space determines boredom (Knight 2016) as much as it reveals it. The cell remains for most detainees a space of constraint, lack, transit and boredom. The depersonalisation of space intended by the institution (Baer 2005) works here fully.

## Unequal and Negotiated Domestication of the Cell

Some foreign nationals, however, change the layout and decorate their cell. They all stayed for a long time in the Romanian detention centres and managed to be granted individual cells after negotiations with the police (Michalon 2015). A long presence in the facility and good relations with the police are determining factors for the practical and symbolic relationships with the cell. Vernacular objects play a major function here. They are very few and standardised from one cell to another and are the means of an investment that makes the cell habitable. The material changes of the cell highlight two registers of power.

The bed is of central importance for the domestication of the cell. It is the detainees' only personal space, which they do not have to share. Fellow detainees are not allowed to sit or lie down on anyone else's bed. Although informal, this rule appears to be broadly shared and the guards say they ensure it is respected. The bed is the space-time continuum for withdrawal and return to oneself: 'It's very hard when it's time to go to bed. You think about several things, including the day when you will leave' (Interview, former detainee, 2009). Faced with the process of de-individualisation and objectification of foreign nationals by the detention policy (Hall 2012), the bed is also the one space that helps them to find a bit of privacy:

> During the day we lay stretched out on the bed and wait … If you are doing well inside your head, you like to have company. Otherwise you don't. That is why people remain silent most of the time. (Interview, detainee, 2009)

If the detention is long term, the bed can be appropriated and become a vector for self-affirmation. An old detainee, having spent five years in prison and then two years in a detention centre, explained how he had moved the beds in order to create a more private space in the cell he occupied on his own. As in other prisons and detention centres, where cohabitation with strangers is obligatory and marked by promiscuity and lack of space, beds seem to be the most important items in appropriation strategies for cell space (Buslé and Morelle 2014; Dirsuweit 1999). Some hang sheets or covers around the lower bunk beds to hide themselves from sight. This search for privacy runs through custodial environments, whatever their architecture resembles. For instance, prisoners in French prisons built on a cell model, say they feel a complete lack of privacy and use spatial strategies to find or create private spaces; the same is true for prisoners in Russian prisons, who are locked up in communal detachment blocks (Milhaud and Moran 2013).

Some detainees, although more rarely, decorate their cells as a way of taking them over. A foreign national who spent two years in one of the establishments described his living space and insisted on the fact that he had put a map of Romania and a calendar on the wall, where he crossed off a date every day at noon. He emphasised how dirty the cell was when he arrived and the small arrangements he had been able to make. Not only did he tell this with pride, but he explained that 'You feel better that way; you feel a bit like you're at home, and you do what you want' (Interview, former detainee, 2009). Another person, whose detention lasted six months, also seemed proud to explain that his cell was 'different from other people's' (Interview, former detainee, 2010). He cleans it carefully every day and arranges various small objects around it that he had in his luggage or had asked visitors to bring. Very pious, he lays out religious books on a small table. A carpet taken from a common room adds a final touch. Religious objects are exchanged between detainees and between detainees and staff, as in prisons (Rostaing et al. 2014).

Small re-arrangements and decoration of cell space do not just improve everyday life during detention, making 'one's own territory' possible (Sibley and Van Hoven 2009: 202). As in prisons (Baer 2005), any additional vernacular objects are mostly donated by outside visitors, who generally do not come empty-handed. Various items, clothes and cigarettes are given to detainees to improve their everyday life, after being subjected to checks and approval by the management. Asking relatives or acquaintances to bring objects forges a link with the outside, both on a social and a material level. The setting of the cell thus reveals the social disparities between detainees: only those who have spent long enough in Romania, or who have strong links with travelling companions, benefit from these material circulations.[8]

The objects brought from outside generally remain in the facility when their owner is released. The connections made inside are useful for re-arranging cells. I often heard of a Koran circulating from one cell to another. Two young Afghans sharing the same cell were able to organise a prayer corner: 'An Iraqi gave us his carpet, he spent two years here and his friends brought him things from the outside' (Interview, former detainee, 2010), which he gave them upon release. The circulation of objects between detainees shows that those who have the means to personalise their cell are those who have external relationships and/or can negotiate with the staff. Most of the detainees are therefore excluded from these exchanges, which benefit those who bear the brunt of the detention policy and spend a long time in the detention centres.

On a second register, domestication practices are at the heart of negotiated power relations, rather than at the core of resistance. The circulation of objects and the changes in the furniture are limited to what is tolerated by the police, who monitor the daily state of cells.

As previously noted, the upkeep of cells is not the duty of the guards but that of their occupants. The detainees know that guards confer considerable importance to the state of cells. Ensuring that this space is clean, tidy or decorated is a means of being seen positively by the staff. A detainee who had spent two years in one of the establishments, and therefore was entitled to an individual cell, said that it was so well-maintained that he earned praise from the police and that the director of the establishment himself congratulated him. His cell was according to him the one shown when visitors came. Having a clean, decorated cell helps create a positive image with fellow detainees. Another foreign national, having spent time in both establishments, explained how he was able to obtain an individual cell, cleaning and arranging it according to his taste. He insisted on the fact that he made it so much more pleasant than the others that his fellow detainees came to visit him every day, taking care to remove their shoes and admiring the tidiness and decoration.

Objects generally circulate among foreign nationals, but also pass via the staff. The cells do not have television; however, in the context of inactivity and boredom experienced in detention, the right to watch TV means a great deal. It is sometimes possible to negotiate with guards to move the television from the common room to a cell: 'You know that when a prisoner has a TV in his cell, he has won!' (Interview, former detainee, 2009). Not only is television used as a privilege to reward detainees for their good behaviour and have them quiet in their cell, it is for detainees a means to minimise the psychological and emotive effects of confinement (Knight 2016). Likewise, the chairs are moved from the common areas to cells, where seating is not always provided. Aware of the lack of equipment in cells, police officers allowed this, while lamenting that 'Chairs can become weapons in case of a fight: the detainees throw them at others or bang them against doors, which is why almost all the chairs are broken' (Interview, policeman, 2010). Some conditions must however be respected by the occupants of the cells so that the tiny changes in the cell and the circulation of objects are tolerated: 'as long as it does not endanger other detainees or the staff, or is not disruptive, and as long as they respect the daily schedule and do not damage the cell' (Interview, policeman, 2009). Vernacular objects in cells, such as televisions, are supposed to lighten the burden of the custodial environment (Tassin, 2014); however, they express the coercive nature of detention by highlighting the social inequalities and hierarchies that run through it. These few examples lead to the conclusion that the police officers define the contours of the relations of the detainees with their cell; they allow them some room for manoeuvre as a means of pacification. Domestication of the cell occurs under control and works for the smooth running and maintenance of the institution.

## Conclusion

Contrary to what civilian terms such as 'room' or 'dormitory' imply, the elementary architectural unit of detention centres—the cell—is a place of power over the confined foreign nationals. It is an important instrument for the police officers who keep watch over the detainees on a daily basis, because some of their prerogatives can only be exerted by the material and symbolic intermediary of the cell. Since detention is characterised by a seminal ambivalence that seeks to distinguish it from imprisonment, the cell is also the medium for the discourse that wants to present it as a place of respect for the privacy of the detainees and thus provide the proof that the wellbeing of the persons confined is supposedly taken into greater consideration than in prison establishments. In fact, when it is possible, domestication of the cell is important for those who carry it out. It improves the living conditions inside the cell walls, as well as making it possible to possess a personal space that is necessary in maintaining a sense of self in the struggle against the depersonalisation imposed by the institution. However, the cell concretises the rationality of control. The majority of foreign nationals confined in these Romanian detention centres cannot personally engage in this space because the constraints weighing down on them fly in the face of any appropriation of the space. For the small number of persons confined who nonetheless succeed in doing so, domestication of the cell is only possible via negotiations with the police officers and within the limits that they set. Domestication of the cell therefore does not appear to be a process of emancipation, but rather a method for distinguishing and creating a hierarchy of the people confined. It proves to be a subtle but efficient way of maintaining order within the cell's walls. This reading of the cell invites us to analyse the role of space in the changing power in carceral settings and its evolution towards governmentality (Crewe 2011). There is, for instance, room for thinking what the cell is and means when confined persons are granted a greater right to mobility (Mincke 2017) and when the walls inside the facilities seem to lose their power.

**Acknowledgements** I thank Jennifer and Victoria for their careful review and stimulating advice on this chapter.

## Notes

1. The Romanian General Inspectorate for Immigration is part of the Romanian Ministry of Interior. Its staff is mainly composed of police officers, whose missions are exclusively dedicated to migration policy.

2. The second underwent considerable extension work in 2015 and now has a capacity of 160 places.
3. In order to preserve the anonymity of the interviewees, the locations of the interviews and the functions of the police officers are not specified.
4. The interviews in detention were conducted outside the cells, in visiting or meeting rooms. I was able to approach the cell space during visits to the centres or wandering in the corridors. I was allowed to enter unoccupied cells. I was not formally forbidden to enter occupied cells, but the police discourse on the private nature of this space was delivered to me from the very first moments in the centres and none of the detainees invited me to enter a cell. Therefore, I considered the cell threshold as the limit to my physical movements in the centres.
5. Foreign nationals receive blankets, sheets and some toiletries when they arrive in detention.
6. For a maximum length of detention of 6 months, extended to 24 months under certain circumstances. Information transmitted by the Romanian authorities.
7. Mobile phones were allowed at the time of the fieldwork, provided they did not include a camera.
8. Domestic space is highly gendered and detention in Romania is mainly a place for men. Though the data gathered didn't allow me to work on the issue of gender, there would be room for thinking about how the uses of the cell in detention takes part in shaping/reshaping gender roles and how the gender issue contributes to the micro-geography of this institution.

## References

Anderson, S., & Ferng, J. (2013). No Boat: Christmas Island and the Architecture of Detention. *Architectural Theory Review, 18*(2), 212–226.

Baer, L. D. (2005). Visual Imprints on the Prison Landscape: A Study on the Decorations in Prison Cells. *Tijdschrift voor Economische en Sociale Geografie, 96*(2), 209–217.

Besson, E. (2018). Quand la cellule devint la norme. Théories de l'architecture carcérale au XIXe siècle. *Métropolitiques*. Retrieved July 5, 2018, from http://www.metropolitiques.eu/Quand-lacellule-devint-la-norme-Theories-de-l-architecture-carcerale-au-XIXe.html.

Bony, L. (2015). La domestication de l'espace cellulaire en prison. *Espaces et societes*, 102–108.

Bosworth, M. (2012). Subjectivity and Identity in Detention: Punishment and Society in a Global Age. *Theoretical Criminology, 16*(2), 123–140.

Bosworth, M. (2014). *Inside Immigration Detention*. Oxford: University Press.

Bosworth, M. (2017). Immigration Detention, Punishment and the Transformation of Justice. *Social & Legal Studies, 28*(1), 81–99.

Buslé, T., & Morelle, M. (2014). Le lit, un objet entre contrainte et réaffirmation de soi. *Géographie et cultures*, (91–92), 153–174. https://journals.openedition.org/gc/3380.

Chaks, T. (2016). MLC 2015 Keynote: Undocumented: The Architecture of Migrant Detention. *Migration, Mobility, & Displacement, 2*(1). https://doi.org/10.18357/mmd21201615465.

Cliquennois, G. (2006). Vers une gestion des risques légitimante dans les prisons françaises? *Déviance et Société, 30*(3), 355–371.

Crewe, B. (2011). Soft Power in Prison: Implications for Staff–Prisoner Relationships, Liberty and Legitimacy. *European Journal of Criminology, 8*(6), 455–468.

Demonchy, C. (2004). L'architecture des prisons modèles françaises. In P. Artières, P. Lascoumes, & G. Salle (Eds.), *Gouverner, Enfermer* (pp. 269–293). Paris: Presses de Sciences Po.

Dirsuweit, T. (1999). Carceral Spaces in South Africa: A Case Study of Institutional Power, Sexuality and Transgression in a Women's Prison. *Geoforum, 30*(1), 71–83.

Fischer, N. (2017). *Le territoire de l'expulsion: La rétention administrative des étrangers et l'État de droit en France*. Lyon: ENS Éditions.

Flynn, M. (2014). How and Why Immigration Detention Crossed the Globe. *Global Detention Project Working Paper No. 8*. Retrieved July 5, 2018, from https://www.globaldetentionproject.org/how-and-why-immigration-detention-crossed-the-globe.

Foucault, M. (1995). *Discipline and Punish: The Birth of the Prison*. New York, NY: Vintage Books.

Foucault, M. (2001). Préface. In B. Jackson, *Leurs prisons. Autobiographies de prisonniers américains*. Paris: Plon, 1975 (texte n°144). In M. Foucault (Ed.), *Dits et écrits I. 1954–1975* (pp. 1556–1559). Paris: Gallimard.

Goffman, E. (1961). *Asylums. Essays on the Social Situation of Mental Patients and Other Inmates*. New York, NY: Anchor Books.

Grinceri, D. (2016). *Architecture as Cultural and Political Discourse: Case Studies of Conceptual Norms and Aesthetic Practices*. London: Routledge.

Hall, A. (2012). *Border Watch: Cultures of Immigration, Detention and Control*. London: Pluto Press.

Johnston, H. (2010). The Cell: Separation, Isolation and Space in the Architecture of the Birth of the Prison. *Prison Service Journal, 187*, 9–14.

Khosravi, S. (2009). Sweden: Detention and Deportation of Asylum Seekers. *Race & Class, 50*(4), 38–56.

Knight, V. (2016). *Remote Control: Television in Prison*. Basingstoke: Palgrave Macmillan.

Larsen, M., & Piché, J. (2009). Exceptional State, Pragmatic Bureaucracy, and Indefinite Detention: The Case of the Kingston Immigration Holding Centre. *Canadian Journal of Law and Society, 24*(2), 203–229.

Martin, L. L. (2012). Governing through the Family: Struggles over US Noncitizen Family Detention Policy. *Environment and Planning A: Economy and Space, 44*(4), 866–888.

Michalon, B. (2015). L'espace intérieur de la rétention. Policiers et retenus: travailler et habiter dans un lieu d'enfermement des étrangers en Roumanie. *Annales de géographie, 702–703*(2–3), 208–230.

MIGREUROP (Association). (2017). *Atlas des migrants en Europe: Approches critiques des politiques migratoires*. Paris: Armand Colin.

Milhaud, O. (2017). *Séparer et punir. Une géographie des prisons françaises*. Paris: CNRS Editions.

Milhaud, O., & Moran, D. (2013). Penal Space and Privacy in French and Russian Prisons. In D. Moran, N. Gill, & D. Conlon (Eds.), *Carceral Geographies: Mobility and Agency in Imprisonment and Migrant Detention* (pp. 167–182). Farnham: Ashgate.

Mincke, C. (2017). Prison. Legitimacy Through Mobility? In J. Turner & K. Peters (Eds.), *Carceral Spaces: Interrogating Movement in Incarceration* (pp. 236–249). London: Routledge.

Nethery, A., & Silverman, S. J. (2015). *Immigration Detention: The Migration of a Policy and its Human Impact*. London: Routledge.

Pugliese, J. (2009). Civil Modalities of Refugee Trauma, Death and Necrological Transport. *Social Identities, 15*(1), 149–165.

Rostaing, C., de Galembert, C., & Béraud, C. (2014). Des Dieux, des hommes et des objets en prison. *Champ pénal/Penal field, XI*. Retrieved July 11, 2018, from http://journals.openedition.org/champpenal/8868.

Scheer, D. (2016). *Conceptions architecturales et pratiques spatiales en prison. De l'investissement à l'effritement, de la reproduction à la réappropriation*. PhD thesis, Free University of Brussels.

Sibley, D., & Van Hoven, B. (2009). The Contamination of Personal Space: Boundary Construction in a Prison Environment. *Area, 41*(2), 198–206.

Tassin, L. (2014). Ne cassez pas ce qui vous profite. *Champ pénal/Penal field [En ligne], XI*. Retrieved July 11, 2018, from http://journals.openedition.org/champpenal/8851.

Tassin, L. (2016). Les frontières de la rétention: genre et ethnicité dans le contrôle des étrangers en instance d'expulsion. *Critique Internationale, 72*(3), 35–52.

# 9

# A Family Cell: Visual Ethnography in a Prison 'Mothers' Section'

Rossella Schillaci

**Fig. 9.1** A 2-year-old child inside the prison 'nursery'. (Source: Schillaci (2016))


J. Turner, V. Knight (eds.), *The Prison Cell*, Palgrave Studies in Prisons and Penology,
https://doi.org/10.1007/978-3-030-39911-5_9

## Introduction

There are conflicting views about whether children should be permitted to reside in prison. One of the first international studies on children in prison states:

> in the absence of other (or better) options, mothers deprived of liberty very often prefer and choose to keep their babies and small children with them while in custody … It is an accepted but frequently controversial practice in many countries. The opinion whether this is in the best interests of the child varies, resulting in different approaches and policies being undertaken in different countries. (Alejos 2005: 2)

In June 2000, the European Parliamentary Assembly adopted a recommendation in which it recognises the adverse effects of imprisonment of mothers on babies. The recommendation goes on to state that 'early maternal separation causes long-term difficulties, including impairment of attachments to others, emotional maladjustment and personality disorders', and that the development of young babies is hindered by restricted access to varied stimuli in closed prison (Parliamentary Assembly of the Council of Europe 2000: 1). However, many European prisons have adopted a policy of compromise accepting that, while the prison environment is generally unsuitable for children, it may be in the child's best interests for very young children to remain with their mother rather than be separated (Caddie and Crisp 1997). There is also consideration of the need for a 'distinct' or 'gender-specific' approach to respond to the vulnerabilities of imprisoned women (Booth et al. 2018) and to the impact

R. Schillaci (✉)
University of Lisbon, Lisbon, Portugal

The University of Texas at Austin, Austin, TX, USA

University of Turin, Turin, Italy

Azul Film, Torino, Italy

of the emotional aspects of motherhood (regardless of whether they have their children with them) (Pryce 2015).

As a result of these discourses, and in order to protect the bond between mother and child, Italian law allows imprisoned mothers and their children to reside together in designated low-security facilities (called ICAM[1]) or in protected family units.[2] However, the law does not guarantee financial coverage for the building of these facilities. As in other southern European countries, in Italy there are still very few separate jails for mothers and children. Some prisons have sections called the 'nursery' where the cells are larger than the standard ones and can hold up to two mothers and their children (Robertson 2012). According to an Italian law of 1975, these sections must be located on the ground floor and have access to a garden or a green area where the children can play outdoors.[3] However, due to lack of necessary funding, in Italy very few prisons have such features. Currently, there are still only four of these facilities in four different regions of the country (Scandurra 2017). Imprisoned mothers who reside in regions without them are permitted to keep their children in prison inside the old 'nursery' sections until they reach three years of age (see Fig. 9.1).When the child reaches this age, it is separated from the mother and either placed in the care of a family member (if they are able) or a foster care family, or else relocated to a residential care home for children (Scharff-Smith and Gampell 2011).

Accordingly, this particular situation of children in imprisonment raises several questions. Most notably, we might consider: What are the problems of raising children inside prison? What strategies do mothers adopt in response to these? How do they use the spaces of the prison (and in particular the cell) as part of these strategies? Consequently, this chapter explores how mothers in Italy 'do time' with their children. First, this chapter outlines the visual ethnographic approach that was used to generate research data before outlining the contribution that interrogates the relationship of mother and child with the prison cell. Here, I provide details of the daily routine of life in the Mothers' section before exploring the cell as a space for play, for familial intimacy and as a site of contestation for 'home'-making before, finally, concluding with a discussion around the extent to which mothering can take place within the prison cell.

## Research Motivations and Strategy

In 2012, I took part in a baby massage course held in a crèche near the correctional facility in my city, Turin, in Italy with my son. This nursery school was also 'attended' by children of incarcerated mothers. The mothers were not authorised to go outside the prison, but their children could attend the nearby crèche for a few hours a day, thanks to a private foundation that paid two educators to accompany them to and from the prison (see Fig. 9.2). There were seven children of incarcerated mothers of different nationalities, and they could play happily with other children in a colourful and bright environment. At the time, I was unaware that infants can live with incarcerated mothers inside prison. Because I had just become a mother and I had a baby infant with me, this situation echoed with me for a long time. I often reflected on how those women experienced their motherhood behind bars, isolated for 24 hours a day with no other family members to help them. These feelings were also compounded by the lack of academic research in this area at that time,

**Fig. 9.2** Children with their educators going back into Turin prison from the 'outside' nursery. (Source: Schillaci (2016))

which inspired my decision to study the 'Mothers' section' in Turin prison. My objectives were to examine the experience of motherhood and early childhood in conditions of imprisonment. The first general questions raised when I was planning the research were: How are the practicalities of motherhood modified inside the space of a prison? Which strategies do the mothers adopt to build an intimate relationship in the controlled prison environment? And, how do children perceive the modified space-time of the prison?

I adopted a two-phased visual ethnographic approach, which eventually resulted in the production of a feature length observational documentary, which was released four years later with the title *Ninna Nanna Prigioniera* (*Imprisoned Lullaby*)[4] (Schillaci 2016). My approach comes from the participant observation method used in ethnographic film work, as conceptualised by David MacDougall (1998) and Jean Rouch (2003), among others. In the first phase of research, I followed the principles of visual anthropology (Hockings 2009) by working to build a relationship with the inmates[5] and to observe their everyday living conditions. However, as written by Frois during her research in a female prison, it is difficult for officers to accept the idea of 'hanging around' engaging in informal conversations (Frois 2017: 3). In my case, I noticed how it was also difficult for most prisoners to accept the idea of just being 'observed': they wanted to speak and they often requested to be 'interviewed'. Accordingly, I listened carefully to all their accounts: about the difficulties of raising children inside small cells with malfunctioning bathrooms and broken windows, about the lack of possibilities to cook what their children liked most and about how to distract them in the long afternoons or weekends when they do not go to school or cannot play outside. It must be noted that the time I could spend inside the jail was limited. Although authorised by the Prison Director and the Manager of the 'nursery section', the authorisation lacked written formal indication about times or locations that would dictate my research activities. Therefore, I was treated like an ordinary 'visitor' by the guards[6] and obliged to follow the same rules: I could stay inside the prison only for a few hours a day, and often only in a common area in the corridor and not inside the cells.

However, it was unusual for mothers and children to remain in a common space such as the corridor. Their everyday life was primarily inside the

**Fig. 9.3** Children saying hello through bars at 8:00 pm when they got locked. (Source: Schillaci (2016))

cell, and if I wanted to observe their activities in prison—and not simply interview them—research only in the corridors was insufficient. As a consequence, six months later, I asked for a second authorisation to access cell space and for longer periods of time. I asked also to start my visual research, bringing with me all the equipment for the film-making such as the camera and the microphones, as well as a camera operator to assist with this task. Consequently, in this second phase, I was authorised to follow all the everyday activities of the families from 8:00 am when the cell doors were opened until 8:00 pm when inmates and their children were locked again inside the cell for the night (see Fig. 9.3) for a further six months.

Following Jewkes' approach of using autoethnography and emotion in prison research (Jewkes 2012), I kept a diary in order to better understand how the rules of a closed system such as a jail applied to both myself and the people who lived and worked in this space. Indeed, one of the guards once told me quite sincerely that from the moment I passed through the entrance door I should consider myself 'in custody' like the inmates, because they were in charge of my security. My position as a researcher was quite complex. As Jewkes writes, 'our personalities, histories, and emotions penetrate our research' (Jewkes 2014: 387). I believe being a mother helped me in the difficult process of establishing the relationships with inmates: in fact, as mothers, they felt understood and never judged. In addition, being both a parent and an ethnographer helped me in the observation and deciphering of the situations that I encountered. At the time of the research, my son was the same age as some of the children inside the prison. I could not avoid making comparisons between the attitude and the behaviour of the children 'inside' with his that was 'outside'. My feelings were quite disturbing but, instead of trying to remove or ignore them, I decided to write down and use my reactions in the attempt to analyse them and discover why they were negatively affectingly.

Accordingly, throughout this experience, I questioned my positionality frequently (Bonifacio and Schillaci 2017). I was, after all, spending time inside a prison but was decidedly happy to be there, as I thought it was the only way to make a good observational film. After a while, though, coming back home at night paradoxically became harder and harder, as I began to find it difficult to reconcile the privilege of spending time in such different worlds. Jennifer Sloan and Serena Wright (2015) write about the difficulties of not only gaining access to prison but also of 'getting out' when the time comes to leave the field behind. In some ways, we—that is, myself and the camera operator—felt greatly embarrassed to leave in the evening after one full and intense day spent with the mothers and the children. A deep sense of guilt plagued us when the guards locked the cell of the people we had been freely talking to only five minutes previously, and, when after 8:00 pm, we could merely converse between the bars. We needed a long period of 'decompression', before being able to come back to our 'normal' lives and houses, to forget all of the small moments of humiliation and violence we witnessed (moreover without being able to change it or saying anything) and all the suffering we listened to, to re-adapt to different rules of behaviour between human beings. As Sloan and Wright underline, 'getting out—and getting away mentally intact is an important process that is rarely discussed in the research literature' (Sloan and Wright 2015: 153). For me, working on the structure of the film helped significantly in responding to this challenge of 'getting out'. It took me almost a year to watch all the footage. Building a narrative that was sufficiently able to summarise the results of the project and represent the point of view of mothers and children took another two years. More than that, the long process of editing helped me to examine my personal experience 'inside', especially from the emotional perspective, and finally 'get out' of prison.

## Turin Prison and the Routine of the 'Mothers' Section'

The Turin prison is like a small town, built at the edge of the city, with several buildings inside. A white iron fence surrounds the prison area and divides it from the rest of the city space. Inside the prison, there are several buildings where inmates live, depending on what 'classification' they are or the project to which they belong (male, female, project for drug-addicted inmates and so on). Only one building is allocated to accommodate the female section. It has three floors and can accommodate 100 female inmates. On the second floor, two guards surveille all the cells on the floor, which is divided into two corridors that are secured at the end with a large, metal gate. The left corridor houses females from the general population, and the right corridor is designated as the section for mothers and children (see Fig. 9.4).

The location and the layout of the 'Mothers' section' is significant because it has substantial bearing upon the daily lives of mothers and

**Fig. 9.4** The corridor of the nursery section with the gate at the end. (Source: Schillaci (2016))

children. First of all, since it is on the second floor, children do not have access to a garden or a courtyard as prescribed by the law[7] because mothers are not authorised to leave the section and children cannot go unescorted. Secondly, as required by law, guards should spend more time inside the section in order to detect any problems that may affect the inmates and potentially weaken the mother-child bond. However, as the guards' 'station' is some distance from the section, and there is a requirement for them to check both the Mothers' section and the general female population section, the guards often find it difficult to leave their central position. Consequently, the children of incarcerated mothers are very much immersed in an adult prison, with very little respite from it.

In the Mothers' section itself, there are eight cells which open onto a large corridor. The cells are approximately 7–8 $m^2$ in size, with two single beds and two baby cots (see Fig. 9.5). Each cell can therefore accommodate up to two mothers with their children. However, if the section is not full, the mothers with more than one child are permitted to occupy one cell individually with their family. These cells were substantially bigger than the 'standard' cells occupied by the females in the general population corridor on the opposite side of the floor. There, cells were approximately 4 $m^2$ in size, accommodated two women, and there was just

**Fig. 9.5** The interior of a family cell. (Source: Schillaci (2016))

enough space for a bunk bed and a small table. By contrast to the Mothers' section, the doors in the standard female section were always closed. Women were not permitted to leave their own cell outside of the times allocated for receiving meals, showering and 'taking air'. All communications, including delivery of mail, were conducted within the cell space.

Once their children reach three years old and are no longer permitted to reside inside the prison, women are subsequently housed in the standard section. Those that had experience of these cells, such as Joy, reported that in comparison to the much smaller, more sparsely equipped standard cells, the mothers' cells were considered to be the 'five-star rooms' of the prison. However, in my experience, the connotation of luxury is far removed from the reality of these spaces. Despite the perception that this mothers' unit is considered more comfortable than others, there are significant signs of neglect and punitive architecture that signify this space as a prison. The women in the section find several strategies to carry on their everyday life in prison, first and foremost as mothers, in order to raise their children inside as best they can. In my opinion, they develop a form of psychological resilience, using different abilities to cope with the difficult situations they find inside prison and to protect their children from the negative effects of them (Robertson et al. 2015). As I will show, this approach is used to deal with the minutiae of everyday motherhood—that is, the small, ordinary everyday practices of washing, feeding and sending their children to sleep—that can become extremely difficult in a confined environment.

All domestic activities including eating, bathing and sleeping take place in the small space of the cell. The materialities of the prison cell were often prohibitive to family life. Aside from the beds, it is also furnished with some cupboards, a (often black and white) television and a small table. The prison bed linen, as women explained to me, was usually badly laundered. Mothers often did not want to let their children sleep in this bedding and asked relatives to bring linen from home (preferably brightly coloured, and alongside other comforts such as wool blankets and soft toys). All the windows in the cells and on the corridor have iron bars across them, but, during my research, every single window pane was broken. Usually mothers make basic repairs using handkerchiefs. An officer once told me that the prison lacks the money to get them repaired. As a consequence, the section is in a state of neglect: the lavatories are dirty, often broken and without running hot water; and the furnishings are made of rusty iron, as are the doors and the bars.[8]

The inmates' daily life is very repetitive: the days are all similar, punctuated by schedules imposed by the prison administration. As my research revealed, these schedules are not adequate for life with children. The day begins at 8:00 am, when an officer comes to open the heavy iron doors of each cell. The awakening can vary depending on who opens the cell. In some cases, a few words can be exchanged such as a simple 'hello' or, perhaps, an affectionate word addressed to the children. Other guards do not say anything at all. As soon as the door is open, the children—still in their pyjamas—seize the opportunity to rush out into corridor to meet each other. Often mothers find it difficult to bring them back inside the cell to wash and dress them. After the opening, the morning—as one mother said—'passes quickly', because mothers have many duties to address. First, they must wash and dress their children by 9:00 am, when two educators come to pick up the children and take them to the nursery outside the prison for the morning two or three times a week. The small bathroom is accessed via a metal door, which reveals a toilet bowl, a rusty, old bath tub and a sink (both with a single tap but without a plug, which makes it difficult to wash). Sink or bath plugs, in fact, are not permitted. Upon enquiry, I learned that this was apparently a result of one prisoner attempting suicide inside her bath tub. Although no prison officers could confirm this to me, the whole Mothers' section had no bath plugs. This action is one of the numerous unwritten rules, with no precise source, which officers follow in the prison that prisoners have to respect. In the case of the restriction on plugs, some mothers managed to obtain plastic basins from staff to bathe their children. For women with two children, bathing is additionally difficult: they are in charge of both of them and cannot ask anyone to help. Often, they go in the small bathroom with both children, because they cannot leave one of them alone in the cell: 'it's too dangerous for them', as one mother told me. Here, it is the relatively poor infrastructure of the cell that again has a bearing upon daily life.

Once the children have gone to the nursery outside, the mothers can have a quiet coffee, smoke a cigarette, talk with the other mothers and try to put the cell in some order until the children return at lunchtime. At 11:30 am, lunch is served from a cart by a female prisoner employed as a cook, but it is only for the adults. The children must only eat the food outlined in the menu prescribed by the prison paediatrician. This food is prepared by this same cook, and only after she has finished serving the entire women's section of the prison. This usually takes another hour, an hour spent trying to placate hungry children who want to eat from the adults' plates. As a consequence, mothers often refuse to take their meals to prevent them having to eat in front of their hungry children. Moreover, the space designed for meals causes several difficulties. In Turin prison, dining areas are not provided and prisoners have to eat at the small table inside their cells. The provision in the Mothers' section is no different. The cell furniture is awkward and not 'child-friendly'—for example, there are no 'high chairs' which make feeding easier—and so mothers have to encourage their children to adapt to eating whilst standing on the chair (see Fig. 9.6).

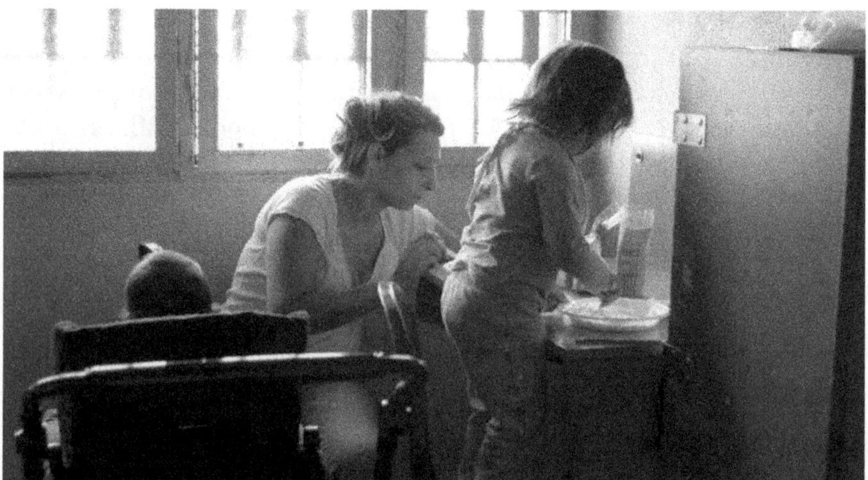

**Fig. 9.6** Child eating standing on the chair as she cannot reach the table. (Source: Schillaci (2016))

For the mothers I spoke to, mealtimes constituted one of the biggest problems of their daily lives and justified one of their most important demands: that is, to have access to the kitchen to be able to prepare the children's meals. Aside from responding to some of the aforementioned challenges, such provision would offer inmates the opportunity to eat in accordance with their different cultural traditions.[9] So far, this request has not been granted, mainly because of the opposition from the officers who think that a kitchen with knives and a heat source will be a source of danger for both mothers and children. Sometimes, with permission, some mothers prepare simple meals for their children themselves by using a small camping stove, one pan and few ingredients (see Fig. 9.7). Recipes such as fried bread are often firm favourites with the children. When cooking is permitted, the mothers typically convene and cook for the unit's children together. Here, they self-organise to ensure the safety of themselves and the children. These moments are precious for the mothers; they are the opportunity to approach a semblance of normal life, as they told me. However, these moments are exceptional because a routine of cooking cannot be assured: the gas bought at the prison store is

**Fig. 9.7** The table with the camping stove. (Source: Schillaci (2016))

expensive, the installation is precarious, and mothers are not permitted access to the fridge.

At 3:00 pm the officers announce—shouting from their position—the hour (although it is realistically often less than an hour time) outside where mothers and children can go in a small courtyard assigned for them. This courtyard is, however, not designed for children since there are no toys or play equipment. This leaves the children to simply run, back and forth, inside the four, grey, concrete walls. During winter, the climate of Turin often renders the hour outside impossible. In this case, all inmates—including their children—will not have the opportunity to go outside until the next day (weather permitting). Nearby there is a bigger yard where all the other women who do not have children inside spend their allotted hour outside. Mothers often told me that they would prefer to join the other women in that yard as it would be 'one hour of freedom' from the obligations of parenthood. Often, mothers have relatives in the general women's section, and this yard time would be a good opportunity to talk to someone—to speak about their problems, confide or exchange information—other than the same few mothers in their section, and not to be forced to have such conversations in front of the children. Unfortunately, for security reasons, children cannot mix, or even interact, with other inmates. On one rare occasion which I observed, where all the women prisoners gathered together to attend a special concert, some of the women did try to speak to and cuddle the children they knew. In this instance, rather than risk an outburst from the children, the officers turned a blind eye.

After this hour in the courtyard, a long and difficult period before bedtime begins. Here, there are many hours to fill with little entertainment. Most mothers wander the corridor, whilst the children amuse themselves by walking up and down on all fours or circling the corridor on a small tricycle, for example. The children often run in and out of the cells where they are then subject to many small reprimands: 'don't jump on the mattress because the bed is metal'; 'don't throw anything through the bars'; and 'be careful not to bump against the doors' especially against the one where the long corridor ends and which gives way to the territory of the officers. At 6:30 pm dinner arrives but this is, again, just for mothers. When the children's meal arrives an hour later, they often are tired and anxious. Shortly after, at around 8:00 pm, the officers come to lock all the families inside their cell overnight. Sometimes children cry because they want to keep playing together in the corridor. Mothers quickly put them into bed in their cramped cells. When night falls and the mothers try to prepare the children for rest, the prison around them does exactly the opposite. Cries redouble where men and women try to communicate by shouting from one building to another. All this theatre ignites the curiosity of the children who try to see what is happening through the bars of the windows. Mothers try to calm their children down by creating an intimate space under the sheets, offering cuddles, soothing words, or sometimes a sweet lullaby.

It is clear that the practicalities of both motherhood and childhood are significantly altered when women undertake parenthood whilst incarcerated. In the following sections, I explore the particularities of how the cell space exists as a space of play, as a space of familial intimacy, but also as a 'cursed' world that both mothers and children should never return to.

## The Cell as a Space of Play

In Turin prison, 'play' is poorly accommodated.[10] In the unit, there is a so-called playground area, created from a designated space in the corridor near to the gate, where there are some toys donated by volunteers.[11] However, the space is not well designed for play, and, annoyed by the noise, prison officers often scold the mothers, or even the volunteers, who are obliged to come back into the cells and try to distract the children with other toys. Aside from this small provision, the Mothers' section lacks any mode of entertainment and the environment is distinctly, as previously noted, not child-friendly and the materiality of the cell has significant impact. At a basic level, there are no carpets, rugs or mats in the section, and mothers often told me that the floor is too dirty and cold for children to play on. In response, mothers usually try to keep their children on the bed. Often this, in itself, presents other problems. More

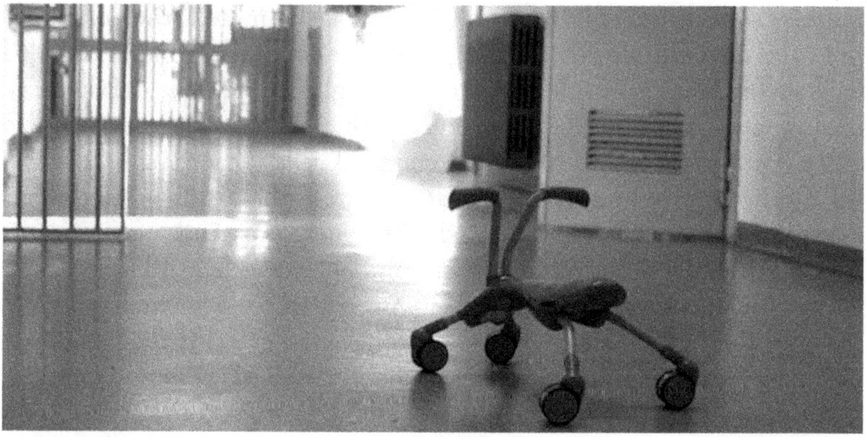

**Fig. 9.8** One of the tricycles used by children in the prison. (Source: Schillaci (2016))

than once I saw children rolling or jumping on the beds, at serious risk of injuring themselves on the metal bed frame. As noted, especially in the long afternoons, children play in the corridor with their small bicycles or tricycles (see Fig. 9.8) in order to, as one mother told me, give them at least a way to 'vent their energy'.

In this endeavour, children unavoidably crash against the doors of the open cells and often hurt themselves. For many of the mothers in this prison, iron was a key metaphor because it characterises prison life: iron beds, irons doors and gates and iron bars—all of which the children are contained by and can hurt themselves on (see Fig. 9.9). As a consequence, the mothers had to act in a way that they called 'keeping the child', which involves holding tightly on to children, containing them in their arms to prevent them from going outside the cell. Whilst in the corridor, mothers also have to keep their children within reach so that they do not try to run off as soon as the section gate is opened. I quickly realised that their major effort and strategy to the prison life was therefore this action of 'curbing' the child as a response to the constraints of the environment. I could understand these efforts only when I started the visual research and I was allowed to spend 10–12 hours with the mothers and their children.

**Fig. 9.9** A child in the corridor near all the iron windows open. (Source: Schillaci (2016))

Only then was I able to share the feeling of an 'eternal' day, with the never-ending difficulties of inventing new ways to allow the child play but also retain control of them.

In spite of all this, the children do not appear perturbed by their environment. Children's resilience has been conceptualised as a 'positive adaptation' to adverse situations (Hopf 2010). I was amazed to discover how they could accept so much time inside a building in comparison to my experience of other children of their age. Surprisingly, children adapt to this new 'home', finding a way to play everywhere and with everything. They devise new games from almost nothing. One of their favourite games was to take all the pencils, pens and every other small object they could find and throw them down through the small holes between

**Fig. 9.10** Children playing at the window. (Source: Schillaci (2016))

the window bars (see Fig. 9.10). They screamed with joy and satisfaction at the sight of an object landing outside the prison. When we came to make the documentary, our equipment bag was a treasure chest for them; we often had to recover batteries that had fallen through the window. Knowing this, and understanding how a culture of deprivation demands that these children adapt and respond in creative ways, I took to hiding a box of coloured pencils in the bag for them to use in their favourite game instead.

## The Cell as a Space of Intimacy

Beyond playtime, there are other aspects of family life that must be conducted within the prison environment: namely, development of personal relationships, family bonds and the enactment of private moments between parent and child. Communications and relations are considerably modified in this environment, and here I discuss how sound and the noise of the prison has significant bearing. The soundscape—the sonic environment as defined by Schafer (1993; see also Herrity, this

**Fig. 9.11** A mother speaking with a prisoner officer through the gate that closes her section. (Source: Schillaci (2016))

volume)—is a key aspect of prison life and has a big impact upon those who spend time there. Such is also the case in the Mothers' section in Turin, where the impact also extends to the children.

Turin prison is noisy, which in some locations is directly attributed to the design of the space. For example, as I have already described, a metal gate separates the Mothers' section from the landing space where the staff are located. Since staff have to observe two different corridors from this location, they rarely leave their station. This means that, in general, all conversations take place through the gate, at a distance between this barrier and the staff desk (see Fig. 9.11).

Such interactions are at a significant volume. Often, inmates speak loudly from their cells and officers reply back, shouting from their desk. The voice of someone calling: 'assistente' (officer) is a constant element in the prison sound experience. Inmates have to call several times before obtaining an answer from the officers, who usually cannot hear them if they have been forced to enter other corridors or relocate to other floors to deal with a particular request. The jangling of keys and the slamming of heavy, iron doors that are constantly opened and closed all add to the sonic experience alongside the guard's telephone ringing, TV audio, chatters and, more often, screams and cries of inmates, children and guards. This creates an uneasy feeling of being forced to be part of other people's private moments and not having your own space, especially in the spring and summer when the windows are all open.

Accordingly then, various strategies are required to undertake the quotidian, yet necessary aspects of motherhood and familial life. For example, every inmate knows that if she feels the need to cry, all the other women and officers of the unit will hear her. There are several strategies that allow 'visual' privacy in the cell: inmates often used sheets as curtains to provide more cover around the area near the bed, especially at night. However, this feeling of the complete sonic pervasion creates a different lack of privacy that is harder to overcome. The sound is all-encompassing: it infiltrates all the open windows and doors; it arrives suddenly, without time to prepare for it. The frustration of hearing people crying or shouting desperately, without knowing where exactly it comes from or what can be done to help, impacts everyone deeply but has the most impact on children, who were very sensitive to the cries of others. Several times when we were filming children playing in the corridor, we heard unexpectedly loud shouting, or even fighting, through the bars. Immediately, the children stopped what they were doing and repeated the sound that they heard: their toys were banged hard against the bars, and they start shouting back. Sometimes, the mothers try to transform this into play, but the children remain overexcited for a long time. Often, in contrast, if the children do hear people crying from the corridor, they stay silent, listening and trying to understand who is making the noise because they know some of the other inmates in the other sections. The pained screams spread and infect everyone's mood, which leads mothers to enact their maternal feelings to protect their children, soothe them and alleviate their concerns. Sometimes mothers take the children inside the cell, where they close their windows, hug the children and let them lie down on the bed in an attempt to relax them and create an affective refuge inside 'their' cell.

In recognising this ambiguous situation where the pains of imprisonment and the practicalities of motherhood both exist and conflict, the next section critiques life in the cell, as a 'cursed' environment, as mothers perceive it.

## The Cell as a 'Cursed' Place

Contrary to the long-term prisoners who may accept prison as a space of the 'home' (see also Marti, this volume), mothers know that the sentence they will serve inside the Mothers' section will be short. Most hope their status as mothers will lead to them being offered either a reduced term of sentence or an alternative method of custody, such as house arrest. If this is not forthcoming, when a child reaches three years old, they must be housed outside of prison, and the mother will move to the section that accommodates the general population of women.

Consequently, the mothers always reiterate that prison is a temporary location. For mothers, there is no acceptance of prison as 'home' both for themselves, but in particular for their children. To give an example, I once brought one mother some photographs of her children that were taken whilst they were in the nursery outside. She loved them but did not put them on the wall of her cell. I asked her why. She answered that she did not want her children to think that the cell was their home. For her, the time spent inside must not be indelible on her children's minds; instead, they must understand that they are merely waiting to go to their 'real' world, their 'real' home.

Goffman claims that, among inmates in total institutions, there is a strong feeling that time spent there is 'time wasted' or 'time taken from one's life' (Goffman 1961). This is true in the case of mothers who do not accept prison as 'home', but their attitude towards their children's experience is more complex. The time spent inside, as mothers explained to me, must not only never create associations of 'home' but also has to be deleted from their mind, 'as if it was just play' and not real life. Here, we find life in prison as an ambiguous existence between 'two worlds' (Agamben and Rueff 2007: 87). Although the educators told the mothers that children do not remember their first three years of life, one mother once told me that she was worried about exactly the opposite because her daughter had, to use her own words, 'witnessed too many tears'.

Such careful considerations about the potential negative attachments to prison cells continue throughout the process of leaving the prison. More than once, I assisted at the release of a prisoner at the end of her sentence. The situation was chaotic. The *liberante*[12] is often shocked, surprised and confused, particularly since little notice is offered—sometimes just one or two hours—about the imminent release. As soon as the other women get to know the good news, the confusion increases. The inmates in the same section rush to the woman who is about to leave, to offer hugs and kisses for her children and at the same time question the rationale for her release in the hope that the same fortune or 'miracle' might befall them in the future. All of them cry both for the joy of this woman and for the renewed hope in their life. The inmates in the other sections start to shout and to make noise with metal objects against the bars. Their screams and shouts echo around the building, and the result is ambiguously both a celebration and, at the same time, a protest. They all shout '*libertà*'—freedom—as if the conquest of one could become the triumph of all.

In this atmosphere the cellmates help the *liberante* to sort all of her possessions. This is where we witness most the tensions of crossing the threshold between 'two worlds', since this transition is often inhibited by the 'residue' of the previous life (Agamben and Rueff 2007: 87). Here, she must collect all her things from her 'life of outside'—from home—and find bags, usually big black plastic garbage bags, to pack them in. At the same time, she must ensure she leaves behind all the objects that come from the prison or have been donated by people connected to the prison. Once I tried to help a woman when I saw a pair of children's shoes had been left on the bed by putting them in the plastic bag alongside other possessions that were packed. For that, I was severely rebuked. The women explained to me that all personal property brought into prison from the outside has to leave with the owner; otherwise, a piece of them will stay in prison and she—or her children—could be 'cursed' and come back in prison. On the contrary, all the objects received in jail—like the pair of shoes—cannot be brought home because they are 'cursed' by the prison. This is as if the objects or 'remnants' from the prison cell were contaminated—or 'sacrilegious' in Agamben and Rueff (2007) words—and cannot stay in the other world, that is, the free world outside the prison.

## Conclusions

As outlined in this chapter, the prison cell—in its form within the Mothers' section—is not designed for children. Mothers must overcome several obstacles in raising their children in such a small place within the prison environment where they are obliged to follow its rules—some of them in evident contrast to children's needs. Therefore, mothers find particular strategies to cope with the minutiae of the everyday life, such as bathing, cooking, giving meals and putting a child to bed. Often mothers, but mostly children, develop a form of psychological resilience using different abilities to cope with the limited space of the cell where they have to live most of the days and night, sometimes for two or three years consecutively. Excluded from the rest of the community and from their families, mothers try to help each other and transform the realities of life in prison into 'playtime'. However, despite these efforts to instill comfort into their children's lives and change their perception of some harsh routines, the actions of the mothers are far from transforming the cell into a 'home'. Although they try to adapt to it, they do so with the clear intention of deleting every memory of life in the prison and the cell from their children's mind, hoping that no remnants of a world that, for them, is 'cursed' will survive.

Although, as I have noted, the cells in the Mothers' section have features such as size, furnishings and sanitation that are more suitable than the standard adult cells, life spent inside it with children is ultimately challenging. In illuminating these challenges and the subsequent resistances to them, this chapter presents reflections about the relationship between the prison cell and the experience of motherhood and childhood as a complex set of negotiations around materiality, legality and place-making. By exploring this example, we can raise further questions about the function of the prison cell in general and its role—for every prisoner—as an important space for building relationships and maintaining privacy, intimacy and dignity within a wider environment of restriction.

## Notes

1. ICAM, Istituto di Custodia Attenuata per Madri (Institute of Custody for Mothers).
2. Law n. 62 of 21 April 2011. The law provides that mothers with children up to six years of age may serve their sentences in custody on remand, at their place of residence, in an ICAM (a 'reduced custodial institution for mothers') or case famiglie protette (protected house for families) where the precautionary requirements of exceptional importance allow these alternative measures to prison.
3. Law n. 354 of 26 July 1975. For the care and assistance of children, the penitentiary administration must organise special kindergartens according to the procedures indicated in art. 19 of the Implementing Regulations—D.P.R. 30 June 2000.
4. The film *Ninna Nanna Prigioniera* had its premiere at the Biografia Film Festival in Bologna in June 2016, where it won the Life Tales Award. It has then presented in several other festivals, like the Cinema Verite Iran International Documentary Film Festival and the NAFA (Nordic Anthropological Film Association) Film Festival. A shorter version of the film, entitled *Les enfants en prison*, has been broadcast by ARTE television in 2016, and it won the Etoile de la Scam, recognition given to the best documentary films broadcast in France.
5. In the Italian language, the terms 'inmate' and 'prisoner' are synonymous and are usually interchangeable without any negative connotation.
6. In the Italian language, the terms 'guard' and 'officer' are also synonymous and are usually interchangeable without any negative connotation.
7. See note 3.
8. There is a new project underway to develop new 'mothers' prisons' in Italy where the designs include aspects such as only providing wooden

furniture and 'soft bars' made with metal mesh to avoid any injury to children.

9. The women housed in this prison represent several different nationalities and ethnicities. Often the cultural traditions associated with these extend to the conventions around and practicalities of dietary choice, cooking and eating. However, the prison environment does not always manage to accommodate such traditions.
10. See Stuit (this volume) for a different conceptualisation of 'play' in the prison cell.
11. Volunteers from NGOs come one afternoon a week for a few hours to play with the children. This makes it possible for mothers to receive visitors and meet with educators.
12. In Italian, this means the liberated person, which describes an inmate that will soon be released. Often this news is unexpected.

## References

Agamben, G., & Rueff, M. (2007). *Profanations* (Vol. 226). New York, NY: Zone Books.

Alejos, M. (2005). *Report on Babies and Small Children in Prisons*. Geneva: Quaker United Nations Office.

Bonifacio, V., & Schillaci, R. (2017). Between Inside and Outside: Projects of Visual Research Inside Italian Prisons. *Visual Anthropology, 30*(3), 235–248.

Booth, N., Masson, I., & Baldwin, L. (2018). Promises, Promises: Can the Female Offender Strategy Deliver? *Probation Journal, 65*(4), 429–438.

Caddie, D., & Crisp, D. (1997). *Imprisoned Women and Mothers*. Home Office Research Study 162. London: HMSO.

Frois, C. (2017). *Female Imprisonment: An Ethnography of Everyday Life in Confinement*. London: Palgrave Macmillan.

Goffman, E. ([1961] 2017). *Asylums: Essays on the Social Situation of Mental Patients and Other Inmates*. London: Penguin.

Hockings, P. (Ed.). (2009). *Principles of Visual Anthropology*. Berlin: Walter de Gruyter.

Hopf, S. M. (2010). Risk and Resilience in Children Coping with Parental Divorce. *Dartmouth Undergraduate Journal of Science, 12*(3). Retrieved from July 18, 2019, from https://sites.dartmouth.edu/dujs/2010/05/30/risk-and-resilience-in-children-coping-with-parental-divorce/

Jewkes, Y. (2012). Autoethnography and Emotion as Intellectual Resources: Doing Prison Research Differently. *Qualitative Inquiry, 18*(1), 63–75.
Jewkes, Y. (2014). An Introduction to "Doing Prison Research Differently". *Qualitative Inquiry, 20*(4), 387–391.
MacDougall, D. (1998). *Transcultural Cinema*. Princeton, NJ: Princeton University Press.
Parliamentary Assembly of the Council of Europe. (2000). Recommendation 1469. *Mothers and Babies in Prison*. Retrieved September 16, 2019, from http://assembly.coe.int/nw/xml/XRef/Xref-XML2HTML-EN.asp?fileid=16821.
Pryce, V. (2015). *Mothering Justice: Working with Mothers in Criminal and Social Justice Settings*. Hook: Waterside Press.
Robertson, I. T., Cooper, C. L., Sarkar, M., & Curran, T. (2015). Resilience Training in the Workplace from 2003 to 2014: A Systematic Review. *Journal of Occupational and Organizational Psychology, 88*(3), 533–562.
Robertson, O. (2012). *Children of Incarcerated Parents*. Geneva: Quaker United Nations Office.
Rouch, J. (2003). *Ciné-Ethnography*. Minneapolis, MN: University of Minnesota Press.
Scandurra, A. (2017). Il ritorno del sovraffollamento. *XIII Rapporto sulle Condizioni di Detenzione*. Retrieved September 16, 2019, from http://www.antigone.it/tredicesimo-rapporto-sulle-condizioni-di-detenzione/01-numeri-del-carcere/.
Schafer, R. M. (1993). *The Soundscape: Our Sonic Environment and the Tuning of the World*. London: Simon & Schuster.
Scharff-Smith, P., & Gampell, L. (Eds.). (2011). *Children of Imprisoned Parents*. Denmark: The Danish Institute for Human Rights, European Network for Children of Imprisoned Parents, University of Ulster and Bambini Senza Sbarre NGO.
Schillaci, R. (2016). *Ninna Nanna Prigioniera (Imprisoned Lullaby)*, Italy–France, 2016, 82', produced by Indyca, De Films en Aiguille, in collaboration with Azul film.
Sloan, J., & Wright, S. (2015). Going in Green: Reflections on the Challenges of 'Getting in, Getting On, and Getting Out' for Doctoral Prison Researchers. In D. H. Drake, R. Earle, & J. Sloan (Eds.), *The Palgrave Handbook of Prison Ethnography* (pp. 143–163). London: Palgrave Macmillan.

# Part III

## The Cell Membrane

This forms the outer boundary of the cell and keeps the cell contents intact, preventing them from mixing with the medium outside the cell or with the contents of neighbouring cells. …One of its principle functions is to exercise control over which substances enter and leave the cell. The wrong type or quantity of a substance entering the cell could upset its delicately balanced chemistry. (Mackean and Jones 1975: 7)

# 10

# Serving Time with a Sea View: The Prison Cell and Healthy Blue Space

Jennifer Turner, Dominique Moran, and Yvonne Jewkes

## Introduction

At 9 a.m. on 13 August 2016, 800 competitors in the 24th annual Alcatraz Sharkfest Swim were dropped just off the rocks of the island housing Alcatraz Federal Prison in San Francisco Bay and challenged to swim 1.5 miles back to the city shore (Terry 2016). This and other challenges taking place since the closure of the prison derive playfulness from the altogether more serious history of its geographical location on an

J. Turner (✉)
Department of Geography and Planning, University of Liverpool, Liverpool, UK
e-mail: jennifer.turner@liverpool.ac.uk

D. Moran
School of Geography, Earth and Environmental Sciences (GEES), University of Birmingham, Birmingham, UK

Y. Jewkes
Department of Social & Policy Sciences, University of Bath, Bath, UK



J. Turner, V. Knight (eds.), *The Prison Cell*, Palgrave Studies in Prisons and Penology,
https://doi.org/10.1007/978-3-030-39911-5_10

island surrounded by deep, cold waters with strong undercurrents. Its nickname, the Rock, is apt, since topographically the island is a drowned mountain, with only a thin strip of dirt that supports little flora and fauna (Jarvis 2004). Some of the USA's most notorious prison were incarcerated here from 1934 to 1963 under the premise that Alcatraz's watery surroundings would make the prison impossible to escape from, although there were in fact 14 documented escape attempts involving 34 prisoners: 23 were recaptured, 6 were shot and killed, but 5 remained unaccounted for. The authorities insisted they must have drowned (Jarvis 2004). In addition, prison folklore held that the waters surrounding Alcatraz were shark-infested. Tales were told of a shark named 'Bruce', said to have been raised with only one fin by the Bureau of Prisons in order that it would swim continually around the island waiting for its prey (Babyak 2001).

The significance of the surrounding water for the prisoners themselves is not something that features prominently in the performance of the site as a destination for penal tourism.[1] Curators have paid attention to the value of the sea in aiding air circulation around the crowded cell block and commented on the chill brought by inclement weather. However, the view—which may be taken from most windows in the building—features less in the narrative of the prison's history. The impacts that a sea view might have had on prisoners are difficult to garner from the prison's archives, but it seems likely that the cold and dangerous waters surrounding Alcatraz could only have exacerbated the pains of imprisonment experienced by its inmates. But can a waterscape have positive effects in a carceral setting? Combining perspectives from sociology, therapeutic and carceral geographies, and criminological studies of the prison, our aim in this chapter is to explore prisoners' rational and visceral responses to a sea view and to discuss the value in interrogating 'healthy blue space' (Foley and Kistemann 2015) under contingent circumstances where individuals cannot choose to accept or reject interaction with their environs and where the very nature of enforced residence can have negative effects on mental health (Jordan 2011).

The notion of 'healthy prisons' is now well established in policy; for example, Her Majesty's Inspectorate of Prisons (2014) employs 'healthy prison tests' as standards against which all prisons in England and Wales are independently inspected. However, the Inspectorate's focus remains on what is 'just' and 'decent', rather than what is 'healthy' in a medical or therapeutic sense. Our aim, in short, is to explore the value of Foley and Kistemann's conceptualisation of 'healthy blue space' and to respond to their call to 'extend the scope spatially, methodologically and in inter-disciplinary ways as part of a broader hydro-social set of therapeutic geographies' (2015: 157). Using empirical data gathered from prisoners and prison staff at a prison located on a seashore in the UK, and drawing on notions of therapeutic landscapes, the chapter theorises the prison cell with a sea view as a potentially nurturing rather than punitive environment, one that might *heal* rather than inflict further harm. After summarising the expansion of inter-disciplinary therapeutic landscape studies from 'green' to 'blue' spaces, we note that the prison disrupts conventional understandings of therapeutic landscapes, as water sometimes engenders negative associations in the carceral environment—associations of punishment and control, rather than the beneficial experiences commonly emphasised—and contend that much existing literature focuses on the health-enabling or therapeutic capacity of blue space via bodily immersion. Although previous research highlights the value of a sea view, for instance, it is the view *in conjunction with* an ability to physically engage with the water that is usually argued to have health benefits. Using interview and focus group data generated from staff and prisoners in a recently built coastal prison in the UK, we will suggest a more complex relationship with blue space; that is, the highly limited, yet powerful visual and sensory interaction that prisoners unable to 'jump in' to the watery landscapes around them (Foley 2015: 219) may nonetheless have—a relationship that complicates individual attachments to the space of their prison cell and traditional understandings of the cell as a 'constant', 'static' space. We conclude by suggesting possibilities for development of theorisations of therapeutic blue space and discussing the benefits that may be generated by a reconsideration of prison location and exterior view outlook.

## Healthy Blue Space and the Carceral Landscape

The concept of therapeutic landscapes was introduced by Gesler (1992) and has subsequently been explored within studies of environment, health and care (Airey 2003; Gesler 1996, 1998, Kearns and Barnett 1999; Kearns and Gesler 1998; Palka 1999; Williams 1999, 2002). Velarde et al. described the main health benefits of exposure to landscapes as being 'reduced stress, improved attention capacity, facilitating recovery from illness, ameliorating physical well-being in elderly people, and behavioural changes that improve mood and general well-being' (2007: 210). The recognition of landscape as a 'key element of individual and social wellbeing' (Foley and Kistemann 2015: 159) has led to policy-level changes concerned with the protection, management and planning of these environments. But while traditional landscape studies have focussed on 'green' space, recent studies have explored the impact of 'blue' vistas (Anderson and Peters 2014; Strang 2004). For example, Luttik's (2000) Netherlands-based study found that houses with views of water cost between 8 and 12 per cent more than those without, while Lange and Schaeffer (2001) reported guests' willingness to pay 10 per cent more for 'lake view' rooms, rather than rooms with forest views in hotels in Switzerland. However, the desire for these rooms may be more than just personal preference. In 2015, Foley and Kistemann coined the term 'healthy blue space'[2] after collating a wealth of documentation about the value of blue spaces including both coastal areas (Depledge and Bird 2009; Wheeler et al. 2012; White et al. 2010) and inland waters known as 'urban blue' (Völker and Kistemann 2011) for health and wellbeing.

In addition to evidence concerning the benefits of views of water, bodily immersion in water has long been considered therapeutic, as witnessed in the development of Victorian spas in seaside towns; lidos, which had become a national institution in the UK by the 1930s; and in the contemporary vogue for outdoor- and open-water swimming (Corbin 1994; Deakin 2000; Parr 2011; Shields 2013). In 2009, Natural England reported that, in the UK, there were nearly 250 million visits to the coast and 180 million to other aquatic environments including rivers, canals and lakes. Aside from the therapeutic benefits of exercise and hydro-immersion, these watery locations 'have wide cultural and emotional resonance' through the health-enabling advantages that derive from the blue components of the water and sky (Foley 2015: 218).[3]

Although blue space literatures conventionally refer to access to and views of bodies of water—which of course frequently appear in shades of grey or green rather than actually being *blue*—the sky is another 'blue' space: access to sight of which is considered therapeutic in a number of ways. Sky views usually coexist with natural light (and dark), which help regulate circadian rhythms and thereby promote wellbeing. 'Sky View Factor' (Oke 1981), a measure defining the fraction of sky visible from a given position on the ground, is used in landscape assessment, and views of the sky, the horizon, slow-moving clouds, sunsets and so on are frequently considered part of therapeutic landscapes (e.g. Lengen 2015). At the horizon where land or water and sky meet, there is a sense of depth which is recognised as 'a primary feature of landscape' (Casey 2001: 690). This enables a sense of reality in space—occlusion of distant objects by closer objects, perspective, shading, motion parallax (Sacks 2010), and an essential sense of reality (Lengen 2015), a sense of belonging and a sense of being (Sacks 2010)—or 'Dasein' (Heidegger [1927] 1962). These intangible yet existential effects of viewing landscapes are reflected in recent studies of therapeutic landscapes, which point out that place is experienced differently by different individuals and therefore may deliver different therapeutic outcomes (Conradson 2005). In other words, and in line with geographical understandings of relational space, environments cannot be fully appraised objectively, but instead must be understood relationally.

So what is the relevance of this discussion to the prison and in particular the prison cell? Prison spaces are also relational. They have 'measurable' qualities, but their punitive and/or therapeutic effect is determined at least in part by their subjective experience or, in other words, how specific individuals experience them: in relation to their own personal characteristics, past experiences and the perceptions of punishment and the role of the institution in enforcing it. Although issues of mental and physical health have been addressed in carceral settings, when specifically juxtaposing carceral spaces and therapeutic landscapes, there are significant issues of extrapolation (Turner and Moran 2019). As Turner and

Moran explain, a barrier is raised 'in terms of the perceived legitimacy of a 'healing' custodial function' (2019: 62). Notably, other institutions, such as hospitals, holistic therapy centres or drug rehabilitation units, have an explicit 'healing' function that encompasses wellbeing, in addition to relief from physical symptoms, illness or trauma. Stress reduction and increased levels of comfort for individuals dealing with emotionally and/or physically demanding experiences are part of their functionality and legitimacy (Cooper-Marcus and Barnes 1995). A therapeutic landscape is, then, one with an 'enduring reputation for achieving physical, mental and spiritual healing' (Gesler 1993: 171). The parallels with prison space may not be immediately obvious. In the above-mentioned examples, there is no overt intent to 'punish' inhabitants, usually viewed as needing and deserving assistance.[4] Conversely, there is little perceived public sympathy for prisoners. With a vigilant(e) media critiquing 'undeserved' 'perks' for prisoners, combined with tight budgets and hyper-attention to security, the penal landscape is rarely 'therapeutic' either in intent or in actual lived experience.

Although emergent research recognises the benefits of therapeutic 'green spaces' in custodial settings (Jewkes and Moran 2015; Wright 2017; Turner and Moran 2019), it is yet to consider 'blue spaces' in a similar manner—perhaps because the relationship between water and carceral space is problematic. The location of a prison near to water is, as far as we can deduce, rarely if ever intended to deliver therapeutic effects. Rather, its proximity necessitates, or is the after-effect of the need for, as an example, prisoner labour when, in the nineteenth century, prisoners built harbours such as at Peterhead in northern Scotland; or water is used as a barrier to escape, as in the island prisons at Alcatraz, at Bastøy in Norway's famous 'eco-prison' located approximately four kilometres from the Norwegian mainland, and at Suomenlinna, a ferry ride from the Finnish capital Helsinki. Proximity can also be the result of sheer coincidence or expediency (if the state already owns land in a coastal or waterfront area, thus avoiding the need to purchase an alternative plot elsewhere). Additionally, even where water appears to be part of a progressive regime aimed at improving prospects of rehabilitation, it can have unintended consequences. For example, Bastøy might seem like an idyll where prisoners can fish from the banks, swim in the water and earn a certificate in maritime proficiency by operating the daily ferry. But the island's water boundness reinforces many of the negative cultural associations of prison islands, and the bittersweet juxtaposition of (relative) 'freedom' and restriction of liberty brings its own insidious 'pains' (Hancock and Jewkes 2011) to the extent that some prisoners simply cannot cope and request a transfer to harsher but more conventional prison conditions on the mainland (Shammas 2014).

Beyond this, as Turner and Moran (2019) explain, the presence of water in the carceral setting is part of an infrastructure of 'careful control'. In particular, 'water may be considered to be an element requiring restriction because it poses some kind of risk, that is, a risk of an individual flooding their immediate environment or the risk of an individual causing bodily harm to themselves or others' (Turner and Moran 2019: 209). This mechanism of control has broadly negative connotations, including the control of behaviour and spatial activities as in the case of water cannons for crowd control or water torture as an interrogation technique (Arntzen and Werner 1999; Rejali 2009). Similarly, water is also 'controlled for the management of prisoner health, such as for cleansing and anti-contagion mechanisms' (Turner and Moran 2019: 209). There are numerous historical examples of the forced bathing of prisoners as part of the reception process (One-Who-Has-Endured-It 1877). Indeed, relics of this infrastructure—for example, communal baths and 'assembly-line' showers—have become a key part of the narrative at penal tourist sites such as Alcatraz. The significance of water and ablutions has featured heavily in the rhetoric for creating humane prison environments, particularly in relation to the focus of the development of the infrastructure of the prison cell. In-cell sanitation poses the risk of an individual flooding their cell or causing bodily harm to themselves or others, a risk averted by providing showers rather than baths, and restricting the flow of taps and showerheads. Guidelines drawn up by the International Committee of the Red Cross (ICRC) in 2012 and the United Nations Office for Project Services (UNOPS) in 2016 are intended to ensure adequate standards are met. From suggestions about the volume of water required per prisoner per day to the litre-per-minute flow and number of taps that should be provided, water has become a quantifiable resource for the maintenance of health and wellbeing. The ICRC also recognises variances in geographical locations and cultural contexts. Although still employed elsewhere (including in Ireland), England and Wales abolished the practice of 'slopping out' (where, lacking in-cell sanitation, prisoners had to urinate and defecate in pots emptied in the morning) in 1996. As recently as 2012, ten British prisons were still believed to be using the practice but, following several legal cases brought by prisoners, in-cell sanitation is the norm for new-build prisons in the UK and, although 'en-suite' cells have received media criticism, such provision is now recognised as essential. Nevertheless, whatever positive prison function may be ascribed to water, it is framed in the language of necessity and minimum standards, or decency, rather than in relation to the notions of leisure and therapy that infuse academic literatures on healthy blue space.

Such therapeutic literature frequently focuses on the necessity of bodily immersion for therapeutic effect, arguing that benefits of seascape generally accrue to individuals viewing a blue space they can also *access* physically. The sight of blue space bolsters bodily experiences of the seashore and memories of aquatic activities (Peters and Brown 2017; Steinberg and Peters 2015). Indeed, Wylie's (2005) exploration of the self and landscape on a coastal path critically interrogated the significance of walking *by* the sea and movement in relation to the sea and the shore. Yet, visual interaction with landscape alone does reduce stress for prisoners, even if they are unable to physically access it. In 1981, Moore found that prisoners who were only able to view the prison courtyard from their cells were 24 per cent more likely to make sick-call visits than prisoners who had a view of surrounding farmland. More recently, Moran (2019) has shown that both access to green spaces and views of large images of nature produce therapeutic effects amongst prisoners. Taking a lead from Moore (1981) and Moran (2019), we interrogate the significance of a sea view from a prison cell in the context of therapeutic landscape, health and wellbeing.

## Data Generation

Fieldwork was carried out at the case study prison in the summer of 2015 as part of a major ESRC-funded project investigating how penal aims and philosophies (what prison is 'for') are expressed in prison architecture and design and the effectiveness of prison architecture and design for conveying and delivering that penal purpose. The UK institution we discuss here houses adult male offenders and both adult and young offender females. Multi-method data collection comprised ethnographic observations, an anonymous prisoner survey ($n$ = 85, 22.6 per cent overall response rate, with 42.5 per cent for females although they represented only 10.6 per cent of the total surveyed population) and focus groups and interviews with staff and prisoners. Data were analysed using SPSS and NVivo. Observations were carried out in individual prison cells, wings, special care units, health centre, visiting suite, education spaces and workshops. Twenty-nine focus groups (2–6 prisoners) were conducted (in prison wing spaces but not in cells), and 42 prisoners and 36 staff participated in one-to-one interviews. For procedural reasons, prisoner interviews took place in interview rooms, that is, away from cells themselves. Although interview questions were not specifically directed towards a 'sea view'—as many cells did not have such a view—blue space proved particularly relevant to discussions surrounding views in general, as well as the notion of colour in the prison landscape.

## 'Escape' on the Horizon

Is blue space meaningful in the prison environment? A prison cell with a sea view came as something of a surprise to our prisoner respondents. Although 75 per cent had been in custody before (an average of eight previous sentences), the fact that the prison was newly built meant that around half of our interviewees had never been incarcerated there before, so its proximity to the sea was unexpected, and was frequently used as a point of comparison to other prisons. Tony's exuberant language clearly expresses his surprise:

> See when you were upstairs [on the upper levels of the accommodation building] you can just see the water and all the boats and that … Seeing like folk on speedboats like racing and that. Holy shit! It's alright, like.

Prisoners were keen to draw such comparisons. In this example from a focus group with male prisoners, participants' language emphatically demonstrated how unusual they found the view of marine life:

**Interviewer**: Does the view out of the window make a difference?
**Harry**: Oh big difference, please believe it. I've been in a while and I'm used to seeing just concrete walls round us or a fence round us.
**Damien**: People like you, you lifers [referring to another member of the group], you could do with a better view couldn't you, to be honest?
**Harry**: Oh definitely…
**Damien**: Like people like us who are doing fours, fives [years], it's not really a big difference …
**Harry**: I've been in nine [years] just now. And as you don't get out this is the first I've ever seen a view like this. …But this is fucking crazy!
**Terry**: See the town, the harbour, the boats …
**Harry**: …it's great. I've seen the dolphins, I've seen the whales out at sea.
**Terry**: It does make a difference doesn't it? It makes it a bit better [you know].
**Harry**: Oh a big difference.
**Sean**: There's not many jails you can see that, you've seen dolphins, whales from your cell window.
**Harry**: It's brilliant man, know what I mean. I stand looking out watching dolphins.
**Sean**: It was last week we were watching the dolphins. Last week we were watching the dolphins!

Although this was not discussed explicitly at the focus group, it could be that in contrast to the apocryphal tale of Bruce the Alcatraz shark circling in search of escapees, the sight of these wild cetaceans out in the ocean on their migratory routes, as well as being a source of amazement and entertainment, was also a poignant sight for their captive viewers.

The experience of this view must be considered in relation to respondents' exposure to it or, in other words, the proportion of their time that was spent in cells and on adjacent landings where such views were available. At the case study prison, regime varied slightly between wings and for prisoners undertaking different forms of work and so on, but, in general, prisoners would be away from their cells and landings for about five hours each day. During the remaining 19 hours, they would be either confined to their own cell (i.e. overnight) or to the space comprising their landing and the unlocked cells—that is, able to look at the view from their own cell window, from the landing windows, and potentially from the windows of other prisoners' cells. This means that, if their own cell had a view of the sea, they would be able to look at this view for the majority of the day—including at night when illuminated by the moon, harbour lights, shipping vessels and oil rigs.

Given this extensive exposure, it is heartening that as well as recounting particularly notable occasions (as in the focus group above), most participants indicated positive associations with the sea view, using words descriptive of a therapeutic effect, including feelings of comfort, ease, relaxation, stress reduction, restfulness and peace, as well as fascination, exhilaration, distraction and excitement. Beyond this, it may be argued that the experience of the sea view from the more private, individual space of a prisoner's cell increased the likelihood of them being able to convert experience of that sea view to these positive emotional and affective responses. Indeed, many prisoners commented on the way the view enabled the passing of time or 'escape' from the monotony of prison life. As Mikey explains:

> A view's a good thing. It makes your time go by. I notice myself just sitting watching stuff outside and an hour or two's gone by. Whereas if you're just looking at your wall downstairs, even just looking out at the main walls, it does your nut in, that.

Additionally, as Jimmy intimates, the therapeutic effects are derived distinctly from the distraction of and association with the sea:

> [I]f I came in at the start of my sentence and having that view it would help me not think of depression and despair and things like that because you're seeing outside. Especially on a stormy night with the sea and things like that.

Prisoners explained that being able to see the sea enhanced their ability to sleep (or that if they were able to move to a cell with a window that overlooked such a view it *would* provide that benefit). Others reflected on the feelings of relaxation and peace derived from the ability to visually interact with the weather or sunsets, augmented by the elemental characteristics of the water (such as the smells and sounds of the sea). As Scott explained:

> I love looking at the sea. I never used to like the sea, it wasn't until I went out there and you see some of the sunsets it is just gorgeous like and even with the thunder and lightning, I liked that as well, but everyone has different… I think when you start getting older you're not young and dumb anymore. I love the sea it's so peaceful like, it's the best thing you can do with the sea, like the fishing boats sailing along the side of us.

These engagements with the landscape hint at the importance of awareness of the passage of time. A wealth of scholarship makes clear the disorientation caused by timelessness in prison and the sense of repetition and being 'left behind' that it causes (e.g. Moran 2012; Kotova 2018). One benefit of nature views is their propensity, in seasonal climates, to enable those who view them to maintain contact with the seasons and thereby the passage of time. In commenting on the apparent progression of the sun and the corresponding patterns of fishing boat trips, Scott gives us another example of the ways in which blue views enable temporal awareness. A firm criterion of a therapeutic environment is the ability to allow the individual to 'escape' from the circumstances that are causing them harm, allowing them to metaphorically cross the boundary between the prison and 'freedom' (Turner 2016). In the prison environment, legitimate escape—that is, which allows an individual to feel removed from the mental or bodily 'pains of imprisonment' (Sykes 1958) without compromising their physical security within carceral space—may be facilitated by a sea view. As prisoners Damien and Stephen recounted:

**Damien**: I can spend ages looking out the window and drifting away...it's made my time a lot better. Especially for long term prisoners, people that have got a large majority of their life stuck in here, little things like that that don't cost anything do make a difference. It helps the time become a bit more bearable, to be honest.

**Interviewer**: What's good about looking at the [sea and harbour area]? How does it make you feel to do that?

**Stephen**: Sort of tranquil. You can gather your thoughts and just think about what you're going to do when you get outside again. It's good to see some civilisation.

Staff members also talked of prisoners and officers 'just daydreaming' while standing at the floor-to-ceiling windows in each living unit, which were likened in one case to 'infinity swimming pools', such was the way the sea view appeared at the end of the corridor (interview, prison officer). However, a sea view is not enjoyed in every area of the prison. Scott explained that unless you are located in the upper storeys of the house block, your cell window looks out only onto the exterior perimeter or internal spaces such as the exercise yard or sports pitch:

**Interviewer**: What view have you got on the ground floor?

**Scott**: The fence, you can't really see much because it's closed off, but I've been upstairs and it's a beautiful view if you're [...] on the left hand side because you've got the harbour, you've got the ships coming in. A lot of people will sit there and just watch the ships coming in and going out. I'm not really too interested in seeing ships moving back and forth or watching people picking up their crab boxes. You see the orange box placed wherever. But I can see where they get the interest from.

Although prisoners' enjoyment of the seascape is arguably a personal preference, this view was coveted by the majority of our prisoner participants. Accordingly, cells without such a view harness fewer positive associations—the outside space is an agent of change upon the inside space of the cell. Reflecting on the limited vistas offered by ground floor rooms, Ali offered suggestions to improve these views, to ensure prisoners were given an equal outlook:

> You can't see past the wall. To me, you could have… say if you're in the Blackpool Tower, I don't know if you've ever been in the Blackpool Tower, you can walk along one part of the section. There's like the four corners, and then one piece of pure glass …And I'm thinking why can't you have a big section of that wall that's glass in that sense? But then again, if that's like the sea, that could be the seaside. Or maybe not the sea, you could maybe look through there to that part, and maybe see a boat. It'd be like a picture. [I'd be] coming alive, looking at it.

There is undoubtedly recognition that this kind of interaction with the sea is different to those experiences discussed in the healthy blue space literature. Prisoners are not able to enjoy physical immersion, and therefore opportunities to enjoy other embodied, elemental entanglements are extremely valuable. A prison officer working in the residential unit explained:

> [C]ertain cells are quite popular … you'd get the ones in the top flat requesting the ones that were facing the sea because they'd have the breeze coming in from the sea, plus the view out … So a view is quite important to a lot of cons [convicts—prisoners].

More than simply contributing to the maintenance of health and well-being, many participants believed the views from their cell windows could have a rehabilitative effect. Being able to see the outside world was something that Benjamin felt was crucial to reduce the 'shock' of release from prison after a lengthy sentence:

> A person that's getting close to their release, maybe they've been in for a long time, it's going to be quite daunting for somebody just to walk straight into the garden, things have changed outside that you can't see past the

> walls. So stuff like that you can see outside, see the countryside and that, at least you can see changes. Somebody could be in prison for 10, 20 years, there's a lot of massive changes.

Jimmy described the enjoyment that he felt when he was able to visit another prisoner's cell, which had a sea view. Reflecting on his own experiences as a long-term prisoner coming to the end of his sentence, he explained that a cell with a similar view would likely be more beneficial to a person *entering* the prison, at the *beginning* of a long sentence:

> If I knew I was going to be here for over a year I'd have took the opportunity for one of the cells that had a sea view because I've sat in one of my pal's cells and you see the boats and that coming in. And I haven't seen the sea since 1994, so when I seen the sea and seen boats coming in. Well, one guy said "look at the smirk on his face". You know? It was just... my eyes were just taking it in. It was nice ... I can move just now if I wish it. But the same again, I'm going to be here for hopefully just a year, so I'd rather somebody else gets that cell if they're doing a big, big sentence because it would be better for them.

We explore the ways in which prisoner culture and the relative 'values' placed on cells with different views by different prisoners elsewhere (Jewkes et al. 2019). Here, we consider the cell space in conjunction with the sea view, performing itself as a liminal carceral space (Moran 2013) of transformation and mobility, which is inherently contra the traditional view of the prison cell as the most static, replicated or 'constant' space within the prison. However, while the benefits of a sea view for health and wellbeing were clearly expressed by many participants, such opinions were not universal. In the following section, we explore how, for some prisoners, the sea view could be viewed as negative, even detrimental.

## A View Too Far?

The relational nature of cell space means that its experience is akin to a transaction between its observable qualities (such as the presence or otherwise of a sea view) and the subjectivity of the occupant (such as whether or not they personally find a view of the sea relaxing). In our study, some responses indicated that the waterscape was far from therapeutic and some prisoners emphasised that the sea view—no matter how temporarily interesting or momentarily beneficial—may eventually form part of the monotony of a prison sentence (as is often the case with other aquatic landscapes that become unnoticed after a period of time [Steinberg and Peters 2015]). For example, Duane juxtaposes the seemingly always mobile landscape of a working port to his own stasis. Here, he makes a critical link between the present blue space and his memories of life working on oil rigs prior to prison:

> I can see the compensators for the gates at the harbour …But now and again looking out our window does your head in. Because I can see our compensators and the cranes so that reminds me of the oil rigs. So then it puts my head back to where I've come from and where I am now.

In this respect, blue space may reinforce the loss of liberty and autonomy. Despite its positive connotations for individuals outside of prison, the coastline is a barrier and obstacle to physical escape. A seemingly endless horizon reinforces the closed space of the prison cell from which it is viewed. Much like the 'shark-infested' waters around Alcatraz Island, the seascape becomes imbued with messages of stasis and helplessness, creating a juxtaposition between past life and current life in the prison cell.

The ability of blue space to act as a memorial landscape, as it does for Duane, is similarly frustrating for other prisoners. When talking about the proximity of the sea, Melody was initially positive, but was adamant that it would have detrimental effects over the longer term. From her cell, she was only able to see the perimeter wall, internal fences and a small portion of the garden area designated for use by female prisoners. She recalled an occasion where she visited another prisoner's cell:

> I went upstairs last week to speak to a friend of mine, [name], who got out yesterday, and what a view you had from her room. You can actually see the whole harbour and see some of the town. It was pretty, it was nice, but I wouldn't like to look at that all the time, I think it would drive me nuts. Because you can see daily life going on out there. I prefer the regime, I think. … It's nice to look at, but I would just want to be out there all the time. It would drive me crazy.

Melody went on to recall her feelings when a local festival was held in the adjacent town. As well as events on land, power boats and acrobatic planes circled the harbour. Although she did not have a direct view, the sounds of the water sports carried into the prison. She explained:

> Last week they had some boat ride or something, some fayre, and it was like next to the window. And that was at eight o'clock, and as soon as I opened the window and looked out, all my heart was melting away, I just felt like my heart was racing, I had to pull the blind down. It was just too much. I had to lie there. It was like I shot [sic] it down, just pulled down the curtain.

For Melody, the cell's permeability rendered its ordinary purpose as a private, sanctuary space impossible. These sentiments take us back to San Francisco and the well-known (perhaps apocryphal) story that the least popular cell in Alcatraz was the one at the end of the facility from which holiday-makers could be seen and heard enjoying themselves on the beach across the bay and where, on New Year's Eve, prisoners reported hearing the tinkling of champagne glasses and laughter carried across the water by sea breezes (Jarvis 2004). The sound of others' enjoyment was simply too painful to bear and only exacerbated inmates' sense of enforced isolation. In addition to the activities associated with blue space, prisoners and staff also commented on several other negative 'effects' of living and working within close proximity to the sea. These ranged from inclement weather to the presence of pestilent seabirds and the unpleasant smells of seaweed and sewage effluent in (particularly urban) coastal areas. These sentiments are contra to the literature that describes the sea as a space of freedom, openness, vitality and lack of restriction (Anderson and Peters 2014; Hastrup and Hastrup 2015). Here, we may draw on work that focuses on the capacity of water/sea to evoke fear, sickness and other less positive notions (Anderson and Peters 2014). In this vein, the physical porosities of the prison architecture create a blurred boundary between sea and cell space.

These types of unwelcome interaction are significant in that they lead us to appreciate that the blue space relationship for incarcerated individuals is at best ambiguous. It is apparent that what at first glance appears to be merely a visual interaction with blue space is in fact manifest in wider embodied interactions. Additionally, it is the lack of agency in relation to blue space that affords opportunities to reconsider how 'healthy blue space' might be interrogated under contingent circumstances. Our research found that, although visual interaction with seascapes *can* have therapeutic effects and engender feelings of freedom, it may also reinforce insidious aspects of carceral control and loss.

## Managing Viewpoints

The absence of a pleasant outlook from certain cells seemed to send a clear message about the treatment that prisoners could expect and about penal philosophy more broadly. As Kyle pondered:

> I think it helps … what you can see outside the window. …Because some jails you go to all you can see is a wall and that's not helping at all. It reminds you you're in a cage within another cage.

So, in relation to this, as part of an architectural design strategy that may serve to send a rehabilitative message to incarcerated individuals, the following question may be asked: could a seascape aid rehabilitation? Both staff members and prisoners agreed that top floor cells with a sea view could be used to incentivise prisoners. In a performance of disciplinary power, good behaviour could be rewarded with allocation of these cells, which were described as having the best atmosphere, outlook and 'ambiance' (interview, security staff member). In relation to the seascape at our case study prison, one support staff member suggested that it was simply 'bizarre' that the whole prison wasn't facing the water as he '[couldn't] see any negative aspect of prisoners … looking at the sea' (interview, non-custodial staff member). However, the relatively limited number of cells with coastal views was clearly intrinsic to the, arguably tension-filled, behavioural compliance model operated in this prison, where prisoners could be incentivised to exhibit good behaviour through offers to move to cells with a sea view, or be down-graded to units without such a view if they failed to comply. In this final excerpt, a prison officer highlights this element of 'choice':

> As yourself, you go on holiday, if you get a choice, say you go away to Spain or wherever, and they say to you in the hotel "what would you like to face?" ...You'd pick the sea, of course you would. Every time. So I think prisoners are like that.

It is this assumption—that a *purposeful* location of carceral space within healthy landscapes, in particular, blue space, may be beneficial to those working and living there—that we take forward in our concluding comments.

## Conclusion

Prior discussion of sea views tends to highlight the benefits for individuals located close to blue spaces they can also access physically, with visual experience complementing therapeutic immersion. In this particular prison environment, although prisoners have limited interaction with the blue landscape from their cells, it nevertheless enables 'escapes' and freedoms for some, whilst this has a counter-therapeutic effect for others that often results in a complicated relationship with the space of the prison cell—the space in which prisoners spend the majority of their time. As such, we may question whether Foley and Kistemann's (2015) notion of healthy blue space can be wholeheartedly adopted. In concluding this chapter, we call for the expansion of inquiry into therapeutic landscapes to the notion of the healthy blue space *under contingent circumstances*, for example, in conditions of incarceration where individuals cannot choose whether to accept or reject interaction with these cell landscapes and/or where access to such landscapes may be part and parcel of a system of behavioural control. With this in mind, we would welcome the expansion of healthy or therapeutic landscapes into other arenas of study that may exhibit conditions of lack of agency and enforced geographical location, for example, hospitals, care homes, hospices or social housing, and in particular where waterscapes do not necessarily meet the conventional definitions of therapeutic, such as industrial coastlines or landscapes with particular dangers, such as coastal erosion or water pollution.

Additionally, while recognising that a sea view from a prison cell is not necessarily a priority for a successful prison, we are confident that proximity to and views of blue spaces may be managed in order to maximise their potential positive impacts on health and wellbeing. In a recently designed prison in Denmark, architects developed a staggered, 'saw-tooth' design to ensure that each cell window has a view of the surrounding countryside and does not overlook any of the prison buildings, thus forcing an exterior view away from the prison itself towards the 'outside' world. In a similar way, blue landscapes may be incorporated into the design of a prison, such as the lake that forms a central feature of The State Prison of East Jutland at Enner Mark, Denmark, which opened in 2006. In taking a lead from such examples, we believe that intentional use of blue space in a custodial setting could serve to reinforce the values of the justice system inasmuch as it facilitates health and wellbeing among prisoners, which form a core component of the wider aims of rehabilitation and reduction of recidivism among offenders.

## Notes

1. See Strange and Kempa (2003) for a critical analysis of tourist experiences on Alcatraz Island.
2. For Foley and Kistemann, 'blue' is used in reference to 'its established associations with oceans, seas, lakes, rivers and other bodies of water' recognising also 'the myriad shades and forms (grey, brown, dark, oily, muddy, clear) that are recognisable dimensions of water bodies at different scales' (2015: 158).
3. For a comprehensive review of therapeutic blue space, see Foley and Kistemann (2015), where examples range from interactions with European rivers to Canadian lakes.
4. Here we consider that although, in some cases, such spaces may be experienced negatively, their healing intention usually prevails.

## References

Airey, L. (2003). 'Nae as Nice a Scheme as It Used to Be': Lay Accounts of Neighbourhood Incivilities and Well-being. *Health & Place, 9*(2), 129–237.

Anderson, J., & Peters, K. (Eds.). (2014). *Water Worlds: Human Geographies of the Ocean*. Farnham: Ashgate.

Arntzen, E., & Werner, S. B. (1999). Water Mist Punishment for Two Classes of Problem Behaviour. *Scandinavian Journal of Behaviour Therapy, 28*(2), 88–93.

Babyak, J. (2001). *Breaking the Rock: The Great Escape from Alcatraz*. Oakland, CA: Ariel Vamp Press.

Casey, E. S. (2001). Between Geography and Philosophy: What does It Mean to Be in the Place-World? *Annals of the Association of American. Geographers, 91*(4), 683–693.

Conradson, D. (2005). Landscape, Care and the Relational Self: Therapeutic Encounters in Rural England. *Health & Place, 11*(4), 337–348.

Cooper-Marcus, C., & Barnes, M. (1995). *Gardens in Healthcare Facilities: Uses, Therapeutic Benefits and Design Recommendations*. Concord, CA: The Center for Health Design.

Corbin, A. (1994). *The Lure of the Sea: The Discovery of the Seaside in the Western World 1750–1840*. Cambridge: Polity Press.

Deakin, R. (2000). *Waterlog: A Swimmer's Journey Through Britain*. London: Vintage.

Depledge, M., & Bird, W. J. (2009). The Blue Gym: Health and Wellbeing from Our Coasts. *Marine Pollution Bulletin, 58*(7), 947–948.

Foley, R. (2015). Swimming in Ireland: Immersions in Therapeutic Blue Space. *Health & Place, 35*, 218–225.

Foley, R., & Kistemann, T. (2015). Blue Space Geographies: Enabling Health in Place. *Health & Place, 35*, 157–165.

Gesler, W. M. (1992). Therapeutic Landscapes: Medical Issues in Light of the New Cultural Geography. *Social Science & Medicine, 34*(7), 735–746.

Gesler, W. M. (1993). Therapeutic Landscapes: Theory and a Case Study of Epidauros, Greece. *Environment and Planning D: Society and Space, 11*(2), 171–189.

Gesler, W. M. (1996). Lourdes: Healing in a Place of Pilgrimage. *Health & Place, 2*(2), 95–105.

Gesler, W. M. (1998). Bath's Reputation as a Healing Place. In R. A. Kearns & W. M. Gesler (Eds.), *Putting Health Into Place: Landscape, Identity and Well-being* (pp. 17–35). Syracuse, NY: Syracuse University Press.

Hancock, P., & Jewkes, Y. (2011). Architectures of Incarceration: The Spatial Pains of Imprisonment. *Punishment & Society, 13*(5), 611–629.

Hastrup, K., & Hastrup, F. (Eds.). (2015). *Waterworlds: Anthropology in Fluid Environments*. Oxford: Berghahn Books.

Heidegger, M. ([1927] 1962). *Being and Time* (J. Macquarrie & E. Robinson, Trans.). New York, NY: Harper.

Her Majesty's Inspectorate of Prisons. (2014). *Expectations: Inspection Criteria*. Retrieved August 26, 2018, from https://www.justiceinspectorates.gov.uk/hmiprisons/about-our-inspections/inspection-criteria/.

International Committee of the Red Cross (ICRC). (2012). *Water, Sanitation, Hygiene and Habitat in Prisons*. Geneva: International Committee of the Red Cross.

Jarvis, B. (2004). *Cruel and Unusual: Punishment and US Culture*. London: Pluto Press.

Jewkes, Y., & Moran, D. (2015). The Paradox of the 'Green' Prison: Sustaining the Environment or Sustaining the Penal Complex? *Theoretical Criminology, 19*(4), 451–469.

Jewkes, Y., Moran, D., & Turner, J. (2019). Just Add Water: Prisons, Therapeutic Landscapes and Healthy Blue Space. *Criminology & Criminal Justice*. https://doi.org/10.1177/1748895819828800.

Jordan, M. (2011). The Prison Setting as a Place of Enforced Residence, Its Mental Health Effects, and the Mental Healthcare Implications. *Health & Place, 17*(5), 1061–1066.

Kearns, R. A., & Barnett, J. R. (1999). Auckland's Starship Enterprise: Placing Metaphor in a Children's Hospital. In A. Williams (Ed.), *Therapeutic Landscapes: The Dynamic between Place and Wellness* (pp. 169–200). Lanham, MD: Rowman & Littlefield.

Kearns, R. A., & Gesler, W. M. (Eds.). (1998). *Putting Health into Place: Landscape, Identity and Well-being*. Syracuse, NY: Syracuse University Press.

Kotova, A. (2018). 'Time… Lost Time': Exploring How Partners of Long-Term Prisoners Experience the Temporal Pains of Imprisonment. *Time & Society, 28*(2), 478–498.

Lange, E., & Schaeffer, P. V. (2001). A Comment on the Market Value of a Room with a View. *Landscape and Urban Planning, 55*(2), 113–120.

Lengen, C. (2015). The Effects of Colours, Shapes and Boundaries of Landscapes on Perception, Emotion and Mentalising Processes Promoting Health and Well-being. *Health & Place, 35*, 166–177.

Luttik, J. (2000). The Value of Trees, Water and Open Space as Reflected by House Prices in the Netherlands. *Landscape Urban Planning, 48*(3–4), 161–167.

Moore, E. (1981). A Prison Environment's Effect on Health Care Service Demands. *Journal of Environmental Systems, 11*(1), 17–34.

Moran, D. (2012). "Doing Time" in Carceral Space: Timespace and Carceral Geography. *Geografiska Annaler: Series B, Human Geography, 94*(4), 305–316.

Moran, D. (2013). Between Outside and Inside? Prison Visiting Rooms as Liminal Carceral Spaces. *GeoJournal, 78*(2), 339–351.

Moran, D. (2019). Back to Nature? Attention Restoration Theory and the Restorative Effects of Indirect and Vicarious Nature Contact in Prison. *Health & Place, 57*, 35–43.

Natural England. (2009). *Coastal Access.* Retrieved April 6, 2009, from http://www.naturalengland.org.uk/ourwork/enjoying/places/coastalaccess/default.aspx.

Oke, T. R. (1981). Canyon Geometry and the Nocturnal Urban Heat Island: Comparison of Scale Model and Field Observations. *Journal of Climatology, 1*(3), 237–254.

One-Who-Has-Endured-It. (1877). *Five Years Penal Servitude.* London: R Bentley and Sons.

Palka, E. (1999). Accessible Wilderness as a Therapeutic Landscape: Experiencing the Nature of Denali National Park, Alaska. In A. Williams (Ed.), *Therapeutic Landscapes: The Dynamic Between Place and Wellness* (pp. 29–51). Lanham, MD: Rowman and Littlefield.

Parr, S. (2011). *The Story of Swimming.* Stockport: Dewi Lewis.

Peters, K., & Brown, M. (2017). Writing with the Sea: Reflecting on In/experienced Encounters with Ocean Space. *Cultural Geographies, 24*(4), 617–624.

Rejali, D. (2009). *Torture and Democracy.* Princeton, NJ: Princeton University Press.

Sacks, O. (2010). *The Mind's Eye.* London: Picador.

Shammas, V. L. (2014). The Pains of Freedom: Assessing the Ambiguity of Scandinavian Penal Exceptionalism on Norway's Prison Island. *Punishment & Society, 16*(1), 104–123.

Shields, R. (2013). *Places on the Margin: Alternative Geographies of Modernity.* Abingdon: Routledge.

Steinberg, P., & Peters, K. (2015). Wet Ontologies, Fluid Spaces: Giving Depth to Volume through Oceanic Thinking. *Environment and Planning D: Society and Space, 33*(2), 247–264.

Strang, V. (2004). *The Meaning of Water*. Oxford: Berg.
Strange, C., & Kempa, M. (2003). Shades of Dark Tourism: Alcatraz and Robben Island. *Annals of Tourism Research, 30*(2), 386–405.
Sykes, G. (1958). *The Society of Captives: A Study of a Maximum-Security Prison*. Princeton, NJ: Princeton University Press.
Terry, H. (2016). *Swim with Sharks: Fire Captain Douses Doubts as He Returns to Sport in Race Near Alcatraz*. Retrieved September 1, 2018, from http://bouldercityreview.com/community/swim-sharks-fire-captain-douses-doubts-he-returns-sport-race-near-alcatraz.
Turner, J. (2016). *The Prison Boundary: Between Society and Carceral Space*. London: Palgrave Macmillan.
Turner, J., & Moran, D. (2019). Careful Control: The Infrastructure of Water in Carceral Space. *Area, 51*(2), 208–215.
UNOPS. (2016). *Technical Guidance on Prison Planning*. Copenhagen: United Nations.
Velarde, M. D., Fry, G., & Tveit, M. (2007). Health Effects of Viewing Landscapes: Landscape Types in Environmental Psychology. *Urban Forestry & Urban Greening, 6*(4), 199–212.
Völker, S., & Kistemann, T. (2011). The Impact of Blue Space on Human Health and Well-being: Salutogenetic Health Effects of Inland Surface Waters: A Review. *International Journal of Hygiene and Environmental Health, 214*(6), 449–460.
Wheeler, B., White, M., Stahl-Timmins, W., & Depledge, M. (2012). Does Living by the Coast Improve Health and Wellbeing? *Health & Place, 18*(5), 1198–1201.
White, M., Smith, A., Humphreys, K., Pahl, S., Snelling, D., & Depledge, M. (2010). Blue Space: The Importance of Water for Preference, Affect, and Restorativeness Ratings of Natural and Built Scenes. *Journal of Environmental Psychology, 30*(4), 482–493.
Williams, A. (Ed.). (1999). *Therapeutic Landscapes: The Dynamic between Place and Wellness*. Lanham, MD: Rowman & Littlefield.
Williams, A. (2002). Changing Geographies of Care: Employing the Concept of Therapeutic Landscapes as a Framework in Examining Home Space. *Social Science & Medicine, 51*(1), 141–154.
Wright, H. (2017). *Outside Time*. HMP Coldingley: Placewise Press.
Wylie, J. W. (2005). A Single Day's Walking: Narrating Self and Landscape on the South West Coast Path. *Transactions of the Institute of British Geographers, 30*(2), 234–247.

# 11

# Hearing Behind the Door: The Cell as a Portal to Prison Life

Kate Herrity

> I came one time with a friend who had to do a workshop … and somebody pushed their flap down, and my friend, he got really scared, and it was only then that he realised. He said: "Oh my, there's people in there!" I didn't understand. I mean, I knew, but I didn't expect him to say that. But then when I thought about it, and him having no idea what prison is and the idea and concept of being locked in a cell. To him that was like "Wow. Oh, there's actual people in there?!" And I chuckled, so yeah, I think the environment is not just one thing is it? It's many things. (Tone,[1] prison officer)

Tone's reflection on the particularity of prison spaces illustrates the centrality of the cell to 'what prison is'. Frequently, and to their detriment, accounts of prison life focus on shared spaces of association—the wings, landings and connecting walkways—forgetting that 'there's people in there', beyond the peripheries of vision. Tone's account of his friend's surprise provides a useful means of sensitising and sharpening our focus on those out-of-sight spaces. Foregrounding accounts of these lesser-considered prison spaces provides a portal to often over-looked

K. Herrity (✉)
De Montfort University, Leicester, UK
e-mail: Katherine.herrity@dmu.ac.uk



J. Turner, V. Knight (eds.), *The Prison Cell*, Palgrave Studies in Prisons and Penology,
https://doi.org/10.1007/978-3-030-39911-5_11

aspects and textures of prison life. Shifting attention to these hidden spaces, beyond our vision, prompts consideration of how they are experienced sensorially; to how they smell, feel and sound. Don Ihde (2007) argues the auditory imagination straddles imagined and perceived realms of experience and is rich with possibilities for exploring our understanding of time and space. The auditory imagination refers to those aspects of thought and experience which are interwoven with sound, a facet of understanding uniquely placed to bridge our private, inner worlds and external social spaces (Eliot 1933; Toop 2010). This presents additional value in the context of prison, where the specificities of how time and space are experienced are particularly acute (Moran 2012).While prison is a powerful totem of the state's power to punish, characterised by stark power relations, its spaces nevertheless echo the array of life conducted within its walls. As Crewe et al. (2014) illustrate, the prison is not a monolithic space but, rather, one characterised by contrasting emotional topographies within which all manner of identity performance must be managed.

This chapter draws on a research project on the significance of sound in prison using aural ethnography, conducted over seven months in a local[2] prison: HMP Midtown, UK. I briefly introduce the project and methodology before going on to focus on sound as a means of foregrounding the cell as a lens for understanding prison life. The prison population in England and Wales spends up to 22 hours a day behind the door (HMCIP 2018) which necessitates communication behind, between and through walls. I consider the implications of this for how we understand the shape of prison life, arguing that the cell features the use of sound as a system of signification, is a place of sanctuary and a site of 'sousveillance'. *Listening* more closely, I argue, adds depth and texture to our understanding of prison life, as well as the space it inhabits, as 'not just one thing… but many things' (Tone, prisoner officer).

## The Project

The material and inspiration for this chapter originated in doctoral research (Herrity 2019) to explore the significance of sound in prison spaces. I spent over seven months exploring the soundscape[3] by listening to and observing the role of sound in the social life of the prison, complementing this with ethnographically informed interviews. While 29 members of the prison community (10 members staff with assorted grades and roles and 19 prisoners) were interviewed, I spoke to most people moving through the prison spaces during my time there. All accounts were taken from interviews or conversations recorded in my field notes collected in the course of the project.

HMP Midtown, where I conducted my research, is an unusually small prison, comprising one main wing. While the 'churn' or turnover of prisoner population was typically high for a prison of its type, there was a certain consistency in the community while people remained there, allowing me to develop a more intimate acquaintance with its soundscape. I carried keys and was generously granted an unusual degree of latitude in my movements, including spending a night listening to the shifting soundscape. However, I remained restricted by an awareness of the precariousness of my position as an outsider and the need to prioritise security concerns. While I had remarkably free rein, I felt unable to accept frequent invitations to enjoy coffee and a gossip in people's cells: first because all within the prison fall under the relentless scrutiny of security and, second, because remaining in clear sight lessened the strain on resources my presence represented. The men often wanted to show me artwork and photographs of loved ones but were generally obliged to bring these treasured items out to me. Pride taken in personalising and maintaining these cramped spaces was a frequent topic of conversation, as were the ways in which the cell, unsurprisingly, featured in navigating prison life. Regrettably I was largely unable to see—or hear—the cell for myself, though the No. 1[4] and I conducted our interview within a locked cell as a means of eliciting reflection on the sonic environment. Privileging sound went some way to compensating for these physical constraints, harnessing the auditory imagination to increase the capacity to invite imaginings of those I spoke with (McNeill 2018: 156).

My research concerns a broad examination of the significance of social aspects of auditory experience for how we understand the prison. In this chapter I am particularly interested in examining the ways the prison soundscape brings the concealed social life conducted within the cell to the forefront of prison life, rather than relegating it to those unseen and unknowable spaces beyond the limits of our vision. I now turn to one aspect of the prison soundscape—banging—as a means of demonstrating the significance of sound for understanding the cell.

## BANGBANGBANG

In prison, where 'sound rules' (Kelly 2017: 3), the function of sound as a system of signification—a system of both representation and communication of meaning (Chion 2010)—is particularly potent. The lexicon of banging—a constant feature of the prison soundscape—is both an explicit and easily accessible demonstration of this point. As is well-documented, prison offers limited access to goods and services; in addition, mobility and consequently vision are restricted for much of the prison day (HMCIP 2018; Sykes 1958). In the prison environment banging—most often on the inside of a locked cell door—was a means of compensating for lack of visibility behind it (in both directions). Imposing a presence on the soundscape presented a challenge to the constraints of being 'behind the door'. Quantity of banging as well as tone, frequency, context and quality denoted the wider emotional climate: 'a bad day, I s'pose the sounds that relate to a bad day is banging, constant banging, unified banging is terrible, that is, it's not a good sound' (Tone, prison officer). For others, banging denoted a wider set of meanings depending on the context in which they were interpreted:

> You could hear banging now and it wouldn't necessarily bother you, but in those situations when you're walking on the landing to drop something off, it's a different type of banging. It can be quite intimidating.... It's just the type of bang, isn't it, and you know, the atmosphere when there's been lots to go in to that full lockdown. (Joanne, drug support worker)

Banging represented an act of insistent communication in opposition to the constraints of the physical environment and in that sense constituted an act of resistance with a variety of discernible messages: a system of meaning (Chion 2010). Here, I use two examples as a means of illustrating both how sound is used within prison to compensate for the restrictions of imprisonment and how the cell operates as a site of self-expression. However, this is far from a comprehensive key. Not only do specific meanings vary according to context of regime and individual circumstance, but the array of banging extends considerably beyond the two examples referred to here. Nevertheless these were amongst those heard during fieldwork at HMP Midtown and provide a useful means of illustrating the social significance of sound in the cell.

## Rapid, Rhythmic (BangBangBangBang)

Rapid, rhythmic banging denotes frustration and irritation. The banging may indicate the regime is running a little behind, that the person within has urgent business to attend to and/or wants out. Frequently this banging erupts in short bursts. It may be echoed by a number of cell occupants depending on what else is occurring. It can go on for prolonged periods of time, particularly if items are used to do the banging rather than fists or feet.

As sound can impact cognitive function and concentration, as well as being a nuisance causing distress and adversely affecting health, this effect could be keenly felt (e.g. Klatte et al. 2013; Munzel et al. 2014). This was underscored by Claire, a senior psychologist who had not long been at Midtown and had moved from a far larger and better equipped prison:

> I mean there's so much about the place that is just really impractical for doing my job, so things like I had an IQ assessment to do with a guy a few weeks ago. So firstly I need him to be able to concentrate, secondly I need somewhere relatively quiet because if I'm asking him to repeat back strings of numbers that I've just read to him and there's people bashing on the door shouting, that's not fair on him and that's going to bias the assessment. (Claire, senior psychologist)

The adverse impact banging could have on the nerves was precisely why it was such an effective means of making the presence of the cell occupant felt and *heard*. Prolonged banging was difficult for those it was imposed upon. Staff, as well as prisoners, were generally stuck on the wing for the duration of their shift and attempting to attend to the needs of nearly two hundred men to the backdrop of a harsh, repetitive soundtrack frayed the nerves and made it difficult to concentrate.

## Rapid, Moving (Bangbangbangbangbang bangbangbangbanG)

Unlike the rapid, rhythmic banging, rapid banging that moves location is always celebratory, like a sonic Mexican wave, and normally heard during sporting events. I stayed behind one evening to listen to the men as they enjoyed a radio broadcast of a Midtown football match on home turf. I was able to monitor the progress of the game by standing on the wing, as the men's response—to goals, near misses, unpopular referee decisions and the other team scoring—effectively relayed the game. I was advised by a number of staff as well as one or two prisoners that I ought to make sure I was there for such an event: 'when the football's on, or the tennis, the atmosphere's brilliant… you hear the cheers, you hear the chants and I can remember feeling really buzzing after that. And like the guys. It was so powerful' (Joanne, drug support worker). The emotional climate of the prison sounded markedly different. This was an evening match and, despite it being an important Midtown game, the volume declined as the evening wore on. There was, seemingly, a collective code about noise levels and disturbance after certain hours (the match concluded after ten).

While celebratory banging was less common, it served as a means of illustrating the ways in which sound could be used from within the cell to positively impact on the community soundscape as well as to convey frustration with prison life. Banging conveyed a complex range of information and emotion, acting as a means of amplifying discontent and shaping the 'feel' of social spaces beyond the cell. It could also function as a means of redressing unequal power relations by imposing an effect on others through noise, despite the limitations of mobility imposed by being locked up. Listening carefully to banging, its purposes and meanings amplifies not only the significance of the prison soundscape but also of the cell to prison life. Banging was a consistent feature of auditory information at HMP Midtown, echoing human ingenuity and the compulsion to communicate. Attending to the importance of banging, which largely occurs behind the cell door, focuses attention on the cell as a site of communication and resistance.

Jennifer Turner (2016) explores the multifarious ways in which relations and culture permeate the porous perimeters of the prison. Banging is one of a number of means of amplifying the extent to which this applies within prison spaces as well as between those and outside. Prisoners could impact on the mood or feel of the wing from within their cell in a variety of ways; in the case of banging, this impact was partially dependent on recognition of a shared system of meanings. Examining this aspect of the prison soundscape reveals an additional facet of navigations of power inside; material constraints of space and goods are circumvented by deploying innovative strategies with sound. Considering these facets of everyday prison life adds nuance to our understanding of the cell, elevating these hidden spaces beyond symbols of imprisonment, and the spaces within which incarceration is most keenly felt. Listening to sound from the cell encourages engagement with the significance of spaces beyond what can be seen. In so doing, attending to sound in cell spaces extends our understanding of imprisonment further than is possible by privileging the visual.

While banging illustrates the ways in which sound could be used in cell to transcend spatial limitations, the prison soundscape also intruded upon the 'sanctuary' that the cell could offer. Sound could present as an inescapable reminder of the wider meaning of imprisonment within the cell space, the clangs, bangs and shouts permeating the walls, vibrating through the body. The materiality of sound could be felt upon the body, reinforcing the pains of imprisonment within the cell. Conversely, while private space was hard to come by, uses of sound within the cell also provided a means for re-inhabiting the self in ways which provided sanctuary. Prisoners reported using sound as a means of carving out space for expressing and exploring their sense of self in opposition to the intrusive effects of the prison environment. Sound here was used as a protective membrane, preserving identity and a means of exercising sonic agency (Labelle 2019).

## Sound, Cell and Sanctuary

Sound could be experienced as reinforcing the pains of imprisonment upon the incarcerated body: 'See, those doors bang. They don't mean it but it goes through you, you feel it in your body' (Clive, prisoner). Attempts to carve out space to reassert the private self could be threatened by the pervasiveness of prison sounds not only reaching the ears but literally imposing the prison environment on and in the body of the prisoner. Clangs, bangs and rumblings in the bowels of the prison could reinforce the sense of imprisonment by reverberating through the incarcerated body. While the mind might find respite and escape from the sights of prison, the intrusiveness of sound could act as an inescapable reminder of the prison surroundings.

Not all sound has profound physical impact, but the absence of 'earlids' ensures the reach of auditory information extends far beyond the limits of vision (Carpenter and Mcluhan 1960). The particular meaning of prison sounds lent them additional force, intruding upon personal space and transgressing boundaries both physical and mental: 'Behind your door, you turn your telly up but you can always hear the keys' (Si, prisoner). At Midtown a number of men reported experiencing the jangling of the keys as an imposition of symbolic power (Bourdieu 1977). The sound of the keys reinforced awareness of prisoner's subaltern status by reminding them of their incarceration. Despite these negative aspects of auditory experience, sound was also harnessed by a number of men as a means of carving out space, peace and solitude. As with a number of prison staff, 'peace' was a complicated and loaded term, often a euphemism for 'quiet'. Conversely, quiet often referred to an absence of trouble (Liebling et al. 2010), a calm and regular day, ironically often the noisiest of all.

Officer Rose explained the satisfaction of a prison day well-managed: 'happiness is door-shaped: that's a reference to, once we've got everybody in a cell, and everybody behind the door then we get that, that peace'. As he also pointed out, it was far from unusual for prisoners to request bang up, particularly if a day felt 'bubbly' (volatile), or they were feeling low or troubled: 'I've had prisoners come to me and say: "Oh Mr Rose, there's something wrong I don't like that, can you bang me up?"' The strains of boredom and the perils of 'bang up' were omnipresent, but time in cell also offered a means of carving out private space in ways which featured in a variety of coping and adaptation strategies which used sound as a means of reinforcing a sense of self. Sound was used by some as a means of creating an insulating cocoon, an additional layer between their person and the prison walls, within which they sought respite from the impact of incarceration.

Sound and the relative amount of control over it behind the door presented the opportunity to transcend the physical constraints of the environment offering partial respite from the prison soundscape. Prisoners utilised the auditory imagination to carve out personal space for themselves within the cell, to detach themselves from the prison environment, using sound to reinforce their separateness. Similar to those Ben Crewe identifies as 'retreatists' amongst his adaptive typology, in that these 'pad rats' were neither subdued nor seduced by prison rules (Crewe 2009: 191). The physical withdrawal of these individuals was echoed in their quietness and lack of contribution to the aural environment. In contrast to both Crewe's typology and much of the local population of Midtown, these men sometimes lacked long-entrenched narratives of drug dependency. Rather than retreating, these behaviours of avoidance of wider prison society in preference of their pads (cells) were about distancing from prison society[5] and the intrusive soundscape which reinforced the sense of imprisonment within it. Urfan spoke passionately about his difference from those around him: 'Yes, change myself to stay in cell and not speak to anyone. Stay in cell, that's it … I don't want involved. Stay inside and do with the reading'. Urfan was keen to emphasise his good character which he marked with his separateness. His expressions of resistance to involvement with wider prison life were framed in this context of quiet separateness. In contrast, Lamar did have a history of drug use. For him withdrawing from prison society was a statement of his desire to move on and be done with this aspect of prison life: 'I'd hardly talk to anyone. I'd come out my cell for my hour, get my shower, go on the phone, and before it's even time to bang up I'm banging up myself cos I just don't want to be around it'. The cell, therefore, featured in identity performance: a means of declaring personhood in contrast to others. Unlike the use of the cell to express a desirable pro-social identity, Urfan and Lamar expressed their good character by drawing on their cells as sites of withdrawal from prison society and the soundscape which lends it shape and meaning. These formed one in an extensive range of adaptive behaviours in which the cell featured in strategies of survival as well as resistance in everyday life (Jewkes 2013).

The relative privacy cells offered were also used to reconstitute the self. Prisoners used these as places to recalibrate, to express their emotions by using sound and its absence to prompt memories of other times and spaces. Lugs explained drug use: 'takes the bars away for the night'. Drugs here provide a means of dulling the senses to the prison environment. Time could move differently in these private spaces, less constrained by intrusive aural markers of the daily regime: 'It goes fast behind that door though Kate. Very fast' (Lugs, prisoner). Tonk, conversely, used his cell differently to carve out space to shore up his emotional wellbeing. He was highly verbal and boisterous, but for him this time served an important function:

> Release… that's what I do, like I need music in my cell. I need music like, I love to just sing and let it out… you know what I mean? If I aint got music I'll either bang my door or shout out my window or shout to other lads like. (Tonk, prisoner)

Sound could be used to carve out separate space. For Tonk the cell was a sonic sanctuary, the absence of which was likely to reduce anyone else's ability to find any. Tonk's feeling of safety derived from the freedom to express himself without fear of censure, a freedom he found within the confines of his cell and the comforts of his own noise. Other than his habitual gym use, his ability to express himself behind his cell door was a necessary means of letting off steam and recalibrating mental balance. For Boyd, time in his cell allowed for auditory imaginings of other times and places:

> Yeah, if I'm listening to CDS, like there's certain songs, when I was with my partner and the kids all doing funny things, and that song comes on again, it reminds you of good times, when we were all doing silly things, like that, that's a good thing I suppose. (Boyd, prisoner)

In the cell, sound was used to summon memories of loved ones and to explore emotions in relative privacy (Herrity 2018). Boyd explicitly refers to the way in which sound, in this case music, was used within his cell to revisit warm memories, the times and places these were made and the feelings associated with them. There was a sociality to sonic memory which eased the passing of time, in contrast to the correspondents who featured in Ian O'Donnell's account of solitude in prison (O'Donnell 2016). Prisoners used their cells to emotionally recalibrate, or to submerge themselves in memories of happier times, summoning temporary respite from the privations of prison.

Difficulty dealing with time 'behind the door' was a profound marker for poor coping with prison more generally, unsurprisingly since this accounted for most of the time. In some ways, coping with and adapting to the doing of time was a solitary process. However, living at such close proximity entangled one another's wellbeing. One man's poor coping could endanger that of the next; expressions of distress and agitation within such confined spaces could prove intrusive. Seamus' account of the difficulty some experienced behind the door demonstrates the inescapable sociality of prison life:

> banging, crying, screaming keeps us awake—they can't do their bang up you see. They should leave the doors open and they'd be okay, it's all those hours locked up by themselves, they can't take it, does their head in then none of us sleep. Keeps us awake all night. Big problem. (Seamus, prisoner)

Changing relationships with the cell also functioned as an indicator that something was wrong. Sabotage of this space could be an expression of profound distress. At the far end of a spectrum of behaviours are 'flat-packing' (destruction of the cell and its furniture), deliberately blocking sinks or setting cell fires where the inhabitant effectively risks self-immolation. Shifting testimony about time in cell was a less dramatic means of illustrating psychological deterioration. Natty, a prisoner on an indeterminate sentence for public protection with a tariff of 18 months but now nearing the 10-year mark of time inside, told me on a particularly bleak day: 'I don't listen to music anymore. I don't watch TV. Just silence and I hear everything going on around me'. Natty seemed particularly prone to mood swings, but on this occasion, his passivity within his space indicated a particularly bad spell. He had, albeit briefly—he was quite hopeful about the latest parole hearing which was keeping him at Midtown on hold—lost the will to assert himself. In talking about his lack of retreat from the sonic assaults of the prison, he appeared to be indicating the soundscape threatened to engulf him in the endless tides of banging, clanging and shouting which dominated the daily symphony of prison life.

Time in cell offered the opportunity to emotionally recalibrate away from the hustle and bustle of the wing. This time could also function as a space for invoking auditory imaginings of other times and places, memories fundamental to the self-narrative. A declining ability to harness these opportunities could serve as an indicator of deteriorating wellbeing. While the cell soundscape featured in individual endeavours to express identity or shore up a sense of self in opposition to the prison environment, sound in the cell was also a key site for navigating wider social relations.

## 'I Can Tell You Exactly What's Happening Around the Prison': The Cell as a Site of Sousveillance

Tom Rice (2013) explores the role of sound in practices of monitoring and surveillance in the hospital setting. As he points out, auscultation—listening to internal sounds of the body—is a feature of medical work. This is expanded externally, he argues, in daily rituals which reify patient identities through the meanings attached to the hospital soundscape, creating what Barry Truax terms an 'acoustic community' (Rice 2013; Truax 2001). Rice focuses on practices of listening and wider epistemological claims remain implicit. Nevertheless his work can be extended to form a proposal for social 'auscultation': a means of discerning the rhythms of daily institutional life by listening (Rice 2010). This is a useful starting point for exploring the significance of sound in the prison institution, but while sound features in practices of surveillance in prison, sound is also integral to practices of 'sousveillance' in which the cell was crucial. Jan Fernback (2012) defines sousveillance as inverse surveillance: acts that resist monitoring practices of power; watching the watched, or in this case, listening to the listeners. The cell was a central site for navigating the tensions inherent in dynamics of power and resistance. Behind the door offered a uniquely privileged listening point for gathering knowledge and a means of circumnavigating surveillance to navigate the prison environment. While the pains of imprisonment were written on the carceral body in the materiality of sound, the intimate familiarity with the sounds of daily life this afforded was a source of knowledge which could be utilised to ameliorate the loss of liberty.

While sound played a fundamental role in monitoring order for staff, it had a more explicit role in gauging what was going on for those confined behind the door. An unsettled, 'bubbly', social climate echoed in the soundscape, a harbinger of incidents to come. The ability to identify and anticipate events was a major preoccupation of the prison community. Officer Rose made this point:

> Some mornings they'll come out and it'll be so subdued, and you just know. Something's gonna go, you just know. Don't know what it is, it'll probably be somebody's gonna come out and batter somebody else, something like that, but you can sense it's gonna happen but you just don't know what it is. (Rose, prison officer)

Officer Rose's account of discerning trouble through the soundscape identifies practices of auscultation as fundamental to the maintenance of order and safety. His account also conveyed a sense of premonitory wariness as central to staff experience. Officer Rose later describes this as predicated on experience, as becoming instinctive… after a while. Officer Tone's remark that 'they know a hell of a lot, they're in tune with wherever you are' amplifies the use of sound as a means of overcoming restricted vision—staff rarely move around the prison without the accompanying percussion of rubber soles on metal, the rustling of uniform and rhythmic jangling of keys. His observation also underscores this distinction between the staff experience of premonitory wariness and that of prisoner's 'consumptive wariness' (Crewe et al. 2014). Ben Crewe et al.

use this term to describe the perpetual feeling of leery discomfort imposed by the prison environment. The intrusiveness of the prison soundscape provides an explanatory mechanism for how this feeling is maintained so consistently behind the door. Conversely participants' reflections on sound and prison life resonate with the contradictions and limits of panoptical power (Foucault 1977). Without acknowledgement of the potential afforded by their sonic skill set, staff were limited by the peripheries of vision and doomed to gauge stability by assessing the whole, rather than drawing on the methods used by the prisoner community. The few were surveilled by the many (Mathieson 1997). Stretch echoed this point:

> I can stand next to staff and have a conversation with you blatantly at this level, and he will not know what I'm on about … the screws? Useless! … I can tell you what they're talking about and I'm on the fours and they're on the threes, you know why? Cos they can't talk to each other like we can, without looking. (Stretch, prisoner)

In recognising a nexus between sound, knowledge and power, prisoners' adaptive behaviours gave them the upper hand: 'I can tell you exactly what's happening round the prison. It's crazy' (Stretch, prisoner). Stretch's account also echoes Sykes' (1958) assessment of the contingent, partial and fluid nature of power negotiations. The cell is a crucial site on which these negotiations are conducted, sound the conduit through which they are contested.

This distinction in experience can be identified as stemming from different ways of knowing. It is worth pointing out too that many of the men I spoke with had extensive experience not only of prison but HMP Midtown specifically. Lugs and Stretch, for example, had clocked up decades of time at Midtown between them, as well as being local men in a local prison largely for local people. Prisoners necessarily spent more time inside, in addition to utilising intelligence gained from that most particular of vantage points, or acoustic 'sweet spots': the cell. Tonk explains: 'this is my… I live here! You [officers] work here, but at the minute I live here more than them'. His intimate knowledge of his surroundings was born of an association with the *rhythms* of daily life uninterrupted by the intrusions of normal existence. Whether or not this determined more was at stake in failing to keep abreast of events, it certainly contributed to an unbroken familiarity with the ebb and flow of prison life. This intimate acquaintance with the everyday rhythms of daily activity provided a uniquely privileged vantage point from which to keep abreast of developments.

Prisoners drew heavily from the particular knowledge derived from what they heard behind the cell door: 'You hear it more in the cell cos you hear like the walls echoing. Outside everyone's talking you can't really hear it' (Mooch, prisoner). Stretch corroborated Mooch's account of sound as a tool for sousveillance when he recounted identifying trouble the night before: 'I was like: the block's getting smashed up … I was only leaning on the wall … but I knew from the vibrations, cos there's different vibrations from music to damage'. Sound, in providing a source of knowledge, was inextricably intertwined with power relations: 'I hear a lot. I know what goes on in here man' (Mooch). Listening out for trouble was a basis for diagnosing its direction, a necessary tool for both monitoring the monitors (where trouble is, staff will frequently follow) and in the ecology of survival (Toch 1992). Sound was a powerful source of knowledge, and ability to interpret the soundscape was intimately bound with assertions of status: 'I can tell you exactly what's happening around the prison … because this is my domain, this is my manor' (Stretch, prisoner).

Recognising the role of the cell as a site of knowledge also adds nuance to understandings of the way in which power operates in prison spaces. The soundscape offers a sonic semaphore with which to navigate prison spaces. Various prisoners reported drawing on sound to keep them abreast of what was happening when confined behind the door, whether listening—and feeling—or more conventionally communicating whether through windows or, as Lugs suggested was a bygone tactic, emptying the loos to talk through the pipes.

Officer Tone rather cynically illustrated the role of sousveillance in avoiding staff attention when he joked: 'mischief greatly heightens the senses'. While the uses of sensory information had far greater scope than this, the men reported the cell as the site of a range of behaviours that might otherwise result in punishment. As Davey explained: 'If I am gonna fight I'll go somewhere where it won't be seen'. This again raised the issue of the degree to which the cells featured in the hidden life of prison, a side of prison society which the staff either struggled to catch up on or remained oblivious or indifferent to: 'A lot of fights happen in pads. And staff don't even know about it' (Tonk, prisoner). Lugs made clear the extent to which these behaviours were adopted as a means of navigating surveillance: "There's cameras so if we do owt we have to go in the toilet or a cell to say "Yo, ra ra ra"'. A whole range of life at HMP Midtown was conducted in cells and out of view both of staff and much of the prisoner population though, in the case of the latter, much could be heard or discerned through the walls or via gossip—a permanent feature of daily routine. Avoiding being seen in these instances also meant retreating to spaces beyond the hearing of those outside the network of cells. Here, sound operates in a number of ways both circumventing and subverting surveillance. Considering the significance of the prison soundscape, then, reveals additional facets of prison life and the way in which hidden spaces—specifically the cell—are utilised in everyday life beyond our line of sight.

Accounting for life out of view adds texture to understandings of daily life inside, but in this particular context also offers instruction on the role of violence in prison. Aside from the suggestion that much violence may be unseen, unchallenged and unrecorded, it also adds nuance to considerations of its function when visible. The No. 1 governor illuminated a central rule of prison life for the whole community: 'People don't want to be mugged off'. Davey examined the particular functions of violence and the role of the cell as a site for negotiating status:

> If someone comes up to you and calls you a dickhead for example, if there was no one there you could just go "shut up, get away from me". But because those people are there you think he's just done that now these lot'll think they can do it to me, so I'll have to do something about it. I think that's how it works in here, what you'll find is they think they're something, in front of all their mates, but if you say to them if you're such a big man you come to my pad, on your own… the people who have got something about them, they will come to your pad. (Davey, prisoner)

His experience prompts contemplation of just how much of prison life, particularly violence, is conducted out of view. This adds to the ways in which violence can be understood, as well as prison life more generally. If much of violence and score-settling is conducted out of view, what challenge does this pose to the way we understand prison life? Considering the role of sound in cell life not only adds nuance to understanding of the functions of violence in prison life but also the ways in which listening and identifying aural cues is an important tool in the armoury of strategies of safety and security. Trouble—a 'bubbly' day—has a sound, and those well versed in the semaphore of the prison soundscape recognise it.

Recognising the role of cell sound in practices of sousveillance adds complexity to understandings of the contingent nature of power in prison spaces. This places sound, and the cell, at the centre of navigations of power and resistance on which order and safety depend. The ability to decipher the soundscape as a means of mapping activity around the space overcame physical limitations of vision and movement. Prisoners used auscultation of their inner world as a means of demonstrating status and negotiating survival, anticipating violence and eluding authority's gaze. Sound illuminated the ways in which the disempowerment of incarceration paradoxically designated the incarcerated body as site of knowledge and power. Considering the significance of the cell in this way illuminated the textures of violence in prison, strongly indicating its social purpose as a means of enforcing social codes as well as navigating the prison social world. Stretch illustrated this point more succinctly than I: 'If you can't hear, you have to feel'.

## Concluding Thoughts

Using sound as a means of casting light over spaces beyond the peripheries of vision offers a means of understanding the ways in which prisoners assert identity in resisting the constraints of imprisonment. Asking about less targeted features of the prison lent greater scope for relaying sonic expressions of identity within the cell. As a result, the ways in which sound within the cell featured in strategies of coping became clearer. In addition to more performative aspects of self, the cell was also central to strategies of self-preservation. The cell could provide physical retreat and emotional respite, an opportunity both to recalibrate and to invoke experience of other times and spaces by harnessing the auditory imagination. Exploring out-of-sight spaces through enquiring about sound emphasised the potential of sound as a way of producing knowledge about how prison spaces are experienced.

The prison community also used sound as a source of knowledge in processes of surveillance and sousveillance. Sound sites the cell at the nexus of tensions between power and knowledge in prison. The cell could be utilised in navigating prison life, in demonstrations of status and practices of survival. Using sound to illuminate the cell acted as a portal to the hidden textures of prison life and strategies of coping. Hearing behind the door prompts us to question what we miss when we fail to take account of what lies beyond the limits of our vision and what implications that has for how we understand our processes of meaning making. Focussing on sound reveals the rich diversity of prison life beyond our line of sight, and the humanity of those forced to exist within it.

## Notes

1. All names are pseudonyms to protect the identity of those I spoke with and are often derived from information exchanged between the participant and I. This extends to the prison which I refer to as HMP Midtown.
2. Local prisons house those awaiting trial, immediately after conviction, or if subject to a relatively short sentence (less than four years) when preparing for release. In practice men—and these are always men's prisons, women's prisons form a separate category within the estate and form a small fraction (approx. 5 per cent of the population)—with a staggering array of sentences and circumstances pass through or become stuck while waiting for parole or appeal hearings.
3. 'Soundscape' refers to aural components of the environment, or landscape. The definition provided by the British Standards Institute includes dimensions of experience (expectation, memory, emotion) which do not reflect sound as it is heard, but rather as it is interpreted within particular spatial contexts (BSI 2014).
4. 'No. 1' refers to the prison governor—head of the prison—overseeing security and day-to-day running.

5. The advent of 'NPS', deepening prison crises and expanding prison population have combined to impose significant changes on the prisoner society in the last decade. 'NPS' refers to new psychoactive substances. These are chemical compounds designed to mimic the effects of other drugs (synthetic cannabinoids with trade names such as 'spice' and 'mamba' are particularly common though compounds change and evolve quite rapidly as well as being highly variable).

## References


Bourdieu, P. (1977). *Outline of a Theory of Practice* (R. Nice, Trans.). Cambridge: Cambridge University Press.

British Standards Institute. (2014). *BS ISO 12913-1:2014 Acoustics—Soundscape Part 1: A Definition and Conceptual Framework*. London: BSI Limited.

Carpenter, E., & McLuhan, M. (1960). Acoustic Space. In E. Carpenter & M. McLuhan (Eds.), *Explorations in Communication: An Anthology* (pp. 65–70). Boston: Beacon Press.

Chion, M. (2010). *Sound: An Acoulogical Treatise* (J. A. Steintrager, Trans.). London: Duke University Press.

Crewe, B. (2009). *The Prisoner Society: Power, Adaptation and Social Life in an English Prison*. Oxford: Oxford University Press.

Crewe, B., Warr, J., Bennett, P., & Smith, A. (2014). The Emotional Geography of Prison Life. *Theoretical Criminology, 18*(1), 56–74.

Eliot, T. S. (1933). *The Use of Poetry and the Use of Criticism*. London: Faber and Faber.

Fernback, J. (2012). Sousveillance: Communities of Resistance to the Surveillance Movement. *Telematics and Informatics, 30*(1), 11–21.

Foucault, M. (1977). *Discipline and Punish: The Birth of the Modern Prison* (A. Sheridan, Trans.). New York, NY: Vintage.

Her Majesty's Chief Inspector of Prisons (HMCIP). (2018). *Her Majesty's Chief Inspector of Prisons for England and Wales Annual Report 2017–2018*. Retrieved November 8, 2018, from https://assets.publishing.service.gov.uk/government/uploads/system/uploads/attachment_data/file/724526/HMI-Prisons_Annual_Report_2017-18.pdf.

Herrity, K. (2018). Music and Identity in Prison: Music as a Technology of the Self. *Prison Service Journal, 239*, 40–47.

Herrity, K. (2019). *Rhythms and Routines: Sounding Order and Survival in a Local Men's Prison through Aural Ethnography*. PhD thesis, University of Leicester.

Idhe, D. (2007). *Listening and Voice: Phenomenologies of Sound*. Albany, NY: State University of New York Press.

Jewkes, Y. (2013). On Carceral Space and Agency. In D. Moran, N. Gill, & D. Conlon (Eds.), *Carceral Spaces: Mobility and Agency in Imprisonment and Migrant Detention* (pp. 127–131). Farnham: Ashgate.

Kelly, L. M. (2017). *Silent Punishment: The Experiences of d/Deaf Prisoners*. PhD thesis, University of Central Lancashire.

Klatte, M., Bergstrom, K., & Lachmann, T. (2013). Does Noise Affect Learning: A Short Review on Noise Effects on Cognitive Performance. *Frontiers in Psychology, 4*, 1–6. Retrieved May 21, 2019, from https://www.frontiersin.org/articles/10.3389/fpsyg.2013.00578/full.

Labelle, B. (2019). *Sonic Agency: Sound and Emergent Forms of Resistance*. Boston, MA: MIT Press.

Liebling, A., Price, D., & Shefer, G. (2010). *The Prison Officer*. London: Routledge.

Mathieson, M. (1997). The Viewer Society: Michel Foucault's 'Panopticon' Revisited. *Theoretical Criminology, 1*(2), 215–234.

McNeill, F. (2018). *Pervasive Punishment: Making Sense of Mass Supervision*. Bingley: Emerald.

Moran, D. (2012). 'Doing Time' in Carceral Space: Timespace and Carceral Geography. *Geografiska Annaler: Series B Human Geography, 94*(4), 305–316.

Munzel, T., Gora, T., Babisch, W., & Basner, M. (2014). Cardiovascular Effects of Environmental Noise Exposure. *European Heart Journal, 35*(13), 829–836.

O'Donnell, I. (2016). *Prisoners, Solitude and Time*. Oxford: Clarendon Studies in Criminology.

Rice, T. (2010). Learning to Listen: Auscultation and the Transmission of Auditory Knowledge. *Journal of the Royal Anthropological Institute, 16*(1), 41–61.

Rice, T. (2013). *Hearing and the Hospital: Sound, Listening, Knowledge and Experience*. Canon Pyon: Sean Kingston.

Sykes, G. ([1958] 2007). *The Society of Captives: A Study of a Maximum-Security Prison*. Oxford: Princeton University Press.

Toch, H. (1992). *Living in Prison: The Ecology of Survival*. Washington, DC: American Psychological Association.

Toop, D. (2010). *Sinister Resonance: The Mediumship of the Listener*. London: Continuum.
Truax, B. (2001). *Acoustic Communication*. New Haven, CT: Ablex.
Turner, J. (2016). *The Prison Boundary: Between Society and Carceral Space*. London: Palgrave Macmillan.

# 12

# Prison Cell Spaces, Bodies and Touch

Elisabeth Fransson and Francesca Giofrè

## Introduction

The prison cell is both a concrete place experienced by physical bodies and an imagined room that we meet in fiction, films and, also more recently, via penal tourism (Turner 2013). The prison cell symbolises penalty (Foucault 1977) and is, in classic penological literature, considered to be the most intimate and private space within the prison where the prisoner rests, sleeps, eats and is alone with their thoughts (Gramsci 1947). Through Jean-Luc Nancy's (2008) concept of *touching*, this chapter disrupts traditional understandings of the prison cell as an isolated unit within the prison by exploring various prison cells, their boundaries and extensions. The analysis is facilitated by material generated through a comparative study in two

The original version of this chapter was revised An correction to this chapter can be found at https://doi.org/10.1057/978-3-030-39911-5_15

E. Fransson (✉)
University College of Norwegian Correctional Service, Oslo, Norway
e-mail: Elisabeth.Fransson@krus.no

F. Giofrè
Department of Architecture and Design, Sapienza University of Rome, Italy



J. Turner, V. Knight (eds.), *The Prison Cell*, Palgrave Studies in Prisons and Penology,
https://doi.org/10.1007/978-3-030-39911-5_12

female prisons in Italy and Norway and highlights three spaces crucially related to the cell: inside cell spaces, corridor spaces and threshold spaces.

Elizabeth Grosz's (1994) concept of *bodies in-place* and *bodies out-of-place* helps to highlight the cultural meanings connected to embodied practices in various prison cell spaces and how such prison cell spaces touch and are touched by female bodies. The intention with this chapter is to develop an analytical optic regarding the relationship between prison cell spaces, bodies and touch. Touch, within this analytical gaze, is not just a concept we use to analyse the material conducted, but is crucial for us as researchers as we touch and are touched by the research field through our mode of study and the classifications and concepts we use. In this way, the chapter explores prison cells by putting ontological and epistemological questions at the core of the analysis. The first section of the chapter introduces the analytical framework related to sensuous architecture and the philosophy of touch. In the second section, we introduce the context and our methodological strategy; and, in the third, we present the analysis of three spaces intrinsic to the prison cell: inside cell spaces, corridor spaces and threshold spaces and their relationship with touch.

## Sensuous Architecture, the Philosophy of Touch and Prison Boundaries

The Finnish architect Juhani Pallasmaa (2005) argues that modern consciousness and sensory reality is dominated by the sense of vision. The power of the eye over the other sensory realms has turned architecture into an art form of instant visual image, leaving out the concept of touch as a multi-sensory experience that is a significant experience of architecture. However, qualities of matter, space and scale are also measured by the ear, nose, skin, tongue, skeleton and muscle (Pallasmaa 2005: 41). All the senses, including vision, are extensions of the sense of touch. The senses are specialisations of the skin, and all sensory experiences are related to tactility, as the anthropologist Montagu argues:

> [The skin] is the oldest and the most sensitive of our organs, our first medium of communication, and our most efficient protector [...]. Even the transparent cornea of the eye is overlain by a layer of modified skin [...].

> Touch is the parent of our eyes, ears, nose, and mouth. It is the sense which became differentiated into the others, a fact that seems to be recognized in the age-old evaluation of touch as 'the mother of the senses'. (Montagu 1986: 3, in Pallasmaa 2005: ii)

Sensuous architecture is closely linked to touch, which in this chapter, will be understood as both physical, emotional and philosophical. Touch can relate to physical, visceral contact: the sensory experience of touching through the skin. Touch is also emotional: we can be touched with or without physical contact, when a feeling arises in us through direct or indirect contact with an object or a person (Derrida 2005). Touch is, then, also philosophical—it is a way of making sense of engagements and relations between things. Moreover, touching is both visible and invisible and requires the movement of bodies, where it is impossible to be in exactly the same place, at the same time. As Nancy explains:

> Two bodies can't occupy the same place simultaneously. Therefore you and I are not simultaneously in the place where I write, where you read, where I speak, where you listen. No contact without displacement. The fax goes fast; but speed is spacing. There is now way that we, you and I, will touch each other, or touch onto entries into bodies. A discourse is obligated to indicate its source, its point of emission, its condition of possibility, and its point of departure. But I can't speak *from where* you listen, and you can't hear *from where* I speak—nor can we, either of us, hear where the discourse is speaking from (and is *spoken from*). (Nancy 2008: 57)

Sensuous architecture and the philosophy of touch opens up for studying the complex relationships between bodies and prison cell spaces. Bodies within prison cells move: they get in and out of beds, walk out of the prison cell, come back inside, look in one direction and then another, eat and think. In all of these activities, bodies with different energies, tempo, rhythms and tones touch and are touched (Derrida 2005; Nancy 2008; Fransson 2018; Rossholt 2012). Some bodies lie in bed and do not want to go out of the cell; others cannot wait for the cell door to be opened in the morning. Others engage with their surroundings and the people in them in less physical ways.

International prison rules, national penal codes and local correctional rules and discourses define when the cell door is open and when it is closed. Old penal discourses mix with new thoughts embodied by prison officers that enter the prison cell. The prison cell context and the numbers of bodies within the prison cell have impact on movements, as well as staff moving in and out of the prison cell. A prison officer coming in to talk, a comment or a certain gaze from another prisoner, a memory or a physical touch can change how a body reacts from one moment to another (Grønvold and Fransson 2019). Anxiety, fear, calmness, hunger and passion are produced in the body by movements within and outside the cell.

Boundaries between the inside and the outside of prisons and other institutions were a key issue in classic sociology (Foucault 1977; Goffman 1961) and have, in later years, been renewed to problematise the "insides" and "outsides" of prisons. In *The Prison Boundary*, Turner (2016) gives an overview of the prison boundary literature and points out that boundaries can be both a hard line and a symbolic construction that often deals with everyday border work (Turner 2016: 54). In this chapter, we are inspired by elements in this literature regarding "inside", "outside" and "everyday border work" as we disrupt traditional understandings of the concept of the prison cell by incorporating the corridor and the threshold as extensions of the prison cell. Through the analytical optic of sensuous architecture and the philosophy of touch in combination with prison ethnography and architectural design, we analyse bodies-space relationships comparing an Italian and Norwegian prison.

## Context and Methodological Strategy

Prison research in Norway and Italy has traditionally been situated in two different penological traditions: Norway in the Nordic and Anglo-Saxon tradition and Italy in the continental tradition together with countries like France and Germany (Fransson, Giofrè & Johnsen 2018). A comparative study of the prison cell in these two countries is interesting because of their differences regarding penal ideologies, prison architecture, correctional care and discourses (Giofrè, Porro & Fransson 2018). The intention with this chapter is to develop an analytical optic regarding the relationship between prison cell spaces, body and touch. Since similarities and differences are constructed and developed through our positions, gaze and conceptual understandings as researchers (Fransson et al.

2018; Giofrè et al. 2018; Krogstad 2000), we need to reflect upon what and how we hear, see, smell and touch. What, for instance, does noise versus silence do to us as researchers? Within the analytical optic of Nancy's concept *touching* (Nancy 2008), we offer an original approach to what a prison cell can become and the various dimensions of prison cell spaces. By thinking philosophically and in a non-representational manner, we follow Deleuze and Guattari (1994) who argue that concepts should be developed by focusing on events that encourage the thought to do thinking. In this research it is not the number of interviews or observations that is most important. The purpose is neither to provide comparisons nor paint a representative picture, since the world does not ask to be observed in certain ways but is constructed by the researcher (Lather 1991; Fransson and Johnsen 2015; Rossholt 2012, Åkerstrøm Andersen 2003). In accordance with this epistemological approach, the empirical material is varied but centred on prison cells and prison cell spaces in two of the largest women's prison in Italy and Norway.

Rebibbia in Rome, Italy, and Bredtveit in Oslo, Norway, are the largest prisons for women in these two countries. Rebibbia was built in the early 1970s, inside a men's district jail built in the 1950s, and designed to accommodate 267 prisoners, but it is often overcrowded. The prison accommodates women in high, medium and low security sections. Bredtveit was originally a farm, taken over by the state in 1929. It has, since 1949, been a prison for women. The prison accommodates 64 women in high and low security sections.

Both in Italy and Norway the methodological approach consists of prison ethnography and architectural design. In Italy, following a period of negotiation of access, we conducted three field visits and held interviews with 14 imprisoned women and five prison staff members in the prison from September 2018 until March 2019. The prisoners were mostly chosen by the prison staff. They were either interviewed individually or in pairs, and some of the interviews were conducted in the presence of staff. In some cases, prisoners were asked to produce sketches or drawings to explain their interactions with the space of the cell and its surroundings. We also observed the prison cells and the spaces connected with them and analysed key policy documents such as the prison rules.

In Norway, we first visited the prison in the early spring of 2018 and spent time observing spaces throughout the prison, including the residential corridors and some of the cells. After our initial site visit, in which we were accompanied by the prison inspector, it transpired that a programme of conventional interviews would be impossible given the various other research commitments ongoing in the prison at that time. Instead, we were offered the opportunity to participate in an event in the prison: the celebration of World Health Day (9 December 2018), which was meticulously planned by both staff and prisoners, in terms of its programme and security arrangements. The day featured a showcase of different activities: poetry readings, singing, discussion around a gardening project, a presentation of the prison radio station, a knitting club and a discussion between prisoners and an inspector about the conditions in the prison. The World Health Day was attended by several external speakers and participants. Here, we were able to converse informally with the women whilst enjoying the activities and sharing food. After this day, we returned to the prison the following week to conduct a focus group with four women. We also subsequently returned for further discussions with the prison administration. In Norway as in Italy, we analysed key policy documents such as the prison rules. As part of the data, our own gaze and reflections as researchers in these two different prison spaces also became crucial to the process of analysing the research material.

## Cells, Corridors, Thresholds

Analysing and comparing the data collected, we found that prison cells must be contextualised and related to various architectonical and cultural settings and movements. Through further analysis, we discerned that prison cells have borders, extensions and "in-betweens". Importantly, then, we attend here to the critical relationship between cells and corridors, which also highlights a third significant space: the threshold. The typical prison cell in the Italian prison is a room of 14 m$^2$ shared by two, three or four female prisoners. In the Norwegian prison women are housed in individual cells, which range from 7 m$^2$ to 20 m$^2$. Accordingly, to be housed alone in the prison cell or to share it with other prisoners reveals important differences in the relationships regarding the body and prison cell spaces in Italy and Norway. Inside the cell, through movements, women create bodily relationships and boundaries to others. Being one or several bodies within the same cell means that cells are touching and touched differently by female bodies. Boundaries, distance and proximity have to be dealt with in different ways, and personal spaces are defined differently in cells shared by women.

In both prisons, the cells are organised along corridors, but the architectural frame of the corridor reveals differences impacting on the concept of what a cell is, its boundaries and extensions. In the Norwegian prison, the cells are organised along a linear corridor. In opening the cell door, the women pass directly out into a corridor, which is usually a silent space. On the other side of the corridor, there is either a wall with windows (Fig. 12.1a) or other cell doors (Fig. 12.1b). The corridor leads to the kitchen or the sitting room, where women can meet other prisoners and staff. Conversely, in the Italian prison, the cells are organised along a corridor that surrounds an "open" courtyard, around viewing balconies. Opening the cell door, the imprisoned body can see and be a part of the bigger prison community, sounds, movements, different languages and conflicts. The prison cell "is the *modus operandi* of the disciplinary powers, but … to make a cell, you need corridors" (Trüby et al. 2014: 941). The corridor is the space that suggests and contains mobility (Armstrong 2015) and has a different meaning according to its role of connection with the cell and other prison spaces. The movement of the body inside the cell changes based on how the outside corridor is articulated. Moving the body from the cell through the linear corridor—as in the Norwegian case (Fig. 12.1a and b)—constructs the corridor as a pathway to get to other rooms like the kitchen, the sitting room or to the education centre or activity rooms within the prison. In the Italian case (Fig. 12.1c), the corridor has an added meaning: it is not only a pathway, but a place where things happen.

Moreover, during our period of onsite observation, we identified another key space that has an impact on the cell by being both a part of it and a link to the corridor: the threshold. Moving from inside the cell into the corridor, the body has to pass the threshold. We relate the threshold to the concept of boundary "as a broad term that refers to any type of

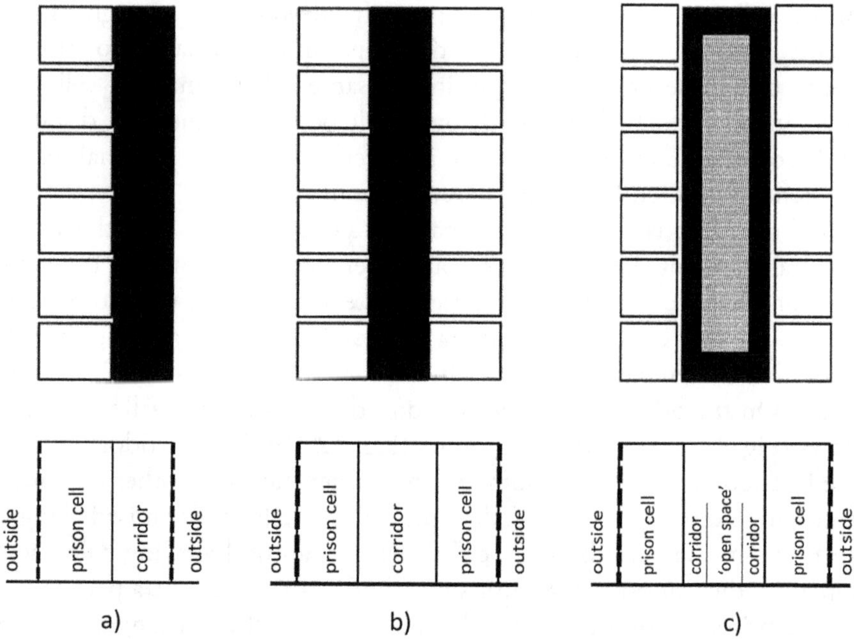


**Fig. 12.1** Cell and corridor: the distribution (Source: F Giofrè)

division" (Turner 2016: 30); however, the threshold also allows the transition from one zone to another. Therefore, threshold is a part of the boundary of the prison cell that sometimes can be perceived as a barrier and in other times perceived as an element that opens up spaces (Boettger 2014: 10). Accordingly, we define the prison cell threshold as an invisible line dividing the prison cell from the corridor, inside the cell from outside the cell, the body as it is inside the cell from the way the body moves and relates to bodies outside the cell.

All these connected prison cell spaces touch and are touched by female bodies differently in Italy and Norway. In the following section, we begin our analysis inside various cells. We then go out in the corridors and, finally, pause on the threshold between the cell and the corridor.

## Inside Cell Spaces

> My cell is the most beautiful one. I have the orange curtains, before they were yellow. I also made the plastic storage trolley covers. In the bathroom, I made some bags to keep things all in the same colour, even toilet paper holders and carpets, bedspreads. My cell is beautiful, wonderful, protective, there are no suffering walls. I am obsessed with cleaning. (Valeria,[1] Italian prison)

There is something universal and very essential about the way in which Valeria speaks of how she has worked with her cell. By making plastic storage trolley covers and bags to keep things in, she has made the cell her "home". However, in touching these prison artefacts, she is also touched physically and materially by them, and their resonance is clearly felt. In her appreciation of her "beautiful", "wonderful" and "protective cell", it is clear that aesthetics plays a central role and gives her dignity. Through the items that she is permitted to contain within her prison cell, she has used her senses, her hands and thoughts: touching, arranging and rearranging, choosing the colour orange. It is a will, a pulse, an energy and a passion here that speaks of existential matters. In her choice of textiles, making covers and bags and through decorating and cleaning, she has worked to create a space for herself without being touched by "suffering walls".

Lucia, another prisoner, says it like this:

> We are two in the cell. I furnished my room in light blue, all in lace including the curtains. I have photos of my grandchildren. The cell has a toilet. I write and read about two hours every day. (Lucia, Italian prison)

Even if Lucia shares the prison cell with another woman, she only talks about how she has furnished *her* room. Her colour is light blue. Similar to Valeria, aesthetics plays a central role for Lucia. By touching the cell—making it as she wants it, creating a suitable atmosphere and organising her days with different activities—she has found a way of touching and being touched by her cell.

Finding a suitable way to exist within, or to touch, the prison cell is crucial to daily life. Nancy, a newcomer in the Italian prison, says: "When they close the door, I feel as a butterfly in a box. I spend the time writing, drawing, and going around the cell". Antonella, another woman in the Italian prison, says: "In the cell I feel relaxed now, but sometimes I still feel anxiety and stress, like as I am going to die". A third woman, Isabella, says: "I am so tired after working that I sleep immediately". This situation becomes more complex when we take the duration of prison sentences into account. There is a big difference between having to spend some weeks or months in a cell and having to spend 26 years like Fabiana, a prisoner serving a long sentence in Italian prison. Subsequently, women often identify their cell according to the prison section they are accommodated in as a result of their sentence duration. "My cell is in camerotti", some of them say. Camerotti are the cells for women with short sentences or for women still awaiting trial or final sentencing. They will touch and be touched by their prison cells only for a limited time. Others say: "My cell is in cellulare", which are cells for sentenced women "with long sentences" or "indefinite sentences". With few possibilities for release from prison, their cells become the closest they get to a "home" and the prison society becomes their society. Subsequently, the very naming of the cell in different ways positions the body, touches it and tells something about what kind of body you are and what kind of future you have in the prison indicated through the time you will spend in it.

We asked Fabiana to sketch her cell (see Fig. 12.2), which was located in the "cellulare" section, and to say something about her feelings and

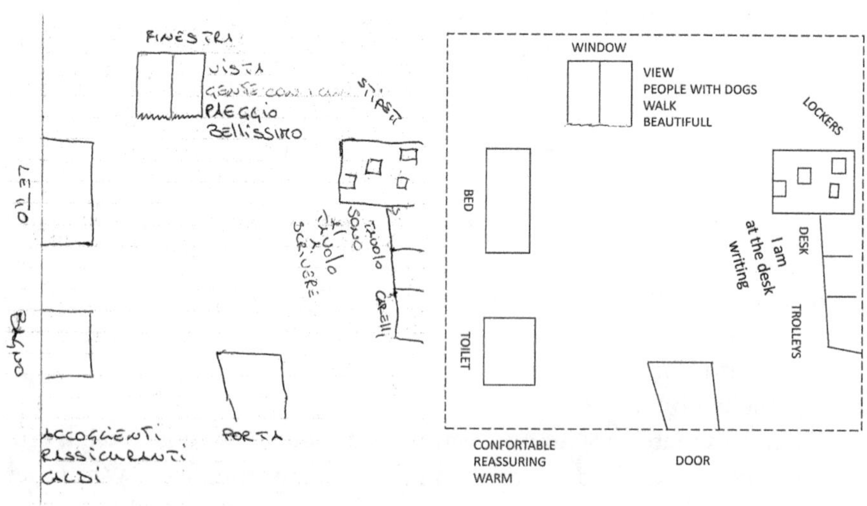


**Fig. 12.2** Sketch of the cell by Fabiana, prisoner in Rebibbia, Italy

how she positions herself inside her cell. For her, the inner cell space is important. The door and the window seem to be the core elements in the cell: the entry and the exit. It is possible to read the "sense of place", "in and out" through these two elements. The adjectives written near the door and the window suggest a positive relationship with the space: "the cell is comfortable, reassuring and warm, but through the window, I can see outside, people walking with their dogs, and the view is beautiful". An interpretation could be that everyday life is inside and leads out the door to the prison community, while the "outside" the "other life", which isn't for her, is outside the prison. Fabiana, despite sharing her cell with another prisoner, has only drawn one bed and she also seems to be alone while she is writing. The curtains in the window are important, because as she says they give the cell "a sense of home".

Fabiana has touched the cell through the way she has decorated and organised it. The cell contains her life and becomes a place for reading, watching TV, exercising, making coffee, drinking, eating, washing and for sharing dreams and fears. The cell is also touching her: making her feel comfortable, reassured and warm. But, there are interruptions. Every morning an event occurs, where one cell is inspected by the police staff to verify that there is no contraband such as drugs or unauthorised personal items inside. Here, the staff touch personal belongings and also sometimes the women's bodies. This means that, after the inspection, the cell must be reorganised so that the body can once again feel in-place.

Touching practices can also be analysed through Grosz's (1994) concepts of *bodies in-place* and *bodies out-of-place*. The concepts help us to see that we are always situated in place and how bodies are constituted by and constitute discourses (Grosz 1994; Rossholt 2012), here, of cultural values and correctional regimes. A *body in-place* in the Italian prison is a body that cares for the cell and for herself: keeping herself clean, communicating and relating to the formal and informal rules. Through the quotes we see how the limited place are divided and organised in ways that makes it possible to create private zones inside the prison cells, which is particularly important given cells usually house more than one prisoner. In the case of these multiple-occupancy cells, odours, language and food all exist in close proximity, meaning that closeness and distance have to be carefully regulated inside the cell space. Flexibility seems to be important and organising the cell giving meaning to small details. A *body out-of-place* is, on the other hand, is a body that smells bad, does not communicate in the "right" way and who does not relate to the rules. A *body out-of-place* might create conflicts, threaten the atmosphere, the rhythm, the tone and disturb the private zones within the prison cells.

The Italian prison staff explained to us that conflicts within the cell are usually due to cleanliness, both related to personal hygiene and to the importance of keeping it tidy. Other types of conflict can be related to the different daily rhythms among women that share the same cell, because those prisoners who are employed have to wake up early in the morning and might disturb sleeping bodies. In addition, thefts inside the cell occur and create conflicts. In this way, it is clear to see how the prison cell touches women. Fear, anxiety, sweat and aggression can be smelled and felt; both the physicalities of bodies and their emotional states literally 'sit in the walls'.

In the Norwegian prison, women usually have single cells and the cells are considered private zones. In some units, the women also have their own key so that they can lock the door when they are outside during the day. In accordance with the Norwegian penal code, women who have been sentenced are obliged to have some kind of purposeful activity during the day such as work or education, amongst others. If a woman does not come out of her cell in the morning, a prison officer will go in and try to motivate her to come out. If this is unsuccessful, and the woman does not wish to take part in her designated activity, she has to stay in her room that day. Unlike in the Italian prison, where women can go out in the corridor, this means being alone in the prison cell.

Beyond the usual expectation for multiple-cell occupancy, conversely, in Italy, being alone is considered problematic in certain cases. One interesting comparison to Norway is that, in the Italian prison, women who might be suicidal are always placed together with other women. They are never alone. In this way we also see how the prisoners use other "women's touch" as protection and shelter. This touch can relate to the skin in the way that the women come very close to each other's bodies through movements and smell, but it can also refer to a more invisible movement, a shared feeling of connection of knowing that there are other bodies around reacting if someone feels the urge to hurt themselves.

The women taking part in the focus group in the Norwegian prison were curious about why we were interested in speaking about the prison cell in such detail. "There isn't so much to say", said Anna. On one occasion, Victoria set the agenda and reversed the questioning by asking Elisabeth, one of the researchers, "How would you react to being in a prison cell?" The exchange occurred as follows:

**Elisabeth:** At first, I maybe would feel claustrophobic, and then maybe I would begin to dream …
**Anna:** You cannot dream. Dreaming is just sad. It is better to follow the routines and be distracted. Time goes faster in this way.
**Irene:** I am also a dreamer, but within the prison it is difficult. (Focus group, Norwegian prison)

The issue around dreams opened an intense discussion about the prison cell, how it touches the body and how women with their bodies touch the prison cell. As Anna explained, the space of the cell often gives way to dreaming, but this is seldom a positive experience:

> In my cell I pull the curtains, lie down on the bed and keep myself occupied with television or music. I don't want to dream, look out or being reminded by the life outside. It makes it worse. It just makes me sad and more aware that I am here and outside life goes on. It is important that the times go fast. That is a paradox. Because, in one way you don't want it to go fast because you get older. But being in here you want it to go fast. And it goes faster if you distract yourselves. (Anna, Norwegian prison)

It has been recognised that in many difficult circumstances—such as those young women dealing with social class and sexual issues—dreams point and direct to a "way out" (Walkerdine 1993; Fransson 1996). However, for Anna, dreaming touches her body in a negative way. It is almost as if she avoids dreaming to keep her *body in-place*. Conversely, one of the other women, Rosa, finds it hard to be alone: "I hate to be alone", she says. In contrast to the others she defines herself as a dreamer. She stands in the window looking out and thinking. She says that this might be because she is an illegal immigrant and that she will perhaps be sent out of Norway.

The cell is also a space where time is passed and it often lingers. Anna wants the time to pass quickly, but this also means that she becomes older, and it reminds her of time passing her by. The time passing is prison time, and not of value for her as a woman in the world. Being in prison and inside the prison cell, her freedom is taken away from her. She knows that the time she spends inside the cell she cannot get back.

As also James finds in another study of a female prison, women actively make time pass by watching television and keeping themselves busy to "keep themselves together" so that they will not "lose themselves" (James 2018: 161–162). The women in our material constantly move around their cell: moving on and off the bed, changing position, thinking, looking out of the window, looking around, watching the television and listening to music. They need to find ways of moving their bodies—that is, the outside and inside of the body in visible or invisible ways—to cope with the situation of being locked up inside the cell. Here, the distraction is important. It seems that without it, the women are afraid of losing control and in danger of becoming a *body out-of-place*. However, beyond this movement inside the cell, movement outside of the cell is crucial for it to exist as a space where an individual does not "lose themselves". A correctional discourse related to the importance of purposeful activity can be read out of the comments from our Norwegian participants:

> It is nice to go back to the cell and know that you have done something useful, used your body and you can go to sleep with a good consciousness. (Victoria, Norwegian prison)

The women explained that the best situation to be in is where you return to your cell, feeling tired and ready to sleep. This means that you have been doing something useful and can be pleased with yourself and you are less tempted to think too much about guilt and sadness. For tired women returning to the cell after a long day, the cell can also be a good place to come back to after work or school and, in this way, a mode of keeping the *body in-place*.

Although these examples of life inside the cell each have standalone significance, what a prison cell can be and how it touches and is touched by the body also has to be understood in relationship to the space outside the cell. In this case, we draw attention to corridor spaces.

## Corridor Spaces

One of the surprising things we found from our research was the difference in respect of the corridor spaces in the Italian and the Norwegian prison. This can be illustrated from notes in our field diaries:

> Walking through airy corridors, our bodies nearly bomb into other bodies. We hear strong noises, a mix between voices and metallic sounds. There are no particular smells, but our eyes appreciate the natural light. We don't feel secure. All the cell doors, situated around the corridor, are open and inside we see a lot of bodies. We are allowed into a prison cell. Stepping over the threshold three women immediately surrounds us. It is like the cell is crowded with bodies and objects. The private space inside the cell is well-organized around each bed. (Field diary, Italian prison)

Lucia, one of the Italian prisoners says:

> Every day when I come back from my work crossing the corridor, I like to see all the women chatting along it. I use to tell them: "Are you waiting for the bus? Look today there is the strike!" (Lucia, Italian prison)

Moving through the corridor on her way back from work Lucia passes a lot of bodies with different forms and shapes, languages, dialects and sounds. Indeed, as we were escorted around the prison, the women barely moved so we could squeeze past. The corridor space in the Italian prison gives connotations of the Italian piazza. The word piazza comes from the Greek word "via larga" which means a big road. People usually associate a piazza as a place on the street where people go outside their house to spend time and meet people: to talk, gossip, debate and interact with others. The prison corridor has some of the same function. Here the women can keep up with what goes on within the prison. The corridor offers extra space and represents "society". Women seem to touch and be touched by each other differently outside in the corridor than inside the cell. While the cell space needs to be well organised and clean, the corridor space is more unregulated and the women can interact with bodies other than those of their cellmates. When asked about the significance of the courtyard space and the impact of its potential absence, Mara, from the Italian prison, explained that this space was extremely important. She argued that she would not like to live in a place where the corridor provided only a restricted view and, without it, she would sincerely miss fresh air and seeing people.

In contrast to the Italian prison corridors, the Norwegian corridors have another atmosphere, with other rhythms and sounds. While the Italian corridor space was full of people, the corridor space in Norway seemed to us as silent and empty:

> Walking through the narrow corridor we don't meet any bodies. It is silence and no particular smells. Our eyes meet a bit dark, but cosy corridor with some pictures on the painted walls. We feel secure. There are cells along the corridors, the doors are closed. Anne is waiting for us to show us her cell. We step over the threshold and into her cell. It is nice, clean and well-organised. We see books and pictures of her parents. The view from the window is pleasant. (Field diary, Norwegian prison)

The corridors in the Norwegian prison seemed much narrower, darker and, according to both the women and the staff, "nothing happens there". It is not usual for women to gather in the corridors. When we asked what was outside the women's prison cells, the women in the focus group in Norway first didn't understand the question. There wasn't anything there! As Irene said, with puzzlement, "the corridor leads to the kitchen". The silence in the Norwegian prison corridors was a huge contrast to the high noise levels in the Italian prison corridors. The silence can be read as a cultural expression of important values such as peace and quiet in the Norwegian culture (Gullestad 2002), but also have to do with how prisons control their prisoners. In Norway, for instance, prison rules prohibit high security prisoners from walking around the prison unescorted. While a body in-place in the Italian case is hanging outside in the corridor and shouting to other women in another floor, this would, in Norwegian prisons, definitively be a *body out-of-place*. This illustrates how bodies in prison corridors move related to prison architecture and correctional discourses regarding what is considered a *body in-place* and a *body out-of-place*.

Given the varying purpose of the corridors in our case studies, our research also revealed the significance of the space between the corridor and the prison cell. Both in the Italian and the Norwegian case, the "threshold" comes forward as an important space to further understand the prison cell. It is to this that we now turn.

## Threshold Spaces

A threshold is traditionally understood as the strip of wood or stone forming the bottom of a doorway, which must be crossed in entering a house or room. Although the cell threshold might not have a physical manifestation—there is no stone strip between the prison and the corridor when the cell door is open—its symbolic presence is acutely felt. In the case of the prison, the threshold is a boundary with meaning both in Italy and Norway. Although bodies have to step over the threshold to reach the corridor in both prisons, the movements related to the threshold space are different in Italy and Norway.

During the day all the cell doors in the Italian prison are opened, as per the internal rules. Going around the Italian prison, we noticed that many women were positioned on the threshold or immediately outside their cells. As Laura explained, this positioning was deliberate:

> I like to spend time on the threshold, because I can see and hear what is happening outside, and at the same time I can stay close to my cell to control it. (Laura, Italian prison)

In the Italian context, a body that moves beyond the threshold is ready to represent itself to the "prison society" with the risk and the possibilities it gives. Here, prisoners may feel the risk of interacting with unknown women, but this brings with it the opportunity to discover what kind of place the prison is and for getting to know other prisoners. A body that remains on the threshold is not ready or does not want to be too involved in what happens in the corridor. By standing the threshold, the woman can step back, at any time, into the prison cell space and into her "private zone".

A body on the threshold moves between the "inner world" of the prison cell and the "prison community" consisting of the corridors. In that respect, women seem to be fiercely territorial about ensuring that nothing might enter the cell and compromise its condition. There, on the threshold acting as an obstacle or barrier between the corridor outside and the cell inside, women can control their cells, their personal belongings and their privacy. In this way the threshold becomes the space between the private zone and "outside life". However, despite using it to maintain the security of their cell, the women also use the threshold space as a mechanism for access to and communication through prison spaces.

The inside cell is opened to the outside prison community and the outside is brought inside the cell. Here on the threshold women can talk both to a cell mate lying on the bed inside and to women on another floor outside. They can both participate and withdraw from the community, so, on the threshold, bodies are inside the cell and outside at the same time without being too involved either in the cell or the corridor. The threshold spaces illustrate that prison boundaries are of various kinds and of importance for everyday border work. Following Turner, the threshold cell spaces are one boundary among many other prison boundaries, connected to cultural symbols, performance, embodied practices and materiality (Turner 2016: 53). The threshold evokes an invisible and permeable line that allows an osmotic and constant movement, touching the cell inside and opening up the prison cell (Boettger 2014).

The threshold space has a different meaning in the Norwegian context. Here you either arrive, and step over, or you remain inside the cell. Bodies do not usually pause on the threshold and spend time there. In Norway there is a saying "to get over the doorstep", which symbolises the effort it may be to cross over the threshold and go out. It seems that, in Norway, the threshold is culturally, and in terms of embodied practice, a more distinct border that can be perceived as a real barrier (Boettger 2014) limiting bodies to remain within the prison cell.

To take part in obligatory activities, such as education and work, or to have breakfast or a coffee in the common kitchen, the bodies have to reach and step over the threshold and go along the corridor. For some bodies this can be a challenge. Prison officers, in particular, said that it was important to observe whether imprisoned bodies "cross the threshold". Staff explained that they prefer women to come out of their cells because spending too much time in them is "not healthy".

Arriving and stepping over the threshold tells us, in the Norwegian context, something about *bodies in-place* or *bodies out-of-place*. In Norway, as in Italy, crossing the threshold and moving into the cell means moving into a private zone. To go into another woman's cell, you usually need to be invited. Women in the focus group said that they rarely invited people into the cell, into their private space. Consequently, a body crossing over the threshold and into the cell without permission therefore could be a *body out-of-place*. Anne explained: "I hate it when someone comes in and stands in the doorway". She says she feels suffocated. Irene says: "It is the same if another woman wants to drag me into her cell to tell me something. I feel that I am trapped".

The threshold in the Norwegian prison therefore seems to be a clear boundary between the inside cell space and the prison community outside, a clear marker between "the public" and "the private space" that helps to keep the right closeness and distance between the bodies.

## Conclusion

In this chapter we have focused upon prison cells and the areas immediately around them through a comparative study of two prisons in Italy and Norway. The goal has been to develop new knowledge about how female prisoner's bodies touch and are touched by these prison cell spaces. The research findings demonstrate that bodies move differently in, touch and are touched by prison cell spaces in various ways under influence from prison architecture, prison design, prison discourses, culture and prison rules.

The chapter therefore reveals a complex relationship between the prison cell and its more peripheral spaces such as corridor spaces and the threshold space. The cell is not necessarily the smallest and most intimate space within the prison. It is both open and locked, connected and disconnected; it has boundaries, extensions and in-betweens. By incorporating the corridors and the threshold spaces into the concept of *prison cell*, we expand its meaning and open up the limited and singular understanding of what a prison cell is and can be. Through highlighting various prison cell spaces and exploring the connotations of "inside cell spaces", "corridor spaces" and "threshold spaces", we have reinterpreted the concept of a prison cell. Through Nancy's concept of *touching* and Grosz's concepts of *bodies in-place* and *bodies out-of-place*, the chapter disrupts conventional understandings of the prison cell and casts light on the relationship between prison cell spaces, bodies and touch in a Norwegian and Italian prison. Accordingly, this chapter contributes in advancing the academic literature regarding sensuous prison architecture and the philosophy of touch. By putting ontological and epistemological questions at the forefront, the chapter is also a contribution to the existing research literature regarding prison boundaries within sociology, criminology and carceral geography. This work broadens our conceptual understanding of the prison cell and points to the importance of how it works in conjunction with spaces at its periphery. Findings suggest that the way prison cell spaces are used has a bearing upon the socialisation of prisoners, their emotional and physical health and their attitude towards their time in prison. In this respect, the comparative analyses of prison cell spaces in Italy and Norway may assist with proposing new questions related to prison cell spaces and how their design is potentially related to correctional progress and reentry into society. More than this, the experience of these spaces is often individualised and varies by geographical context. This chapter therefore highlights the importance of studying prison architecture beyond its technicalities, using an embodied and interdisciplinary approach. For these reasons we argue the importance of studying how bodies move, touch and are touched within various prison spaces and the importance of the user-oriented design, bringing prisoners into the planning process of renovation, extension and building of prisons.

**Acknowledgements** The authors would like to thank Doris Bakken, Deputy Governor at Bredtveit prison, for reading through and checking the details about Bredtveit in this chapter.

## Note

1. Pseudonyms have been used throughout.

## References

Åkerstrøm Andersen, N. (2003). *Discursive Analytical Strategies: Understanding Foucault, Koselleck, Laclau, Luhmann*. Bristol: Policy Press.

Armstrong, S. (2015). The Cell and the Corridor: Imprisonment as Waiting, and Waiting as Mobile. *Time & Society, Sage Journal, 27*(2), 133–154.

Boettger, T. (2014). *Threshold Spaces: Transitions in Architecture. Analysis and Design Tools*. Basel: Birkhäuser.

Deleuze, G., & Guattari, F. (1994). *What is Philosophy?* New York, NY: Colombia University Press.

Derrida, J. (2005). *On Touching, Jean-Luc Nancy*. Stanford, CA: Stanford University Press.

Foucault, M. (1977). *Discipline and Punish: The Birth of the Prison* (A. Sheridan, Trans.). New York, NY: Vintage Books.

Fransson, E. (1996). Room for Girl Life? A Sociological Study of Relationships in a Child Welfare Institution. *NOVA/BVU Report No. 3*. Oslo: Norwegian Institute of Child Welfare Research.

Fransson, E. (2018). The Lunch Table: Prison Architecture, Action-Forces and the Young Imprisoned Body. In E. Fransson, F. Giofrè, & B. Johnsen (Eds.), *Prison, Architecture and Humans* (pp. 177–199). Oslo: Cappelen Damm Akademisk.

Fransson, E., Giofrè, F., & Johnsen, B. (Eds.). (2018). *Prison, Architecture and Humans*. Oslo: Cappelen Damm Akademisk.

Fransson, E., & Johnsen, B. (2015). The Perfume of Sweat. In D. H. Drake, R. Earle, & J. Sloan (Eds.), *Handbook of Prison Ethnography* (pp. 187–198). London: Palgrave Macmillan.

Giofrè, F., Porro, L., & Fransson, E. (2018). Prisons between Territory and Space: A Comparative Analysis between Prison Architecture in Italy and Norway. In E. Fransson, F. Giofrè, & B. Johnsen (Eds.), *Prison, Architecture and Humans* (pp. 39–64). Oslo: Cappelen Damm Akademisk.

Goffman, E. (1961). *Asylums: Essays on the Social Situation of Mental Patients and Other Inmates*. New York, NY: Anchor Books.

Gramsci, A. (1994/2011). *Letters from Prison* (F. Rosengarten, Ed., R. Rosenthal, Trans.). New York, NY: Columbia University Press. Orig: Lettere dal Carcere (1947).

Grønvold, M. & Fransson, E. (2019) Meetings in Between: A Study of How University College Students in Correctional Studies Understand Milieu Work in Prison. *UNIPED*, 2, 180–193. Retrieved September 25, 2019, from https://www.idunn.no/uniped/2019/02.

Grosz, E. (1994). *Volatile Bodies: Toward a Corporeal Feminism*. Sydney: Allen & Unwin.

Gullestad, M. (2002). *Kitchen-Table Society*. Oslo: Universitetsforlaget.

James, F. (2018). "It's important not to lose myself": Beds, Carceral Design and Women's Everyday Life within Prison Cells. In E. Fransson, F. Giofrè, & B. Johnsen (Eds.), *Prison, Architecture and Humans* (pp. 151–176). Oslo: Cappelen Damm Akademisk.

Krogstad, A. (2000). Antropologisk sammenlikning i tunt og tykt: ti kjetterske teser. *Norsk Antropologisk Tidsskrift, 11*(2), 88–107.

Lather, P. (1991). *Getting Smart: Feminist Research and Pedagogy with/in the Postmodern*. New York, NY: Routledge.

Nancy, J.-L. (2008). *Corpus*. New York, NY: Fordham University Press.

Pallasmaa, J. (2005). *The Eyes of the Skin. Architecture and the Senses*. West Sussex: John Wiley & Sons.

Rossholt, N. (2012). Food as Touch/Touching the Food: The Body In-Place and Out-of-Place in Preschool. *Educational Philosophy and Theory, 44*(3), 323–334.

Trüby, S., Werlemann, H., Mcleod, K., AMO., Harvard Graduate School of Design, Koolhaas, R., & Boom, I. (2014). *Corridor*. Venice: Marsilio.

Turner, J. (2013). The Politics of Carceral Spectacle: Televising Prison Life. In D. Moran, N. Gill, & D. Conlon (Eds.), *Carceral Spaces: Mobility and Agency in Imprisonment and Migrant Detention* (pp. 219–247). Farnham: Ashgate.

Turner, J. (2016). *The Prison Boundary: Between Society and Carceral Space*. London: Palgrave Macmillan.

Walkerdine, V. (1993). Girlhood through the Looking Glass. In M. de Ras & M. Lunenberg (Eds.), *Girls, Girlhood and Girl's Studies in Transition* (pp. 9–25). Amsterdam: Het Spinhuis.

# 13

# PrisonCloud: The Beating Heart of the Digital Prison Cell

Jana Robberechts and Kristel Beyens

## Introduction: The Multifunctional Cell

The use of information and communication technologies (hereafter, ICTs) is deeply embedded in modern social life. Investment in ICTs has evolved to such an extent that the environment in which citizens interact with public authorities and administration is one which is heavily dependent on them (Scharff-Smith 2012: 467). The positive attitude towards the benefits of ICTs is less apparent in the context of the prison setting, where its rarity is notable (Johnson and Hail-Jares 2016: 284). Although the principle of normalisation—that life inside prison should as far as possible resemble the positive aspects of life outside prison—is promoted from an international perspective, the issue of technology usage is a sensitive one (Council of Europe 2006). This is largely related to the fact that prisons are managed from a control and security position which establishes limits to normalisation (Vollan 2016; Maes et al. 2019). By

J. Robberechts (✉) • K. Beyens
Department of Criminology, Vrije Universiteit Brussel, Brussel, Belgium
e-mail: Jana.Robberechts@vub.be



J. Turner, V. Knight (eds.), *The Prison Cell*, Palgrave Studies in Prisons and Penology,
https://doi.org/10.1007/978-3-030-39911-5_13

denying prisoners' access to new technologies, however, a new level of disconnection had emerged, 'demarking a distinctive pain of modern imprisonment' (Johnson 2005: 257) and leaving prisoners as 'cavemen in an era of speed-of-light technology' (Jewkes and Johnston 2009: 135). The more recent introduction of ICT to the prison context has attempted to bridge the digital gap.

The principle of normalisation that gradually penetrated the Belgian prison system since the 1970s led to ICTs such as televisions and phones becoming fully embedded in the context of prison life (Maes 2009: 340). However, in 2014, the Belgian Prison Service went one step further by introducing a new digital platform called *PrisonCloud*—a digital tool that established an *in-cell* platform—to give prisoners greater responsibility (Belgian Prison Service 2011). A partnership between the Federal government and a private partner (e-BO Enterprises) was introduced to manage this platform (Belgian Prison Service 2011, 2014). The government recommended that the culture of paperwork, so dominant in the Belgian prison system, ought to be overhauled (Belgian Prison Service 2011). Internal prison communications with prisoners were hitherto conducted through pre-printed forms that were handwritten. For example, canteen items and other requests were ordered using proformas, and judicial files were photocopied upon a prisoners' request for consultation. *PrisonCloud*, as an *in-cell* digital platform, aimed to digitise the culture of literacy and become not only more cost-efficient but also one that could give prisoners greater independence over the constructive use of their time (Belgian Prison Service 2011). Furthermore, in-cell access could have tangible educative advantages. It is asserted that *PrisonCloud* could remedy levels of digital illiteracy perceived to undermine reintegration strategies and also guarantee the continuity of education programmes disrupted by strike actions or absence.[1]

*PrisonCloud* had obvious prisoner-related objectives, but it also precipitated changes to the work of prison staff. The government argued that increased in-cell activities created a more secure environment for prison staff but also resulted in their work being less labour-intensive (Belgian Prison Service 2014). This needs to be considered in the context of *PrisonCloud* being co-developed by a private security company—who may be concerned with their staffing expenditure—specifically for the custodial industry. In hindsight, however, the potentialities of *PrisonCloud* appear to have been more ambitious than the reality: there is a significant lack of fit between what is provided and the applications that have been actually used in practice. Nonetheless, there is still a tangible difference between the standard equipment of a prison cell in digital and non-digital prisons.[2] In a digital cell:

> The following items are part of the standard equipment of the living area, in particular: a table, a chair, a bed, a washbasin and a toilet. In the prison [...], the cells are also equipped with a *shower, refrigerator, pin board, plasma screen, headset, thin client, keyboard*, basic dishes, cutlery, toilet brush, bucket, window extractor and two waste bins with hinged lid. (Federal Public Service of Justice 2014: 6, our emphasis)

In a digital prison, each incoming prisoner receives a personalised USB stick with a password, which for security and privacy reasons can only be accessed by their own in-cell *PrisonCloud* device. Prison cells occupied by more than one prisoner are consequently equipped with the appropriate number of devices to individually access the platform. Although prisoners have access to a secured cloud via the platform, *PrisonCloud* does not currently give prisoners access to the Internet (with the exception of the local library catalogue through the library application).

At its most basic level, the use of *PrisonCloud* is limited to facilitating prison life and acting as an information provider; prisoners can find information on relevant legislation, the internal prison rules, the prison services, the catalogue of the local library, phone rates, and the daily menu. Furthermore, with just a few mouse clicks, prison staff can easily post announcements on changes to the regime or new activities. The platform thus provides a fast distribution of information relative to non-digital prisons. Alongside these informatic functions, the platform can be used for recreational purposes as it gives prisoners access to television, films, meditation audio, and games. The digital platform also includes an alarm clock, calendar, and canteen applications that aim to empower prisoners to take responsibility for their daily lives. For example, prisoners can directly order canteen products instead of having to hand over their handwritten requests to the prison officers. Furthermore, *PrisonCloud* gives prisoners access to courses and paid work. Since 2017, a small selection of prisoners have been allowed to work as call centre agents from within their cell. These in-cell facilities are promoted as an advantage, especially in the event of strikes of the prison staff or shortages of staff hampering movements of prisoners. Indeed, *PrisonCloud* can (partly) resolve the problem of prison staff refusing to organise prisoner's movements, because they are not always required to undertake this work.

The biggest change however is that *PrisonCloud* facilitates communication not only with internal prison services but also with the outside world. Through *PrisonCloud*, prisoners are able to make phone calls to the outside world[3] from within their cells and directly write messages to the internal prison services with no intervention or control by intermediaries. Communication from prisoners in non-digital prisons takes a protracted route and involves several prison officers—all of whom are able to read them—to correctly deliver the messages to the relevant services. When implementing *PrisonCloud*, this direct way of communication was raised and discussed by policy makers as a matter of privacy (Knight and Van De Steene 2017). For example, prisoners can now make an appointment with the medical service directly, and with the advantage that communications do not get lost, or mislaid, which regularly happens in non-digital prisons and thus causes daily discussions between prisoners and officers.

*PrisonCloud* thus covers the range of services that are available in non-digital prisons albeit accessed directly from a digital cell. In this sense the large range of applications available is not immediately innovative, but the relocation of how to access these facilities to the prison cell is. One example is the simple change around telephone usage; previously limited to a small number of handsets located on communal landings, phone calls are now accessible with more privacy in the individual cell through *PrisonCloud*. Alongside the traditional functions of the prison cell as a room to sleep and eat in, the introduction of digital infrastructure has transformed it into a multifunctional workplace, classroom, and recreation room. In this context, this chapter illustrates how ICT in general, and *PrisonCloud* in particular, has the potential to broaden the functions of the prison cell[4] and how the idea of multifunctionality is situated in the ongoing discussions about how digitalisation might affect the prison experiences of both prisoners and prison staff.

Although the focus here falls primarily on the digital infrastructure of the prison cell, we believe other features of the cell also contribute to understandings of multifunctionality and its consequences. Moreover, the specific configuration and use of digital platforms in each prison is decided by the local prison administration and thus differs between digital prisons in Belgium. Amongst other things, it means that decisions of local prison administrations can have a direct impact upon the lived experiences of users by deciding what information is displayed on *PrisonCloud* and which services prisoners can access. Furthermore, the Belgian penitentiary landscape adds a distinctive flavour to discussions surrounding digitalisation and multifunctionality. Certain particularities of the Belgian context are important to bear in mind when considering experiences with *PrisonCloud*, as many of these have also been influenced by prior experiences in non-digital prisons. Belgium currently has 35 prisons, 17 of which are located in the Flemish-speaking part of Belgium (Flanders) and 16 in the Southern, French-speaking part of Belgium (Wallonia). The remaining two prisons are located in Brussels (Belgian Prison Service 2018: 8). Many Belgian prisons were built in the nineteenth century and have suffered from overcrowding since the late 1980s. While the overall overcrowding rate was still 24.1 per cent in 2014, in 2017 it decreased to 11.8 per cent. However, in some prisons, and particularly in the remand prisons, the overcrowding rate still varies between 20 and 40 per cent. In 2017 the average Belgian prison population totals 10,471 prisoners for an average capacity of 9231 places (Belgian Prison Service 2018: 8).

As a direct response to overcrowding, three new prisons were built between 2013 and 2014 and provided an opportunity for the Belgian Prison Service to take a first step in the digitalisation of prisons. It was arguably questionable to invest in an ambitious digital platform, an initiative that sat uncomfortably with the poor living conditions in most existing prisons to date. Nevertheless, the new prisons were equipped with the digital platform, and currently most, but not all, prisoners are detained in single-occupancy cells. This is seldom the case in many of the older non-digital prisons, where a single cell is shared between two or more prisoners.

This chapter is based on the findings of an ethnographic study in one digital Belgian prison that has implemented *PrisonCloud* since 2014. After describing the research design, the data section will focus on the impact of the prison cell as a 'self-providing' place on the detention experiences of prisoners, staff-prisoner interactions, and the shifting prisoner's position of dependency.

## The Study: A Digital Research Context

The empirical findings discussed here were derived from a wider project[5] that studied the impact of *PrisonCloud* on the experiences of prisoners, prison staff, and the prisoner-staff relationships in one digital prison. The institution was a closed prison (with a capacity of 300) for long-term male prisoners serving sentences from five years to life imprisonment and was comprised of four wings—two with an open-door regime and two with a closed regime. Between June 2017 and August 2018, a total of 63 interviews were conducted with participants who were selected by a non-probability purposive sample of 36 prisoners, 12 prison officers (with different rankings), and 15 other members of various prison services including prison governors (3), accounting services (1), religious services (3), local prison administration (1), ICT services (2), medical services (1), psychosocial services (2), and social and welfare services (2). Prior to the interviews, observations in the prison were conducted by the first author over six months between January and June of 2017 to develop a clearer contextual picture of this uniquely digitalised prison.

Information and communication technologies were central to the research and were also used to inform and contact potential respondents who worked with *PrisonCloud*. Prison staff were contacted by e-mail, and those who responded to our call for participation (with a few exceptions for practical reasons) were interviewed; prisoners received a general message through *PrisonCloud*. The invitation to participate included the conditions attached to taking part in the research, and informed consent was orally discussed and elicited prior to the interview commencing. The local prison administration agreed for the ICT service to create a new account for Robberechts, who conducted the empirical research. This way, prisoners were able to directly message her without mediation or official monitoring, to confirm their willingness to participate. In just a few days, over 50 of the 300 prisoners replied positively to the invitation, of which 36 were interviewed. The messages automatically included the cell number of the prisoner, showing whether or not the prisoner was sharing a cell, and if the prisoner was detained on an open or closed wing. Following the findings of the initial observations and considering the extant literature, the type of prison regime and the form of cell occupancy proved to be important to the prison experience (Molleman and van Ginneken 2014). So, the interviewees were evenly distributed between those on open and closed wings and those sharing or occupying single cells.

The ICT service was asked to post a new message on *PrisonCloud* to confirm, as agreed with the local prison administration, that the required number of prisoners had applied. At an elementary level then, the use of *PrisonCloud* had expedited the dispatch of information to potential interviewees, facilitated the finding of respondents, and gathered essential information on some of the relevant variables for the research. However, as prisoners gave consent to their participation directly from their prison cell, full anonymity of their involvement was not initially guaranteed. Eventually 36 prisoners participated—some initial respondents were lost to a combination of prison transfers and conditional release—and whose identities were not communicated to the local prison administration. A list of the prisoners wishing to participate was however given to the prison governors, as their permission was required for the research to continue. Furthermore, the prison officers needed to open the cell door and thus knew where the interviewed prisoner was at the time of the interview, because of the routine counting of prisoners on the one hand and the fact that interviews took place in separate rooms across the prison on the other. Thus, it was difficult to ensure privacy within the prison setting, as everyone sees who moves where and knows what the movements mean. Furthermore, it is possible that we did not reach prisoners who were not using the digital platform, the so-called refusniks (Selwyn et al. 2005: 18). However, in discussions with prison staff, we learned that this was likely a small proportion of prisoners and so no further elaboration on the experiences of this group is necessary here.

## The Digital Infrastructure of Isolation

Although the outside world increasingly enters the prison (Farrington 1990; Baer and Ravneberg 2008; Moran 2013), isolation in prison settings is still commonplace. Physical isolation in prisons is twofold. First, although the walls become more permeable, the prison is still largely closed for the outside world. On top of that, the cell door provides another boundary for the prisoner towards the other people living and working in prison. The physical isolation affects the social isolation as the possibility to interact with other human beings becomes more limited. In most Belgian prisons, it is quite common for prisoners to spend most of their time behind the cell doors. Whilst open and closed prisons exist, the capacity of the former is very small (about three per cent) compared to the latter. Closed regimes are the general rule in the context of Belgian penitentiaries, with the exception of a few prisons with wings where an open regime allows prisoners to walk freely on the landings during the day. These regimes affect both the level of physical and social isolation of prisoners. As alluded to above, the prison under consideration here was a closed prison with both open and closed wings.

We have suggested that the provision of in-cell ICT facilitates a connection between the prison world and the outside world. However, the introduction of *PrisonCloud* had additional consequences. First, in-cell technology can counter isolation due to the easy and permanent access to virtual communication. Prisoners can stay informed about life outside prison through media such as the television, radio, and the phone, where the sound and images can 'create some kind of presence in the prisoner's cell' and 'suppress feelings of isolation' (Vandebosch 2000: 537). *In-cell* television is now fully embedded in contrast to *in-cell* telephone (Knight 2005; Maes 2009). In non-digital prisons, telephones are limited and are commonly shared limiting the opportunity to make long calls.[6] The *PrisonCloud* phone function was therefore welcomed by the prisoners, as it offered the privacy and the freedom to call when it was most suitable.

In spite of the physical isolation then, the in-cell phone and television provided a potential 24/7 social connection with the outside world. As one interviewee explained, having immediate access to a phone can even compensate for the feelings of isolation than watching television can evoke:

> Sometimes you think of, or you see something nice on television that reminds you of conviviality and then indeed you feel alone. Then I pick up the phone and it is alright again. (Interview prisoner 14)

Both prisoners and prison staff pointed to the use of the phone as a medium to counter not only feelings of isolation but also feelings of boredom (Knight 2012). By way of killing time, and its 24/7 availability, the use of the phone increased for many prisoners despite the associated costs of expensive phone rates. This was also mentioned by a prison officer:

> It is good that you can always make a phone call, but soon there is no money left. And this is very strongly present here. Here, there is no money left all the time. They are always complaining about having no money to make a phone call. Why? Because out of boredom, they will say. They start calling their family and friends out of boredom. (Interview supervising officer 5)

Prisoners found the permanent in-cell access difficult as their (limited) budget prevented them from making a phone call. Through the in-cell access of the digital platform, prisoners are constantly reminded of the possibility for instant connectivity, which could cause additional frustration. In-cell television and phone certainly countered social isolation, but only within the constraints imposed by the prisoner's budget.

By introducing technologies into the prison setting, the idea of prisons as 'communication poor environments' weakens (Knight 2015: 3). However, we found that the introduction of technologies in prisons had unforeseen and somewhat contradictory effects. Moreover, our findings suggest that the gradual introduction of in-cell access to virtual communication with the outside world has not necessarily led to more, or better quality, social interactions within the prison setting. Previous prison research has shown that the introduction of television has served as a tool for 'boredom management', an 'electronic babysitter', or an in-cell 'care deliverer' that made prisoners invisible to each other as they remained inside their cells watching television (Jewkes and Johnston 2009; Jewkes and Reisdorf 2016: 3; Knight 2012). Johnson, for example, states that 'the appeal of TV is that it entertains and distracts [...], while demanding little from the viewer' (2005: 265). In this sense, prisoners are *passing* time than *doing* time in any active way (Jewkes 2002: 10–11). The introduction of technologies then played a role in shaping prisoners' preferences so that a greater proportion of their time was occupied by passive activities in their cells (Vandebosch 2000). However, this was not necessarily a voluntary choice. For vulnerable groups, such as sexual offenders, *PrisonCloud* allowed them to increasingly spend time in their cells and withdraw from the public life of the prison as a means to avoid conflicts with other prisoners and thus protect their safety. Again, the digital platform, whilst offering many applications that encountered some forms of isolation for some prisoners, became a new feature of segregation that although voluntary was intrinsically structured around *PrisonCloud* because it decreased the necessity to leave their cell.

> Some people don't even dare to go to the library anymore—mainly the sexual offenders—and have their books brought to their prison cell. There are a number of people that I know have not put a foot outside their cell for maybe three or four years. And the comfort of *PrisonCloud* and the in-cell shower makes them [prisoners] indeed feel comfortable, but makes them also... There is definitely detention harm there. It makes total isolation possible. (Interview chaplain 1)

Although not being the only factor that plays a role in facilitating the voluntary isolation, the above quote illustrates that most prisoners and prison officers criticised its effect of increasing the time that was spent inside the prison cell. And although PrisonCloud is welcomed by the prisoners for the in-cell access to facilities, the following quote shows how *PrisonCloud* also impedes prisoner's movements:

> This prison is made to stay in your cell. You know? Everything is in your cell: a shower, a phone. Everything is in your cell. In the old days you could go outside to take a shower, you could go outside to make a phone call. But now, you're always in your cell. That is fucked-up. (Interview prisoner 2, closed regime)

By reducing the daily, albeit small interactions, prison officers lost the everyday contact and affinity they once had with the prisoners, which increased their capacity to check on the prisoners' moods. This was particularly the case on the closed wings. Consequently, they no longer know what to expect when they open a cell door, which increases their feelings of unease and safety. Jewkes and Reisdorf (2016) referred to the situation of when prisoners had received bad news from outside, that left 'the recipient alone and in a heightened stage of anger or anxiety, with no officers able to observe and intervene' (Jewkes and Reisdorf 2016: 12). This contrasts with the situation where phone calls are made on the landings and where prison officers can easily overhear prisoners' conversations, monitor their emotional state, and thus anticipate their reactions:

> I find the in-cell phone a disadvantage. Let me give you an example. In N (non-digital prison) I saw a prisoner who heard that his brother died through the phone and he just collapsed on the landing. I was nearby, and I immediately took him into my office. You have more feeling, more contact. You can talk with them. You can share their happy moments and bad moments in which you can react and tell them it will be okay. I think this is the greatest disadvantage of *PrisonCloud*.[…] If you hear that a father, even though he is a prisoner, is telling his kids "You did that well, buddy". And then he goes back to his prison cell and you walk together and then you will ask: "Has he been good?" And then you see the prisoner cheer up because he will say, oh she is interested in my life. "Yes! He had gotten an A on his school report and normally it is quite difficult for him." The prisoner will appreciate it that you show interest for his life outside prison, that you do not only see him as a number. (Interview supervising officer 5)

This officer's quote thus explains that the location of the phone on the landings also offers an additional opportunity for meaningful prison officer—prisoner interactions, enhancing the dynamic security in prison.

However, it is also true that in non-digital prisons, phone conversations are not systematically overheard by staff. Phone calls are neither routinely recorded due to data protection legislation, and the system only records the called numbers and the duration of the calls. So in-cell phone conversations increase a prisoner's privacy.

## Shifting Prisoners' Position of Dependence

Staff-prisoner relations are often said to be at the heart of prison life (Crewe et al. 2015; Liebling et al. 2012). After all, prison officers are the first point of contact within the prison setting. But as the cell has become ever more a 'self-providing' place, prisoners rely less on the prison officers to organise their life in prison. So, *PrisonCloud* even becomes the centre of the prison cell:

> Due to *PrisonCloud*, the prison officers hardly ever have to do anything. They never have to collect or distribute the report messages, or when you ask if they can phone the psychosocial service, they will say, "no, send a message through PrisonCloud". So, everything has to … I think it is like the **beating heart of our cell**. Because whenever you need something, you have to do it through *PrisonCloud*. (Interview prisoner 5, closed regime, emphasis added)

The key role of the prison officer was historically related to a certain level of prisoner dependency. However, *PrisonCloud* initiated a partial shift in the dynamics of that dependence, away from officers and toward the digital platform: new forms of dependence were beginning to become established through the technology. This shift reduced the opportunities for meaningful social interactions through the mundane routines of prison life. This was found to be more detrimental on the closed wings, where prisoners were locked behind their cell doors for long periods with few opportunities to leave their cells (e.g. visitation, participation activities). In these circumstances, tendencies toward isolation were more marked.

Although the digital platform had provided instant connectivity with both the internal prison services and the outside world, it simultaneously fostered the idea that the landings were spaces of disconnectedness. In the wings with the open regime, the cell doors were opened for longer periods. We observed that fewer electronic report messages were sent from here than in the closed wings. Observations on the open wings revealed that, during opening hours, prisoners had short conversations with other prisoners or staff and that many issues were resolved during these interactions. During the interviews it was also confirmed that more report messages were sent from the wings with the closed regime. We would argue that the findings strongly suggest that prisoners on the closed wings had become more dependent on virtual forms of communication.

With the introduction of *PrisonCloud*, the Belgian Prison Service has pursued a policy that decreases the movements of prisoners inside prison. This has been confirmed by the Minister of Justice during an intervention in the Chamber of Representatives in 2016:

> In addition, access to an in-cell phone and other services (education, ordering canteen, etc.) can reduce the number of internal movements within the establishment, which has an impact both on the required staff and on the peace and quiet within the establishment (less stress related to access facilities). (The Chamber of Representatives 2016: 143)

It was asserted by the Belgian Prison Service that reducing the workload of prison officers would give more opportunity, among other things, for developing and maintaining social interaction with prisoners. Prison research shows that 'besides quality time, "quantity time" is important in relationships' (Beijersbergen et al. 2013: 6). The relocation of daily activities to the prison cell did indeed lead to a decreased workload for the prison officers. However, our observations revealed little evidence that this prompted more, or better quality, social interactions between prisoners and prison staff (Robberechts forthcoming). It has been described above how the relocation of activities to the cell through *PrisonCloud* diminished the opportunities for face-to-face prisoner-staff interactions and conversations. We cited how in non-digital prisons messaging demanded a higher level of social interaction. Although very long-winded, this form of organising the prison created space for a lot of micro, yet positive, social interactions.

Through the digitisation of the internal communication system, prison officers and supervising officers are eliminated from the line of communication, which impacts on the daily operation of the wing. The advantages however were evident to one supervising officer familiar with the communication process in a non-digital prison:

> "I did not get my canteen order, why didn't I get my canteen order?" [the prisoner says]. And then there will be a report message from the accounting service, saying that there is only 25 cent left on their bank account. And you are always somewhere in between. Because you will open the doors, telling them they only have 25 cents. "It is not true chief, I received 20 euros!" And then you have to start ringing around and you are in fact the mediator between the two parties. You do not know anything about it. You do not know whether the story of the prisoner is true, or whether the accounting service [administrators] just made a mistake. You put a lot of energy in these situations and get zero energy in return. You will be the losing party. And I knew, this is not going to happen to me in here. (Interview supervising officer 7)

Besides this, we also found that, whilst direct digital communication with the internal prison services eliminated negative staff-prisoner interactions, *PrisonCloud* entailed a systemic problem of a different kind: an overload of messages from prisoners. This led the local prison administration to limit the number of messages that could be sent to each service on a daily or weekly basis. Moreover, the in-cell access to several facilities impacts the work of the prison officer. Although prisoners were still dependent on prison officers to open the cell doors, accompany them to other parts of the prison, and for various informal requests, the perception of prison officers was that their discretionary powers were decreasing. The in-cell accessibility to services then had an impact on the self-governance of the prisoner, and also the nature of their dependency on prison officers had shifted.

Jewkes and Reisdorf (2016: 541) have pointed out that (selective) access to ICTs could serve as an incentive to good behaviour. However, this was not the case in Belgium when discussing the use of *PrisonCloud*, as each incoming prisoner was permitted the same access to all available services from the beginning—there was no incentive in place that 'rewarded' prisoners with *PrisonCloud* time or facilities. Technologies that promote the self-reliance of prisoners, according to Jewkes and Reisdorf, could divest the guards of their authority, as they find themselves defenestrated by the simultaneous movement of powers upwards to the prison administration and downwards to the 'newly self-empowered prisoner' (Jewkes and Reisdorf 2016: 7).

## The Limitations of Self-Empowerment

Mass media is an important source of empowerment for prisoners. In its various forms, it grants them the possibility to make choices that sustain and develop their identities (Jewkes 2002; Knight 2005: 89). By providing facilities within the prison cell through the digital platform, the prison administration has claimed that it will enhance the reintegration, self-reliance, and self-empowerment of prisoners (Snacken and Beyens 2017: 119). And indeed, at first glance, *PrisonCloud* provided prisoners with considerably enhanced autonomy at different levels. For example, they were able to make appointments with the medical service directly, order products via the canteen function, continue to work, or follow courses during prison strikes. However, whilst it increased the responsibilisation of prisoners (Crewe 2011), the autonomy provided by the digital platform was not infinite. Also Bosworth notes that although prisoners indeed have the right to order some goods and services, 'they have little means of ensuring their delivery' (2007: 73), and their access to certain information or facilities remains restricted. Similarly, and as already mentioned, communication with the internal prison services through *PrisonCloud* has been limited. The normalisation process envisaged with the introduction of *PrisonCloud* has thus been subordinated to organisational constraints. The following quote also illustrates how the use of the in-cell *PrisonCloud* phone is still hampered by other factors which maintain the prisoner's dependency:

> The guards there [non-digital prison] also have much more contact with the prisoner because you have to call on the guards first and foremost. And

> here you are much more in the cell and you have to do everything yourself. But you can't always do that. For example, you may make phone calls 24 hours a day. But you do not have a phonebook and 1207[7] is a blocked number. That means that you always have to ask someone for a phone number. But if you want to do that in N [non-digital prison], it is much easier. There is the phone book next to the phone and if you are allowed to make a phone call, you can at least look up a phone number. (Interview prisoner 27, closed regime)

While prisoners can contact the internal prison services themselves, they are still dependent on the reaction of the users on the other side of the line. Crewe (2011: 519) points to this new pain of imprisonment in that 'now the prisoner is given greater autonomy—in a limited and localised way—but is enlisted in the process of self-government and held responsible for an increasing range of decisions'. In this case, to assume responsibility is to use *PrisonCloud* to act. The digital platform is the only way to access certain services to realise their own prison regime (e.g. in order to receive visits from the outside world, prisoners have to send a formal request through PrisonCloud).

However, there is a certain danger in leaving the initiative with the prisoner; some will simply do nothing. As one Chaplain suggested:

> They will never write a report message. So, if you do not take the initiative to see the man… They never say 'long time no see'. But they will say: 'you are the only one I talk to'. *PrisonCloud* strengthens the possibility of total isolation. (Interview chaplain 1)

## Conclusion: The Emergence of the 'Total Cell'?

In his classic study, Goffman (1961: 71) argued that prisons are total institutions since all matters of different spheres of life are exercised in one place. These total institutions implied that a certain barrier separated prisoners from the outside world. In the nineteenth century, the Belgian penitentiary policy was one of individual segregation that forbade any contact between prisoners (Snacken and Beyens 2017). Sykes (1958: 65) argued that 'the loss of liberty is a double one—first, by confinement to the institution and second, by confinement within the institution', pointing at the importance of the fabric of the prison cell. Indeed, as he explains:

> if men in prison were locked forever in their cells, shut off from all intercourse with each other, and deprived of normal life, the dimensions of the cell would be the alpha and omega of life in prison. (Sykes 1958: 5)

The prison remains a closed place to wider society, but today the walls between and within the prison and the outside world have become more permeable. In addition, activities are now organised to humanise the detention conditions of the prisoner, and digital media makes it possible for those on the inside to maintain connected with the outside world. Nevertheless, we found that the increase in the multifunctionality of the prison cell, where all aspects of life can be exercised from the inside, had changed the situational geography of the prison cell. Multifunctionality had involved a relocation of certain facilities to the prison cell, and the different applications of *PrisonCloud* gave a new virtual dimension to the prison cell. The possibility of a *total cell* within the total prison institution thus became a reality for some prisoners or in those parts of the prison with a closed door regime. Particularly vulnerable prisoners, for whom *PrisonCloud* was a tool to function from within their cell, disappeared into this new prison context. Also, in general, we found that the effect of physical or social isolation became, on the one hand, weakened by the increasing possibility to interact with the outside world (e.g. in-cell phone) and, on the other hand, strengthened by the decreasing necessity to leave the prison cell for or to directly communicate with the prison staff on the landings. The increasing access to digital communication, both internally and externally, thus has had (in)direct consequences for the (feelings of) isolation of the prisoners, voluntarily or involuntarily. So, paradoxically, the possibility of greater virtual communication has the potential to create physical and social isolation in this prison context.

Furthermore, our findings show that *PrisonCloud* entailed a shift in the position prisoners took, within the limitations of the broader prison context, towards independence and self-government. The use of technology then created some elements of self-governance for prisoners; however, they remained heavily dependent on the reactions to any request or question that they used it to address. Also, in this respect, the digital platform created a paradoxical relationship: the claim that it increased the autonomy of the prisoners was found to be related to the dependency that *PrisonCloud* established between the prisoner and the platform. *PrisonCloud* offered the prisoners the freedom to communicate virtually both with the outside world and with the prison services, but only at the expense of face-to-face communication with the prison staff, whose tasks were partly taken over by the platform and who felt threatened in their professional roles.

To end, we argue that it was the *relocation* of the activities to the prison cell due to the use of technology, rather than technology *per se*, that has made the greatest impact on prison life. The new form of interaction and isolation is mainly due to how technology is used and that it is not the technology in itself that has generated these effects. This is in line with our findings that the normalisation process is indeed being pursued through the platform, but in practice is limited by local policy. Our analysis thus confirms that technology is not neutral, but only acquires meaning through its use by human actors and within an organisational context (Orlikowski and Robey 1991).

## Notes

1. In Belgium, prison officers are allowed to strike and it is not uncommon. As the Belgian government has repeatedly been criticised by the European Committee for the Prevention of Torture (CPT) for the detrimental consequences of striking upon prisoners, mandatory guaranteed minimum service of prison officers during strikes has been introduced by law in 2019.
2. In this chapter, we will use the term 'digital prison' for prisons where *PrisonCloud* is installed and 'non-digital prisons' for prisons where *PrisonCloud* is not installed.
3. The standard phone system is based on a blacklist, allowing prisoners to call anyone but the numbers on this list. This can however be adjusted to

the use of a white list, allowing prisoners only to phone the numbers that have given consent.

4. The chapter does not specifically elaborate on the access to media in prison but rather focuses on the digital infrastructure in general.
5. The research 'Digitalisation in prison' (Nr. G024316N) is funded by the Research Foundation Flanders (FWO) and promoters Prof. Kristel Beyens (Vrije Universiteit Brussel (VUB)) and Dr. Eric Maes (National Institute for Criminalistics and Criminology (NICC)). Researcher: Jana Robberechts (VUB).
6. Since 2019 in-cell telephones have been gradually implemented in non-digital prisons.
7. 1207 is a free service directory providing phone numbers and addresses.

# References


Baer, L. D., & Ravneberg, B. (2008). The Outside and Inside in Norwegian and English Prisons. *Human Geography, 90*(2), 205–216.

Beijersbergen, K. A., Dirkzwager, A. J. E., Molleman, T., van der Laan, P. H., & Nieuwbeerta, P. (2013). Procedural Justice in Prison: The Importance of Staff Characteristics. *International Journal of Offender Therapy and Comparative Criminology, 59*(4), 337–358.

Belgian Prison Service. (2011). Internal Document.

Belgian Prison Service. (2014). *Annual Report 2013*. Retrieved October 31, 2018, from https://justitie.belgium.be/sites/default/files/downloads/nl_small.pdf.

Belgian Prison Service. (2018). *Annual Report 2017*. Retrieved January 16, 2019, from https://justitie.belgium.be/nl/nieuws/andere_berichten_131.

Bosworth, M. (2007). Creating the Responsible Prisoner. *Punishment & Society, 9*(1), 67–85.

Council of Europe. (2006). *Recommendation Rec(2006)2 of the Committee of Ministers to Member States on the European Prison Rules* (Adopted by the Committee of Ministers on 11 January 2006 at the 952nd meeting of the Ministers' Deputies). Retrieved from https://rm.coe.int/european-prison-rules-978-92-871-5982-3/16806ab9ae.

Crewe, B. (2011). Depth, Weight, Tightness: Revisiting the Pains of Imprisonment. *Punishment & Society, 13*(5), 509–529.

Crewe, B., Liebling, A., & Hulley, S. (2015). Staff-Prisoner Relationships, Staff Professionalism, and the Use of Authority in Public- and Private-Sector Prisons. *Law & Social Inquiry, 40*(2), 309–344.

Farrington, K. (1990). *The Modern Prison as a 'Not-so-total Institution': Impacts upon Transactions with, and Penetrations into the Larger Community*. Paper presented at the Annual Meeting of the American Society of Criminology, Baltimore.

Federal Public Service of Justice. (2014). *Internal Rules* (Unpublished Document).

Goffman, E. (1961). *Asylums: Essays on the Social Situation of Mental Patients and Other Inmates*. New York, NY: Doubleday Anchor.

Jewkes, Y. (2002). *Captive Audience: Media, Masculinity and Power in Prisons*. Oxford: Willan Publishing.

Jewkes, Y., & Johnston, H. (2009). Cavemen in an Era of Speed-of-Light Technology: Historical and Contemporary Perspectives on Communication within Prisons. *Howard Journal of Criminal Justice, 48*(2), 132–143.

Jewkes, Y., & Reisdorf, B. C. (2016). A Brave New World: The Problems and Opportunities Presented by New Media Technologies in Prisons. *Criminology and Criminal Justice, 16*(5), 534–551.

Johnson, R. (2005). Brave New Prisons: The Growing Social Isolation of Modern Penal Institutions. In A. Liebling & S. Maruna (Eds.), *The Effects of Imprisonment* (pp. 255–284). Oxford: Willan Publishing.

Johnson, R., & Hail-Jares, K. (2016). Prison and Technology: General Lessons from the American Context. In Y. Jewkes, J. Bennett, & B. Crewe (Eds.), *Handbook on Prisons* (pp. 284–305). London: Routledge.

Knight, V. (2005). Remote Control: The Role of TV in Prison. *Criminal Justice Matters, 59*(1), 28–29.

Knight, V. (2012). *A Study of In-cell Television in a Closed Adult Male Prison: Governing Souls with In-cell Television*. PhD thesis, De Montfort University, UK.

Knight, V. (2015). Some Observations on the Digital Landscape Today. *Prison Service Journal, 220*, 3–15.

Knight, V., & Van De Steene, S. (2017). Digitizing the Prison: The Light and Dark Future. *Prison Service Journal, 231*, 22–30.

Liebling, A., Price, D., & Shefer, G. (2012). *The Prison Officer*. London: Routledge.

Maes, E. (2009). *Van gevangenisstraf naar vrijheidsstraf. 200 jaar gevangeniswezen*. Antwerpen/Apeldoorn: Maklu.

Maes, E., Robberechts, J., Beyens, K., & Robert, L. (2019). PrisonCloud voor gedetineerden. Grenzen aan digitale normalisering? *Panopticon, 40*(1), 29–45.
Molleman, T., & van Ginneken, E. F. J. C. (2014). A Multilevel Analysis of the Relationship between Cell Sharing, Staff-Prisoner Relationships, and Prisoners' Perceptions of Prison Quality. *International Journal of Offender Therapy and Comparative Criminology, 59*(10), 1029–1046.
Moran, D. (2013). Between Outside and Inside? Prison Visiting Rooms as Liminal Carceral Spaces. *GeoJournal, 78*, 339–351.
Orlikowski, W. J., & Robey, D. (1991). Information Technology and the Structuring of Organizations. *Information Systems Research, 2*(2), 143–169.
Robberechts, J. (forthcoming). Van het veld naar de theorie. Het gebruik van grounded theory in onderzoek naar digitalisering in de gevangenis. In K. Verfaillie (Ed.), *Nieuwe uitdagingen, nieuwe perspectieven*. Antwerpen: Gompel & Svacina.
Scharff-Smith, P. (2012). Imprisonment and Internet-Access: Human Rights, the Principle of Normalization and the Question of Prisoners' Access to Digital Communications Technology. *Nordic Journal of Human Rights, 30*(4), 454–482.
Selwyn, N., Gorard, S., & Furlong, J. (2005). Whose Internet is It Anyway? Exploring Adults' (Non)use of the Internet in Everyday Life. *European Journal of Communication, 20*(5), 5–26.
Snacken, S., & Beyens, K. (2017). Het Belgische beleid ten aanzien van de gevangenisstraf en haar alternatieven. In K. Beyens & S. Snacken (Eds.), *Straffen. Een Penologisch Perspectief* (pp. 95–136). Antwerpen: Maklu.
Sykes, G. M. (1958). *The Society of Captives*. Princeton, NJ: Princeton University Press.
The Chamber of Representatives. (2016). *Question nr. 896 of Mr. Philippe Pivin of 4 March 2016*. Retrieved January 16, 2019, from https://www.dekamer.be/kvvcr/showpage.cfm?section=qrva&language=nl&cfm=qrvaXml.cfm?legislat=54&dossierID=54-B069-866-0896-2015201608207.xml.
Vandebosch, H. (2000). Research Note: A Captive Audience? The Media Use of Prisoners. *European Journal of Communication, 15*(4), 529–544.
Vollan, M. (2016). Widening the Scope of the Principle of Normality. *Advancing Corrections Journal, 1*, 90–100.

# 14

# Carceral Projections: The Lure of the Cell and the Heterotopia of Play in *Prison Escape*

Hanneke Stuit

## Introduction: Reading the Cell

Approaching the city centre of Breda, the Netherlands, from the east, its skyline is dominated by the dome of the prison. The prison was built in 1886 and designed by J.F. Metzelaar, who closely followed Jeremy Bentham's famous design of the domed panopticon (Van Traa 1987). In 2001, the prison was declared a monument by the Dutch government and in 2016 it was repurposed, like many other prisons in the Netherlands. Many former prisons offer office space, have housed refugees or sport coffee bars, restaurants and hotels. In some, musical recitals, art exhibitions and tours of the premises are also organised. An emerging trend is to utilise them for explicitly lucrative entertainment purposes, particularly escape room games.[1] The panoptic prison in Breda houses *Prison Escape*, a game in which participants are locked up with sometimes as many as 200 other players. In three hours, players try to escape by way of

H. Stuit (✉)
University of Amsterdam, Amsterdam, The Netherlands
e-mail: H.H.Stuit@uva.nl





J. Turner, V. Knight (eds.), *The Prison Cell*, Palgrave Studies in Prisons and Penology,
https://doi.org/10.1007/978-3-030-39911-5_14

role-playing and following narrative strands acted out by almost 80 actors. These actors portray guards (including those handling sniffer dogs), a hostile warden, a psychologist, other prisoners, administrative staff and janitors. Like escape room games, *Prison Escape* leans on the basic tenets of popular conceptions of the cell: the base of the game is a small, locked room with escape as the most desirable outcome. It differs, however, in that escape is not achieved by solving puzzles, using small key-like objects and cracking codes, but instead relies on the heterotopic interplay of space and the imagination.

From the outside, the prison in Breda emanates the ambiguous atmosphere of a churchlike fortress. Inside, gazing up at the visually and aurally overwhelming dome inspires awe and triggers the imagination. Indeed, as Wilson has remarked: 'The physical prison tells stories. Or rather, it *implies* them' (2008: 333). According to Roux, too, 'one of the characteristics of a prison is that it demands a narrative: to write about the experience of prison is, in a sense, to explain how one ended up there' (2014: 255). However, prison narratives, especially those prevalent in popular culture, do not only describe what happens before confinement. Just as often, they focus on how, when or whether one will get out of prison (Jarvis 2004: 170; Bennett 2018). The meaning of *Prison Escape*, I argue, relies on the entanglement of such imaginaries of escape and the triggering effects of the building itself.

In this chapter, I analyse how *Prison Escape*'s playful engagement with the building offers new perspectives on how shared carceral imaginaries influence player experiences. Following Fludernik (2005), I interpret the carceral imaginary as a discursively circulated repository of images, tropes, themes, narratives and genres that relies on and elicits specific affective and embodied responses that may have ideological orientations. Of course, the penitentiary is imagined and experienced in radically different ways by various individuals and communities alike. The cell as an everyday and embodied space, for instance, is likely to feature more prominently in the experience of less privileged communities (Alexander 2010; Fassin 2017), while the playful carceral atmosphere of a repurposed prison may be the closest more privileged people will ever get to a cell. In the face of this differentiation in 'closeness' to the penitentiary, it is all the more important to analyse how cultural expressions like *Prison Escape* are constructed and what insights they allow into the ideological and affective charge of conceptions of the prison.

Through an analysis of the interplay between the panoptic dome and the cell in the imaginaries the game references and produces, I argue that the game relies on what I call the lure of the prison cell. This lure consists of popular narratives of prison escape, combined with metaphorical constructions of transcending the cell, both of which are familiar from an exoticised and exoticising carceral imaginary. In the game, the prison comes to function as a screen on which specific imaginations and expectations of it are projected. Yet, this spectacular use of the metaphor of the cell and the trope of escape is countered by the experience of the game enacted in the enclosure of the cell itself. It is thus also an interface that connects the scripting force of the space and the carceral imaginaries of the individual player in a space of play. This space of play, following De Cauter and Dehaene, is profoundly heterotopic and thus 'entails an always faltering, incomplete process, without synthesis, a dialectics at a standstill, an unstable interruption or suspension' (2008: 94). To be sure, the game risks exoticising the cell as a creative and connected space, rather than as just having a 'containing power' for those incarcerated (Levine 2015: 8). Yet, through the heterotopia of play, it also creates an open-ended embodied experience that mediates prison space with the carceral imaginary and disrupts passive 'penal spectatorship' (Wilson et al. 2017: 5).

In order to get at the detailed texture of the game experience, I analyse my own participation in and contact with the game by considering myself an educated 'reader' of its forms; I played the game with the intention of studying it. My analysis is a close reading, which is a method central to Cultural Analysis (Bal 2002). In this method, the cultural object or phenomenon under consideration is seen as a 'text' that can be approached through detailed attention to the mesh of structures, forms, intertextual relations and metaphorical layers that determine a specific object's or phenomenon's meaning (Bal 1999, 2002; Barthes 1957; Culler 2007; Geertz 1973: 10). Close reading is based on the premise that cultural expressions are always situated, delivered and received in a form (McLuhan and Fiore 1967; see also Morton 2011). This form, like language, is multifaceted and sometimes even resistant to understanding (Culler 2010), requiring close and detailed analysis before its affective, theoretical and political effects can be grasped. Cultural theoretical insights are used as a crowbar to prise open the complex ways in which cultural objects do more than just mimetically reflect the culture in which they have been formed. The analysis also seeks to unearth objects' performative and reiterative functions (Butler 1996) in generating new meanings that may circulate beyond their direct contexts in politically or theoretically relevant ways (Bal 1999: 10; Peeren 2007: 3). By studying *Prison Escape* in this way, I show how conceptions of the prison travel through bodies and through the imaginaries and spaces these bodies frequent.

## Carceral Imaginaries and the Lure of the Prison Cell

*Prison Escape* is an elaborate and complex real-life game consisting of roughly ten stages. All of these stages, from first contact on the company's web page to the final escape on site, are heavily scripted (see Table 14.1).

**Table 14.1 Overview of game stages in *Prison Escape***

| | | |
|---|---|---|
| Immersion | 1. Pre-game priming and logistics | Player finds website, buys tickets, story is sent over mail, signing of waiver |
| | 2. Arrival and entry into the complex | Instructions by game organisation |
| | 3. Entry into the prison building | First encounter with actors (guards) |
| | 4. Check-in | Locker room, overalls, mugshot, name tags, fingerprints |
| | 5. Orientation | Orientation by guards, arrival in dome, instructions by warden |
| Material exploration and storylines | 6. The cells | Exploration of cell, collecting objects for kick-starting player narratives |
| | 7. Recreation | Players are in the dome and courtyard figuring out how to escape |
| | 8. Escape (or not) | Players run away from the prison |
| Postgame (cooling down) | 9. Celebration | Everybody is in the dome again, drinks and merchandise are offered, group photo is taken |
| | 10. Postgame marketing | Questionnaires and so on are emailed to players, mugshots and group photos are posted on Facebook |

Interestingly enough, the script does not reference Breda prison's most infamous function of detaining Nazi collaborators after WWII nor the successful escape of some of these men to Germany in the 1950s. There is no mention of the fact that they were never extradited back to the Netherlands, causing heated political debate for almost 20 years (Olink 2004). Significantly, the game interpellates its mostly Dutch-speaking players by relying on the trope of prison escape and the way prisons appeal to the imagination, rather than on this particular site's history.[2] Examples of this are the character of the bad warden (who had me searched for contraband without provocation), the sympathetic or perhaps corrupt guard (who returned that contraband to me as soon as the warden turned his back) and the possibility of joining a prison gang (Jarvis 2004: 168). The focus on gangs, particularly—which are much less prevalent in Dutch prisons than in some other countries—seems to suggest scripts familiar from US prison narratives. Most crucial, however, is the reliance on the canonical narrative climax ending in the escape itself (Jarvis 2004: 170).

The specificity of the site qua architecture, however, does feature heavily in the game and plays a crucial role in how the notion of escape is figured for the player. This is highlighted by the game's home page (see Fig. 14.1), showing an almost full-screen image of a prisoner trying to escape from their cell, accompanied by the following line: 'Can you escape from the domed prison in Breda?'[3]

At face value, this text can be read as an exciting challenge aimed at drawing visitors in as future players of the game. On closer inspection, however, the phrasing is puzzlingly specific. Apparently, it matters that the game takes place, not in any prison, but in the 'domed prison in Breda'. Indeed, the interior of the monumental building's dome takes up most of the space on the home page. The railing flanking the cells starts on the left hand side, a natural starting position for 'reading' the image that guides the gaze of the viewer along the gallery into the larger space of the prison. Yet, more than half of the left side of the image is blurry, directing attention to the right. There, the prisoner, clearly engaged in escaping from their cell, is rendered in full focus. The cell door, too, is sharp, giving it prominence in the image as a whole. Whether the prisoner is looking at the gallery or the guards is not clear, as they are seen

**Fig. 14.1** Image of a prisoner escaping from their cell used on *Prison Escape*'s home page (Source: Sander Erdmann/Prison Escape)

from behind. In any case, the guards' haziness turns them into an integral part of the 'architectural apparatus' that needs to be subverted in order to achieve escape (Foucault 1975: 201).

It is precisely the focus on the prisoner's ability to *look* that determines this image's content because it reverses how panoptic surveillance induces 'in the inmate a state of conscious and permanent visibility that assures the automatic functioning of power' (Foucault 1975: 201). The prisoner in the panoptic prison knows that they are always potentially seen, but does not know exactly when they are being watched. As Božovič points out in his introduction to Bentham's panoptic writings, the panopticon thus relies on the fiction that the guard is always there as an 'invisible omnipresence' in the panoptic function of the dome in general (Bentham 1995: 9). Bender describes this as 'an imaginative projection in the subject's consciousness of the jailer's eye watching, as if eternally' (1987: 23–24). By having an escaping prisoner look at the dome and apparently loitering guards, the image on the *Prison Escape* home page stages an individual defying a blurry panoptic power by looking directly at the apparatus that should be invisible. Considering Foucault's claim that the panopticon is 'a diagram of a mechanism of power reduced to its *ideal* form', the escape from this cell becomes an attractive display of resistance to how power functions on individual bodies in panoptic settings (Foucault 1975: 205, emphasis mine).[4] The placement of the camera behind the figure further invites viewers to identify with this defiant position, looking with them, over their shoulder, rather than at them.

The small silver ring in the figure's left ear works as a further individualisation: a shimmer of choice in an environment otherwise represented as bleak and static. This situation is communicated through the blandly coloured overalls and the grey filter reminiscent of the American *Prison Break* television series, which sports a similar use of both. Because of this intertextual relation, the image becomes further infused, not just with bleakness but more specifically with that series' foregrounding of the protagonist's bold ingenuity in purposefully getting arrested in order to escape and break his brother out of prison. The image thus taps into a more general turn in prison narratives in popular culture towards 'the heroism of characters' (Aitken and Dixon quoted in Turner 2013: 224) expressed through a focus on 'the dangerous, violent, atomised experience of imprisonment … against which a "prison innocent" can endure and then overcome the indignities of a brutal prison regime' (Kearon 2012: 6).

*Prison Escape* is thus ultimately not about doing memory or educational work for the situatedness of the site, like a prison museum would (Wilson et al. 2017: 5), although it does offer an opportunity to see a prison from the inside—'a space usually deemed wholly inaccessible to the "law-abiding" public' (Turner 2016: 98). Even before the visitor has set foot anywhere near this prison, the monumental aesthetic of the building is put on display as the setting of a heroic attempt to escape. The game ultimately stages an imagined prison within the material and architectural confines of the disused penitentiary, and the building itself becomes a screen on which the trope of prison escape is projected. In other words, the game invites players to live through imprisonment in the panoptic prison and escape from it in a metaphorical sense.

This fantasy of escape is part of an historically persistent metaphorical construction of the cell as a site of transcendence. Like escape tropes, these metaphors are stored in what Fludernik has called the carceral imaginary: 'a collection of culturally relevant images and associations that define our society's *idées reçues* about imprisonment' (2005: 16–17). Having studied prison metaphors in English literature from the Renaissance to the twentieth century, Fludernik shows that the images in this repository rely on a number of popular metaphors including the connection of prisons to hell, marriage, a tomb, the workings of society at large, a ship, a university or academy and a sanctuary or refuge (Fludernik 2005: 10). The lure of the prison cell is indeed a dominant feature of the carceral imaginary and themes of liminality play an important role. Particularly cell walls and windows are made permeable 'either through the mental/spiritual projection of the prisoner into the realm of the transcendental (God, peace, love), or through the consolatory ingress of spiritual help, visions of God, of angels providing food, etc.' (Fludernik 1999: 51). In his study of American literature and film, Jarvis foregrounds instances of the cell as a monastic and snug space that can be longed for by some prisoners (Jarvis 2004: 153, 154 and 163). In addition, the iconic chipping away at the cell wall in order to tunnel out of prison (Jarvis 2004: 204) further imbues the cell with utopian, resourceful and heroic narratives of hope and futurity. In this sense, prison cell imagery features more than just the containment of bodies. It also foregrounds liminal themes of escape and transcendence that 'disrupt the prison cell's containing power' (Levine 2015: 8).

Other prison metaphors also rely strongly on the cell, using images like prison bars, in order to transfer a 'sense' of being incarcerated to contexts that have very little to do with the penitentiary (e.g. Alber 2011: 222). Props associated with the prison cell (and dungeon), like blank walls, closed doors, scant sanitation facilities, austere beds and small windows, also frequently occur. Jarvis also points out that:

> Bodies will be glimpsed in tiers of cells, through bars, crowded by bunks, basins and toilets. In a formal mirroring of its subject's predicament, the camera in most prison films is fixed and largely restricted to tight, interior shots. (Jarvis 2004: 170)

Here, it becomes clear that imagery of the prison is the result of a negotiation between an external gaze looking at the cells, while the forms used usually mirror looking at the prison from within, as if *from*, a cell. In the image from the *Prison Escape* website, the centrality of negotiating the limits of the cell is clearly visible through the foregrounding of the prisoner and cell door against the backdrop of the blurry threat of guards and dome. Besides a prisoner hiding in a cleaning cart elsewhere on the website, it foregoes generic images of prisoners crawling through sewage pipes, climbing fences or running away from the prison with the shackles still around their wrists.[5] The website thus suggests that the rebellious image of escaping the cell is expected to connect to the carceral imaginaries of future players so strongly, that it alone will suffice to pique their interest.

According to Fludernik, this focus on the cell as liminal in carceral metaphoricity tends to be produced and circulated by groups whose social standing means they are unlikely to end up in a prison cell themselves (2005: 21). This disjunction causes Fludernik to conclude that:

> The carceral imaginary remains a fantasy world, an exotic heterotopia that displaces our real-world emotions into the safe and apolitical realm of fiction. Its historical veracity is minimal and so is its immediate impact on our actions. At the same time, carceral metaphors help to engage our emotions and, much like the sublime, seem to cleanse us from a set of psychological ambivalences. (Fludernik 2005: 24)

Here, Fludernik alludes to the cathartic properties of the carceral imaginary. She finds this process deeply suspicious because it contains 'a spectacle of suffering which we vicariously enjoy as heart-rending and then, purged from our emotions, set aside to go back to business as usual' (Fludernik 2005: 24). Following Lakoff and Johnson's take on metaphoricity, her suspicion makes sense. Apart from yoking disparate materials and meanings, metaphoric constructions make visible certain aspects of a concept while simultaneously hiding others (Lakoff and Johnson 1980: 12). Thus, the positive and exciting imagery of the cell as a site of sanctuary or spectacular escape for a privileged elite simultaneously obscures the conditions of those who actually dwell there. Considering Lakoff and

Johnson's claim that metaphors structure thought, carceral imaginaries thus may indeed have 'no purchase with the real, but nevertheless determine our political, moral and social actions because they become reified in our thinking' (Fludernik 2005: 21).

In this sense, *Prison Escape* problematically reifies the prison as an 'exotic heterotopia' structured by the ambivalent fascinations and interests of a largely white, middle-class experience. It merges the traditional association with the cell as an 'idyllic situation of refuge, peace and creativity' with the titillating display of escape from prison (Fludernik 2005: 15). Tickets are expensive and, in its leanings towards the spectacular, it exoticises and glorifies criminals.[6] It commodifies prison life through selective representation (Wright 2000) and may uncritically tap into punitive or voyeuristic desires on the part of the visitor.[7] However, faulting the game for these reasons does not reveal how imaginaries projected on the prison are structured or what kind of effects they produce. As Turner points out in the context of televised prison settings, staging the prison as a spectacle may actually be preferable over not making the penitentiary visible at all; even if the spectacle obscures actual experiences of incarceration, it may also include ironic or destabilising aspects that make the mechanics of 'particular distribution[s] of exposure and denial, reveal and [hiding]' visible (Turner 2013: 224).

As I will discuss in the next section, working through imaginings of the cell is important in assessing how the spectacle of the carceral imaginary, and the aspects it foregrounds and forgets, can be negotiated. By further developing Fludernik's suggestion that the carceral imaginary is an 'exotic heterotopia', I will investigate the effects and critical potential of the otherworldliness of the cell in the game. Through the involvement of the cell in the game script, the building becomes tactile to the player as its panoptic power enforces itself on the carceral imaginaries brought to it. Because the cell offers an intersection of multiple heterotopia (that of the carceral imaginary, the prison itself and the space of play), I argue that it offers an experience of surveillance as it is inscribed on the body that is capable of disrupting fantasies of escape and undermines the spectacular mechanisms of the game's carceral imaginary.

## The Cell and Heterotopic Experiences of Play

As Turner points out in *The Prison Boundary*, a visit to a repurposed prison can be seen as a double heterotopia, 'wherein we trace the subversion of an already subverted space' (2016: 103). This is certainly the case in *Prison Escape*: visitors are confronted with the architecture of a former heterotopia of deviation in the Foucauldian sense (1967: 18) while also being triggered to reflect on the re-imaginings of the space. Indeed, heterotopias, as described by Foucault, exist 'in relation with all other sites, but in such a way as to suspend, neutralise or invert the set of relations designated, mirrored, or reflected by them' (1967: 17). The point, then, is not necessarily to use the concept to designate a type of space (Wesselman 2013: 22), but to read spaces for their reflective and relational effects. Heterotopias make visible how space and discourse work together and how 'spatial configurations (be they material/physical or social)… establish a certain order' in society at large (2013: 22). In *Prison Escape*, several spatial configurations interact and create an intensified heterotopic experience that further complicates 'the subversion of a subverted space' of 'normal' prison tourism. It does so most clearly in the cell, which is central to the game experience because the narratives and plots that carry the game towards possible escape only kick into action once the player has entered it. Without the actions carried out there, immersion is reduced and the game experience would be considerably impaired.

The cell blends several heterotopias together, ordering the space in a way that actively subverts player fantasies of transcendence and escape. First, there is the appearance of the cell itself, which mixes architectural features of different historical periods and enforces multiple temporal realities of the prison as a heterotopia of deviation on the player. Second, the cell functions as a playground, offering objects that induce game immersion and play, which, according to De Cauter and Dehaene, is fundamental to understanding the unsettling effects of heterotopia as an 'unstable interruption or suspension' (2008: 94). Finally, the cell forms an interface for the expectations of the role-playing individual, partly determined, as I have shown in the previous section, by the exotic heterotopia of the carceral imaginary. In the cell, all these threads work together. As I will analyse below, 'touching' the cell and the scripting power of the panopticon in play creates a safe, cathartic engagement with the prison that might uncritically 'reconstitute the myth of the place' (Turner 2016: 118). However, it also provides 'opportunities for spiritual and political reflection' (Turner 2016: 116) on alternative conceptions of the workings of the cell through the embodied experience of multiple heterotopias.

Before I enter the cell, the game is already well under way (see Table 14.1). From first entering the prison, I have been forced into a passive role and my fantasies of escape are consistently curtailed. I am handed orange overalls and my mugshot is taken. I am fingerprinted and lectured by the warden during a prolonged line up in the courtyard of the dome. I am made to perform physical exercises like push-ups and interpellated as a troublesome prisoner. Unless instructed otherwise, the player is to keep their hands along their sides at all times and look straight ahead. The sound of shouting guards in the panopticon's dome is overwhelming; it causes an uncomfortable pressure on my eardrums that makes me cringe. Beyond tactical resistance within the boundaries of this heterotopia of deviation (Foucault 1967: 18), there is little room for strategic action or secondary adjustments (De Certeau 1984; Goffman 1961).[8] The first opportunity I get to move and look around without being shouted at is when I am brought to my cell. There I can finally use my hands and touch things.

The cell is very white. It has a light-grey tiled floor that looks worn. Immediately to my right is a built-in cupboard. To my left there is a sanitary unit behind a partition; the sink is visible, the toilet is not. Like the floor, these things look worn from years of daily wear and tear. There is no bed in the cell, although it must have stood against the wall on the right, since the wall on the left has a desk-like structure fixed to it. Directly above the desk are some shelves, and fixed to the bottom of the shelves are a desk light, an intercom and some sockets. The built-in furniture and sanitation unit have a distinct 1970s institutional feel to them. The only things that really 'say' I am in a nineteenth-century building are the barrel vault and the paned window directly opposite the door. It has a curve on the top that mirrors the shape of the ceiling. Below the window is a radiator; above it, an empty curtain rail. Despite having seen prison cells in other settings before, I am confused by the historical mix of architecture. It occurs to me that the building must have been repeatedly adjusted to incorporate modern improvements like central heating systems and electricity while also having to maintain its historical value as a listed building when it was still in use. This makes me think about the generations of prisoners that must have been housed here in varying conditions. There is no visible trace of them though. There are no apparent markings on the wall or furniture, which gives the cell a particularly sanitised, unsettling atmosphere.[9]

When I arrive, there is already someone in there. I did not expect this and it is something of an unpleasant surprise. Perhaps I have a carceral imaginative preconception of cells as solitary.[10] The other person is wearing orange overalls, like me. We shake hands and look at each other's nametags. I wrote a fake name on mine; I don't know about hers. We chat a little about where we are from, why we came and what we expect. Time is ticking, however. There might be objects in the cell, the other player could already have found some and might be putting me at a disadvantage by hiding them from me. I start looking around and tell her what I find in order to make her tell me what she has in her pockets. The objects could be valuable contraband later on and I want to get my hands on as many as I can. I also want to see how she will respond, testing her in case I need to rely on her later in the game. We find a poker chip, some pills, something that looks like cannabis but smells like oregano, a map of the prison, a letter to a prisoner who supposedly was in this cell before us and a flyer advertising group therapy. Later, when the cells are opened for recreation, I become aware that the objects are in fact narrative clues or triggers; handing over the 'right' object to the 'right' person will kick-start 'my' narrative within the game.

A double process is going on. On the one hand, the cell functions as a material interface for the carceral imaginaries I bring to the game: like my assumption of cells being solitary and contraband being useful in prison. On the other hand, these thoughts and strategies come to mind because of the objects and the other person present. Rather than triggering an unencumbered playfulness, the other player awakens a competitive and strategic streak in me, immersing me more fully in the game. In this sense, the way the cell functions in the game turns it into a play space.[11] Play is ambiguous. It is central to culture, but also partly exists outside of society's rules. It suspends reality in a way that is strongly reminiscent of fiction's suspension of disbelief, but is at the same time very serious (Huizinga 1950: 8–11).[12] In their discussion of Foucault's notion of heterotopia, De Cauter and Dehaene point out that the space of play 'is fragile and unstable and can at any time be dispelled' (2008: 96). As such, the space of play in the cell is a kind of 'magic circle': a 'liminal space' that, 'in its formal separation from the rest of the world, presents a world of instability and possibility' (De Cauter and Dehaene 2008: 96). This possibility, which De Cauter and Dehaene consider a basic tenet of Foucault's notion of heterotopia in general, opens up 'a profoundly ambiguous terrain marking both the moment of man's imprisonment within the norms of culture and the threshold of liberation, or, more likely, temporary transgression' (2008: 96). In *Prison Escape*, however, the ambiguity of play as both unsettling and laced with possibility has more sinister inflections. Being serious about my play alienates me from my surroundings, suggesting that the prison setting influences care-free inflections of play.

This type of 'serious' play is most significantly represented in the entanglement of the cell with the panoptic power of the dome. The cells are not locked: no doubt due to fire regulations. Every now and then the metal panel in the door of the cell is lifted and a guard looks in. The continuous slamming of the panels echoes through the dome; I cannot tell where the guards are. I am reprimanded twice: once when I want to look through the keyhole and cannot be surveilled because I am too close to the door to be seen, once when I push open the door in a gesture reminiscent of the prisoner in the website image analysed above and two guards immediately come running. The guards call me a troublemaker and I am threatened with 'solitary' if I transgress a third time. Even without locks, the architecture of the building makes it impossible for me to go anywhere without being noticed. There are guards on all the tiers. There is even a guard in the middle of the floor, overseeing the whole panopticon.[13]

I oscillate between wondering whether a third reprimand leading to solitary will increase my chances of escape and thinking about the cell's eighteenth-century design, its nineteenth-century stones and its twentieth-century additions in the form of toilet stall and wall plugs. I have no idea how much time passes. Indeed, as Hardt points out, 'time is the measure of power' (1997: 65). Once again, I wonder what it must have been like for the people who dwelt here. Although I am not locked up in the literal sense of the word, the wait really drives home that, despite my fantasies of escape, panoptic surveillance keeps me firmly in place and that the threshold of the cell is 'the locus of a power contest' (Fludernik 2005: 15). I get frustrated because I will just have to wait for the next phase of my imprisonment, hoping it might offer further clues to win the game. I am fully immersed and working on my escape, but I also wonder throughout (as I sit through therapy sessions that feel like an eternity or explore the prison yard, right up until the moment when I finally bolt for the prison gates in the pouring rain almost two hours later) what is happening to me. Why am I so engrossed? Why do I resent being seen? Why do I feel trapped? Which parts of my responses are scripted by the game, which come from the building, which originate in what I have seen and read about prisons, and, finally, which are my 'own' responses? There is no way of knowing.

Miguel Sicart, in *Play Matters*, describes this process as a bleed, when 'the transmission of experiences and knowledge from the activity of play [transfer] to our worldview' (2014: 67; see also Waern 2010). Within the boundaries of the game, it is perfectly possible to hover between the different 'layers' of the situation in the cell, to move in and out of the suspension of disbelief needed to complete the story of the game. The cell in *Prison Escape* becomes both a containing space and an interface for the projection of fantasies about incarceration. Play relies on this state of limbo: you play without losing grip on reality. In this game, play can be productive precisely because it creates a heterotopic space in which the player negotiates the materiality and delimitation of the playground with what they know of the carceral imaginary:

> A playful technology can allow a material-based critique of a context by highlighting its own existence through play. What we can do unwillingly or what we take for granted can be revealed playfully, and so a space for conversation is created. (Sicart 2014: 65)

*Prison Escape*'s experience, because the panoptic building and the prison setting in general complicate a care-free liminality of play, allows players to come close to prison. It allows them to perceive their own heterotopic blend of material impressions and discursive constructions. In *Prison Escape*, the Sicartian bleed involves taking on board the effects of the play setting such as the history and architecture of the building, the interpersonal relations created by this setting and the embodied disruption of the carceral imaginary. The cell foregrounds the realisation that the fantasy of escape launched by the lure of the prison cell literally bounces off its walls. This imaginary ultimately comes up short against the architecture of the panoptic prison and the unsettling experience it triggers. The experience of incarceration, in this case, may not be about enclosure per se but rather about knowing what it feels like to be interpellated as someone who needs to be surveilled and kept in place.

## Conclusion

By analysing the various heterotopic qualities of the cell in *Prison Escape*, I propose that spatial experiences of the prison always partly travel through the imagination, especially if one holds a privileged social position and is unlikely to come into contact with it in other ways. These experiences need to be emphatically read as personal declensions of a larger carceral imaginary. As such, the prison cannot be known without understanding the assumptions implied in this imaginary. The website image of the prisoner exiting their cell engages the historical and metaphorical construction of the cell in the carceral imaginary by inviting a voyeuristic view that foregrounds the cell as a liminal and exciting space. It does so not by focusing on properties of the cell itself, however, but by depicting the fantasy of escape *from* the cell and the subsequent subversion of panoptic surveillance as an attractive escape fantasy.

Yet, in the otherworldly experience of the cell in play, these fantasies are also disrupted by the prison's material and architectural qualities. Despite a limited mobility in the cell, players are decidedly stuck until the larger script moves on. In bouncing off the cell walls, stereotypical imaginations of the prison make way for an experience of the cell as a miniature of intensified surveillance as it is scripted on the body. More precisely, in the interaction between the cell and the inevitable ordering power of the prison dome, players undergo the panoptic gaze of the heterotopia of deviation and, due to the bleed from play to preconceptions, are made gratingly aware of what it feels like to be surveilled. Even if these experiences are undergone from a privileged position of volition and thus may invite voyeuristic qualities of cathartic release for the player, the fact that they take place through a serious playfulness also allows for a touching of the prison in Turner's terms. Even without real incarceration, the embodied experience of the cell in *Prison Escape* is a harbinger of what it feels like to inhabit deviation in a space that is only partly visible to society at large.

**Acknowledgements** Thanks to the members of The Peripheries Project research group at the Amsterdam School for Cultural Analysis (ASCA) who read and discussed earlier drafts of this text with me. Thanks also to the editors of this volume who have been immensely helpful and constructive in their feedback. Special thanks to Alex Niemeijer-Brown, Daan Wesselman and Rik Stapelbroek for helping me understand the game.

## Notes

1. Other examples of escape room-like games in repurposed prisons exist in Utrecht (Wolvenburg), Amsterdam (Bijlmerbajes) and Arnhem (Koepelgevangenis).
2. For a discussion on globalised scripts of imprisonment, specifically in the mugshot genre, see Stuit (2020).
3. 'Kun jij ontsnappen uit de koepelgevangenis in Breda?' See prisonescape.nl, accessed 29 November 2018.
4. Browne has argued that the panoptic model needs to be put 'under erasure' (2015: 41). It is still relevant in understanding contemporary conditions of surveillance, but does not have universal valence. The notion of the panopticon historically coincided with other forms of incarceration, like the slave ship and the plantation, that also influence contemporary experiences and imaginations of capture and escape.

5. Relevant examples here are *The Shawshank Redemption* (1994), *Escape from Alcatraz* (1979) and *O Brother, Where Art Thou?* (2000).
6. For further elaboration on cultural representation's paradoxical fascination with criminals, see Duncan (1996) and Hobsbawm (1981).
7. For a more elaborate reading of punitive desires and the representation of prisons, see Kearon (2012), King and Maruna (2006) and Cheliotis (2010). For an angle on voyeurism, see Ross (2015).
8. Options I tried out were faking to do push-ups, not shouting 'Sir, yes, Sir' or rolling up the sleeves of the overalls because the guards only mentioned that the collar should be in order. The first two went unnoticed, the third raised annoyance in the guards.
9. In her analysis of prison graffiti in Australian prisons, Wilson mentions that the walls of cells open to tourists are often repainted (2008: 334). Graffiti is only preserved in places closed to the public. In the prisons I visited in the Netherlands, notably Bijlmerbajes and the panoptic prison in Haarlem, the opposite is true. In the first, graffiti was eminently visible in the holding cells, and in the latter, the graffiti in solitary confinement was elaborately discussed by the former prison guard giving the guided tour.
10. This may be a Dutch imaginary, considering that cells have only recently become shared in the Netherlands (Thie 2013).
11. A play space is less formal than a game space. Sometimes the play space and the game space intersect. A game is always a space for play with its own logic, materiality and rules (Begy 2017: 722), but a play space is not always a game. A playground as a play space is more susceptible to what Sicart calls 'free play', which is determined by the space and context, but not by any rules (2014: 51).
12. Consider Sutton-Smith's remark that 'the playful nip may not be a bite, but it is indeed what a bite means' (1997: 1).
13. This confirms Foucault's suggestion that the panopticon not only scripts the behaviour of the person being watched but also of the person doing the watching (1975: 202).

## References

Alber, J. (2011). Cinematic Carcerality: Prison Metaphors in Film. *The Journal of Popular Culture, 44*(2), 217–232.

Alexander, M. (2010). *The New Jim Crow. Mass Incarceration in the Age of Colorblindness*. New York, NY & London: The New Press.

Bal, M. (1999). Introduction. In M. Bal & B. Gonzalez (Eds.), *The Practice of Cultural Analysis: Exposing Interdisciplinary Interpretation* (pp. 1–14). Stanford, CA: Stanford University Press.

Bal, M. (2002). *Travelling Concepts in the Humanities: A Rough Guide*. Toronto: University of Toronto Press.

Barthes, R. ([1957] 1972). *Mythologies* (A. Lavers, Trans.). New York, NY: The Noonday Press.

Begy, J. (2017). Board Games and the Construction of Cultural Memory. *Games and Culture, 12*(7–8), 718–738.

Bender, J. (1987). *Imagining the Penitentiary: Fiction and Architecture of Mind in Eighteenth Century England*. Chicago, IL and London: University of Chicago Press.

Bennett, J. (2018). Representations of Prison Escapes in Films. In T. M. Martin & G. Chantraine (Eds.), *Prison Breaks: Towards a Sociology of Escape* (pp. 265–290). London: Palgrave Macmillan.

Bentham, J. (1995). *The Panoptic Writings* (M. Božovič, Ed.). London and New York, NY: Verso.

Browne, S. (2015). *Dark Matters: On the Surveillance of Blackness*. Durham, NC and London: Duke University Press.

Butler, J. (1996). *Bodies That Matter: On the Discursive Limits of Sex*. London and New York, NY: Routledge.

Cheliotis, L. K. (2010). The Ambivalent Consequences of Visibility: Crime and Prisons in the Mass Media. *Crime Media Culture, 6*(2), 169–184.

Culler, J. (2007). Text: Its Vicissitudes. In J. Culler (Ed.), *The Literary in Theory* (pp. 99–116). Stanford, CA: Stanford University Press.

Culler, J. (2010). The Closeness of Close Reading. *ADE Bulletin, 149*, 20–25.

De Cauter, L., & Dehaene, M. (2008). The Space of Play. Towards a General Theory of Heterotopia. In M. Dehaene & L. De Cauter (Eds.), *Heterotopia in the City. Public Space in Postcivil Society* (pp. 87–102). London and New York, NY: Routledge.

De Certeau, M. ([1984] 1988). *The Practice of Everyday Life* (S. Rendall, Trans.). Berkeley, CA and London: University of California Press.

Duncan, M. C. (1996). *Romantic Outlaws, Beloved Prisons: The Unconscious Meanings of Crime and Punishment*. New York, NY: New York University Press.

Fassin, D. (2017). *Prison Worlds: An Ethnography of the Carceral Condition* (R. Gomme, Trans.). Cambridge, MA and Malden: Polity.

Fludernik, M. (1999). Carceral Topography: Spatiality, Liminality and Corporality in the Literary Prison. *Textual Practice, 13*(1), 43–77.
Fludernik, M. (2005). Metaphoric (Im)prison(ment) and the Constitution of a Carceral Imaginary. *Anglia. Journal of English Philology, 123*(1), 1–25.
Foucault, M. ([1967] 2008). Of Other Spaces (L. De Cauter & M. Dehaene, Trans.). In M. Dehaene & L. De Cauter (Eds.), *Heterotopia in the City. Public Space in Postcivil Society* (pp. 13–29). London and New York, NY: Routledge.
Foucault, M. ([1975] 1995). *Discipline and Punish: The Birth of the Prison.* New York, NY: Vintage Books.
Geertz, C. (1973). *The Interpretation of Culture.* New York, NY: Basic Books.
Goffman, E. ([1961] 1991). *Asylums: Essays on the Social Situation of Mental Patients and Other Inmates.* London: Penguin.
Hardt, M. (1997). Prison Time. *Yale French Studies, 91*, 64–79.
Hobsbawm, E. J. (1981). *Bandits.* New York, NY: Pantheon.
Huizinga, J. ([1950] 2014). *Homo Ludens: A Study of the Play Element in Culture.* Mansfield Centre: Martino.
Jarvis, B. (2004). *Cruel and Unusual: Punishment and US Culture.* London: Pluto Press.
Kearon, T. (2012). Alternative Representations of the Prison and Imprisonment: Comparing Dominant Narratives in the News Media and in Popular Fictional Texts. *Prison Service Journal, 199*, 4–9.
King, A., & Maruna, S. (2006). The Function of Fiction for a Punitive Public. In P. Mason (Ed.), *Captured by the Media: Prison Discourse in Popular Culture* (pp. 16–30). London and New York, NY: Routledge.
Lakoff, J., & Johnson, M. (1980). *Metaphors We Live By.* Chicago, IL and London: University of Chicago Press.
Levine, C. (2015). *Forms: Whole, Rhythm, Hierarchy, Network.* Princeton, NJ and Oxford: Princeton University Press.
McLuhan, M., & Fiore, Q. (1967). *The Medium is the Massage: An Inventory of Effects.* New York, NY: Random House.
Morton, T. (2011). Sublime Objects. *Speculations II*, 207–227.
Olink, H. (2004). De zeven van Breda. *Nrc.nl.* Retrieved December 6, 2018, from https://www.nrc.nl/nieuws/2004/02/07/de-zeven-van-breda-7673142-a833464.
Peeren, E. (2007). *Intersubjectivities and Popular Culture: Bakhtin and Beyond.* Stanford, CA: Stanford University Press.
Roux, D. (2014). Inside/Outside: Representing Prison Lives after Apartheid. *Life Writing, 11*(2), 247–259.

Ross, J. I. (2015). Varieties of Prison Voyeurism: An Analytic/Interpretive Framework. *The Prison Journal, 95*(3), 397–417.

Sicart, M. (2014). *Play Matters*. London and Cambridge, MA: The MIT Press.

Stuit, H. (2020). The Prison as Playground: Global Scripts and Heterotopic Vertigo in *Prison Escape*. In S. Ferdinand, I. Souch, & D. Wesselman (Eds.), *Heterotopia and Globalisation in the Twentieth Century-First Century*. London and New York, NY: Routledge.

Sutton-Smith, B. (1997). *The Ambiguity of Play*. Cambridge, MA and London: Harvard University Press.

Thie, M. (2013). Wie gaat straks met wie in de cel? *Nrc.nl*. Retrieved December 21, 2018, from https://www.nrc.nl/nieuws/2013/03/29/wie-gaat-straks-met-wie-in-de-cel-12637038-a555682.

Turner, J. (2013). The Politics of Carceral Spectacle: Televising Prison Life. In D. Moran, N. Gill, & D. Conlon (Eds.), *Carceral Spaces: Mobility and Agency in Imprisonment and Migrant Detention* (pp. 219–247). Farnham: Ashgate.

Turner, J. (2016). *The Prison Boundary: Between Society and Carceral Space*. London: Palgrave Macmillan.

Van Traa, P. C. (1987). *Bouwhistorische Documentatie en Waardebepaling Koepelgevangenissen*. Den Haag: Ministerie van volkshuisvesting, ruimtelijke ordening en milieubeheer, Rijksgebouwendienst.

Waern, A. (2010). 'I'm in love with someone that doesn't exist!' Bleed in the Context of a Computer Game. *Nordic DiGRA*. Retrieved July 15, 2018, from http://www.digra.org/wp-content/uploads/digital-library/10343.00215.pdf.

Wesselman, D. (2013). The High Line, 'The Balloon,' and Heterotopia. *Space and Culture, 16*(1), 16–27.

Wilson, J. Z. (2008). Transgressive Decor: Narrative Glimpses in Australian Prisons, 1970s–1990s. *Crime Media Culture, 4*(3), 331–348.

Wilson, J. Z., Hodgkinson, S., Piché, J., & Walby, K. (2017). Introduction: Prison Tourism in Context. In J. Z. Wilson, S. Hodgkinson, J. Piché, & K. Walby (Eds.), *The Palgrave Handbook of Prison Tourism* (pp. 1–12). London: Palgrave Macmillan.

Wright, P. (2000). The Cultural Commodification of Prisons. *Social Justice, 27*(3), 15–21.

# Correction to: Prison Cell Spaces, Bodies and Touch

Elisabeth Fransson and Francesca Giofrè

**Correction to:**

Chapter 12 in: J. Turner, V. Knight (eds.), *The Prison Cell*, Palgrave Studies in Prisons and Penology, https://doi.org/10.1007/978-3-030-39911-5_12

The original version of the chapter was revised: The figure 12.1 in Chapter 12 has been replaced with an updated version of the figure.

The updated version of the chapter can be found at
https://doi.org/10.1007/978-3-030-39911-5_12


J. Turner, V. Knight (eds.), *The Prison Cell*, Palgrave Studies in Prisons and Penology,
https://doi.org/10.1007/978-3-030-39911-5_15

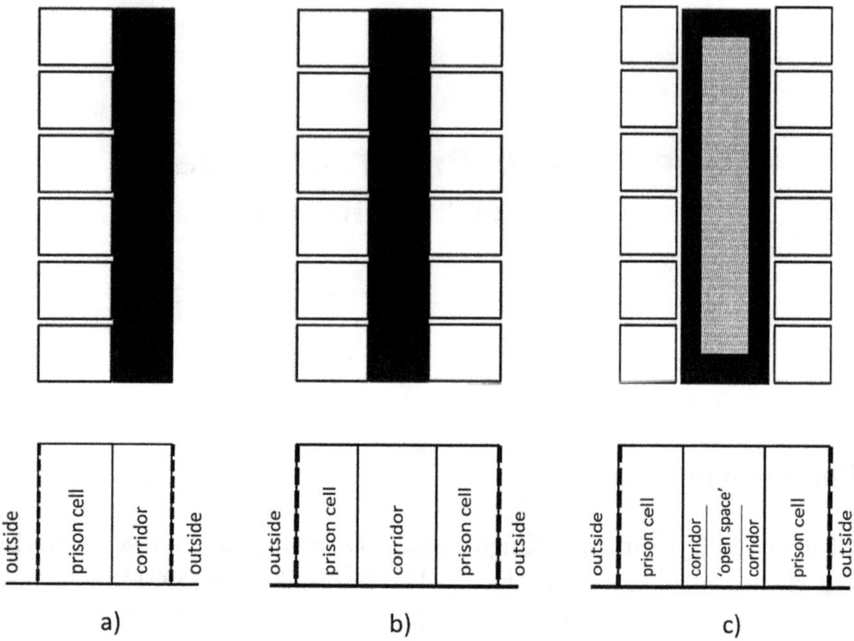


**Fig. 12.1** Cell and corridor: the distribution (Source: F Giofrè)

# The Cell: Afterword

Ben Crewe

Some of the moments in my research career that have lodged themselves most firmly in my mind have involved cells, and the interactions in and around them. Several years ago, during a short research visit, I sat on a prisoner's bed while he told me about the state of his life and his mental torment. His mother, the only family member with whom he was in contact, was dying, and he was contemplating life without her. In a bare and joyless cell, in a segregation unit for his own protection, in a ragged local prison—all of which he commented upon, and which contributed to his sense of desolation—his situation felt about as bleak as was imaginable. More recently, researching in very secure units within high-security prisons, one interviewee told me, without direct hostility, that had there not been a second protective door between us when officers had opened his cell for me to speak to him, his sense of threat meant that he would have attacked me immediately. He went on to describe the terms of his

B. Crewe
Institute of Criminology, University of Cambridge, Cambridge, UK
e-mail: bc247@cam.ac.uk



J. Turner, V. Knight (eds.), *The Prison Cell*, Palgrave Studies in Prisons and Penology,
https://doi.org/10.1007/978-3-030-39911-5

existence: he was confined to his cell for around 23 hours each day, and due to the abuse he received from other prisoners, had chosen not to use the prison's exercise yard for several months. He left his cell only to shower and collect his meals, which he took back to his cell to eat. Yet within his cell, he found little comfort: he had severe mental health problems, and said that he could not remember the last time he had felt relaxed: 'everything is a struggle'. He could not spend time reading, because the text 'all merges into one', and he made 'a point of not watching the news': 'I feel like I've been left to rot, really'. In such circumstances, the cell is the penal space *par excellence*, a distillation of its core qualities and effects.

Cells are also a frontline site of various symbolic and material tussles between prisoners and staff. In England and Wales, the imposition of rules about how cells should be arranged (e.g. whether prisoners are allowed to put up makeshift curtains, or put certain posters on certain walls) represent much more than their ostensible objectives of health, safety and security. The fact that keeping a 'clean and tidy cell' is often used in wing reports as a signifier of positive conduct and compliance is in itself instructive. Meanwhile, the flashpoints that result from cell searches are emblematic of the psychological boundaries that prisoners construct to mark out private and customisable territory, and the moments when it becomes clear that such space is never truly theirs.

Even if only temporarily, then, cells are 'homes': places where individuals get on with their everyday lives. In his research in Oslo prison, in Norway, Ugelvik describes spending long periods of time in prisoners' cells, while they cooked improvised meals, played chess, watched television, showed him their artwork, rehearsed stories that reinforced aspects of identity and morality and talked about 'football, politics, literature, stuff on TV' (Ugelvik, personal communication, 2014). Cells can also be places of warmth, humour and relational generosity. In various semi-ethnographic research projects, I have often seen prisoners in cells playing chess or cards in companionable silence, or laughing raucously as they watch television together or chat about their lives. In interviews, I have been told about the forms of compassion that are expressed beyond the public gaze: emotional support, material kindness and the micro-intimacies of making someone else a cup of tea or trying to grant them some privacy in light of 'bad news'. In a medium-security prison for men, one interviewee described to me his attempt to minimise the distress of his vulnerable, illiterate cellmate, by strategically editing the content of a letter he was reading out to him, from his girlfriend, in which she was terminating their relationship. Despite a prevailing idea that prisons are places that are emotionally suppressive, clearly there are zones of exception.

As in this example, much of the time, my understanding of the role of cells in prisoners' lives—their emotional consistency, the social and personal dynamics within them—has been based only on prisoners' descriptions rather than direct observation or experience. In England and Wales, researchers are generally not allowed to spend time in prisoners' cells or can enter them only for brief periods when invited to do so: to be furtively shown prisoners' photographs or get a sense of their living conditions. The irony, then, is that cells sit at the heart of the prisoner experience, and yet they have very been the focus of serious scholarship relatively infrequently. This skews the field. Within prison research, the neglect of the cell relative to 'the wing' or 'unit' means that we have a clearer sense of the public and social dimensions of imprisonment than the private and existential. As Herrity argues, in her chapter in this volume, 'Foregrounding accounts of these lesser-considered prison spaces provides a portal to often over-looked aspects and textures of prison life'.

To do so seems particularly important given both the amount of time that most prisoners spend in their cell, and the fact that the crux of imprisonment is that they cannot open the door. When prisoners berate researchers for being 'part-timers'—'if you really want to know what it's like, you should commit a crime and find out for yourself'—at some level they are emphasising the importance of a form of comprehension that starts with the cellular experience: sleeping in a locked chamber, often with a stranger, in whose company one has to eat, defecate and inhabit a space of intense emotional humidity. Goffman's (1961) characterisation of the total institution as a place in which daily activity is carried out in the immediate company of others, with almost no separation of the normally distinct domains of work, leisure and sleep, applies with all the more intensity when prisoners are required to co-habit.

In this respect, the increasing input of people with lived experience into academic and non-academic accounts of imprisonment is important and exceptionally insightful. In a recent podcast about prison cells, part of a series called *The Secret Life of Prisons*, a panel of former prisoners talked about the mundane stress of cellular existence: being locked up overnight with a pad-mate who snores, or with toothache ('you are not getting out, you are not getting painkillers'), and the need to cope with the endless present that results from being restricted within a very limited space. Most strikingly, their recollections bring into light the cell's axiomatic role as the communicator of the prisoner's status and situation. One unnamed contributor described the process of confronting her new living conditions:

> When they first took onto the wing and put me in that cell, I was mortified. It was just absolutely disgusting, it was filthy. Oh, the *smell*. There was a toilet in the corner that was just minging. [...] I felt physically ill. I sort of stood there hugging myself in the middle of the cell. I didn't even want to touch anything. And I thought 'right, well I'm gonna have to get over this, because this is my new home for the foreseeable'. (Maguire and Harriott 2019: n.p.)

Others emphasised elemental themes of constraint and captivity. Former prisoner, David Breakspear, explained that 'When you've got that door closed, and you can't see a handle on your side of the door, you've lost control, you're not in control anymore. Someone else is in control of everything about you' (Maguire and Harriott 2019: n.p.). Two further contributors likewise recalled their feelings of powerlessness and confinement:

> I remember the sound of the cell door closing, a big clump of metal behind you. You have to wait for someone to open that door for you. It is a strange thing, looking at a door, a big clump of metal, and knowing that you can't open that. (Unnamed former prisoner, from Maguire and Harriott 2019: n.p.)

> The one thing that struck me more than *anything*, having been a free person, if you like, was going into this space, which was now confined to 9 by

> 6, and that closed in on me, as a 20-year-old, immediately. There was nothing worse, you know. Seeing this green knitted blanket and the black foam mattress and the plastics and the bars was one thing, but the *space* that my life had been confined to now, behind this closed metal door, was probably the most harrowing. (Raphael Rowe, former prisoner, from Maguire and Harriott 2019: n.p.)

In many respects, the cell is the essence of imprisonment. This book goes a long way towards ensuring that it is seen as such.

## References

Goffman, E. (1961). *Asylums: Essays on the Social Situation of Mental Patients and Other Inmates*. Garden City, NY: Anchor Books.

Maguire, P., & Harriott, P. (2019). Episode Two: The Cell. *The Secret Life of Prisons*. Retrieved November 27, 2019, from https://prison.radio/the-secret-life-of-prisons/.

Ugelvik, T. (2014). *Power and Resistance in Prison: Doing Time, Doing Freedom*. London: Palgrave Macmillan.

# Index[1]

A

Agency, 10, 46, 49, 60, 89, 114, 145, 147, 148, 154, 157, 158, 168, 232, 233, 245
Alcatraz prison, USA, 215, 216, 220
Architecture of the cell, 23, 28, 29, 173, 195, 266–268, 315, 316

B

Bastøy prison, Norway, 220
The birth of the prison, 24
Boredom, 79, 104, 107, 113, 147, 177, 178, 181, 247, 291, 292
Bredtveit prison, Norway, 265

C

CCTV, *see* Closed-circuit television
Cells
  assignment, 170–172, 232
  Belgium, 284, 287, 300n1
  in biology, 14
  as a 'cursed' place, 207–209
  as 'escape,' 225, 226, 233, 307, 309, 313, 320
  as 'home,' 11, 121–140, 151, 156, 158, 207–209, 269–271
  imaginaries, 307–314, 317, 320
  Italy, 11, 12, 189, 261, 265, 266, 270, 279, 280
  The Netherlands, 13, 305
  Norway, 12, 46, 261, 265, 266, 276, 279, 280

[1] Note: Page numbers followed by 'n' refer to notes.



J. Turner, V. Knight (eds.), *The Prison Cell*, Palgrave Studies in Prisons and Penology,
https://doi.org/10.1007/978-3-030-39911-5

Cells (*cont.*)
  Philippines, 9, 71–91
  as 'palimpsest,' 143–159
  Romania, 10, 167, 168, 170, 174, 175, 177
  as 'sanctuary,' 12, 153, 231, 240, 245–250, 312, 313
  Scotland, 97, 102, 108
  as a space of play, 201–204, 315, 318
  Switzerland, 10, 121, 123
  UK, 6, 217, 240
  USA, 46, 144
Children, 188, 200, 203, 209
Cleanliness, 138, 155, 175, 179, 180, 201, 272
  *See also* Hygiene
Closed-circuit television (CCTV), 97, 102–105, 110, 112, 113
Contraband, 4, 55, 73, 84, 125, 132, 154, 271, 309, 317
Coping mechanisms, 73–75, 77, 85–87, 91, 134, 150, 156, 196, 209, 247, 249
Cost of facilities and services, 51, 60, 67n5

D

Daily routine, 11, 50, 189, 196, 197, 200, 225, 252, 254, 271
Decency, 217, 222
Dependence on staff, 107, 284–286, 293, 294, 296, 297
Detention centres, 10, 165–171, 177, 180, 181
Deterrence, 2, 31–34, 38, 47
Domestication, 10, 11, 144, 145, 154, 165–182

E

Eastern State penitentiary, USA, 60
Emotion, 33, 95–98, 100, 104–106, 108, 109, 114, 129, 139, 152, 153, 158, 192, 206, 225, 231, 244, 248, 249, 256n3, 263, 313
Escape games, 305, 321n1
Etymology of the cell, 2

F

Food, 72, 77, 83, 84, 132, 156, 198, 199
Furniture/furnishings, 10, 39, 45, 52, 54, 56, 63, 65, 66, 122, 123, 125, 126, 129, 131, 169, 180, 196, 197, 209, 211n8, 285, 316
  *See also* Architecture of the cell

G

Gladstone Committee, 31, 38, 40
Guidelines for prison cell conditions, 123

H

Halden Prison, Norway, 46, 48, 51, 52, 56, 57, 65
Healthy blue space, 215–234

Heterotopia, 306, 307, 314, 315
Holford Committee, 26
Hygiene, 110, 156, 221, 271, 272
*See also* Cleanliness

I

Inhabitation, 122, 126, 127, 139
Intimacy, 132, 189, 201, 204–207
Isolation, 2, 8, 13, 24, 26–41, 108, 167, 173, 231, 290–294, 298, 299

J

JVA Lenzburg and JVA Pöschwies, Switzerland, 123

K

*Kubol* system, 71–91

L

Labour, 30–32, 67n5, 161n7, 220
*See also* Work
Long-term imprisonment, 122, 227, 270, 288
Lure of the prison cell, 307, 312

M

*Mayores* system, 9, 77–81
Memory, 133, 154, 209, 222, 230, 248, 249, 256n3, 264, 311
Mental health, 30, 90, 99, 102, 111, 146, 148, 152, 216, 220, 280
*See also* Physical health
Methodological approaches, 191, 192, 265, 288, 307
Millbank Penitentiary, UK, 26
Mobility, 7, 150, 156, 173, 177, 182, 200, 202, 222, 229, 230, 242, 244, 263, 267, 274–277, 286, 292, 295, 320
Multi-occupancy cells, 72, 74, 75, 85, 166, 170, 271

N

Neighbourhoods, 144, 145, 148–150, 152, 161n8
Noise, 29, 111, 149, 201, 204, 206, 208, 244, 248, 265, 275, 276
Normalisation, 123, 132, 166, 283, 284, 297, 300
Norwegian Correctional Service (NCS), 46, 49, 50, 58, 63

O

Oregon State Penitentiary, USA, 144
Overcrowding, 9, 71, 73, 76, 91, 265, 287

P

Pains of imprisonment, 75, 140, 153, 207, 216, 221, 226, 245, 246, 251, 298
Panopticon, 25, 152, 169, 173, 305, 310, 311, 316, 318, 321n4
Parenting in prison, 204, 209
Penal ideology, 9, 45–66, 264

Pennsylvania Department of Corrections (DOC), USA, 49, 51, 54, 64, 66
Pentonville penitentiary, UK, 29, 30, 35
Personal belongings, 77, 125, 129, 130, 155, 177, 179, 180, 208, 271, 278
Personal space, 82, 126, 138, 152, 178, 179, 182, 246, 247, 267
Peterhead prison, UK, 220
Physical health, 24, 219, 221, 228, 234, 280
  *See also* Mental health
Police cells, 5, 9, 16, 96–98, 102, 108, 110, 111, 113, 114
Power, 7, 8, 10, 14, 30, 38, 40, 60, 61, 80, 86, 90, 96, 97, 105, 107, 109, 110, 113, 114, 115n1, 126, 144, 147, 149, 151, 158, 159, 168, 174, 178, 182, 232, 240, 244–246, 251–253, 255, 256, 262, 267, 297, 307, 310–312, 314, 316, 318, 319, 321
Prison
  boundary, 5, 208, 245, 262–264, 278, 280, 290, 299
  reform, 24, 76
  tourism, 216, 315
PrisonCloud, 283–300
Privacy, 10, 58, 59, 62–64, 82, 97, 104, 121, 138, 139, 146, 149, 150, 152–158, 173–175, 178, 179, 182, 206, 210, 247–249, 271, 277–279, 285, 286, 289, 290, 294
Privatisation, 83, 88, 284

R

*Rancho* system, 83–85, 88–90
Rebibbia prison, Italy, 265, 270
Rehabilitation, 9, 38, 46–48, 60, 62–64, 66, 74, 75, 78, 79, 85, 220, 228, 232, 234
Relationships with people and space, 209, 233, 247, 254, 267, 271, 275
  *See also* 'Neighbourhoods'
Resistance, 6, 8, 13, 14, 34, 96–99, 101, 109–114, 130, 137, 140, 146, 161n10, 176, 180, 209, 242, 245, 247–249, 251, 255, 311, 316
Role of religion, 27

S

Sanitation, 149, 197, 209, 221, 222, 316
Security, 5, 6, 16, 47–50, 52, 54, 58, 61, 62, 64, 66, 73, 75, 83, 86, 92n5, 122, 149, 150, 152, 160n4, 192, 200, 220, 227, 241, 255, 256n4, 266, 276, 278, 283, 285, 293
  *See also* Surveillance, 5
Self-governance, 75, 86, 87, 91, 296, 300
Self-harm, 96, 99, 103, 105, 114, 197, 272
  *See also* Mental health
Senses, 3, 12, 52, 55, 64, 77, 108, 129, 133, 156, 219, 239, 246, 248, 253, 262, 263, 265, 269, 272
  *See also* Sound

The separate system, 23, 26–31
The silent system, 27, 28
Sound, 12, 30, 38, 129, 133, 140n5, 156, 204, 206, 226, 231, 240–256, 256n3, 267, 275, 276, 290, 316
  *See also* Noise
Standardisation of cell architecture, 6, 123, 148, 158, 167, 176, 178
State Correctional Institution (SCI) phoenix, 46, 49–51, 53, 58
The State Prison of East Jutland at Enner Mark, Denmark, 234
Suomenlinna Prison, Finland, 220
Surveillance, 13, 25, 51, 58, 61, 146, 152, 170, 172–175, 194, 250–252, 254, 256, 310, 314, 319–321, 321n4

T

Technology, 5, 12, 13, 51, 102, 283, 284, 288, 290–292, 294, 297, 299, 300
Therapeutic green space, 220
Therapeutic landscape, 11, 217–220, 222, 233
Time, 5, 16, 24, 27–29, 40, 46, 48, 51, 80, 97, 103–105, 108–111, 114, 122, 127, 134, 136, 139, 140n6, 145, 150–154, 158, 172, 173, 176, 177, 180, 207, 226, 227, 240, 248, 249, 270, 273, 274, 278, 291, 292, 319
Touch, 12, 261–280, 316
Turin prison, Italy, 190, 191, 194–201, 205

V

Violence, 64, 73, 90, 91, 99, 109, 157, 160n6, 173, 193, 254, 255

W

Wellbeing, 85, 114, 182, 218–221, 228, 229, 234, 248–250
  *See also* Mental health
Work, 27, 36, 79, 80, 151, 161n7, 272, 286

CPSIA information can be obtained
at www.ICGtesting.com
Printed in the USA
LVHW021007130721
692566LV00010B/853

9 783030 399139